PRINCIPLES OF CONVERGENT JOURNALISM

JEFFREY S. WILKINSON
AUGUST E. GRANT
DOUGLAS J. FISHER

SECOND EDITION

New York Oxford
OXFORD UNIVERSITY PRESS

Oxford University Press, Inc., publishes works that further Oxford University's
objective of excellence
in research, scholarship, and education.

Oxford New York
Auckland Cape Town Dar es Salaam Hong Kong Karachi
Kuala Lumpur Madrid Melbourne Mexico City Nairobi
New Delhi Shanghai Taipei Toronto

With offices in
Argentina Austria Brazil Chile Czech Republic France Greece
Guatemala Hungary Italy Japan Poland Portugal Singapore
South Korea Switzerland Thailand Turkey Ukraine Vietnam

For titles covered by Section 112 of the US Higher Education
Opportunity Act, please visit www.oup.com/us/he for the latest
information about pricing and alternate formats.

Published by Oxford University Press, Inc.
198 Madison Avenue, New York, New York 10016
http://www.oup.com

Library of Congress Cataloging-in-Publication Data
Wilkinson, Jeffrey.
Principles of Convergent journalism / Jeffrey S. Wilkinson, Auggust E. Grant, Douglas J. Fisher
p.cm.
Includes bibliographical references and index.
ISBN 978-0-19-983865-3 (alk. paper)
1. Reporters and reporting. 2. Journalism—Authorship. 3. Online journalism.
4. Broadcast journalism, I. Grant, August E., 1956- II. Fisher, Douglas J., 1953- III. Title.
PN4781.W615 2012
070.4—dc23
2011026826

Printing number: 9 8 7 6 5 4 3 2 1

Printed in the United States of America
on acid-free paper

CONTENTS

PREFACE

Media convergence has transformed journalism in the twenty-first century. When the first edition of this book was released, innovations such as Twitter and Facebook were new or in development. Today they are a common presence in many news media organizations and are routinely used by audiences seeking the latest and most up-to-date information.

But with the flood of change we also continue to see the need for basic journalism practices including strong writing, careful observation, and the ability to ask clear and appropriate questions. Convergent journalism is just the latest tool to keep people informed in a free and open society.

Much of journalism is about identifying the things that affect people's lives—whether witnessing events or finding information others want to keep hidden—and providing meaning and context for others. The theory is that the better you are at reporting, the more likely you will eventually command a larger audience than those who are not.

But even as certain skills mirror those in public relations or advertising, journalism in the digital age remains different in important ways. A fundamental journalism skill is interviewing and reporting. Journalism at its best remains largely a field where you must pull information from people who often don't want to share it. But additional needed skills now include being able to adapt your storytelling to whatever media are the best for conveying the information at hand. In fact, you may have to completely rethink the idea of "story." You also now have to be adept at thinking interactively. That might mean taking photos, whether with a high-end, high-definition digital camcorder or the quick point-and-shoot on a mobile phone, or recording audio. It might mean remembering to get documents in a digital form so they can be shared with your audience. It could mean getting geolocative information to help produce a map, and it definitely means paying attention to linking to other sources of information that can expand context and bring greater clarity.

In our democratic society, the role of journalists to counterbalance and provide checks on those in power remains important, but the digitization of media has caused many organizations to rethink what stories they report and how they report them. It also has caused fundamental changes in where and how people get those stories. News is as likely to be consumed online as through traditional media, and with increased mobility through cellphones and other devices.

Much journalism instruction has coalesced around online without losing the strengths of print and broadcast media, a point we tried to stress in the first edition of *Principles of Convergent Journalism*. In the past four years, we've watched journalists increasingly incorporate social media and mobile technologies into news practices, and this edition not only brings a converged perspective but also seeks to seamlessly incorporate social and mobile media practices across all forms of journalism.

New to the Second Edition

The original twelve-chapter edition has been expanded to fifteen chapters. Here are the most important additions:

- Instead of one chapter on journalism basic skills, there are now two. The new chapter 2 provides greater depth on writing, reporting, and interviewing. The companion chapter 3 takes a more detailed look at other important skills identified in convergent journalism such as basic photography, audio and video editing, and using graphics—all with an eye toward online—as well as new newsroom roles.
- There is a new chapter detailing social media and journalism, including a discussion of how mobile technologies converge with Facebook and Twitter in newsrooms.
- We have added a chapter examining the business of journalism, with emphasis on emerging business models of convergent journalism. This chapter also explores the ways the Web is being monetized by news organizations and includes some suggestions on how these business models may evolve.
- There is a greater emphasis on ethics. Some chapters now have a new box that takes a real-world incident or event that affects convergent journalism practices. Each box presents the issue in a way designed to help the student see how emerging technologies bring about unexpected ethical challenges. Other chapters explore ethics in a more general sense. These can be used as a springboard for discussion or as assignments to develop critical thinking skills.

In addition, each chapter has been extensively revised to reflect the latest practices and trends in convergent journalism. For example, chapter 7, "From Broadcast to Internet: New Types of Content," presents recent research on specific ways that television and radio stations are using the Web. The expanded chapter 15, "Your Future in Convergent Journalism," now includes suggestions for careers in journalism-related areas such as sports or even the management of social media.

As it was in the first edition, the book is organized in a flexible but nontraditional way. Basic skills tend toward the front of the book; the middle chapters reflect current practices related to print, broadcast, and online; and the chapters near the end try to bring important "big picture" issues back to the reader exploring careers, business models, and new and emerging practices. Throughout these chapters, the emphasis is on practical, "hands-on" skills and techniques. These must be combined with ethics, responsibility, the role of journalists in society, and the business requirements of news organizations in order for you to fully apply them in practice.

We believe the principles presented in this text provide a foundation for current or aspiring journalists. Society needs journalists and news organizations to inform people as well as keep an eye on other institutions of power. The overriding purpose of journalists shall always be to provide the information needed to help people improve themselves and participate in a free and democratic society. How they effectively gather, make sense of, and deliver that information, however, is likely to be a process of constant change.

Acknowledgments

This text has been improved by contributions from a great support team. We are grateful for the suggestions from the scholars who provided significant input during the review process, including: Robert Schmuhl, University of Notre Dame; Holly K. Hildreth, West Virginia University; Fred F. Endres, Kent State University; Robert Dunn, East Tennessee State University; Peggy Dillon, Salem State University; Karen Isaacs, University of New Haven; Dee Drummond, University of Toledo; and six anonymous reviewers. We also want to express our appreciation for the team at Oxford University Press, including John Challice, Mark T. Haynes, Caitlin Kaufman, and their production team, all of whom smoothed the transition of the raw text to the final tome you are reading.

Dedications

This book was inspired by journalism and mass communication professors from around the world who participated in the annual "Convergence and Society" conferences and the Newsplex Summer Seminars at the University of South Carolina. The passion for studying and advancing journalism practices by the participants of those seminars inspired the first edition of this book, and the continuing dialogue among those scholars inspired this edition. Journalism is practiced globally, and if you've ever stood in front of a group of students and wanted to spend the next term inspiring them to become the best journalists they can be, this book is dedicated to you.

The book is also dedicated with thanks to Dean Charles Bierbauer of the College of Mass Communications and Information Studies at the University of South Carolina (USC). Since the birth of USC's Newsplex facility in 2002, Charles provided encouragement and resources to allow his faculty and others to pursue the next generation of journalistic practices. This environment helped produce this book and dozens of other activities aimed at helping faculty prepare students to be next-generation journalists.

Finally, this book is dedicated to you, the reader, as a member of our journalism community. We hope that you find a blend of inspiration and instruction that will help define your role as a journalist, as well as providing a vision of your future in our evolving field.

ABOUT THE AUTHORS

Jeffrey S. Wilkinson is a professor of Journalism and Mass Communication at Houston Baptist University in Houston Texas. Wilkinson is a specialist in international journalism with more than a decade teaching and researching mass media in China and Hong Kong. At United International College in Zhuhai he served two years as acting dean for the division of humanities and social sciences. He earned both his Master's and Ph.D. from the University of Georgia and areas of interest include Web journalism, video applications, writing, and reporting. Before that, he worked in radio and television news as a reporter, presenter, and talk show host.

August E. ("Augie") Grant is J. Rion McKissick Professor of Journalism at the University of South Carolina. Grant is a technology futurist who conducts research, teaches, and writes regarding convergent journalism, media technologies, audience behavior, and media organizational behavior. Grant created the *Communication Technology Update and Fundamentals series, The Convergence Newsletter*, and the Newsplex Summer Seminars. He earned his M.A.J.C. at the University of Florida and his Ph.D. from the Annenberg School at the University of Southern California, and serves as a consultant to media and high-tech organizations.

Douglas J. Fisher is a senior instructor at the University of South Carolina where he specializes in editing, new media, and community journalism. He spent 30 years as a broadcast, newspaper, and wire service journalist and is a former Associated Press news editor. He was a Kiplinger Fellow at Ohio State University, founded the Hartsville Today community journalism site and belongs to the NuzBiz consulting group. He writes the "Common Sense Journalism" blog and monthly column and is executive editor of The Convergence Newsletter.

CHAPTER 1

INTRODUCTION TO CONVERGENT JOURNALISM

The practice of journalism is undergoing a paradigm shift as new media expand the ways journalists can tell stories and also how the public can interact with those stories and provide quick and continual feedback. In an era of limited media, journalists could specialize in a single medium. But as things like web apps and social networks have become widespread, both the public and journalists see the potential for increasing journalism's reach with new forms that take advantage of an interconnected society.

The now almost limitless ability, in both quantity and form, to distribute news and information—coupled with the public's growing desire to consume that content digitally and to share it, comment on it, and re-form it—has produced four trends:

- Traditional media, especially print and broadcast outlets, are using websites, digital apps, and social networks to distribute the news they gather.
- News outlets using the Internet for distribution have sprung up to compete with traditional media.
- Individuals, some without any intention of becoming part of "the media," are creating their own repurposings, "mashups," and commentaries that sometimes are far more popular than the original offerings.
- The public is playing an increasingly important role in journalism, sharing stories via social media; adding opinions and interpretations in comments and blogs; and serving as a primary source of video, pictures, and information for breaking news stories.

One of the most immediate impacts is the emergence of *convergent journalism,* defined in this book as the practice of simultaneously using multiple methods to report and produce news and information so the resulting content can easily be distributed in numerous forms.

Many books and scholarly articles have sought, with varying success, to define "convergence." One set of definitions is provided in box 1.1. Our goal, however, is not to focus on definitions as much as on the practical considerations of being a journalist expected to produce multiple forms of content. The material presented here provides the information and thinking to help you develop basic journalistic skills for creating content in forms that allow multiple ways of delivery and methods of interaction.

This book is designed to complement what you may have learned in other courses. Depending upon the extent of your training, you might have already encountered some of the basic skills. But our goal here is to cover all the basics so that you and your peers obtain a comparable degree of insight into the creation and distribution of news and related information in broadcast, print, online, and emerging media. Even if you've encountered similar material before, you should find helpful information in each chapter that will assist you in applying that knowledge to new contexts. The remainder of this chapter will provide an overview of the book and its approach to convergent journalism.

OVERVIEW OF CONVERGENT JOURNALISM

The Internet, as the distribution medium for a wide range of new media technologies, is the most basic force behind the trend toward convergent journalism. Almost every news

Box 1.1 Dimensions of Media Convergence

"Convergence" has been defined in so many ways that a single definition does not exist. These different definitions are distinct "dimensions" of convergence. Rather than using the generic term "convergence," it may be more useful to use a more specific term identifying the specific dimension. Here are a few:

Technological Convergence: The application of digital technology to media content, resulting in media messages being stored and manipulated in a similar fashion by computers and computer algorithms.

Multimedia Journalism: The practice of gathering news and reporting it across multiple media.

Cross-Ownership: The ownership of different media outlets serving the same audience by a single company.

Collaboration: Two or more separately owned media companies working together to share stories or exchange content.

Source: A. E. Grant, "Dimensions of Media Convergence," in A. E. Grant and J. S. Wilkinson, eds., *Understanding Media Convergence: The State of the Field* (New York: Oxford University Press, 2009).

organization in every market has added an online component, allowing redistribution of content from the organization's other media plus additional content and, in many cases, public comment. Broadcast and print outlets can post online content that may not fit the space or time requirements of their primary medium. Additionally, newspapers can distribute audio and video along with text to more directly compete with broadcasters, while broadcasters can provide depth to be more competitive with newspapers. And with lowered distribution costs, new organizations with no roots in either traditional medium can form more easily to compete.

In addition to giving news organizations an opportunity to redistribute the content published in traditional sources, the Internet provides four new opportunities:

- Expansion of news coverage beyond the limits of news holes in newspapers and broadcast media.
- Ability to distribute virtually any type of content, including text, pictures, graphics, audio, and video.
- Interactivity so that readers can contribute content, giving the entire community wider perspectives, or alter content, offering each person a different experience.
- More frequent and faster updating.

Of these four, probably the most important in practical terms is the opportunity to provide any combination of text, pictures, graphics, audio, and video. One indication of the degree to which an organization has converged its news operations is the diversity of content types it provides.

True convergence, however, is not limited to adding a website to a print or broadcast operation. Rather, convergent journalism presumes multiple distribution media are available for any story and can include print, broadcast, online, and emerging platforms like mobile devices, message boards, and digital signage. The convergent journalist does not become comfortable with one or even a few technologies but is constantly looking at innovations and how they can be applied to a better practice of journalism. Convergent journalism thus focuses on the story, giving reporters, photographers, and editors the capability of communicating it in ways that best fit the story's nature and the audience's needs.

In addition to the traditional roles of reporter, editor, assignment manager or assignment editor, copy editor, producer, and photographer or videographer, converged newsrooms need new editorial functions. Many are evolving and titles may vary, but some specific functions, as discussed in chapter 3, have been identified. For example, a "newsflow editor" is needed to oversee when and how individual stories and updates are delivered through each individual medium.

A second new role is the "story editor," who focuses on individual stories, making sure the journalistic team gathers all of the relevant interviews, pictures, background information, and other elements that contribute to each story.

The third new role is "multiskilled journalist," responsible for gathering, organizing, and reporting information in a wide range of media. (This role is discussed in more detail below in the section titled "The Multiskilled Journalist.")

Another role discussed in chapter 8 combines the supervisory functions of a broadcast field producer with the skills of an editor, resulting in a person who uses a

Figure 1.1 ■ Although newspaper and television websites can contain almost the same information, they can be designed to emphasize the content of the parent medium. These two websites illustrate how different newspaper and television websites can be. A: The Oregonlive.com home page is an index of dozens of stories, with complex navigation listing each of the sections of the website. B: The KYW-TV website, on the other hand, emphasizes video stories, with simpler navigation and fewer stories on the home page.

combination of on-the-scene insight and field equipment to generate content that can move directly from the scene to consumers in multiple forms.

The increasing importance of content contributed by readers often requires a "user-generated content editor," someone responsible for moderating the flow of comments, tips, and other user-generated content. This role is distinct from traditional reporting and focuses on gatekeeping functions such as editing and verifying information rather than generating news stories. And as discussed in chapter 11, many newsrooms are also adding specialists in social networks and managing online communities.

Another emerging role in news organizations is digital rights management, the process of making sure the organization has the legal right to distribute content in each of the individual media served by the organization. Other roles include online advertising sales, interactive content design, and social media coordinator.

These new roles represent a set of tasks that can be performed by a number of individuals or combined into a single individual's job description. For instance, many social media managers also help manage user-contributed content. Regardless of the organization chart, the most important difference between converged and traditional newsrooms is the focus on storytelling in many ways.

IMPORTANCE OF STORY

Let's look at the ways a news platform or medium can affect how you report on a story. Assume you are a reporter driving through town when you see a train stopped and blocking a road, with a half-dozen emergency vehicles surrounding it. A reporter focused only on a newspaper report might stop and ask questions about what happened and why it happened so that she or he can write an in-depth explanation. A reporter focused only on a broadcast of the event might grab a camera to shoot some video for the 6 o'clock news. Finally, a reporter focused on getting a report in online media might quickly shoot and transmit a few pictures, then text a three-line story that could be immediately posted with the pictures on the website, Twitter, and Facebook.

The point is that three reporters, working for three different media, should logically focus on different aspects of the story, providing information that will be relevant to their audiences *at the time the audience members get the story from a particular medium.*

Increasingly, however, that newspaper has a website that also carries video and slideshows. The TV station's site also carries video, but its text stories are more like print. And both are likely to have a Facebook page and a Twitter stream. They might even have a mobile application that requires yet a different story form.

Your job as a reporter now is more complicated. You must deliver the immediate story information for posting to Twitter and Facebook, probably followed by posts to the website and a mobile device. At the same time, you must do your basic reporting: getting in-depth information that answers your audience's questions, which may also require that you obtain the best pictures and video you can.

Some of this information parsing may be done by technology. For instance, a posting to Twitter might automatically be routed to Facebook, or a posting to a Tumblr or Posterous blog might go as well to several social media outlets. But it still requires thinking about a story in additional dimensions, ideally so you gain a more complete understanding that you can communicate using all the media available to you.

There is a weakness in this scenario, however; it frames the discussion of story through incremental advances in existing media. That's the way much of media history has evolved—as new technologies have been invented, they have tended to supplement the older ones, not supplant them. Some theorists and practicing journalists, however, think the digital age might be different. They argue that as mobile devices and social networks become ubiquitous, completely new forms of storytelling are required.

Perhaps that train wreck story is not told in the typical text-plus-multimedia way at all. Maybe you click the story link and, instead of a text story, up comes an animation showing you exactly how witnesses say it happened. The animation might change as more information becomes available, with a timeline that lets you return to previous versions to see how things evolved. You might be able to touch the screen to hear a witness describe what happened, then touch another link to call up a map of where the victims are from. Touch yet another and you might see a data visualization of train crashes in your area for the past 10 years.

This approach requires a journalist who thinks not only across media but also in terms of detailed data. Creating such products remains labor- and time-intensive, but if we continue on the same technological trajectory, they will become easier and faster to generate.

Even today there are opportunities to try such innovative storytelling. For instance, what U.S. news organization is bold enough on the Fourth of July to blow up its home page and replace it with an interactive map showing where all the holiday parades, fireworks, and festivals will be? Click on a marker and up pop the details, maybe with video, pictures, or some text added throughout the day. After all, barring some disaster, isn't this the story most of your readers want when they go online that day? It might be jarring to the traditionalists, even those for whom tradition means a series of short stories and links on a home page. But if your focus is truly on storytelling, and this is the story your readers want, shouldn't you consider innovative ways to tell it?

As discussed in the next section, this focus on the story requires converged journalists to have a range of skills. Perhaps more importantly, it also requires converged journalists to know the capabilities and limitations of each individual medium served by the converged newsroom, as well as the type and timing of information the public is looking for from each output medium. The starting point for converged journalism is the multiskilled journalist who has this range of skills.

THE MULTISKILLED JOURNALIST

Almost every discussion of convergent journalism introduces a new type of journalist who is adept at reporting stories across multiple media. In this text, we will refer to this role as the "multiskilled journalist." This term describes reporters skilled at two or more of these tasks: interviewing; collecting audio, video, and still images; editing those images; producing interactive elements (such as graphics and online-accessible databases); and writing stories for delivery across multiple media. Focusing on these tasks, however, ignores the most important role of the journalist in a converged environment: to be able to look at a situation and determine what elements are needed for the various ways that media might be used to disseminate the story.

Journalists have traditionally had to know a great deal about a wide range of subjects without being expected to be an authority on each one. The same now holds for content creation skills and expertise. The multiskilled journalist should know writing and editing across media, interviewing, photography, video creation and editing, public speaking, creating simple graphics, and creating interactive elements and should have some technical knowledge of how to use wired or wireless networking to post or send material remotely. One of this book's authors has described this as the migration "from story generalist and media specialist" to "story specialist and media generalist." Naturally, no one can be expected to master all these skill sets, but a modern journalist can reasonably be expected to excel in two or more according to training, experience, inclination, desire, and natural ability.

Consider everyday situations. The first one on the scene of any breaking story needs to be able to capture as much information as possible, including pictures, videos, and interviews, along with an ability to clearly deliver the story right away. Freelancers carry this combination of skills onto a battlefield or into remote regions, sometimes being the sole witness to a story that can and should be delivered across media. Even routine coverage of a city council meeting could reach more people if the reporter filed short updates for Twitter and Facebook and maybe even an audio report for radio or Web streaming, along with a broadcast package for the next newscast or a story for the next day's Metro section. The reporter also should remember to get digital copies (or paper ones that can be scanned in) of relevant documents to be linked to the online stories and help make them more interactive.

The perspective of the multiskilled journalist is vital for being able to look at all the possible forms a story may take and how each would best be disseminated. In practice, that means the ability to identify all of the elements of a story, including interview sources, photographic subjects, video or audio opportunities, documentary sources, and so forth.

The next skill is the ability to tell the story in the appropriate format, ranging from an inverted pyramid for newspapers or Web text to a linear broadcast narrative. Writing across media may be one of the most difficult skills to master, but the task is made easier by the presence of storybuilders, editors, and others who can help refine the presentation.

Each reporter need not be an authority on photography and other technical skills, but in the absence of a photographer, videographer, or audio engineer, the multiskilled journalist must be capable of capturing the images and sounds that will help tell the story, especially with breaking news when he or she may be the first—and only—journalist on the scene.

Time is critical for multiskilled journalists. At the scene of an event, they need to know which medium needs to be fed first—the website, social media, the radio station, the television broadcast, or the newspaper. It's not unusual for a journalist working for an organization such as CNN to first feed a live television report and then record a follow-up report, which is followed by rewriting the script for the website and finally sending a voice report to a radio network—all in the space of an hour or two.

The idea of having to learn so many skills can be intimidating to both experienced and new reporters. Our experience in training journalists suggests this barrier can be overcome. The most exciting part of training journalists to report across media is watching them take on multimedia reporting skills to deliver pictures and sound along with text. As the technical skills are absorbed and practiced, they become increasingly automatic as the focus remains on the story and how it is delivered across each medium.

(A)

(B)

Figure 1.2 ■ A: In the field, multiskilled journalists sometimes resemble ordinary journalists. B: However, breaking news and new technology now often thrust the ordinary person into journalistic roles. (Source, 1.2B: Richard Puffer; used by permission.)

Few topics in convergent journalism have generated as much debate as the role assigned to the multiskilled journalist. This position has also been referred to as a "backpack journalist" or "one-man band," implying that one person can take on the roles formerly filled by two or more individuals. Generally speaking, a reasonable division of labor produces the best product.

Tools

Certainly, a few reporters and editors are also accomplished photographers, just as some photographers are excellent reporters and writers. But the norm is not, and never will be, a person who has mastered all the skills related to gathering information. On the other hand, the norm in converged newsrooms is likely to be that all journalists will share a basic set of technical skills to enable them to be more effective at gathering information for distribution across media.

That brings up the issue of equipment. Electronic equipment, from digital cameras to laptop computers and cellphones, is becoming more compact and less expensive, making it easier to equip all journalists with cameras, recorders, and other tools that contribute to the process of gathering news. Multiskilled journalists must know basic equipment operation and principles of image composition in order to use this equipment, but they need not be masters of each craft (similar to the argument that photographers and audio engineers need basic writing and interviewing skills).

The lower cost, small size, and ease of operation of the cameras and other equipment used by these backpack journalists enable an organization to equip all of its journalists so that breaking news is more likely to be captured anytime, anywhere. The key skills are not technical; the equipment itself is fairly easy to operate. Rather, they are organizational. You must know how to organize your own time and the story elements so that the story is told in an appropriate manner by the appropriate deadlines in all of the media you reach.

Again, the primary concept of the multiskilled journalist is not to simply master a particular set of skills but to have the mind-set that the information being gathered will be distributed through a variety of media. This perspective understands and recognizes the individual elements that must be captured in order to bring the story to the consumer.

Recognizing Stories for Each Medium

As discussed earlier, the second most important skill (after great storytelling) is the ability to recognize the stories that will work best in each medium. Although almost any story can be told in a variety of forms, characteristics of individual stories can make them work better in some media than in others (see table 1.1). Breaking stories are more appropriate for initial distribution via text messages and social media, as well as on broadcast, because these media are most immediate (keeping in mind that the story will also quickly appear on the news organization's website as well). On the other hand, stories that involve a great deal of detail, analysis, or background can work better in print, where readers tend to spend more time with a story, and online in layers, links, and other innovative ways that let users explore in whatever depth and breadth they desire.

Stories that have compelling visuals still tend to attract audiences to the "big screen" of television, although the "small screen" of online video has become a force, especially

Table 1.1 ■ Examples of Stories That Work Well in Different Media

	Online	Broadcast	Print
Politics	Comparison of candidates, links to related information, real-time vote counts.	Profiles, polls, and debates; announcements and press conferences; voter reactions.	In-depth analysis of platforms, messages, etc.; comparisons with other candidates.
Business	Stock quotes, detailed financial information, breaking news.	Impact of stories on consumers; events with keynote speakers, new product launches.	Analysis of regulations, identification of trends in consumption or spending; global comparisons across markets.
Sports	Scores and statistics; links to team sites; photos of favorite players, fantasy leagues.	Highlights, key plays, live events, championship games.	Analysis and strategy, "business side of sports" (trades, contracts, arrests, marriages/divorces and their impact).

with the spread of high-speed Internet connections. The online medium (including mobile applications) is the only one that allows user interaction to customize a story. As tools allowing user feedback and input into stories are developed, news-oriented websites are offering increased opportunities for visitors to contribute content, register their opinions, and customize the news they get.

Gathering Information

The skills common to all forms of reporting are those of gathering and organizing information. There are four basic steps:

1. Identifying and interviewing individuals with knowledge about the story.
2. Searching information libraries, databases, and other sources of archival information for background details.
3. Contextualizing the story to give it meaning (the "So what?" test).
4. Writing the story.

Converged journalists exercise these skills in the same manner as traditional journalists did when they focused on one medium. The difference is that each skill must now be developed for use in each respective medium. As later chapters of this book detail, important differences among media affect each of these practices. Among the four, writing offers perhaps the biggest challenge, with differences in format, storytelling style, and depth, depending upon the medium.

Writing the Story

For now, the most basic journalistic skill remains writing. The biggest challenge for experienced journalists adapting to new media is learning new formats and new ways of organizing information. Print reporters learning to write for television, for example, might be more likely to start by writing a script and then looking for visuals to fit the story. An experienced television reporter would typically start by combining the most compelling video with the most important elements of the story and then creating a script and visual sequence that weave these two elements together.

Time

The first difference in writing across media is the time element—when the story will be delivered to the public. Websites, social media, and radio allow information to be delivered or updated almost instantaneously. With the exception of major breaking stories and 24-hour cable channels, television news reports are limited to regular broadcasts in the early morning, at noon, in the early evening, and following prime-time entertainment programming. Most newspapers are delivered only once a day, in the morning. In writing stories for each medium, you have to consider (1) the lag between when you write the story and when it will be delivered to the public; and (2) what people may be doing when they receive it.

As a side note, there is some debate whether websites should be updated on a schedule or whenever new information becomes available. Anecdotal evidence suggests that websites should generally adhere to a schedule so that the public can learn to expect when updated information will be posted. There is obviously an exception for major breaking news (election results, outbreak of war, significant disaster, etc.), which calls for updated information as soon as it is available. Mobile devices also may be changing how often new information is updated as the public, now "always on," expects an information stream and not just periodic updates.

Actual practices can vary within a website as well as across news organizations. For example, some TV stations and newspapers provide continuous updates on national stories, sports scores, and other information from outside the organization; but most of the locally generated information is not posted online until after a story has been broadcast or printed. For breaking news, however, immediate publication on the website and other Internet-based media has become the norm.

Length

The next critical difference among media is the story length. Broadcast stories are typically measured in time, while print stories are measured in column inches. Online stories are sometimes measured in "screens," or how many full screens it takes to show something when the reader scrolls. When these numbers are converted to the number of words, a sharp difference emerges.

As illustrated in figure 1.3, radio stories are the shortest, typically averaging 10 to 30 seconds, which translates to 25 to 100 words. Television news stories are also fairly short, ranging from 15-second "readers" to four-minute "packages," with 40 to 500 words. Newspaper stories can run from one column inch (about 25 words) up to dozens of column inches (1,000 words or longer).

Format

Print stories are often told using an "inverted pyramid" style, in which the most important information (who, what, when, where, why, and how) is communicated in the lead

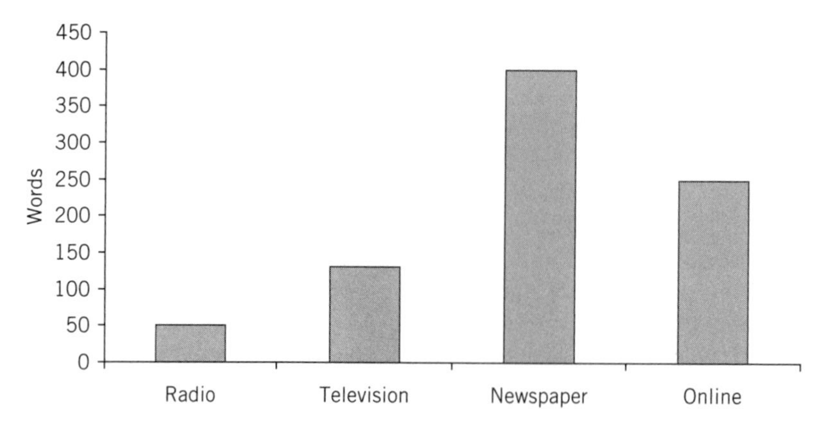

Figure 1.3 ■ Comparing the typical length of stories.

sentence or, if an anecdotal lead is used, still very high in the story. Broadcast stories, on the other hand, are typically told in a linear format, often as a chronology. Computer software used in writing stories also functions somewhat differently for each medium.

Elements

The last major difference among media concerns the elements that can be included in a story. Newspapers and magazines emphasize text and still images or graphics to accompany a story and a short headline draws attention to it. Television news stories make the most extensive use of video but increasingly use still images and graphics. In addition to the text in the script, television reports can include text superimposed over pictures to help viewers understand information being presented. For breaking stories in remote areas, telephone voice reports over an image may suffice.

One of this book's goals is to explore in more detail how these elements differ for each medium. In studying and practicing writing for each medium, however, it is also important to identify shared elements among media platforms.

Much of what we discuss will lie within the frame of incremental advances from current media because, frankly, that is the state of affairs in most of the media world. We realize there is criticism of this approach from those who argue that it hinders experimentation with truly new forms of storytelling they see as necessary for journalism to survive and thrive. As we have mentioned in this chapter, we will from time to time suggest completely different ways of looking at storytelling, but we encourage you to examine the stories happening around you and regularly ask yourself, "If I had any tool I needed, how would I tell this story?" Feel free to mentally invent some of those tools and then check around. You might be surprised to see some of them are already available.

Other Journalistic Skills

In addition to writing, this book will address other critical skills for journalists. For instance, the basics of setting up and conducting interviews are similar for all media, but there are also distinct differences in how the interviews themselves are captured and used by the reporter. We will also address how archival sources—especially electronic information sources—can and should be used to contribute to the depth and perspective provided in each story.

Capturing visual images is a major part of any converged news operation. We will explore those things that are common to capturing still pictures and video and creating graphics that combine a range of visual elements, but we will also explore differences.

The need for ethics is also constant across media, but ethical challenges vary considerably. We will explore some of the ethical challenges that you will face, along with possible solutions to these dilemmas.

Finally, there are practical dimensions to convergent journalism that may be particularly relevant to you, the reader. Understanding the business side of journalism and how to get a job as a converged journalist will be explained to help round out your convergent journalism training.

MOTIVATION FOR CONVERGENCE

There is a critical question to answer for yourself: Why converge? From a practical perspective, few job listings today require all the skills discussed in this book. This will certainly change as more organizations expand their reach across media. For now, though, consider that when managers choose from available candidates, hiring decisions will tend to favor journalists grounded in the basics who also bring additional skills to the newsroom. That's perhaps the best reason for making sure you are ready to work in a converged newsroom.

SUMMARY

This chapter has provided an overview of convergent journalism practices and the thinking behind being a multiskilled journalist. While all the basic and traditional journalism skills are still needed, changes in technology and the economics of news are bringing about new practices, new organizational structures, and even new positions and roles. Newspaper and broadcast organizations no longer have the luxury of seeing themselves as confined to a single medium. Online, mobile, and social media technologies enable today's journalists to bring the news to almost anyone at any time in any form. Because of human limitations, it is doubtful many journalists will be expert in reporting for all media. But we suggest it will become standard to be expert in one platform and competent in the others while continuing to experiment and adapt.

EXERCISES

1. Look at how the same story is covered in your local newspaper, on a local television newscast, and on the websites of both the newspaper and the television station. How do these stories differ in depth? How are visuals used in each medium? Is the Internet just repeating the content from the other media, or does it include unique content?
2. Observe the timeliness of stories reported in the newspaper, on television, and on both newspaper and television station websites. How different are these media? Is the

timeliness of information in the online stories significantly different from the parent newspaper's or television station's?

3. If you've been trained as a television reporter, choose a newspaper story and write a television news script based upon the newspaper story. If you've been trained as a newspaper reporter, choose a television news report and write a newspaper story based upon the television news report. Analyze how the stories differ across media. What do you need to write your story that you didn't find in your source material?
4. Choose a local news story of interest to you. Keep track of the number of times during the next week that this story appears in the media that you use regularly. Compare the frequency and depth of coverage for these media.
5. Look at a friend's Facebook page and/or Twitter account. How frequently do they link to or discuss news stories? Then compare the types of stories you find. What is the relative importance of each of the major categories of news: international, national, political, business, sports, local, entertainment, lifestyle, health, and science/technology?

CHAPTER 2

JOURNALISM BASICS: WRITING, REPORTING, INTERVIEWING

No matter the medium, the underlying skills related to gathering information do not change. While every journalist must have basic skills in writing, editing, interviewing, and verifying, converged newsrooms create a special challenge for reporters because they are expected to have a wider range of skills than those who produced content for only one medium. As news organizations have embraced the Web, reporters, editors, owners, and academics have debated the skill set needed. As noted in chapter 1, reporters working in a converged media operation are not expected to be expert in every skill for every medium, but a basic working knowledge (and appreciation) of a wide range of skills across media is expected. The next two chapters focus on these skills.

It is increasingly common for the public to perceive that journalism is not all that different from other types of content such as talk radio, comedy shows presented as news, and "spin" from public relations. But journalists have a different set of assumptions regarding opinions and spin. For example, while journalists strive to be fair, fairness doesn't require all sides to be presented equally in a story. A dictator (or a school bully) can justify his or her behavior, but the journalist is not being unfair to say that behavior is wrong. When different perspectives on an issue can be measured against information known to be true, journalists have the responsibility to provide that context, even if (some would say "especially if") it demonstrates the fallacy of one or more arguments.

Today, anyone can use clever writing and editing software to pull a quote out of context and push a particular agenda or deliver a funny punch line. But the journalist prefers that the sides compete to a draw in a fair fight rather than one side winning on a technicality. The journalist also has to be open-minded enough to admit a preconceived position is wrong and then provide the facts to support an opposing view that may be closer to the truth.

Critics may deride such "flip-flopping," but sometimes the best reporting makes everyone unhappy. Human experience is complicated, so there are multiple sides to stories. Truth is evasive. Events are not single stories; they change over time and evolve. A seemingly simple story about a federal income tax increase might meld with foreign policy and military funding issues to become complicated and muddy, with no clear-cut good guys, bad guys, winners, or losers.

This traditional "hard news" approach is the essence of basic journalism. Journalists provide an account of an event, sometimes from eyewitnesses, sometimes from official reports, and sometimes from seeing and hearing it themselves. Journalists often blend two or more of these sources and incorporate remarks from key people with whom they have spoken. This type of reporting rarely wins awards, doesn't pay well, and doesn't make friends. But it is the starting point and foundation of an informed public in a post-modern world of ongoing conflicting agendas.

One of the best ways to understand journalistic skills and how they are interrelated is to consider a specific story. Suppose you're on the way to your converged newsroom when you see traffic stopped in front of you. A train is off the tracks. You hear sirens. You see smoke. And you have your basic reporting tools with you. How will you proceed?

Figure 2.1 ■ Some events we know are newsworthy and part of history. Some events are mundane and quickly vanish from our collective memory. Sometimes an event turns from one into the other with no notice. That's the excitement of reporting.

HOW TO HANDLE "THE STORY

The first tool you need as a journalist is judgment regarding what constitutes a news story (see box 2.1, "What is Journalism"). Stories are accounts of things that come to your attention in one of the following ways:

1. Unexpected and surprising events are referred to as breaking news: floods, crashes, scandals, earthquakes, scientific breakthroughs, etc.
2. Scheduled events: elections, anniversaries, budget cycles, Super Bowl games, Christmas events, etc.
3. News releases: an organization or group announcement of interest.
4. Ideas or tips from others: people come to you and volunteer information.
5. Your ideas: limited only by your creativity and hard work.

Box 2.1 What Is Journalism?

Journalism is the business of telling true stories about things that are *News*. News is something you hear, see, or read about that is important to you. Common news values have been identified to help you determine whether something is newsworthy.

A. *Proximity or location.* Something that happens near you geographically (a local festival) or psychologically (research findings on a disease specific to your age group, gender, ethnicity, or affecting someone you know).

B. *Significance and impact.* The greater the significance and the greater the number of people affected, the more newsworthy it is. National elections and disasters, for example.

C. *Conflict.* When parties disagree or fight, we pay attention. Interest can be increased when the focus goes beyond "who wins" to detail what the conflict was about.

D. *Timeliness.* Something happening now or that just happened. Anniversaries are also timely because they highlight an event that should be remembered.

E. *The unusual, unexpected, or unique.* Anything that makes you say, "That's different!" Unexpected outcomes can be when a favored side loses and an underdog wins. Another classic example: "When a dog bites a man, it's not news. When a man bites a dog, that's news."

F. *Prominence or celebrity.* We often show interest in famous or familiar names. The universe of celebrities now includes people who are famous for being famous.

G. *Need versus want.* Sometimes there are developments the news organization decides people need to know, even if they don't realize it. A great deal of reporting on government activities falls under this category.

H. *Emotional appeal via the medium (visual/aural emphasis).* Some events are newsworthy because of the sights or the sounds. Any story where you might have said, "You had to be there" (such as a balloon race or a concert of barking dogs).

I. *Voyeurism.* Sometimes we want to look into other people's lives to see their struggles and triumphs.

At least two sets of questions should go through your mind as you look at the wreck. One set consists of the "**5 W's & the H**"—who, what, when, where, why, and how—concerning the train wreck itself. What happened? Is anyone hurt? Is anyone in danger? Why did it occur? The other set of questions concerns your **coverage**—where you want to take the story. What should you text and to whom? Do you post photos immediately to the Web or gather information first? Does it justify a live broadcast? How should it be reported in tomorrow's newspaper?

A converged journalist serves multiple media, and capturing images (and sometimes sound) is as important as getting the story's details. This chapter looks at the basic skills of writing, reporting, and interviewing. The next chapter covers taking pictures, recording video and audio, graphics, and performance.

WRITING

Writing is probably the most basic skill expected of all reporters. Most writers are made, not born, and becoming a good writer follows two rules:

1. Learn the basics of written communication.
2. Do it. Over and over and over.

If you take two people of equal writing ability and have one write 1,000 words over a semester and the other 20,000, it's obvious which one will probably be faster, more confident, and more creative.

Journalism professors often encourage students to write every day. One professor is known to advise students to use Friday nights to sit and rewrite stories until either the sun comes up or they fall asleep. This technique is a bit harsh, but effective.

Although each medium is a bit different in how a story is packaged or what points are emphasized, all media and all newsrooms expect proper grammar and punctuation, correct word usage, and clear organization.

Grammar is placing words in the correct order so that the message the writer seeks to convey is the message received by the reader, user, or viewer. It includes such things as proper subject-verb agreement, correct modifier placement (avoiding "squinting" adverbs between two verbs, for instance, or dangling participles that modify the wrong thing), and proper verb tense.

Punctuation is an aid to understanding and as such is best used sparingly. A text riddled with commas, for instance, is like running into a bunch of speed bumps, but failing to use one where needed can produce a mashed-up, jumbled set of thoughts that are difficult to follow.

Correct word usage can help you stay credible. While many newsrooms have their own stylebooks, most rely on the *Associated Press Stylebook* for their foundation. See http://apstylebook.com for details about print and online versions. The *AP Stylebook* can answer a number of style and usage questions, including things such as the difference between a "tornado warning" and a "tornado watch," "affect" and "effect," or "premier" and "premiere." A dictionary and a thesaurus are also common resources. Finally, spell check and grammar check on your computer's word processor can warn you of things to check further, but don't rely on the suggestions alone. Spell check often misses homophones, for example, and some of the grammar advice is sketchy or just plain wrong.

Clear organization of your story guarantees better understanding. How you organize the story can vary depending on what impression you want to leave, but some basic principles still apply: All stories should have a logical and interesting beginning, smoothly move to the heart of the matter, and end with some sort of resolution or conclusion.

Some standard questions can help guide you. Do you answer a reader's or viewer's questions where they are likely to be raised, or do you force the person to wait—or worse, not answer them at all? Do you pile on background information too early in the story, or do you give just enough so the person continues reading or viewing? Do you use just a few quotes and keep them pointed, or do you let talking heads drone on with information that you as a journalist could more clearly and efficiently summarize yourself? Do you vary your sentence and paragraph length to create a cadence, and do you use primarily active subject-verb-object sentence structure?

For online stories, organization also includes some techniques not seen as often in traditional print. Subheads, highlighted words, and bulleted lists help "open up" a story for people who tend to scan more for information on the Internet. Subject-verb-object sentence structure also is highly prized in a medium designed for fast absorption of essentials.

The Writing Process

According to *Coaching Writers*, there are five basic steps to writing a story:[1]

- Idea: generate your own or take one from the editor
- Report: gather information
- Organize: decide what to say and how to say it
- Draft: write the first version(s)
- Revise: polish until finished

The challenge is deciding when a story is "done." It's easy to stop editing and rewriting after a first or second draft, especially when the pressure is on to publish online quickly. Although controversial, some news organizations increasingly are rushing stories online with minimal rewriting and editing, the philosophy being that it is easy to revise and update and that the expertise of the public can be brought into the process of refining the story.

But experienced writers know that good copy is the result of a process of rewriting and editing that can focus or balance a story or make a story "come to life" by making it more relevant to the public. In a converged newsroom, rewriting may become ingrained in the process because each medium may have a different deadline, with a story changing in depth, detail, and format as it spreads from one medium to the next.

Basic Differences Among Print, Online, and Broadcast

Knowing which medium you're writing for is important, because each medium has specific formats, structures, and constraints. Newspapers, for example, rely on text and still images to delve deeply into an event or issue.

---

[1] R. P. Clark and D. Fry, *Coaching Writers: Editors and Reporters Working Together Across Media Platforms* (New York: Bedford/St. Martin's, 2003).

Three common formats used in print reporting are:

Inverted Pyramid: The most important facts and information come in the very beginning, then comes less important information, and finally, at the end, the least important information appears.

Hourglass/Martini Glass: Start with the inverted pyramid, go to a chronological narrative of the issue, then finish off with a kicker/surprise ending or quote.

"Circle"/Dollar Sign: This format gained recognition in the *Wall Street Journal's* elegant use of it for longer feature stories. It begins with a quote or anecdote involving a specific individual, broadens to a general discussion of the topic while weaving more about the individual in, and at the end comes back to the specific individual again (there is more on these story forms in chapter 9).

Radio demands brief accounts using colorful wording to paint pictures in the listener's mind. Some common radio news formats are:

Reader: Copy read by an anchor without any **sound bite** .

Donuts: A reader with an actuality (sound bite, audio quote) in the middle.

Wraparounds: Same as a donut except it's delivered by a reporter in the field so it demands an anchor introduction (these story forms are explored in more detail in chapter 8).

Television news stories supplement words with a wide range of visual content. The most common television news formats are:

Reader: The same as in radio, copy read by an anchor without any video or graphic resulting in the famous "talking head." Viewers don't mind a reader as long as it's relatively short (30 seconds or less).

Voice-Over (VO): Similar to a reader, except after the first sentence or two the viewers see video while the story is being read.

Voice-Over/Sound on Tape (VO/SOT): The TV version of the radio donut, a VO with a sound bite in the middle.

Package: A self-contained reporter story from the field, requiring an anchor introduction or lead-in (these story types are explored in more detail in chapter 8).

The Internet combines elements of all the formats discussed above. Jonathan Dube, publisher at cyberjournalist.net has identified several forms of online storytelling[2]. Some are more difficult to create than others, but all are possible thanks to the Web.

1. **Print plus**. A basic text article (broadcast reader or newspaper article) that then adds additional elements such as a photo, video clip, animation, or clickable interactive.
2. **Clickable Interactive**. Combines linear and nonlinear storytelling to include audio, video, images, or graphics. Time intensive.

---

[2] Jonathan Dube (July 10, 2000), "Online storytelling forms," Cyberjournalist.net, retrieved from http://www.cyberjournalist.net/news/000117.php.

3. **Slideshows**. Using multiple images with captions to tell a story. Easy to do, hard to do well.
4. **Audio Stories**. Expertly uses sound sources to tell a story more powerfully than simple text. Can be augmented by photos, text, and even video, but the key selling point is sound—the way something is said or the way it sounded when it transpired.
5. **Narrated Slideshows.** Combines audio and video to tell powerful stories.
6. **Live Chats**. An interactive version of the Q&A story format. Like the slideshow, easy to do, very hard to do well because being a good moderator is harder than most people think.
7. **Quizzes and Surveys**. One of the most engaging ways to present information, either as part of a story or can even be the entire story itself.
8. **Animated Stories**. When there are no photos or video and you want to recreate an event that has motion or action. You can also use animation to show how something happened or works.
9. **Interactive Webcasts**. Online video news but adds interactive elements like chat or polling to make it a true interactive experience.
10. **Multimedia Interactives**. This time and resource intensive form combines everything into a complete package.
11. **Other forms**, such as Stories without words, Weblogs, Interactive memorials, and even Games.

Figure 2.2 ■ Whether your story is for print, broadcast, online, or social media, it is important to be a good listener and careful observer.

By reporting on actual news events, you will eventually practice many of the story forms listed. Common elements include having a good lead or introduction; a logical story structure; appropriate quotes or sound bites and visuals; and a solid, thoughtful conclusion.

Basics of Good Writing

In Robert Gunning's classic "The Technique of Clear Writing,"[3] 10 basic principles suggest how you can become a good writer. These rules are still useful because human nature has not changed.

1. **Keep sentences short, on the average.**
   Generally stay below 20 words in a sentence. But vary the length because the best writing mixes 10-word sentences with 35-word sentences.
2. **Prefer the simple to the complex**.
   Simple sentences are easy to understand and encourage people to continue reading. Long and complicated sentences do not. Use short and simple sentence structure as often as possible: subject-verb-object. Example: "The Senate passed the bill."
3. **Prefer the familiar word.**
   And by implication, eschew the unfamiliar, for example:
   Hide, don't *obfuscate*; *chew*, don't *masticate*,
   An accident victim has *cuts and bruises,* not *lacerations and contusions*.
4. **Avoid unnecessary words.**
   Master the language and eliminate redundancies in your writing: Don't say "dangerous weapon" (all weapons are), or "young child." Numerous online sources list the most common errors, and *Strunk & White*[4] is particularly popular among journalism professors for recommending ways to tighten up your writing. For example, "in spite of the fact that" can be simply changed to "although." More examples can be found at the Strunk & White website at http://www.bartleby.com/141/index.html.
5. **Put action into your verbs.**
   Generally, use active, not passive, voice. Active voice is stronger and uses fewer words.
   Passive: The bill was passed by the Senate.
   Active: The Senate passed the bill.
   However, there may be times when the subject receiving the action is more important than the actor so passive voice is better: "Smoking in restaurants was outlawed by City Council today." (Smoking is more likely to get your audience's attention than the City Council.)
6. **Write the way you talk.**
   Broadcast style has always encouraged this approach. Write tight. Use contractions. Use natural expressions but avoid cliches. Put attribution first. For example:

---

[3] Robert Gunning, *The Technique of Clear Writing* (New York: McGraw-Hill, 1952).
[4] W. Strunk and E. B. White, *The Elements of Style*, 3rd ed. (New York: Macmillan, 1979).

Don't say: "Smith caused the accident, according to police."

Better: "Police say Smith caused the accident."

7. **Use terms your reader can picture.** The way to create word pictures is detailed in chapter 8. The best writing from reporters around the country is also identified in the yearly competition by the American Society of News Editors (ASNE).
8. **Tie in with your reader's experience.**
   For example, if taxes are going up, explain what that means in real terms. If the city cuts the budget by $10 million, how will that affect services? Fewer firefighters? Fewer police? Longer wait for those in an emergency? Dimming streetlights after midnight? Something must be affected. Be specific.
9. **Make full use of variety.**

   All writing is communication, and each of us develops a unique way or style of communicating. We begin by trying to imitate others, but over time and with experience we gain mastery over language and wording. The best writers work hard at the craft and experiment with ways of expressing themselves and their ideas.
10. **Write to express, not to impress.**

    It is tempting to bloviate. Computer software allows us to replace simple words with longer, impressive-sounding ones. Don't do it. Clear communication requires small words, not big ones.

The Lead

The lead (still spelled in some newsrooms as "lede" to distinguish the word itself, such as in an editor's query, as a term not to be published) is the first and most important sentence of your story. The lead must grab people's attention and set the tone for the rest of the story. If it doesn't entice readers, they'll give up and move on. If it grabs attention but doesn't accurately reflect the rest of the story, they'll feel misled and stop reading. The result is the same: Your time and effort are wasted.

Writing an effective lead can be the hardest part of writing a story. But a good lead can also help you complete the rest quickly. As you gather information, you should continually be thinking how it all fits together and what it means for others—the "so what" test.

The process of thinking-then-writing is done in stages:

Stage one: As you're collecting as many facts as possible you are also thinking about what is most newsworthy. At some point you must determine when to stop collecting facts and begin the writing process.

Stage two: Begins when you first attempt to write down the most essential facts—the 5 W's and the H—and prioritize which ones you think are most important right now (or will be most important when the story is actually published, posted, or broadcast).

Stage three: If you're up against a deadline and there's little time, revise quickly so it is at least well-written and professional. But if you have some time, rethink and revise, allowing yourself to be appropriately creative. A well-written creative lead makes a huge difference.

The most basic lead is the newspaper "summary lead." The summary lead often contains the who, what, when, and where, and even the why or how.

Here is a 39-word summary lead example by Griff Witte of *The Washington Post:*[5]

> CAIRO—The Egyptian military moved on multiple fronts Sunday to display its strength and consolidate support as factions within the government and on the street vied for control of this strategically vital nation at the heart of the Arab world.

You can easily identify the who (Egyptian military), when (Sunday), and where (Cairo, Egypt), and even the why (to consolidate support as factions within the government and on the street vied for control). The what (moved on multiple fronts) and how (display of strength) may be a little less clear and arguably interchangeable in this example, but the facts are there.

But summary leads don't work very well in broadcast or online formats because they tend to be longer than normal writing, averaging 35 words or more. In broadcast and online writing, leads may contain only one or two W's. Often the Why and How are left for later in the story. Some leads may provide even less information, especially those involving sports or entertainment celebrities:

> *Justin Bieber has done it again.*

Other types of leads

Besides the summary lead, with practice journalists also learn to vary the approach to stories with different leads. Depending on how deeply one wants to study the art of crafting a lead, there are several subtypes. Probably the most important consideration is the urgency of the story. If it's a serious story, write a direct lead and get to the point. But if you're writing a feature and want to draw readers in, there are a number of techniques that are pretty much self-explanatory:

a. Delayed identification lead. Useful when you purposely leave out the "who" or "what" until the second or third sentence.
b. Anecdotal lead. Begin with a specific anecdote or story to provide some context for the reader. But be careful to bring the person involved in the anecdote back into the story elsewhere.
c. Scene-setter leads start with providing useful context for the reader.
d. Direct address lead. Relates the story directly to the public, emphasizing "you." Common with consumer-oriented features.
e. Blind lead. The first sentence provides only a provocative detail. In the second or third sentence the five W's and the H are then provided. But you have to be

---

[5] Griff Witte (January 30, 2011), "Egypt's Military Shows Its Strength, Not Its Hand," *The Washington Post*, retrieved from http://www.washingtonpost.com/national/egypts-military-shows-its-strength-not-its-hand/2011/01/30/ABAJCME_story.html.

a little careful so as not to unintentionally mislead your audience. In broadcasting, listeners or viewers can be distracted and miss the second part, which can leave a wrong impression. ("Another world war is on the horizon. That's what a local professor is predicting.")

f. "Wordplay" (creative) leads. Puns and wordplay are generally enjoyed but try not to overdo and be too cutesy. Your work could end up in the legendary Bulwer-Lytton Fiction Contest for bad writing (or, if under 200 characters, its cousin, the Lyttle Lytton).

Some types of leads don't work as well and writers should think twice about using—or overusing—any of these.

a. Topic lead. Criticized because it is boring and does not say enough to keep interest. An example is "The City Council met last night." Instead, tell us what it did or whether anything important happened.
b. Question leads. What's wrong with a question lead? The problem with a question lead is that it wastes time and space and is generally answered in the second sentence (like this).
c. Quote leads. One of the authors of this book once led a story with "I'm sorry baby, but I've got to kill you." It may be a good quote, but a lousy lead. (This is different from using part of a quote in a lead if it is really pointed or poignant, but the entire quote from which the partial quote came should then be used later in the story.)

Rewriting

You should seldom go with your first version of a lead. Good writing is the practice of revising and improving. Generally speaking, it's not until your third version or so that you get a lead you're comfortable with. But sometimes it takes much longer and several more tries. In college, one of the authors remembers 16 attempts before finding an acceptable lead for a story. And acceptable does not mean good or even great.

How do you know when you've found the best lead? Maybe it can be best described as "when the rest of the story writes itself." In other words, when the lead helps you almost effortlessly write the rest of the story, you know you've found a great beginning.

REPORTING

Good writing starts with good reporting. If the right stuff isn't in the notebook or the recorder, all the skill in the world isn't going to turn dull facts into sparkling prose. Reporting starts with gathering information. Three basic sources of information enable the reporter to produce a news story: interviews, documents and archives, and the personal observations of the journalist. Another way to think about it is:

(a) Information you get from actively asking questions (interviewing);
(b) Information you get from gathering data, reading any and all related documents and other written material, listening to archived audio, and viewing archived video; and

(c) Information you get from what you see or hear (observation), which includes the common sense and knowledge you have built from your life's experiences to provide understanding of the event (for instance, you know when and why graduates throw their mortarboards in the air).

Reporters are often said to be eyewitnesses writing the first draft of history because they go where significant events are occurring or have occurred. Reporters write down the things they see and hear, the mood they feel, and the actions and atmosphere of their surroundings. They then judge how to best convey "what happened" for those not there.

Often, simple observation is not enough for the reporter to get all the necessary information about an event. The reporter has to actively gather information either from a newsmaker or from those who witnessed or knew what happened.

Selecting Sources to Interview

During the course of information gathering, the reporter will identify and interview people who are familiar with the story or the facts surrounding it. They can be **newsmakers**—firsthand sources such as officials and celebrities, but also inventors, survivors, and participants or witnesses—or they might be **spokespersons**, **experts**, and "**ordinary folks.**" In that case, which ones are the best and how many should be interviewed? Generally more is better, but other factors should be considered:

- *Time to deadline:* More time allows you to talk to more people.

Figure 2.3 ■ Professional reporting is methodical and rarely done from memory. Journalists write down key details like correct spellings of names, titles, addresses, and precise wording of statements about sensitive issues.

- *Availability*: If they can't or won't speak before your deadline, they can't be a source for that day's story (although don't overlook the possibility they might provide good follow-up material if you can finally get hold of them).
- *Expertise vs. relevance:* A person with greater expertise tends to provide better information, allowing you to finish your story sooner, but "ordinary folks" can better express the views of what concerns "nonexperts."
- *Topic complexity:* A complicated event or topic demands more perspectives from more sources.
- *Degree of controversy:* The greater the controversy, the more care needed to make the story balanced and understandable.

Deadlines and Sources

Print stories often have a single evening deadline, which affords greater depth of reporting. Broadcast stories may have several deadlines throughout the day, so fewer individuals appear or are quoted on camera. Online posting policies vary among news organizations, so the answer is still "it depends." But what has not changed is that journalists produce accurate stories quickly and then post, publish, or broadcast the stories when they are most timely.

It's still best to directly contact an eyewitness or expert for insight into the story you are working on. Talking to people—either in a formal interview or a casual chat—helps develop personal networking, builds credibility, confirms facts, provides follow-up leads, and often gets you the best sound bites or quotes to air or publish. Two invaluable aids are the telephone and the Internet-connected computer.

Telephone-Assisted Reporting

The best reporting occurs by witnessing and experiencing the event, but often reporting staffs are stretched thin by practical considerations and lack time or resources to send someone. If a reporter cannot be someplace in person to do interviews, the telephone is used to quickly get quotes or sound bites. Interviewing by telephone can save time and works well for getting clarification about events that are not controversial. Interviewing by telephone does not work well otherwise, because a source can easily avoid you and your questions. Even if you do have a source on the line, he or she can decline to comment or simply hang up. In addition, it is not possible to get video from a telephone interview, so a reporter may still have to make a trip to some locations.

Computer-Assisted Reporting

Another valuable tool for collecting and verifying information is your computer connected to the Internet. The term "computer-assisted reporting" was coined when the use of computers in reporting was not so common, but now using them has become commonplace (more on CAR is provided in chapter 10).

Given the nature of deadlines, it is tempting to go to the Internet first to find and quote information. But keep in mind that many of your best sources may not be available online. People who don't have an active online presence may not turn up in an online search. Also, your competition has access to the same online resources that you do, so limiting yourself to people and sources you find online will rarely give you an edge. That's why a good reporter's best resource is his or her personal network. You don't have to know everyone who has an answer as long as you know people who can direct you to those who have information you need for your story. In practice, when you need a source or an interview but don't know whom to call, you can start by calling the person who is most likely to give you a name or other lead.

Regardless of the output medium, it is critical to verify information from personal interviews before putting that information into a story. Traditionally, controversial information requires at least two independent sources. Sometimes one source has such a high degree of authority or expertise that another is not needed. In the train wreck example, the fire chief's telling you when and how many fire units responded is enough.

With the advent of the Internet, search engines, and news databases, accessing background, or archival, information has become easier, sometimes too easy. Social networks have made it easier to find out even normally private details about people. It cannot be stressed enough that just because something has been published and pops up in a search engine or database search, or is found on a social networking site, it is not automatically true. Let's say you have the name of the engineer in the train wreck, "Jim Wilson," and you put it into a search engine or a database. Results come back showing a Jim Wilson has been involved in a previous wreck with intimations of drinking beforehand. You publish this without checking at your peril.

First, Jim Wilson is a common name. Second, maybe a father and son have the same name, but the archives don't reflect Jr. or Sr. (a news organization once spent thousands of dollars defending itself after mistakenly leaving a Jr. off a name). The bottom line is that archives and databases are great places to start amassing background, but all the information obtained online should be checked as thoroughly as you would any other fact in a story.

Don't forget that, as a reporter, you have more background knowledge about most stories you will cover than the people who will hear or read them. Some information can simply be presented as fact, but other information, especially information new to the reader, should reference the source.

PRACTICAL INTERVIEWING

Interviewing is the art of interpersonal communication. Getting people to talk and provide the information or emotion you want to capture or record is not easy. Each interview is different, but some general guides or approaches can help you become an expert.

First, understand what type of interview you are doing. There are time, place, and manner restrictions that give more or less freedom in how you ask questions. For example, the classic ***formal interview*** affords you the time to get depth and detail. You can clarify points and repeat lines of questioning, and even if you ask a difficult question, it's not so easy for the person to walk away. A second type of interview, the ***foner*** (***telephone interview***) mentioned earlier, allows you to get needed information quickly. A third type, the ***walkaround,*** is often used at scheduled events where a variety of people and newsmakers can be informally approached and spoken with. Another type, ***on-the-fly chat***, occurs spontaneously and while newsmakers are in motion. You may not have a chance to formally write out questions and you are literally "winging it." Finally, reporters often have to talk to people because they don't understand something or are unfamiliar with the background. These ***backgrounder interviews*** help educate the journalist so better questions can be formulated for the appropriate newsmaker to answer later.

There are three general approaches to interviews, and the situation dictates how free you are to probe and ask follow-up questions. These approaches are easy to remember and cover most situations. They are only guides to help you keep your questions on track and on target.

Approach A: Asking questions as an "expert." This is the preferred approach because you do your homework first, become informed about the topic, and ask deep, insightful questions. The "expert" approach is good when time is limited because it helps push the discussion forward. It also helps you control the interview and avoid dismissive or overly simplistic analyses or solutions. A caution is that you can get overly complicated or focus on matters that are beyond what most people care about. Even worse, if the question becomes complicated and wordy, people can become impatient. The authors have attended news conferences where reporters were cut off in midquestion and even ridiculed by other reporters.

Approach B: Asking questions as "common folk." This approach tries to ask the types of basic questions most people want to know. If the county commission votes for a property tax rate increase, tell us how much it will cost the average homeowner. If the city is buying new police cars, tell us why—do they have high-tech weaponry, or is it to replace the old gas-guzzlers? This interview approach gets you the quotes to help nail down the essence of the story. The downside is that, while the questioning strives for simplicity, you must not be perceived as ignorant or uninformed.

Approach C: Past Present Future (PPF): When all else fails and you're unprepared (shame on you, but hey, it happens), this is an easy-to-remember structure to generate dozens of questions. For example, you stop in to see the mayor and coincidentally she shows you the first draft of the proposed city budget. She has to run but you've got five minutes for an exclusive interview. What to ask? Tackle the topic according to Past, Present, and Future:

Past: What were the biggest things addressed in this budget that were not addressed in last year's budget?
Present: Where are the major increases? Where are the major cuts?
Future: Will there be chances for the public to react? When will we see the effects of these changes?

This approach is also useful for features (like interviewing a local celebrity).

Past: Talk about how you became interested in your work; reactions by parents, siblings, neighbors, teachers; early inspiration, successes, encouragements, disappointments; key development points or events.

Present: How do you feel about your work/success now? What are you doing now? Recent/current/immediate plans, successes, failures, accomplishments? Key people or projects?

Future: What's next? Goals, aspirations, fears, greatest success, greatest failure, desire, wish, hope for the future, and anything about how to spend retirement?

And finally, finish by asking, "Anything we missed or you want us to know that we've not covered?" Sometimes you're rewarded with a golden factoid, like finding out a custodial staff member once did lighting with the Grateful Dead in the 1960s.

There are of course other approaches to interviewing, and with practice you'll develop your own method for asking the right questions that get you the best answers.

Time and Space Constraints When Interviewing

You don't have the luxury of spending an hour with each person you interview. In a deadline-oriented business, things move fast. Forget 20-minute interviews for TV news; it's a waste of time sifting through that much recorded material. Professional TV reporters often record only one or two questions for sound bites, but those two are the *best* questions. In radio, it depends on whether the interview is live or recorded and how much time you have. Some people speak in short, clipped sentences. Some don't know how to speak in sentences shorter than a minute (complete with "uhs," "ums," "you knows," etc.).

Newspaper reporters, as discussed further in chapter 9, will spend extra time asking questions—sometimes the same one in different ways—looking to get just the right quotes that capture the moment. Those quotes often are the linchpins in holding a longer text story together while also getting readers to stick with it.

Figure 2.4 ■ There are standard ways to interview people. Be interested in the person, be sincere, make eye contact, and most important—listen.

Basics of Asking Questions:

a. Keep questions short and to the point.
b. Avoid yes-no questions.
c. Avoid double-barreled questions (asking two questions in a single sentence).
d. Avoid leading questions.
e. Ask easy questions first, tough questions at the end, but if you can ask only one question, ask the toughest one.

Interpersonal Skills:

a. Make frequent eye contact.
b. Occasionally you may nod or briefly smile (unless inappropriate; probably not good for interviewing convicts on death row).
c. Don't be afraid to firmly but politely cut off someone if they're being long-winded, deviating off-subject, or simply not answering the question.
d. Be skeptical but don't show any skepticism unless you have to.

Capturing the Interview

The mechanics of capturing an interview can be as complicated as the interview process itself. A multiskilled journalist should always carry some type of recording device, be it a cellphone, still or video camera, or digital audio recorder. We'll discuss specifics of editing and uploading in chapter 6.

Recording the interview helps you in a number of ways. Recording helps you to get your facts straight. The recording can verify what you wrote down was accurate. It can also provide the context for opinion or reactions to sensitive topics. Recording also helps you generate stories for multiple platforms. You can pull audio quotes for online as well as broadcast.

It is also important to remember that recording someone is a legal issue. You must let the interviewee know in advance he or she is being recorded and obtain his or her consent. Most of the time newsmakers are fine with it, but occasionally you'll suddenly be confronted with someone demanding that you "turn that thing off!"

Finally, last but not least, know how to operate your recorder. Sounds too obvious? Students routinely tell us they missed recording an interview because "the equipment didn't work." We call that "operator error" and it happens to us all. Many years ago one of the authors made the same mistake, conducting an interview with a state representative with the recorder in pause the entire time. There was no retake and no soundbites ever aired. The lesson is to know your equipment and don't get distracted by the pressure of the interview.

Specialized Types of Interviewing

News Conferences: Group Interviewing

This is probably the most intimidating experience for young reporters. You're in a group situation with a famous person and the older, more experienced reporters talk over each other (even yell) and jostle to be in front and get the questions in. You might not get to ask a single question. But there are some ways to improve your place in the scrum.

Box 2.2 Ethics in Journalism

By Chris Roberts

Journalists gather information, decide what's important, and present it in useful ways. So do lawyers and public relations practitioners, which may be why many journalists eventually go to law school or take PR jobs.

The difference lies in their loyalties, a primary consideration when making ethical decisions. While lawyers and PR practitioners feel primary loyalty toward their clients, the Society of Professional Journalists' code of ethics says its members' top obligation is to "public enlightenment." Bill Kovach and Tom Rosenstiel, writing in *The Elements of Journalism,* made it plainer: Journalism's "first loyalty is to citizens."

This doesn't mean law or PR is inherently unethical. It means that journalism's public-first loyalty affects its values, the bedrock beliefs that lead to our actions. Journalism's "first obligation is to truth," Kovach and Rosenstiel wrote in defining a journalist's key value.

The SPJ code describes four overarching values, but a close examination reveals that those four values often conflict with one another. The code calls for journalists to:

"Seek the truth and report it," but also to "minimize harm." Individually, each value brings its own set of ethical issues, but efforts to tell the truth while minimizing harm is often the crux of dilemmas. And notice that it's about minimizing harm—not eliminating it—because truth-telling often harms people (whether they deserve it or not).

"Act independently," but also to "be accountable." Journalists cannot be beholden to anyone other than the public in order to tell the truth, but they also must be accountable to the public and others.

The essence of doing journalism ethics is finding the justifiable balance between these sometimes-competing values is. It's always been difficult, and in today's convergent media environment of speed and competition, it's never been harder.

But never more important.

Chris Roberts, Ph.D., is an assistant professor of journalism at the University of Alabama and co-author of *Doing Ethics in Journalism: Theories and Practical Applications* (Routledge, 2011).

Arrive early and stake out a place in the front. Be serious, be friendly, but hold your ground. Watch out for other reporters who will try to step in front or use body contact to jostle you to the side or to the back.

When it's time to ask questions, be sure you are ready. Write out the question word for word or mentally rehearse it. Follow the rules set earlier—for example,

Figure 2.5 ■ Public group interviewing is still the best and most efficient way for newsmakers to get their message to people. Journalists judge and verify information so people tend to trust it more than when it's a simple news release or posted through social media.

avoid leading or double-barreled questions. Focus on asking a why or how type of question. Seek a response that captures opinion or emotion. When you're actually able to ask the question, use a clear voice in a moderate volume and be as succinct as possible. Make eye contact with the speaker. Record the response or make sure you write it down.

Sports Interviewing

Because of the nature of sports, it's often difficult to be a tough interviewer. Especially when starting out and covering local sports, there is often pressure to boost the local team. Then there is the need to fight through the thicket of clichés like "We're just going to take it one game at a time," or the classic "We gave it 110 percent tonight."

Sports reporters learn to be focused, often asking "why" and "what" questions: Why did you make that pitching change? Why did you throw to Jones when Smith was open in the end zone? What, exactly, was going through your mind when that putt was rolling toward the cup for the title?

The worst kind of question often is, "How do you feel about (fill in the blank)." That's usually a cliché generator.

Interviewing is essentially the same no matter what area you're in. Sports coverage is just as much a part of journalism as government or natural disasters. Be friendly, be confident, talk to as many people as possible. Don't get carried away by the thrill of victory. Be sympathetic, because for every winner, there's a loser. Be a good listener, and be ready to ask intelligent follow-up questions when the quotes and anecdotes come forth.

Weather Interviewing

Stories about the weather are easy to do but hard to do well. When weather is bad, it's easy to get people to comment and say the obvious, such as, "I've never seen storms this bad before." But it's difficult to sustain interest if nothing new is happening.

On the other hand, when bad weather causes destruction and death, it's too easy to lapse into the "how do you feel about this" mode, which can be seen as insensitive. You also want to avoid making victims seem like objects of pity with your questioning. The Dart Center for Journalism and Trauma (http://dartcenter.org) provides guidance on how to handle sensitive situations. (It's also an excellent place for journalists to find ways to minimize the psychological scars that can result from covering disasters and human suffering.)

A common mistake during hurricane season is to make it sound as if an approaching storm is the apocalypse when it's not. Avoid the "urgent voice of doom" approach while showing us video of gentle waves and sunshine.

Entertainment Interviewing

Interviewing actors, musicians, comedians, artists, dancers, authors, and other celebrities can be difficult because there are two distinctly different agendas. The celebrity is seeking publicity and promotion. You want something newsworthy. In between, especially with higher-profile individuals, there often is a protective public relations person.

Usually you and your subject can compromise and get insights into his or her private life and public persona that make a great feature story. But you'll also meet those with stars in their eyes who equate "fan buzz" to newsworthiness. One of the authors once got the helpful suggestion that the lead should be "This band is hot and tickets to tonight's show are going fast."

Anyone in the spotlight for more than a short time has probably been asked the same questions repeatedly. You need to think hard about what those are and come up with fresh material. Some of the shopworn queries just have to be asked, but it's best not to lead with them so the person being interviewed doesn't lapse into "oh no, not again" mode and spit out canned answers. Many entertainers love being asked about their art more than about themselves. Those can be great icebreaker questions, but only if you actually have read, watched, or listened to their work and can talk intelligently about it. Otherwise, they can spot a faker a mile away.

SUMMARY

This chapter presented four of the most basic elements to being a journalist and reporting about news events. First, it is important to know what about an event turns it into "news" for you and the community. News is more than simply information; it is timely information about something of interest to people. Second, good journalism is also good storytelling. To tell a story well, it's important to use appropriate words carefully. Writing well is attained by practice and attention to detail. Good writers are made, rarely born. Third, a journalist is a gatherer of information, and there are guidelines to help you get the information you need. Knowledge is power, and the best information is not easily uncovered. This brings us to the fourth basic element: Interviewing. A journalist is only as good as his or her sources, and sources are people too. How you ask questions, how you cultivate professional sources, and how you interact and talk with your sources can greatly influence your career. The next chapter will provide the other essential skills you need to be a truly converged journalist.

EXERCISES

1. Reporting. Attend a scheduled event on your campus that has some degree of controversy or difference of opinion. Was one side supported by facts more than the other? Which one seemed closer to "the truth", and why? Next, exchange stories with one of your classmates and look for evidence of bias or favoritism. Discuss with each other the type of impression your readers may take away from your story.
2. Interviewing: Theory into practice. Each of the scenarios listed below places ever-increasing demands upon you as an interviewer. By the end of the fourth interview you should be noticing some clear differences in the interviewing experience. Discuss these differences in class or in groups. What was the biggest issue you had to deal with in the fourth interview?
   a. First, interview *someone you know* about a topic he or she is *willing* to talk about (or at least, they probably won't resist answering questions). For example, interview a friend about what he or she did last summer.
   b. Next, interview *someone you don't know* about a topic he or she is *willing* to talk about. For example, interview a professor you've never taken a class with about his or her research, professional experience, or hobbies.
   c. Third, interview *someone you know* about a topic he or she is *less willing or reluctant* to talk about. For example, talk with a friend or acquaintance about a topic that could be painful or difficult to talk about. This can be anything from personal pain, loss, or failure to something related to politics, sex, or religion.
   d. Finally, interview *someone you don't know* about a topic he or she is *less willing or reluctant* to talk about. For example, schedule and arrange a short interview with a university official about specific types of campus crime, future tuition increases or budget problems, or even identifying a program that is underperforming and may be shrunk or cut entirely.

CHAPTER 3

CONVERGENT JOURNALISM SKILLS AND ROLES

"Tell me a story."[1] That was the mantra of Don Hewitt, creator of *60 Minutes* and the program's longtime executive producer. Hewitt argued that *60 Minutes'* success was due to its focus on telling stories to the audience, skillfully weaving interviews, narrative, and video of events to draw viewers into a story and make them care about a subject and those affected by it.

You can tell the stories you report on in many ways. The most common is to write it, and later chapters in this book discuss differences in writing news for different media. But you're not limited to text. Pictures and video tell stories too, frequently conveying emotion more powerfully than through a textual description. Graphics show how the elements of a story are linked together, helping news consumers make sense of complicated stories.

In this chapter, you'll learn a set of basic technical skills so that you're prepared to gather information and share it in whatever medium is most appropriate. You'll then read about new roles in converged newsrooms to gain a better understanding of the tasks involved in editing and delivering these stories to the public. Finally, you'll have a chance to consider the importance of teamwork in a converged newsroom.

[1] D. Hewitt, *Tell Me a Story: Fifty Years and 60 Minutes in Television* (New York: Public Affairs, 2002).

CONVERGENT JOURNALISM SKILLS

The set of basic skills everyone needs in a newsroom is evolving. For example, copy editing was once considered such a fundamental skill that many copy editors never envisioned their jobs would be in jeopardy. Even now, the annual awards given by the Southeast Region of the Society of Professional Journalists are known as the "Green Eyeshade Awards" after the iconic visors editors used to wear to reduce eyestrain.

But when job cuts hit newsrooms during the Great Recession of 2007–2009, copy desks were hit especially hard. Copy editors learned that, no matter how much they identified themselves as journalists, those running news organizations identified them as part of the production chain in creating newspapers. When economic times are tough, the goal of any industry producing a good, in this case the newspaper, is to reduce production costs.

Many news companies have now consolidated their copy desks so that fewer and more harried editors serve multiple newsrooms. There have even been suggestions to do away with most editors.[2] The lesson to take away is that if you define yourself as a journalist by just one skill, you are more likely to become digital roadkill.

You need to be familiar with a range of skills in order to be a multimedia journalist. You can't be expert at everything, but you need to know the basic principles behind them all. Then you can work effectively as a solo "backpack journalist" when conditions demand it and also as part of the team needed to produce today's journalism across media.

Editing

Your first editing decisions take place even as you are planning the story: What elements will be included? Will there be video, audio, or maybe a photo slide show? How you begin framing the story at this point affects the reporting you do. You must also consider the filing schedule: Will you go immediately to the Web with a short item, building it as the story progresses, or will you seek to break it in print or on TV and then move the items to the Web (a workflow that is less common each day)?

Depending on that filing schedule, once you have completed enough interviews, taken pictures or maybe shot video, and gathered the background information on your story, it's time to write. You must decide what information is to be included and what is to be left out. You might work with a "line editor" at this point, or you might be left to your own devices. (A line editor in newspaper newsrooms is generally the direct supervisor of a group of reporters. In broadcast, a "producer" may assume this role, but reporters tend to have a bit more autonomy.)

Eventually, and primarily in newspaper newsrooms, your well-honed story will go to a copy editor. Copy editors used to be typecast as grammar and style nerds who nitpicked, enforced arcane style rules, and wrote the headlines. That was never true—copy editors have always been the readers' surrogates, making sure stories are complete,

---

[2] A. Mutter (February 2008), *Can Newspapers Afford Editors?* Reflections of a Newsosaur blog, http://newsosaur.blogspot.com/2008/02/can-newspapers-afford-editors.html. See a rejoinder, D. Fisher, *Let's Fire All the Copy Editors* (February 2008), Common Sense Journalism blog, http://commonsensej.blogspot.com/2008/02/lets-fire-all-copy-editors.html.

concise, and coherent, even after line editors directly in charge of the reporters take a first crack at structural and content issues.

In the modern newsroom, the copy editor's job has expanded. In some cases, only a copy editor may see a story—if it is edited at all—before it is posted online. (Stories usually are given at least one more look by an editor, often a copy editor, before they are printed in the paper.) At smaller papers, copy editors are being pressed into service to post content (including video) on the news organization's websites; to monitor comments; and to write two sets of headlines, including one for the online posting specifically designed to be search engine friendly (more on that in chapter 4). And at papers large and small, some copy editors are being redesignated as "curators" who not only do traditional work editing stories but also find or confirm related links and monitor online posts for relevant content from other sources such as blogs and Twitter feeds.

One thing is certain, especially in large newsrooms: The number of editors looking at a story before it is published has been cut. Reporters are now expected to scour their copy for many of the same issues that previously might have been left to a copy editor.

Copy editors follow a hierarchy of issues when they look at a story (or photo and caption or graphic). These issues should also be considered by the multimedia reporter:

Legal issues and fairness: Is this defamatory or does it invade privacy? Have all sides been given a chance to present their views? Does the writing make sure not to convict someone before a trial? Nothing else matters if you leave your newsroom open to expensive legal action.

Accuracy in fact, tone, and display: Are all the facts right, names spelled correctly, places located correctly, etc.? Are the correct words and idioms used? Do the numbers add up; are the percentages right; are there logical impossibilities, such as saying something decreased more than 100 percent; and if the copy lists four things, does it say "four" or "five"? Are the tone of the story and the headline appropriate? (A New Jersey paper once ran the headline "Roasted Nuts" over a story about a fire at a mental hospital. The public outcry led to an apology in the paper the next day from the editor.) Will any juxtaposition of elements on the page—printed or online—cause a misunderstanding or, worse, derision?

Completeness: If the story says an accident happened at one of the interchanges on the interstate highway, does it tell you which one? If it says traffic was backed up, does it say how far? If it says the fire station is moving "down the road," does it tell you which road? The copy editor must, and the reporter should, anticipate readers' questions throughout the story and make sure they are answered.

Length and conciseness: Is the wording concise and are the quotes to the point? One big job for any editor these days is to try to squeeze more into less space (even online, where studies show that reading drops dramatically after scrolling past the first screen). As Ruth Walker put it so well in her "Verbal Energy" column in the *Christian Science Monitor*: "Editing is often the point at which the irresistible push for shorter, simpler ways of saying things meets the immovable object of the need for standards, accuracy, and precision."[3]

---

[3] R. Walker, *Politically Incorrect in Holland and Ulster, Christian Science Monitor* (June 2005), http://www.csmonitor.com/2005/0617/p18s04-hfgn.html.

Language issues: So far, we haven't mentioned grammar, style, spelling, usage, punctuation, and similar issues. They are important, but good editors take care of many of them when they are dealing with the larger things. It's like the tableside chef at a Japanese hibachi restaurant. Amid all the whirling knives and spatulas, flipping of pieces of meat or fish onto your plate, and flames shooting from the food, it's easy to forget the main thing, which is that the chef is also cooking that food just right.

English is a polyglot language, having borrowed many of its words and conventions from other languages. As a result, the guidelines of grammar and correct word usage (saying a tense situation was "defused" not "diffused," for instance) are wide and deep and take up entire books. There are plenty of good texts out there. But remember this basic concept: Grammar is the order in which words go together to create meaning, and it is the editor's job to ensure that the meaning the writer intended is the one the reader receives.

Style sits on top of grammar and language issues. It will vary from publication to publication. Many newspapers use the *AP Stylebook* (AP style), but some online operations use the Yahoo! Style Guide and some book publishers use the *Chicago Manual of Style* (CMS or Chicago style). Most news organizations of any size have a local stylebook that covers things like names unique to your area.

Style sets the tone of a publication and provides consistency both for production and for the reader. It's a referee. Do we spell the word "canceled" or "cancelled," for instance? There is no correct answer, so the style guide, after considering how various others use it, generally chooses the first-listed spelling in the dictionary.

Style changes have speeded up as the Internet allows lightning-fast dissemination and adoption of new usage. For instance, in 2010 AP style made a change to "website" from the previous "Web site," the latter having long been derided in parts of the online community. You may have to learn several styles during your career. They will differ, and it's pointless to argue too strongly about things like whether to use a comma before the conjunction in a series. But there is one truism: *The only style you have to follow is the one used by the person signing your paycheck.* If you run your own publication or blog, feel free to set your style but make sure you can explain the decisions behind it.

Language and style issues can be scary, especially because journalism tends to be more "prescriptive" than you might have encountered in high school writing assignments. But the pressure is on more than ever to get it right—the first time—and that means reporters no longer can say they'll leave it to the copy desk to fix because they need to move on to the next assignment.

Photography

Taking pictures is now a basic skill for every journalist. Good photography has two dimensions: mechanics and aesthetics. The mechanics deal with the basic use of the camera to capture an image. Aesthetics deals with the subjects themselves and how the picture is composed. Great photographers not only know the mechanics but also sense when the moment should be captured, the best angle and lighting, the elements that should or should not be included, and how those elements should be arranged.

Photojournalists generally do not have the luxury of positioning their subjects but must capture them in real time, using available angles and often without a second chance.

The three rules for good general photography (excepting the occasional artistic shot) are:

1. The image must be in focus.
2. The image must be lit using natural or artificial light so that it can be clearly seen from the angle of the camera.
3. The subject must be within the frame.

Many other tips for taking good photographs can be found in photojournalism or photography textbooks, but let's look at these three in more depth, with illustrations of each in figure 3.1.

Focus: To understand how to focus a camera, you must understand "depth of field," the distance between the closest and farthest points at which an image is in focus. Many factors affect a camera's depth of field. The more light reflected from a subject to the camera, the greater the depth of field. As more light is available, the camera's iris, the opening that controls the light from the lens to where the image is captured, can become smaller, allowing a sharper image.

Expert photographers manipulate the depth of field to draw attention to specific objects in a picture, but most other photographers prefer to have as much depth of field as possible, reducing the likelihood that anything will be out of focus. The simplest

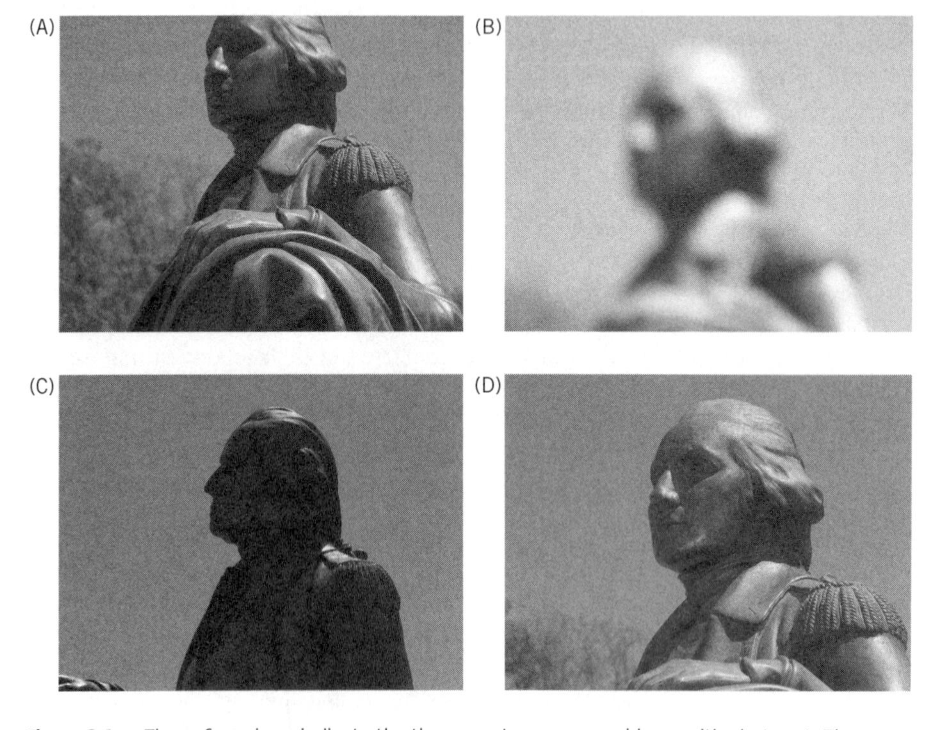

Figure 3.1 ■ These four views indicate the three most common problems with photos. A: The subject is out of the frame. B: The subject is out of focus. Neither of these problems can be fixed in editing. C: This is an illustration of bad lighting; in some cases, the photo can be improved with a great deal of editing. D: The last photo has the subject in frame, in focus, and well lit.

cameras have a single lens that allows images to stay in focus from about 10 feet from the camera to as far as the camera can see. Most cameras used in photojournalism, however, have advanced lenses containing multiple elements that can be adjusted to focus light from different distances.

Those lenses usually have a ring that is turned in order to bring an object into focus. Increasingly popular automatic focus cameras allow less experienced photographers to more easily capture images without having to manually focus the camera. The downside is that they can miss the shot because of the time it takes the camera to focus or because the camera focuses on the wrong object.

Lighting: Two principles should be followed. First, there must be enough illumination for the image to be captured. Second, the lighting must create shadows so the two-dimensional image will appear to have the depth we're used to seeing in 3-D real life.

You never want the light coming from behind a subject because the side of the subject seen by the camera, usually a face, will be darkened like a silhouette. The light should come from behind the photographer so the part of the subject facing the camera is most illuminated. But if the light comes from directly behind the camera, there are no shadows on the subject, and the subject appears to be flat. The best lighting is behind and slightly above the camera, both illuminating the subject and creating enough shadow to create some depth in the two-dimensional image.

When natural light is not sufficient, photographers use a flash, but a flash has limited range. Most flashes will illuminate objects between five and 20 feet from the camera; anything farther will be in shadow. Sometimes photographers will use a flash even when there is sufficient natural light in order to provide additional illumination to fill in harsh shadows on the subject.

Framing: The third basic principle of good photography is that the subject must be included in the frame of the picture. Photo editing tools such as Photoshop let you cut out, or crop, parts of the picture that you don't want seen—in essence you can enlarge any part of a photograph to become a new photograph on its own. But you can't add elements that don't appear in the photograph originally. Besides any technical questions, adding them would raise ethical issues. Therefore, always frame your subject wider than you expect the final picture to be, ensuring that movement by the subject won't take it out of the frame.

Beyond focus, lighting, and framing, good photographs must also include certain aesthetic elements. The most basic of these is the set of subjects you choose to portray. For example, if you're trying to illustrate a particular automobile, don't take a picture of the car in heavy traffic or the viewer's attention might shift to other automobiles or to the relationship between the cars. Similarly, if you're trying to take a picture of an individual, consider whether other people should be in the photograph. The presence of others may help illustrate a particular story or may detract attention from the central subject, confusing the viewer. Also, pay attention to the background so that, for instance, it doesn't appear like you have a tree growing out of someone's head. Photo editing tools allow you to eliminate extraneous subjects, but these should be used sparingly and almost always introduce ethical issues. As a photojournalist, your job is to capture a moment or event, not create a moment or event with photographic wizardry.

The angle of the shot also can affect our perception of the subject. Shooting while looking up at an object or person makes them seem bigger, more powerful. Positioning the camera high and shooting down makes an object or person seem smaller and less powerful. The best angle for news is straight on at eye-level.

Box 3.1 Ethics of Photography

Ethics for Visuals in a Converged World

By Denise McGill

We work in an amazing time for creativity in visual media. Sometimes the field is so open, it feels like the Wild West. But the new frontier is not a lawless free-for-all.

Here are some guidelines to help sort out ethical standards at every stage of production. As a general rule, be honest about the content and where it came from. Protect your credibility at all costs.

Gathering content: Document what's going on; don't move things around or tell your subjects what to do. You'll get the best moments when you let things unfold in front of you. The exceptions for set-ups are portraits, interviews, and illustrations.

Post-production: All files need to be processed for things like color correction. But fundamental changes are *verboten*. Don't change the color of someone's outfit or remove clutter in Photoshop. For video, make sure your cuts don't change the meaning of a story.

Be sure captions and credit lines are accurate. Make an effort to trace the source as far back as you can, not just to the first Web site you find on Google.

Publishing: Respect copyrights. Give credit (and fees) to the copyright holder. It's illegal to shoplift from a brick and mortar store, and it's illegal to steal files online.

Remember that anything can go viral. You are more likely to get sued when your creation gets a lot of page hits. Ask yourself, "What would happen if 1,000,000 people view this?" If you've used a song or an image without permission, someone will likely come knocking to cash in.

For more information, contact the National Press Photographers Association (NPPA). Their Code of Ethics and Business Practices are the standard for still photography, video and online visual journalism. http://www.nppa.org/professional_development/business_practices/ethics.html

Because each photo tells a different aspect of the story, most photographers take dozens of shots, allowing their editors to choose the one or two that combine with the text to tell the most complete story. Figure 3.2 illustrates how two pictures of the same scene tell a very different story.

In a converged newsroom, the number of photos used may be much greater than one or two. In traditional print media, there is rarely enough space to print more than one or two photos to accompany a story. But online media allow the use of as many photos as the editor thinks will help tell the story. These photos may be presented in a gallery (as clickable thumbnails that expand to full size that the user can navigate around) or as a slideshow (in which the editor or photographer decides the order in which the photos are

(A)

(B)

Figure 3.2 ■ These two photos were taken a few minutes apart to show the same scene. The difference between the two is that the one on the top shows a densely packed set of remote trucks, and it is difficult to make out any details regarding any specific truck. The one on the bottom shows just one of these trucks, but this time the truck appears separated from others so that the focus is on the parts of this remote truck. If the goal is illustrating intense media coverage, the picture on the top is much better. But if the goal is showing what a remote truck looks like, the picture on the bottom is much better.

seen). It is rare that every photo taken for a story would be used, but using more photos increases the angles and dimensions of the story portrayed.

A photojournalist must abide by the same ethical rules any journalist follows. Your photographs, and the subsequent photo editing process, must accurately depict the subject or events in your story. It is often possible to capture a subject during an inopportune moment, creating a memorable image that misrepresents the subject or event. Don't do it. Rather, consider the maxim that "a picture is worth a thousand words" and use your camera to help people who were not there to see, feel, and understand the story.

Videography

The basics of good videography are the same as those of good photography: Your images must be in focus, well lit, and in the frame. With videography, however, you have less ability to edit what is seen inside the frame. When combined with video's lower resolution than still photography, framing becomes a more important element in videography than in photography.

As with photography, having the image in focus is critical in videography. Again, the more depth of field you have, the more likely any image is to be in focus. How you use your zoom lens on a video camera has a big effect on the depth of field. The more you zoom to capture a distant image, the more the iris opens to capture the restricted light, resulting in a decreased depth of field. But when the camera is zoomed out and is closer to a subject, the iris is closed down, creating more depth of field and making it easier to keep objects in focus.

Getting close to the subject also reduces the image shaking caused by camera movement. When the camera must be handheld, any slight motion will result in a shaky picture. The more you zoom in on the subject, the more the shaking of the camera is magnified. But if you zoom out all the way, using the widest angle setting, and getting as close as possible to your subject, any camera movement becomes less perceptible, creating a more stable image.

The best practice is to use a tripod whenever possible to keep the camera stationary. The viewer's attention will then remain on the subject of the picture, not on the inexperience of the videographer.

Editing video also is different from editing photographs. Instead of cropping and retouching an individual image, editing video consists of putting together a sequence of moving pictures to tell a story. As discussed in chapter 8, the editing process begins with analysis of both the story and the video, with the object being to use the video to illustrate the news story being told.

Today's high-definition video also lets editors capture individual video frames for use as photographs with enough resolution for print, websites, and other online media.

Graphics Design

Graphics are an increasingly important tool across all media. They can simplify complex quantitative information, illustrate a place or event, diagram relationships among subjects of a news story, or highlight specific story elements. A good graphic:

1. Is simple so that the reader can easily grasp the point being made.
2. Uses multiple colors to illustrate differences among subjects or areas of a graphic, but not so many that the viewer becomes confused.

3. Cites the source of the information contained in the graphic.
4. Tells a story on its own without needing explanatory information. (There may be such information, but it should extend the storytelling, not be required for understanding.)

As a convergent journalist, you don't need to be a graphics artist, but you do need to know when graphics can be used to enhance a story or help simplify complex elements. Your most important skill will be how to relay information to a graphic artist, allowing the artist to create the image that will accompany your story. But remember, this is your story and you must make sure the graphic accurately represents the information available to you. Figure 3.3 illustrates the power of a graphic to communicate simple information.

Web Design

In the Internet's earliest days, individuals posting information on a Web page were expected to know the underlying HTML language that determines how a browser displays things. Now, things are simpler, and the most important thing is to know your website's capabilities.

Most news organizations employ professional designers to create a website's look and feel. What you need to know—and think about during your reporting—is what elements are on a particular Web page and how they are likely to be edited and arranged. For greater depth and detail, you should consult a more comprehensive text that focuses on Web design.

	Radio	Television	Newspaper	Online
Measurement unit	# seconds	# seconds	# column inches	# screens
Typical length	20 seconds	90 seconds	12 column inches	1 screen
Typical length—words	50 words	130 words	400 words	250 words

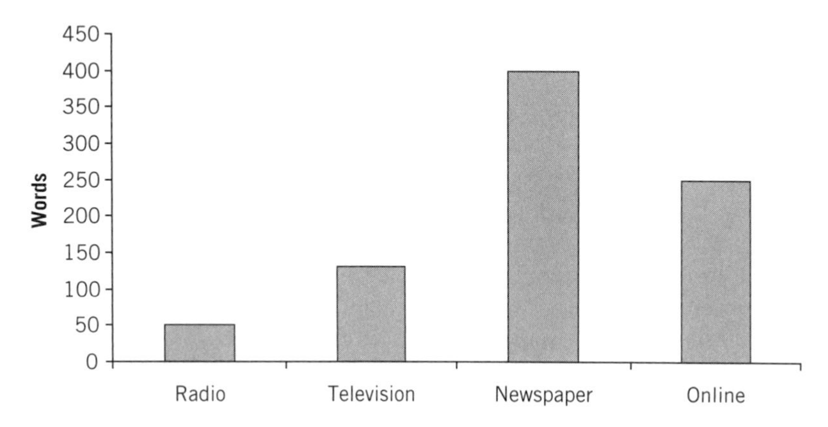

Figure 3.3 ■ Here are two views of the same information (in this case, an illustration from chapter 1). The numbers in the table tell the same story as those in the bar chart, but it is much easier for a reader to understand and interpret the bar chart than the table.

NEW ROLES IN A CONVERGED NEWSROOM

In a converged newsroom, the flow of stories to multiple media creates a need for two new types of managers introduced in chapter 1, the *storybuilder* and the *newsflow manager*. These roles are not job titles, but rather functions that must be fulfilled in order to manage the flow of content.

New Role: Storybuilder

The storybuilder combines a number of traditional newsroom roles, including the copy editors and assigning editors in newspaper newsrooms and the producers in broadcast newsrooms. The storybuilder role addresses how today's multimedia news workers might deal with information and story flow differently from a decade ago. Then, the media employed linear, assembly-line models where quality control occurred at specific points (producers or copy editors). Now, multimedia elements of the same story flow at widely differing times and, sometimes, locations.

Instead of managing multiple stories across a specific medium, the storybuilder manages fewer multimedia "streams" on specific topics. The output is either filed directly or the elements are made available to other more media-specific desks.

Thus, the storybuilder must have a copy editor's eye for detail, the producer's acumen for flow and pacing, and the assigning editor's skill in seeing the various paths a topic might take, then matching resources to those possibilities. The challenge of the storybuilder is to recognize what aspect of a story is best told in each medium and then differentiate content across media.

New Role: Newsflow Manager

The newsflow manager has the role of directing the stories produced to all of the different output media available in a converged newsroom. In a newsroom that might serve a print product, a broadcast outlet or digital video channel, a web-based app, and one or more websites, the newsflow manager would direct individual stories and story elements to the most appropriate output media. The newsflow manager oversees the flow of information collected and processed by journalists and storybuilders to the production side of the operation, where it is then delivered to the public.

The comparable role in a newspaper is that of the managing editor and for a television station that of an executive producer or managing editor. The key difference is that in a converged newsroom the newsflow manager looks at the mix of available stories with an emphasis on delivering them through multiple media, not just one. In this respect, the role is most similar to that of the television executive producer who decides what stories will be delivered during which of three to five evening newscasts.

In a multimedia newsroom, where the newsflow is asynchronous, someone still must be in charge. According to journalism futurist Kerry Northrup (the visionary behind Newsplex at the University of South Carolina), the newsflow editor looks at the management of a story from 30,000 feet while the storybuilder is looking at it from 10,000 feet and the multimedia reporter is on the ground.

In some ways, this position may be the most important in transitioning news operations where different editors in the same organization are responsible for content in different media. This is a structure that leads to territoriality, where content is embargoed rather than shared. Work is duplicated. The synergies of convergence are harder to achieve, as editors make decisions based upon the best interests of their individual work unit instead of the broader news organization.

One media house that has confronted this problem is the Nordjyske Medier in Alborg, Denmark, one of the most converged news organizations in the world. Its 250 journalists are organized by content area and produce content for print, online, radio, TV, and mobile. The former editor-in-chief, Ulrik Haagerup, described himself as a "media conductor." Individual editors are responsible for each medium and report to him. Haagerup says different media have different demands, so he sees a need for these platform-specific editors to "refine" the Nordjyske's content.

The newsflow manager must have a detailed knowledge of the different audiences for and capabilities of each output medium. The timing of each story's delivery must be determined and communicated with appropriate newsroom personnel. Each reporter, storybuilder, photographer, and others must also communicate with the newsflow manager regarding updates, angles, and breaking information to ensure that stories are delivered as planned or that adjustments can be made with minimal disruption. Accordingly, the newsflow manager has the greatest need for management skills in a converged newsroom.

A newsroom might have several newsflow managers working together. Responsibilities might be divided by subject matter (metro news, sports, national news, lifestyle) or by output medium (television, digital, print).

New Role: User-Generated Content (UGC) Editor

News organizations have always relied upon news tips and leads from the public, but the flow of information from the public continues to increase as cameras shrink and mobile devices equipped with cameras proliferate. Now, almost every breaking news story is captured by someone's cellphone (or a security camera).

A decade into the 21st century, newsrooms remain conflicted over what to do with this material, and relatively few have an editor devoted solely to this function. Some of the content needs to be verified and some needs to be selected or edited, especially when the news organization has asked people to contribute material (such as after a major storm). But while this potentially complicates the flow of information into a newsroom, much of this content remains walled off in separate sections of news organizations' websites, such as CNN's iReport (http://ireport.cnn.com), with little oversight. Figure 3.4 illustrates how CNN frames the content provided by these ireporters.

Still, even CNN monitors the stream, looking for significant items, and it bestows a special "CNNiReport" logo on those it has vetted.

Along the way, a new challenge has emerged. Many of these images are heavily edited—or sometimes fabricated—to distort an event or skew coverage of a person or issue. User-contributed content must be verified, and the speed of checking the accuracy of this content can make the difference between being first or last with breaking news.

Some news sites also allow people to create their own blogs, and some even feature the most recent posts on their home page, but little of this content is directly integrated into the normal newsroom workflow.

Comments, which can also be considered a form of user-generated content, are another thorny area that remains unresolved. The Digital Millennium Copyright Act

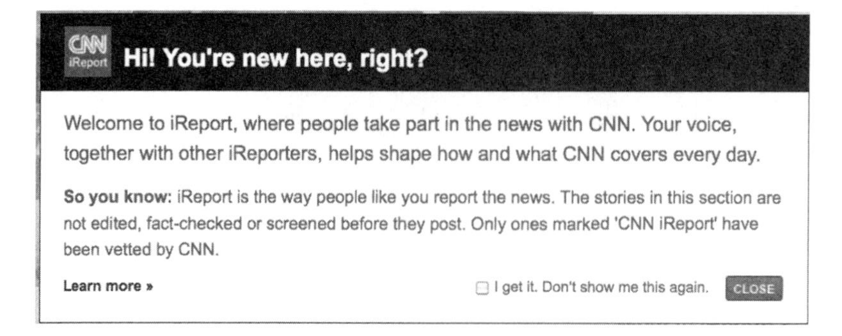

Figure 3.4 ■ CNN's iReport comes with a disclaimer to let readers know that most content has not been vetted and that vetted content gets a special identification.

and Section 230 of the Communications Decency Act largely insulate website operators from liability in U.S. courts if someone else posts copyrighted or defamatory material to a site. The debate continues, however, about whether comments can be anonymous (which proponents say encourages speech but opponents say promotes the nastiness seen in many comment threads) or should be allowed only after registration and identification (which proponents say promotes civility while opponents say it drives people to other sites).

A novel approach by some news organizations (such as *USA Today*) is to allow users to rate comments made by other users—a high ratio of negative to positive comments results in "hiding" the offending comments. Other sites have a "report offensive comment" button.

Some "best practices" have emerged, however:

- Have a code of conduct written in plain, simple language. The code should make clear that harassment of other online community members is not tolerated and that some types of content (such as vulgarity and posting substantial portions of content on other sites) are not allowed. A code also makes it easier for the community manager to take action against violators without seeming to be arbitrary.
- Resist the urge as a journalist to "expose" violators and ban them at the first infraction. The reaction from your other members is not likely to be relief or applause but an apprehension that you could easily do the same to them. The better approach is to remove any offending material and send a note to the offender explaining why. You should also leave a note in place of the removed content explaining why it was removed to address concerns other community members might have.
- If the problems persist, explain to the community in more detail what is happening. Sometimes community peer pressure will work.
- Don't execute the ultimate penalty—banning the person—without fully explaining to the online community why. As in real communities, rumors and misinformation can quickly ricochet around an online community, and

once positions have hardened based on such rumors and misinformation, incalculable damage may have been done.

- In current newsrooms, the task of managing user-contributed content is often distributed among editors, but the increasing complexity of the issues may lead to an opportunity for journalists to specialize in this area. Already we are seeing more newsrooms creating "online community manager" positions that include some of these roles.

New Role: Digital Rights Manager

As photos, video clips, text, and other content flowing into a newsroom increases, "digital rights management" (DRM) systems have been developed to manage these newsroom "assets." They help the news staff keep track of what content is in the system, what rights the organization has to use the content, who created the content, and so on.

For example, content from a wire service or syndicator may be approved for use in print but not online. Or a reporter might need a photo or video clip from a story that ran months or years ago. Digital rights management systems keep track of allowed uses and enable specific content to be found quickly. As these systems become more complicated, newsrooms will increasingly need "digital rights managers."

New Role: Interactive Content Designer

The capability to use Flash, JavaScript, and new versions of HTML to create interactive content such as data visualizations has created a demand for a specialist combining technical software skills and journalism skills to gather and edit the underlying data and other information. Reporters who have this particular combination of skills are a valuable commodity. Although this role is not served in every converged newsroom, it should become more prevalent as more journalists acquire the combination of skills needed.[4]

New Role: Social Media Coordinator

The emergence of social media has created an important new role, the social media coordinator. This role is responsible for sharing information on social network sites such as Facebook and Twitter. As discussed in chapter 11, this role is substantially different from that of a traditional reporter. Rather than gathering and sharing news, the social media coordinator is responsible for creating conversations about the news, linking the work of reporters to the public through conversations, and applying other techniques that enable interactivity. In some newsrooms we're also seeing this position being given the job of managing online communities.

It's not possible to discuss every new role in a converged newsroom—in fact, some new roles will undoubtedly have emerged between the time this book was written and the time you are reading it. One of your more valuable insights may be to spot these new roles as they emerge, training yourself (or obtaining the training) so that you can add the right skills to your repertoire.

---

[4] See Mindy McAdams's website www.flashjournalism.com for a discussion of the complexities in creating interactive news content, as well as how-to training (if you're so inclined).

Although some early speculation suggested that the major challenge of managing a converged newsroom would be the difference in terminology and work style, research has indicated that these barriers are easily overcome.[5] Instead, the primary challenges that have emerged relate to the "ownership" of stories by reporters who identify with a specific medium and to the clash of organizational cultures among print, broadcast, and online.

PERFORMANCE

Just as all journalists should know how to operate *behind* a (video) camera (phone) to record images, so journalists should also know the basics of how to appear and act *in front* of a camera, as in figure 3.5. The structure of video news requires that reporters be able to appear on camera telling a story as well as reading the story off-camera. All converged journalists must have certain basic skills related to on-camera performance.

Speaking clearly is the most important performance tool. You don't have to have a great voice, movie star looks, or a flashy wardrobe to appear on camera. But you must be able to read your script clearly, enunciating your words so that listeners or viewers can clearly understand what you're saying. Many novice reporters make the mistake of trying to sound like a television announcer rather than simply speaking clearly. Once on camera, don't try to be someone you're not. Instead, make sure the words coming out of your mouth are clearly understood by your audience.

Figure 3.5 ■ A multiskilled journalist needs to be prepared to report on camera. Some reporters spend more time on camera than others, but all reporters should be comfortable with on-camera reporting.

---

[5] S. Keith and W. Silcock, "Beyond the Tower of Babel: Ideas for Future Research in Media Convergence," in A. E. Grant and J. S. Wilkinson, eds., *Understanding Media Convergence: The State of the Field* (New York: Oxford University Press, 2009).

The simplest rule of thumb regarding your appearance is to make sure nothing distracts the viewer from the story you're trying to tell. As a general rule, dress conservatively, so that your clothes, jewelry, and makeup do not distract from the information you're reporting. Make sure that your attire is appropriate for the event you're covering. For example, it is appropriate for a reporter to wear a tuxedo to an awards show, but not to a train wreck—unless you came across the train wreck on the way home from the awards show.

TEAMWORK

The days of the lone-wolf journalist are largely gone. Yes, the reporter's trade is still at its heart one-on-one: The relationship with his or her sources is not likely to succeed as a group affair. But once the interaction with sources has given general shape to a story, creating the final version is a team effort. You are part of a team, regardless of whether it is a traditional print or broadcast newsroom, and especially in a converged operation. Teamwork is needed because of the increasing complexity of the technology and the channels by which the final product is delivered.

Teamwork is the last basic skill we want to explore in this chapter. Although many people have the image of a converged journalist as a "one-man band," most journalists are constantly working with others in the process of gathering and reporting the news, as in Figure 3.6. In converged newsrooms, there may be a greater overlap of skills among reporters, photographers, and editors.

Figure 3.6 ■ Teamwork is an essential aspect of any newsroom. Each member of the team has different contacts, skill sets, and expertise. Get to know your colleagues so that you can draw from their experiences and utilize their expertise to improve your reporting.

As with any team effort, the more you have worked together, the better you'll be at coordinating your efforts and generating a high-quality product. In the process, it is critical to know the strengths of the individuals with whom you are working so that you can draw upon their strengths to get the best possible story.

Communication skills become more important for a converged journalist. You must be able to relate information about interviews, images, and other story elements so that everyone on the team is gathering and processing information. For example, a television reporter must know the best shots being obtained by the videographers so the story can be written to use that video. Similarly, a photographer must know which individuals or objects are central to the story so that photographs of those can be taken and prepared for distribution. A reporter whose job includes writing for online—and most jobs do include that now—should know whether the relevant links are to be used within or alongside the story. He or she can then use help from the story's editors in discovering new, relevant links. In today's information-overload world, no one can hope to know enough of everything.

SUMMARY

It is not necessary that you become a master of all the skills discussed in this chapter, but it is important to have a fundamental working knowledge of many of them. That will not only let you work more effectively with others but also assist you in being more effective in gathering the elements you will need to report your story on the Web, on the air, in the newspaper, or in any other medium served by your newsroom. In the process, you will find you are better at some of the skills than others.

If you don't use a skill often enough, however, you might become rusty and forget the basics. Make sure you practice each of the skills discussed in this chapter regularly enough so that you are comfortable doing those jobs.

EXERCISES

1. Take a story from your local newspaper or a local TV report about some government or civic issue. Now put yourself in the position of being a multimedia reporter. What parts of the story would you like to actually see? Hear? Read more about?
2. Outline those multimedia elements you believe increase your desire to see, hear or read more about something. For instance, do you need a map to be able to tell where something is? Do you want to see or hear those angry neighbors protesting a tax increase? Do you want to actually read the parking law the city now says it will vigorously enforce?
3. Discuss where you would get that information and in what format. Discuss what other information you might have to give up. For instance, if you are busy recording audio of protesters and the city council members slip out a back door when you need more clarification on the tax proposal, what do you do?
4. Rank the top five skills you think journalists will need in the next decade and discuss your ranking and those of your classmates.

CHAPTER 4

FROM PRINT TO INTERNET: REPURPOSING CONTENT

It is rare to find a newsroom these days where journalists are not expected to file online. From new operations that exist primarily online, such as Pro Publica, Huffington Post, Politico, Voice of San Diego, and MinnPost, to traditional news operations that have integrated online into their legacy media, moving stories and other information online fast and often is the rule of the day.

Critics have been decrying the use of *shovelware*[1] for more than a decade. But the practice of producing content for another medium and then automatically moving it online by computer with little human intervention remains a powerful force in publishing. This chapter explores moving content online in ways that help a harried journalist on deadline minimize the shovelware.

Mobile devices such as tablets and smartphones demand new thinking about storytelling. New and improved technology, from social networks to a rewrite of the basic building block of most websites, HTML, makes it easier to quickly tell multimedia-rich, interactive stories online. This chapter serves as a bridge between old and new, designed to equip you with the skills needed to operate in that interregnum between legacy media and online while getting you ready to explore new ways of doing journalism in an online world.

---

[1] L. Pryor (April 9, 1999), "Old Media Firms Dig a Grave with Shovelware," *Online Journalism Review*, retrieved from http://www.ojr.org/ojr/technology/1017969861.php.

DELIVERY SYSTEM OR MEDIUM?

The Internet is both a **delivery system** and a **medium.**

As a delivery system, the Internet can provide information in whatever form your readers want, as long as it's available in that form:

- Do you have the spreadsheet from that budget meeting? Some letters or printed emails critical to that investigative project? Scribd or Google Docs is designed for quick uploading of documents to share with readers.
- Do you have video of the wreckage left by that storm? If so, YouTube or Vimeo are quick and easy upload sites, as are some social networks like Facebook.
- Maybe you want to share a PowerPoint presentation? Try Slideshare.
- Photos? Flickr or Photobucket—or Facebook.

The Internet can deliver that 5,000-word, analysis-laden Sunday story from a major newspaper as easily as it can last night's sports scores.

As a medium, digital storytelling has opened a largely untapped frontier. The idea of a daily news report specifically tailored for the reader—the vision of a "Daily Me" popularized by MIT Media Lab founder Nicholas Negroponte—is just beginning to be realized on portable devices like tablet computers. The vision by Tim Berners-Lee (acknowledged as the creative force behind the World Wide Web) of a "Semantic Web," where computers not only distribute information but also read the metadata in it to recognize patterns and make judgments, is not too far away with computer programs, for instance, already able to write simple sports stories about games based on statistical information.

The hallmark of the Internet era is *rapid relevance*—information delivered how you want it, when you want it, and where you want it at previously unheard-of speed.

For now, it seems the economics favor delivering information in bite-sized chunks or something a bit longer, but not the lengthy screeds some newspapers had developed a reputation for writing. Online news is still driven by metrics like unique visitors and page views, although studies continue to show those are relatively crude and ineffective measures, as few people actually click through on the banners and other ads that clutter pages. We are in an environment where routine news itself has largely become a commodity.[2] The result, for now, tends to push us more toward shovelware rather than toward groundbreaking forms.

Having said that, *good, engaging storytelling will work across media, even if it must be reshaped for each one. There are ways to make your storytelling more engaging, even when writing primarily for a more traditional medium and then pushing it online,*

THREE KEY ASPECTS

The Internet is an interactive medium. Studies show that people tend to quickly move among various elements on a page looking for things to click on and read or interact with,

---

[2] B. Grueskin, A, Seave, and L. Graves (May 10, 2011), "The Story So Far: What We Know About the Business of Digital Journalism," *Columbia Journalism Review*, retrieved from http://cjr.org/the_business_of_digital_journalism.

with one researcher noting the persistent F-pattern in found in eye-tracking studies.[3] In addition, search engines, specifically Google, continue to drive a large amount of traffic to news websites,[4] while social media sites are growing in influence. As a result, material online should have **searchability, scanability,** and **linkability.** It should also be shareable, but that is more of a factor of the publishing platform; the journalist's use of services like Facebook and Twitter will be discussed more in chapter 11 on social media.

Searchability

The Internet is a vast sea of information trolled by robots, also known as spiders, reporting back to search engines that display results according to algorithms (a preset process or set of rules) that take into account a site's content and utility, as well as how often it is linked-to from other sites.

Search engine optimization

This has spawned an entire industry, also called SEO, designed to push sites onto the first page of search engine results. (The industry is sometimes vilified as "black hat" manipulation, although, as in any specialization, that overemphasizes the ne'er-do-wells among its practitioners.)

The good news for journalists is that manipulation is not needed—just continuing to put the who, what, when, where, why, and how in the story. Doing that high up in the text (online news has promoted the return of the inverted pyramid form, though not with the massive first paragraphs that once characterized the style), and doing it as specifically as possible, will provide the key words needed to give you a boost in Google News results. Google News gives a bit less emphasis to the "page rank" algorithm (based on incoming links) of its regular search engine and uses other signals such as timeliness and relevance. It already has a built-in preference for "a strong news ecosystem" powered by what it calls "aggregate editorial interest" and favoring original content and local, trusted sources (trust being evidenced by how often users click on a publication's articles when seeking a specific type of information).[5]

This means some care must be taken when writing, especially considering how someone might search for an article. For instance, deciding whether to identify a person as Sam Jones or Samuel V. Jones III can affect whether that story shows up in future searches. And if he's more widely known as "Benny" Jones, then you need to consider whether (and where) to include his full formal name so the person searching in the future for "Samuel V. Jones" can find the story.

---

[3] J. Nielsen (April 17, 2006), "F-shaped Pattern for Reading Web Content," retrieved from http://www.useit.com/alertbox/reading_pattern.html. See also S. Outing and L. Ruel (2004), *Eyetrack III: Online News Consumer Behavior in the Age of Multimedia*, Poynter Institute, retrieved from http://www.poynterextra.org/eyetrack2004/main.htm.

[4] K. Olmestead, A. Mitchell, and T. Rosenstiel (May 2011), *Navigating News Online: Where People Go, How They Get There, and What Lures Them Away,* retrieved from http://www.journalism.org/sites/journalism.org/files/NIELSEN STUDY.pdf. One critic notes several shortcomings of the study: S. Buttry (May 10, 2011), "5 Big Problems with 'Navigating News Online' Study," http://stevebuttry.wordpress.com/2011/05/10/5-big-problems-with-navigating-news-online-study.

[5] Google has posted a video explanation of its system on YouTube: http://www.youtube.com/watch?v=hg8xgoULIIE. It also has a help site for publishers: http://www.google.com/support/news_pub/.

Searchability also is prompting a re-examination of some longtime style rules. For instance, is someone more likely to search for "Calif." (Associated Press style) or "California"? We are likely to see many such re-examinations.

Headlines

In SEO, headlines are critical because they often form the title tags that search engines use to categorize and promote a story or blog entry.[6] The headline may also be all a reader sees when deciding whether to click through to read something.

Websites are now taking a more minimal approach to design and presentation, so headlines without additional explanatory text take on greater importance. The *Bakersfield Californian* was one of the early sites to adopt this strategy under Howard Owens, then vice president of interactive. In an email to one of this book's authors, Owens said this put pressure on copy editors and online production staff to get the headlines right and acknowledged more training in this area is needed.

Newspaper headlines have always tended to use wordplay because space was limited and they needed to entice readers to pick up the paper and read the story. But a person online is already at the site looking at the story, so headlines should be descriptive ("boring")[7] and favor a more natural sentence-like structure. Online headlines need words that might be the terms someone searches for, such as the name of a town or a person.

For example, the headline below might be found in a newspaper. It is imperfect, but it might be the best possible because of design and tight space.

Disarmament Pact Mulled

But this headline will not work well online because it lacks specifics and uses an odd word, "mulled." With the growing awareness of search engine optimization and new editorial systems allowing creation of both print and online headlines, such headlines shoveled onto the Web are less common.

Effective online headlines should:

- Follow conventional subject-verb-object structure.
- Provide a more natural form by using some of the articles and helping verbs we strip from print headlines.
- Avoid "headlinese" that space- and time-challenged editors sometimes resort to for print headlines (instead of "mulled," for instance, "considered" is a more natural verb). Space is not unlimited online (four to seven or eight words still works best), but you won't have the sometimes unnaturally tight space newspaper designers allocate for headlines.

---

[6] For a simple explanation of how Google uses title tags and other elements to decide what gets to the top in a search result, see Google (September 2010), *Search Engine Optimization Starter Guide*, http://www.google.com/webmasters/docs/search-engine-optimization-starter-guide.pdf. Today's journalist should keep up on search engines by checking sites specializing in following the trends, such as searchenginewatch.com.

[7] S. Lohr (April 9, 2006). "This boring headline is written for Google," *New York Times*, retrieved from http://www.nytimes.com/2006/04/09/weekinreview/09lohr.html.

- Provide specifics. In that headline above, who is doing the mulling? How about this:

  United Nations Considers Korean Disarmament Pact

Specifics make the headline not only more understandable but also more searchable.

Why should I care about all this? You need to pay attention at least partly because there may not be an editor there to take care of all this for you. As we'll discuss later, blogging has become an integral part of many reporters' routines, and the blog post title is also a headline. With staff cutbacks in recent years, reporters from Sydney to Minneapolis are being told to file cleaner, Web-ready copy with potential headlines. And some are being warned they might have to take a turn as an editor.

Scanability

Print can be superior for analysis and investigation, while broadcast works best for communicating through emotion. The Internet is unsurpassed in delivering information raw and quickly. When people use the Internet, they tend to look for specific information in small, digestible chunks. As a result, text delivered online has to be formatted so that information can be found quickly.

What has evolved is a form that straddles print and broadcast, with added features to aid navigation—a form sometimes called "printcast."[8]

1. *Tight, bright writing with one idea per paragraph.* Strip away most of the complex clauses that characterize newspaper writing, but with a bit more complexity than typical broadcast writing.

   Online usability expert and engineer Jakob Nielsen says the inverted pyramid has made a comeback because users often will not scroll past the first screen.[9] But the inverted pyramid no longer is the 40- or 50-word behemoth that tried to cram everything in one lead paragraph. It has evolved to more of a "Christmas tree," a series of short, often multiple-paragraph inverted pyramids, each focused on a single idea with the main details of that idea in the top of each section. At each section's end, there is a "turn," be it a pithy quote, a telling detail, or a bit of foreshadowing, that propels the reader into the next section.

   Tight, bright writing also means using subject-verb-object sentences not laden with adjectives or adverbs. Let the verbs do the heavy lifting. (Although when it comes to attribution, be careful; many words have connotations that can introduce bias or editorializing. "Says" and "said" remain the most neutral verbs of attribution.)

   Another idea gaining popularity is to have a summary paragraph at the top of a story, perhaps something like this:

   Sumter's leaders want you to think about living downtown. They're looking for developers to put apartments in buildings' upper floors.

---

[8] S. Attkisson and D. R. Vaughan, *Writing Right for Broadcast and Internet News* (Boston: Allyn & Bacon, 2003).

[9] J. Nielsen (June 1996), "Inverted Pyramids in Cyberspace," retrieved from http://www.useit.com/alertbox/9606.html.

This summary, at 134 units (characters, spaces, and punctuation), also makes an effective Twitter or text message (see more on that in chapter 11) and provides supplemental material that could accompany a headline link.

2. *Break items into bulleted lists.* Traditional "print" writing should also do this more to "open up" pages and provide a little more white space in text. But you can overdo it, too. People like to read lists, which is why you see so many "Top 10 Ways to Do..." and similar stories online—so many, in fact, that there is a slightly pejorative name for them: "listicles." Still, the bulleted list can be used profitably if you remember some basics:

- Keep each item short. Creating lists of long paragraphs isn't creating a list; it's just putting bullets in front of paragraphs.
- Don't use too many lists. They can give the piece a choppy, washboard feel.
- Observe the "rule of three." Psychologically, we seem to like things grouped at least three at a time. Lists with two items seem off-balance and incomplete while those with more than four or five items seem too long.

Lists come in two types, but making sure they stay in parallel structure is important for either. Like the one above, lists can be discrete items, each able to stand alone. But each should still start with the same form of speech. For instance, we wouldn't want a list of items beginning with *keep, don't use,* and *the "rule of three" is important.* The last item would not parallel the first two, which begin with strong verbs. So instead we used the word *observe.*

In the second form of listing, each item can complete an introductory thought.

For instance, remember to:

- *Write tight and bright.*
- *Use inverted pyramids.*
- *Don't forget to employ basic subject–verb–object sentence structure.*

But the last item has a problem. The first two seamlessly complete "remember to" (*remember to write; remember to use*), but *remember to don't forget* is at best clunky. How to fix it? There is more than one answer, but perhaps use *Follow subject-verb-object sentence structure.*

3. *Consider using subheads and boldfaced words.* Subheads have been used by some newspapers for years to break up the text in long stories. On the Internet, they also can be used as links to help a reader navigate through the document, especially a reader quickly scrolling through a page looking for information. Similarly, some publications **put key points in boldface** to help the user pick out the ideas.

Boxes 4.1 and 4.2 show how a story typically written in print style can be easily fashioned into a shorter, easier-to-read online version. The online version would still work well in a newspaper, and it may be time to think about moving traditional "print" writing more toward the easier-to-follow forms that readers increasingly see online.

Linkability

Links are the currency of the online world, prompting one writer to coin the often-repeated phrase, "Cover what you do best. Link to the rest."[10] Depth, breadth, context, and veracity all are developed through the interwoven web of linked information. What makes the online world so rich (and sometimes so addictive) is the user's ability to read the article, see that picture you are talking about, examine that budget document, or read more about the author you have cited—all with a simple mouse click.

Two decades after the World Wide Web became widely accessible, many news sites, especially legacy news media, still shovel "print" content onto the web and struggle with linkability. Some see it as a mistake to send someone away from their site, possibly to the competition. But proponents of linking say it builds credibility. If someone knows he or she can get to other useful sites from yours, that person is more likely to begin at your site (thus increasing his or her exposure to your ads).[11] More research is needed, but one of the authors founded a community news site and heard from people who said they made it their browser's home page precisely because the site's front page linked to other news sources. This anecdote supports the idea that online value comes from utility rather than content and that content is overabundant to the point of becoming a commodity.

Too many news sites also do not effectively link to their own related stories. For example, one city's major employer announced it was renaming a plant after a retired executive. In the story was a paragraph noting the company's namesake also had recently died and that the event was thoroughly covered by this news organization. Yet nowhere was there a link to any of that related coverage.

MSNBC, on the other hand, provides good examples of how to link extensively without being afraid to let readers find their own paths. Not only do bylines link to writers' profiles, many stories have copious links, and even the dateline (the location named at the beginning of many stories) links to a map. One recent analysis piece on the Middle East had 10 links in its first 11 lines, most to previous MSNBC stories. Other links throughout the story went to the BBC, the *CIA World Factbook*, and other sources. The *New York Times* has also vastly improved its linking, mixing links both to outside sources and to its "topics page." The topics page is set up to aggregate stories on the subject as well as other items such as multimedia and the latest headlines. The *Los Angeles Times* has a list of related stories next to what you are reading. But at best it can be said that linking still needs more attention among journalists (figure 4.1).

Much, but not all, of this can be done by computer. It takes human judgment to sift through and judge the relative importance of items, a process called "curation"; otherwise the reader can be just as easily be overwhelmed (as it is easy to become on

---

[10] J. Jarvis (February 22, 2007), "New Rule: Cover What You Do Best. Link to the Rest," BuzzMachine, http://www.buzzmachine.com/2007/02/22/new-rule-cover-what-you-do-best-link-to-the-rest/.

[11] Publishing 2.0 (September 15, 2007), "Drudge Report: News Site That Sends Readers Away with Links Has Highest Engagement," retrieved from http://publishing2.com/2008/09/15/drudge-report-news-site-that-sends-readers-away-with-links-has-highest-engagement/. See also J. Stray (May 4, 2010), "Why Does the BBC Want to Send Its Readers Away? The Value of Linking," *Nieman Journalism Lab*, retrieved from http://www.niemanlab.org/2010/05/why-does-the-bbc-want-to-send-its-readers-away-the-value-of-linking/.

Box 4.1 Original Print Version (448 words)[1]

Would you live in downtown Sumter?

Ray Reich, the city's downtown development manager, and others involved in the redevelopment of downtown are hoping people will.

Reich said putting apartments in the upper levels of some downtown buildings is the next step in the revitalization of downtown Sumter.

"We fully expect a year from now to be well under way with construction of a number of upper story apartments throughout the downtown," Reich said.

He said he expects the main people who will be interested will be young professionals.

"People who welcome the idea of living over the top of a building in an historic area and being able to walk out in the evening, grab something to eat or grab a drink or go to something at the opera house and never have to get in your car," he said.

Jack Osteen, the chairman of the downtown economic restructuring committee, said about $1 million from the local option sales tax passed in the November election will be used to buy existing buildings in the downtown and sell them at cost to developers who will turn the upper levels into apartments.

"We feel like the time is right to do this," Osteen said.

Reich said that since it is harder for young professionals to get a loan to buy a home, he expects the rental market to increase.

"Demand for apartments is probably going to get greater," Reich said.

Osteen said the committee is already looking at some potential properties, and Reich said he has already had conversations with at least two downtown property owners who are interested.

Mack Kolb, a local developer with Century 21 Hawkins & Kolb, said he is interested in the downtown apartment idea.

"The upstairs of these buildings could be something a little more unique," Kolb said.

Kolb, who is also on the downtown economic restructuring committee, said he is just waiting to see what becomes available.

Osteen said the goal now is to find someone with a property that has an upper level that can be used for apartments and someone willing to develop and rent the first apartments.

"The person who does it the first time is going to be the most successful," Osteen said and now it is simply a matter of finding those first couple of buildings.

Reich said he imagines it will start off with a few apartments and then the demand will increase and more will be built.

"My dream is to walk downtown at night and see lights on in all the upper stories and activity in the street," Reich said. "That's something that can be accomplished in the downtown unlike any other part of any town."

[1] Courtesy *The (Sumter) Item.*

Box 4.2 Rewritten for Online (326 words plus 134-word summary)

Sumter's leaders want you to think about living downtown. They're looking for developers to put apartments in buildings' upper floors.

Would you live in downtown Sumter?

City leaders want you and others to consider it. They're **looking for developers to put apartments in the upper floors of downtown buildings**.

Ray Reich, the city's downtown development manager, says he expects some of those apartments to be **under construction within a year**.

He sees **young professionals as the target market**: "People who welcome the idea of living over the top of a building in an historic area and being able to walk out in the evening, grab something to eat or grab a drink or go to something at the opera house and never have to get in your car."

Some **key points**:

- About **$1 million from a local option sales tax** voters approved in November will be used to buy buildings. They will be sold at cost to developers who promise to put in upstairs apartments, says Jack Osteen, chairman of the downtown economic restructuring committee.
- Osteen, also publisher of *The Item*, says the committee is looking at some potential properties. Reich says he's **already talked with at least two interested downtown property owners**.

With home loans harder to get, **Reich expects more people will rent**.

Mack Kolb, a developer with Century 21 Hawkins & Kolb, says he's interested and wants to see what becomes available. He's on the downtown committee with Osteen and says upstairs apartments "could be something a little more unique."

The goal is to find someone with a suitable building and a developer to renovate it, Osteen says. He predicts, "The person who does it the first time is going to be the most successful."

Reich imagines **starting with a few apartments and then building more as demand increases**.

"My dream is to walk downtown at night and see lights on in all the upper stories and activity in the street," Reich says. "That's something that can be accomplished in the downtown unlike any other part of any town."

the *Times*' topics pages). This may be one reason we see it less frequently in strapped local news operations. But for a young journalist who might blog or join a native-to-the-Web news organization, understanding the ethos of the link is critical, and legacy news organizations will have to get better at it to provide full value to users.

As noted earlier, effective headlines can result in more links to your story. Stories with specific information presented as lists and in boldface are also likely to attract more incoming links because these features make it easier for the reader to parse the information.

By Richard Engel
Chief foreign correspondent
NBC News and msnbc.com

Share | Print | Font: A A + –

ANALYSIS

Amel Pain / EPA

An Egyptian voter smiles while proudly showing his ink marked finger after casting his vote for the referendum on constitutional changes at a polling station in Cairo, Egypt, March 19.

BENGHAZI, Libya – The Middle East has seen a blur of activity this year. It's hard to keep track of all that's happened:

- Desperate self-immolations
- The Tunisian president's flight to exile in Saudi Arabia
- Government-sponsored thugs on camels whipping protesters in Cairo's Tahrir Square
- Bahrain bulldozing its version of Tahrir
- Snipers in Yemen
- NATO war on Gadhafi
- Free Benghazi
- Syrian tanks in Daraa
- The birth of new Arabic words like "TWEET-tr" and "FacebOOK"

Figure 4.1 ■ Screenshot of MSNBC
MSNBC makes extensive use of links to help readers find additional information as well as related stories written by the correspondent, in this case Richard Engel.

Here are some key points:

- *Links should be the reporter's job but the editor's responsibility.* Who knows the sources better than the reporter? But the editor has to make sure the links are there and that the reader has enough information to understand where the link is taking him or her.
- *Be specific and link directly.* Effective linking finds the most relevant information and takes users *directly to it.* For instance, if you are writing about business tax deductions, don't just link to the Internal Revenue Service home page. Link directly to that section of the IRS site dealing with business deductions. Even better is a series of links taking your reader directly to specific documents or pages. However, one recent study found that with complicated topics, sending people to other sites for additional information was not as productive as displaying the information in the same context as the story, perhaps in a pop-up box.[12]
- *Warn readers if a link takes them anywhere other than a standard Web page.* Examples include an MP3 audio file, video, a PDF document, or anything else that appears to start a separate program on the user's device.

---

[12] R. A. Yaros (prepublished March 21, 2011), "Effects of Text and Hypertext Structures on User Interest and Understanding of Science and Technology," *Science Communication*, doi: 10.1177/1075547010386803

- *Choose your words carefully.* Especially if linking in-text, make it clear from the words used to label the link what additional value the user gets by clicking through.

THE CONDENSED NEWS CYCLE

We don't own the news anymore.

—Richard Sambrook, director, BBC World Service

In an era of convergent journalism, newsrooms and reporters have had to rethink certain practices as decisions are made, content is approved, and stories are posted much more rapidly.[13] See chapter 11, for instance, on how quickly word spread of Osama bin Laden's death.

For those who remember when afternoon newspapers flourished or who might have worked for a wire service, such as the Associated Press, the Internet is back to the future—get the information, file it quickly, get some more, file it quickly, and so on. Then step back and try to pull it all together. It is rare anymore for a journalist to have a true exclusive for more than a few minutes.

Now, everyone has access to continual updates. It's no longer enough to put one version of a story out per day and update it the next. Even at the local level, where a news outlet might think it still has a monopoly, blogs and discussion groups have formed online around key issues. They are updated easily and are your competition.

The general standard now for all media is that news is broken online first, perhaps with a quick post to Twitter or Facebook that might be fed back into the news organization's website. As seen in figure 4.2, many reporters are expected to feed Twitter or to blog updates quickly and then write the story for the legacy medium. Some newspaper newsrooms have instructed staff to simply keep filing updates online throughout the day. The editing desk then assembles the updates into a story for the print edition, getting more information from the reporter as needed.

This kind of speed, however, poses new challenges for accuracy, completeness, fairness, and other journalistic standards. In the haste to assemble stories, plagiarism can become an issue,[14] prompting one commentator to note that if journalists paid more attention to the ethos of linking (see our earlier discussion), this would be less of a problem. Speed also requires returning to some tried-and-true techniques.

The Return of the "Shirttail"

For years, wire service reporters and those who worked for afternoon newspapers had to update stories on deadline as well as write "shirttails" before leaving for an assignment. The *shirttail* is newsroom lingo for the bottom of a story that is mostly background and will not change. Then it only takes a few paragraphs of newer information to quickly

[13] Sambrook's widely circulated quote about journalists losing control over how news is distributed can be found at R. Snoddy (January 2, 2006), "TV News Looks to the Future," retrieved from http://news.bbc.co.uk/newswatch/ifs/hi/newsid_4540000/newsid_4546100/4546116.stm.

[14] J. Koblin (February 16, 2010), "The Accidental Plagiarist," *New York Observer,* retrieved from http://www.observer.com/2010/media/accidental-plagiarist.

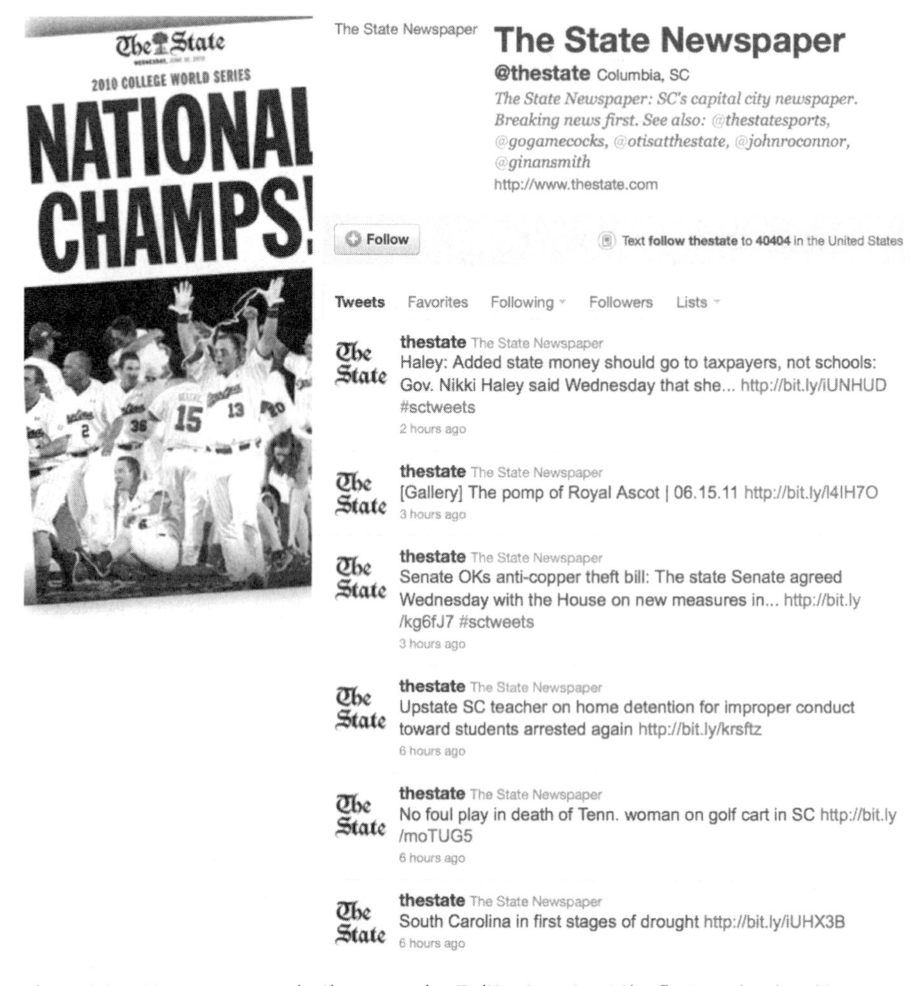

Figure 4.2 ■ Many news organizations are using Twitter to put out the first word on breaking news. This Twitter feed from The State in Columbia, S.C., is typical.

form a complete story. Often, a story was updated several times during a news cycle, and each time editors would integrate the new material and cut away outdated information so a story did not become overwritten and unwieldy.

That skill is making a comeback, with the chief difference being that stories are updated by filing from a computer rather than by dictation over the phone.

Print-oriented reporters sometimes have objected to this increased deadline pressure. They say it takes valuable time that's needed to make additional calls and find information to give a story depth. They also say it can disrupt the flow of their reporting at fast-moving events. There is no easy answer, but the ability to write ahead, move quickly, update constantly, and file from the field using mobile devices is now a core competency. Increasingly, our content is not just being repurposed from print or broadcast to online. Instead, it is created for online and repurposed back to the legacy medium.

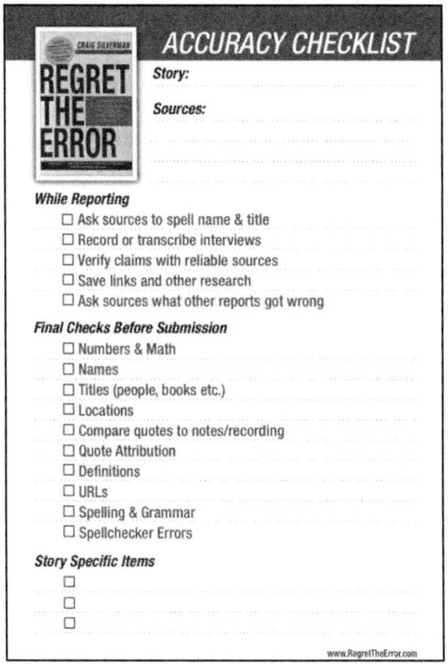

CRAIG SILVERMAN
REGRET THE ERROR

ACCURACY CHECKLIST

Story:

Sources:

While Reporting

- ☐ Ask sources to spell name & title
- ☐ Record or transcribe interviews
- ☐ Verify claims with reliable sources
- ☐ Save links and other research
- ☐ Ask sources what other reports got wrong

Final Checks Before Submission

- ☐ Numbers & Math
- ☐ Names
- ☐ Titles (people, books etc.)
- ☐ Locations
- ☐ Compare quotes to notes/recording
- ☐ Quote Attribution
- ☐ Definitions
- ☐ URLs
- ☐ Spelling & Grammar
- ☐ Spellchecker Errors

Story Specific Items

- ☐
- ☐
- ☐

www.RegretTheError.com

Figure 4.3 ■ This checklist by Craig Silverman, who founded the Regret the Error website, can help you avoid mistakes even when the push is on to file information online quickly.

Making Corrections

Faster and constant updating means errors are more likely to appear in stories. Reporters and editors are rushed, material is put online with little or no editing, and early information from sources may be wrong and will have to be corrected later in the news cycle. Wire services have dealt with this challenge for years, but then the product coming into newsrooms was scrutinized and massaged by editors and copy desks before the public saw it. To correct or just update information, the wire service produced a "writethru" that explained what was wrong and contained the new or corrected material. In serious cases, an accompanying "corrective" reinforced the change and called attention to it.

Newspapers, on the other hand, generally buried their mistakes on page 2 or elsewhere with short, sometimes inscrutable notices. Broadcasters often did not correct at all, figuring they'd get it right in the next newscast. In either case, the public had little or no access to the original story or correction—unless that reader happened to cut it out of the paper—beyond the initial publication.

The Internet challenges us to address the issue of corrections for two reasons. First, mistakes are more easily found when everyone can be your editor and commentator (see sites like the *Regret The Error* blog on Poynter.org). Second, days, weeks, or years after a story is posted, an online user can discover information through a search engine or other means—what Chris Anderson has termed the "long tail" of online content.[15] This discussion about the journalist's and journalism organization's

[15] Chris Anderson, *The Long Tail: Why the Future of Business Is Selling Less of More* (New York: Hyperion, 2006).

duty to correct items has been going on for more than a decade. Yet, sadly, research so far, much of it by Scott Maier, shows that many errors are not even reported by news sources. They consider it an exercise in futility, and even more so when it comes to online stories.[16]

A related issue is how the journalist and news organization react to someone who has been quoted or photographed as part of a story and asks that the quote or photo be deleted because it was not flattering. Perhaps he or she was not one of the central figures, yet the quote or picture keeps turning up in search engines. Known as "unpublishing," it has been debated, and early research suggests most publishers resist such requests.[17]

Here are some of the new challenges online raises:

- How will we make it easy for people to let us know if something is wrong with a story? Will we have a "report an error" button?
- How will we display corrections? Should we strike out the wrong material and insert the new (but leave the wrong material visible so people can be clear as to what we've changed)? Should we note on top of a piece of content if something has been changed? Or should we just correct it and move on since things online are updated more often and people generally understand we make errors?
- Should we have a central place online where a person can go to see all our errors?
- How will we handle "unpublish" requests? What criteria will we use to evaluate them? Who will be responsible for the final decision?

As journalists become more online-oriented, they will have to consider these new dimensions of corrections, changes, and updates more often.

Copyright and Creative Commons

> *But honestly Monica, the web is considered "public domain" and you should be happy we just didn't "lift" your whole article and put someone else's name on it! It happens a lot, clearly more than you are aware of, especially on college campuses, and the workplace.*[18]

The editor of the (now-defunct) *Cook's Source* magazine unleashed an Internet firestorm when she wrote that to a woman who complained the magazine had lifted her article on apple pie recipes from the Web and reprinted it without permission. Angry netizens flooded the magazine's Facebook page, forcing it to shut down, and then turned up other similar suspected cases.[19]

---

[16] S. Maier (Fall 2009), "Confessing Errors in a Digital Age," *Nieman Reports*, retrieved from http://www.nieman.harvard.edu/reportsitem.aspx?id=101903.

[17] D. Fisher (January 9, 2010) "'Unpublishing'—The Growing Challenge for Editors, Publishers," Common Sense Journalism, retrieved from http://commonsensej.blogspot.com/2010/01/unpublishing-growing-challenge-for.html.

[18] D. Kravets, (November 2010), "Cooks Source Copyright Infringement Becomes an Internet Meme," *Wired*, retrieved from http://www.wired.com/threatlevel/2010/11/web-decries-infringement/.

[19] ibid.

The Web is not "public domain," and publishing content online does not mean it is "free to take." The converged journalist must remember this as he or she routinely files a range of content, including visuals, directly online. A *New York Times* reporter was accused of plagiarism after other publications' material appeared uncredited in his financial blog. He said that in the rush, some background material he had intended to re-report unintentionally got mixed in. The retort was that had he used one of the simplest and most native tools to the Web—linking—it would not have been a problem.[20]

Fair Use

There are many myths about "fair use." This section hopes to heighten your sensitivity to such things *but it is not a substitute for consulting a lawyer, or your boss, if you have questions.*

Journalists generally have wider leeway to use others' material as part of newsgathering and publication if necessary to accurately report the story and if it does not gratuitously damage the economic value of the work being cited. Fair use, however, is not a blank check. While it might be asserted as a defense if you are sued, the U.S. Copyright Office lists four key things that must be balanced:[21]

- *The purpose and character of the use, including whether such use is of a commercial nature or is for nonprofit educational purposes.*
- *The nature of the copyrighted work.*
- *The amount and substantiality of the portion used in relation to the copyrighted work as a whole.*
- *The effect of the use upon the potential market for, or value of, the copyrighted work.*

There is a long-established tolerance for quoting text passages if they are used to report the news, and especially if used in criticism or a review of the work. However, note this warning from the Copyright Office: "The distinction between fair use and infringement may be unclear and not easily defined. There is no specific number of words, lines, or notes that may safely be taken without permission. Acknowledging the source of the copyrighted material does not substitute for obtaining permission."[22]

The material need not display a copyright symbol or be registered with the Copyright Office to be covered by copyright.

The danger of a violation is higher with visual or multimedia material. Even the smallest excerpt cropped from a photo, or a few well-known chords from a song, for instance, could damage its value. One of the misconceptions is that if you are criticizing a visual element, like a photo, you can reproduce the photo to illustrate that, but it's the type of criticism that may be key.

For instance, let's say the community was upset because the public art museum had just bought what some people considered salacious paintings. Using a photo of one

---

[20] F. Salmon, (March 2010) *Link-phobic bloggers at the NYT and WSJ.* Reuters. http://blogs.reuters.com/felix-salmon/2010/03/08/link-phobic-bloggers-at-the-nyt-and-wsj.

[21] http://www.copyright.gov/fls/fl102.html

[22] ibid.

of the paintings with a story detailing why community leaders are critical could run into trouble. However, there might be more protection if the article was actually an art critic's review of the technique, style, and so forth.

While a code of best practices drawn up for the use of online video urges that such use of copyrighted material for illustration or example be recognized,[23] and while some legal experts say federal law goes too far in giving creators and corporations stranglehold rights, court rulings often hinge on the economic damage done—not just to the work but also to the creator's ability to make derivative works (in this case, perhaps, prints or posters). That can involve things such as the size or quality of the image.

Even more dangerous for the harried journalist is the temptation to hit the "save as" option on an online photo. Let's say you found a picture of that artist's work on the museum's website. Surely you can use it? It's a public museum, and it clearly had permission to display the photo online, right? But you'd want to keep in mind that the U.S. Postal Service lost a case where it purchased the rights to a photo of a war memorial sculpture but did not get a release from the sculptor.

Fair use rulings vary widely.[24] In this push-to-publish online world, an old journalistic saying still has value: "When in doubt, leave it out."

Creative Commons

The Creative Commons (creativecommons.org) was established to help promote the sharing, reuse, and remixing of various works. Those who assign a Creative Commons (CC) license to a work (see figures 4.4 and 4.5 for illustrations of CC license designations) can specify two conditions (that the work must be attributed is built into all the licenses): whether derivatives can be made from the work and whether the work is licensed for commercial or noncommercial use.

The most open license simply requires attribution, which means you must clearly identify the source of the content if you republish it. The most restrictive, called "attribution, noncommercial, no derivatives," allows the work to be shared for noncommercial purposes only and without any changes. Most journalists, since they work for businesses, will have to stick with those items designated as allowed for commercial use.

Screenshots of CC licenses

Being aware of the Creative Commons framework and some of the ways to use it can be a big help to journalists on ever-quicker deadlines. The image posting and sharing site Flickr.com, for instance, allows people posting images to designate them as "Creative Commons licensed," and they can be searched for that way. In addition, there is a Creative Commons plug-in for the Firefox browser that will let you search the Web for CC-licensed material.

In addition, if you are looking to have your or your organization's work more widely distributed, a CC license might be the thing. Creating a license does not involve lawyers

---

[23] American University Center for Social Media, (n.d.), *Code of best practices in fair use for online video,* retrieved from http://www.centerforsocialmedia.org/fair-use/related-materials/codes/code-best-practices-fair-use-online-video.

[24] Stanford University has an excellent site on copyright and fair use at http://fairuse.stanford.edu/Copyright_and_Fair_Use_Overview/index.html.

Figure 4.4 ■ If you see this on a website, it means the owner is allowing you to share the work, but you cannot make commercial use of it or make any derivatives. It is the most restrictive Creative Commons license.

or massive amounts of paperwork. Just copy the code to your online item. It then points back to the Creative Commons site and its licensing code, which can also automatically be read by a computer.

BLOGGING

Much ink has been spilled and vitriol written about whether blogs are journalism and bloggers are journalists, but that's like asking whether something is newspaper journalism just because it's printed on newsprint. A lot of great journalism has been written on newsprint, but quite a bit of newsprint has also been wasted on sensational gossip, rumor, opinion, and innuendo.

Blogging is both a publishing system and an ethos, a set of ideals that those who blog tend to follow. While much of the discussion about blogging has now turned to new, more nimble social media platforms such as Posterous and Tumblr (see chapter 11 for more), blogging deserves special mention here because it has dramatically reshaped how digital-age journalists do their jobs. Once news organizations got over their apoplexy and stopped sneering about the supposed corps of pajama-clad amateur bloggers, they took to the form in a big way as a quicker and easier publishing platform. As Scott Rosenberg has observed, "Blogging, the first form of social media to be widely adopted

Figure 4.5 ■ This is the least restrictive Creative Commons license. You have to give credit to the creator, but you can create derivatives and use the work commercially.

beyond the world of technology enthusiasts, gave us a template for all the other forms that would follow."[25]

The term "weblog" is generally credited to Jorn Barger and its shortened form, "blog," to Peter Merholz in 1999.[26] But blogging remained in the realm of computer geeks until Pyra Labs released Blogger later that year. Sometimes called "push-button publishing" (although the term encompasses a wider range of content management systems), blogging software's main characteristics are that each post is a separate item with its own Web link, or URL, which allows easy linking to others, and that each post is presented in reverse chronological order. As Rosenberg notes, the reverse order was a natural form to the computer experts of the 1990s because computers process information last in, first out. The software allowed easy formatting and publishing through rich text editing screens, but the big breakthrough was giving each post a URL that allowed easy linking.

Another decade passed before newsrooms widely adopted the form. But blogging caught on because they were looking for ways to bolster their largely static websites, connect with readers, and find new avenues for advertising. By then, the speed and ease of updating combined with availability and low cost made blogging irresistible.

Now, young journalists are urged to establish blogs (see figure 4.6 for an example) so that potential employers have a place to see their work. And in many newspaper and broadcast newsrooms, beat reporters are expected to blog (though in some cases they now use Facebook and Twitter instead). Many say it has enormously changed their relationship with the audience, generated better story ideas, and kept stories "live" long after they were printed or broadcast.

While blogging tends to have more of a personal voice, for journalists all the usual admonitions apply—take pains to be accurate, don't run into publication with unconfirmed rumors, don't attack anyone, and, while you might express a point of view, avoid overtly editorial statements (unless you are being paid to write opinion pieces or editorials).

Some journalists have posted partially completed work online, received feedback, and substantially revised that work before it went into print. That is different, however, from the ill-conceived idea of post first, ask questions later—in hopes the post will generate its own news or leads.

Consider this January 2006 entry by reporter Jason Foster on a blog run by *The Herald* of Rock Hill, South Carolina:[27]

> *The folks at Backyard Burgers told me yesterday that the construction in front of their restaurant... is going to be a CVS Pharmacy. I have a call into CVS corporate headquarters to confirm, but haven't heard back yet. I'll let you know when I get the official word.*

---

[25] S. Rosenberg, *Say Everything: How Blogging Began, What It's Becoming and Why It Matters* (New York: Crown, 2010), p. 16.

[26] Rosenberg discusses the evolution at length. See also Merholz's archived explanation at http://www.peterme.com/archives/00000205.html.

[27] J. Foster (January 2006), "Confirmed: CVS Coming Near Baxter, retrieved from http://community.heraldonline.com/q=cvs_coming_near_baxter (this link has since been removed).

Metro Desk

Blogging local government in and around South Carolina's capital city

About | City Council actions | Campaign disclosures | Columbia's stimulus money

Eau Claire board member resigns because of new boss

By ADAM BEAM | *Published:* JUNE 15, 2011

Realtor Rhett Anders resigned form the Eau Claire Development Corporation's board of directors this morning in response to City Manager Steve Gantt reassigning Tony Lawton as the corporation's director.

Here's his letter, addressed to The Rev. Richard F. Dozier, the board's chairman:

Reverend Dozier,

I just read the announcement of a Director for the ECDC. I am simply amazed. It was my understanding this was going to be process where applications for this position were going to be taken by the city, narrowed to three candidates, and sent to the various neighborhood organizations for "interviews and feedback". I think the City does us a great disservice by hiring a director without the knowledge of the board or any input, especially a director that has been investigated by the F.B.I. and HUD. I am not comfortable with this appointment. I feel that the entire board and development corporation will be put in jeopardy by Mr. Lawton's hiring. Please accept this as my letter of resignation to take effect immediately. It has been a pleasure serving with you and the rest of the board. Thank you for your service.

Sincerely,

Rhett Anders

UPDATE: The city advertised the executive director position a few months ago, and Anders applied. However, the city did not hire anyone and ended up removing the job posting. Anders said he did not resign because he was made Lawton got the job and not him. "This has nothing to do with that," he said.

ShareThis

Posted in *Columbia city government* | Tagged *Eau Claire Development Corporation, Rhett Anders* | *13 Comments*

About

Adam Beam covers the City of Columbia for The State newspaper. Here, he blogs about local government. Reach him at (803) 386-7038 or abeam@thestate.com

Call Me

RSS Links

- All posts
- All comments

Search

To search, type and hit enter

Twitter Updates

- Updated post on Rhett Anders, who resigned to protest Tony Lawton's hiring at Eau Claire Development Corporation http://bit.ly/jgVpT7 about an hour ago

follow me on Twitter

Sewer plant upgrade
4:50

TheMetroDesk
Subscribe
YouTube

Figure 4.6 ■ Many reporters now are expected to blog about things breaking on their beats or about things that might not make it fully into the eventual news story for the paper or online. This example from Adam Beam at The (Columbia, S.C.) State is typical.

A reader, in the blog's comments section, challenged the reporter/blogger. Why, the reader wanted to know, was it OK to print a rumor on the blog when it would not be done in the paper? Could the reporter at least not have waited for the call from CVS? The reporter responded:

"[W]e wouldn't print a rumor in the newspaper. A blog, however, allows for slightly different rules.... The way we see it, there are rumors and then there are RUMORS. We would never, for example, blog that we've heard a rumor about a top elected official being arrested. If the construction isn't a CVS, we'll point that out and, in the long run, there's no harm done."[28]

But is "no harm done" the correct standard for a news organization? How much harm would have been done by waiting until the paper heard from the drugstore chain? These are among the new types of questions raised by blogging and the push for quick filing of stories.

SUMMARY

In this chapter we looked at how content can best be repurposed for online because that still is the practice in many newsrooms. But the power of the Internet is in finding new ways to tell stories. Writing for the Internet must consider searchability, scanability, and linkability. Speed and frequent updating are other important considerations as blogging or other forms of quick online posting have now become common in news organizations. But that also puts pressure on the journalist to separate rumor from fact and avoid costly missteps by being familiar with the basics of fair use and copyright.

EXERCISES

1. Look at the front page of today's newspaper. Which headlines do you think would work well online and get you to click through to the story? Which would not work well? Explain your reasoning in no more than 100 words for each headline.
2. Take the headlines you do not think work well and rewrite them into a form that does. Do each using no more than eight words. Now, show them to a friend. Ask your friend if, based on the headline, he or she would want to read that story online and explain why or why not. Now, show your friend the original newspaper headline and ask, based on the headline, if he or she would want to read the newspaper story. Why or why not?
3. Now that you've heard your friend's reasoning, refashion the online headline and ask that friend again whether his or her attitude has changed. What did you have to do to get the person interested?
4. Each of these is a rumor you have heard from several people, including at least one who has steered you right in the past. Which would you blog about right this minute and why? Which ones would you hold, why, and for how long?
   a. The latest hot band is supposed to be coming to town next week.
   b. The mayor is reported to be having an affair with his secretary.
   c. The university's starting quarterback is injured and can't start.
   d. A local bank is about to close, and its accounts will be frozen.
5. If you do not have a blog, assemble a plan for one. Consider what you want to write about, what your likely audience will be, how you would publicize it and how frequently you would post. If you already have a blog, examine it using those same criteria. Is it meeting your objectives? Why or why not?

---

[28] ibid.

CHAPTER 5

FROM PRINT TO INTERNET: NEW TYPES OF CONTENT

The ongoing changes occurring with newspapers are unsettling if you're not prepared to embrace the possibilities afforded by convergence. This chapter takes some of the traditional newspaper concepts and practices and recasts them to better reflect today's newsgathering environment. A modern multiskilled journalist in a converged newsroom is now free to pursue a story in a number of ways that benefit the individual reporter, the news organization, and the community.

TRADITIONAL NEWSGATHERING MEETS THE WEB

The email from the special projects editor to the newspaper's computer specialists was pleading—the newspaper had done a major series on poverty in its area that was featured on the paper's front page and had generated lots of talk in town. And the series was being lost on the paper's website.

> *I just got my third call on this: People are going to our website and not being able to find the earlier poverty stories. This last call was from a college student.*
>
> *There's not an obvious link (no one but us knows what ENTERPRISE means), and even when they follow the links provided under today's story, they can't find all the rest of the stories....*

> *Is there a way to make a few small changes that would make it easier for our readers to find the stories that are already there?...*
>
> *The reporters have been working SO hard on these, putting in amazing effort, and they deserve to have their concerted efforts displayed in a way that shows the overall pattern of their stories.* (Memo from *The Item,* Sumter, S.C. Used by permission.)

Things are getting better. News organizations are moving toward converged online experiences, giving users clear, coherent, and complete packages of story elements. Mobile tablets and smartphones, with their smaller screens, pose design challenges and are forcing the issue. A changed news ecosystem, with shrunken traditional news organizations and many smaller ones looking for ways to make their mark through innovation, are also forcing things. And technology is making it easier by the month to gather, assemble, and present information in new ways.

The challenge in a convergent world is to understand all the potential elements of a story and decide how each element is best presented. It also means understanding that what you put online will have a much longer life and potentially wider exposure than tonight's newscast or tomorrow's newspaper. It may continue to attract readers from around the corner or from around the world who never before would have seen your work. Now, through search engines and the Web's ever-growing network of links, users can access an online story as easily as one from their hometown news providers.

At the same time, the emphasis on breaking news in this mobile world creates a churn that can drastically shorten the audience's immediate attention span on even the best and most important stories.

SIX GUIDELINES ABOUT PRESENTING WEB CONTENT

- You can't control how readers get your content. Readers are just as likely to come to your stories, photos, and graphics through other ways than the carefully crafted "front door" you have provided.
- As a result, they will need a detailed navigation system that makes apparent not only the interlinking parts of the story but other elements elsewhere online that may bolster or enhance the storytelling.
- Elements need to be crafted with enough context or background so that they can stand on their own but also so that their relationship to other elements is easily discerned.
- "Story" no longer needs to be an 8-, 10-, or 15-inch chunk of words. In fact, some of the most effective storytelling may use no words at all.
- "News has become a conversation" means that the ability to gather audience feedback and to react to it, as necessary, is an important part of the story as well as of site design.
- The importance of all these things persists, especially maintaining the ability to follow interrelationships. Depending on how your site is set up, that story element could be generating interest and revenue for many years.

RETHINKING "THE STORY"

David Gelernter, in a seminal 2003 article in the *Weekly Standard,* challenged readers to think of the "Next Great American Newspaper" as an object not in space but in time, where "story" was defined not as a single silo of information (today's practice of writing a chunk of text and pairing it with some photos or graphics into a static "package") but as a constantly changing slice in time.[1] "Today's web-papers are wedge-ins, stop-gaps, crack fillers, with all the character of putty in a plastic spritz-tube," he wrote. The new paper would need to deliver "timeliness with style." The challenge of such an online site, of course, is the same one faced by that pleading editor: how to maintain coherence in an online world that by its very nature is designed to be a bit chaotic. Things like tags, shells, social bookmarks, and social-ranking tools can help bring some order. But first, let's re-examine the very roots of "story" in this new world.

In most print-oriented newsrooms, a story is still a chunk of text, maybe with graphics or photos, and perhaps with a growing awareness of the possibilities of audio and video on the Web. In broadcast newsrooms, a TV story is still typically voice-over video and sound on tape, and radio news is still reading text and playing actualities. But vast amounts of digital information are now always on and available wherever and whenever we want it. It is especially true inside newsrooms as journalists must now continually monitor their online presence and metrics (see, for example, the projection of online pages onto the walls of London's *Telegraph* newsroom in figure 5.1). Eventually, it will effectively all be coming down the same digital "pipe," and in this confluence of bits and bytes, the definition of "story" is likely to change.

RETHINKING "THE NEWSROOM"

Gannett, one of the nation's biggest media companies, recognized this coming change when in late 2006 it embarked on a massive restructuring to turn its newsrooms into "information centers." It dismantled the newsroom built around newspaper sections, creating a configuration with seven centers:

- *Digital.* "Accelerates the speed and volume of news and information posted on multiple digital and print platforms." This is the heart of the new newsroom.
- *Local.* The closest to the traditional newsroom desks, the focus is to expand coverage to include hyper-local stories. It is based on experiments with mobile journalists, or mojos, at the *Fort Myers (Fla.) News-Press* who cover intensely local news.
- *Data.* Figuring out ways to take the information that is being produced and to create new ways to mine it and present it. This also includes finding new sources of relevant digital information. Think various local calendars, entertainment listings, and similar items.
- *Multimedia.* In charge of the visual presentation in whatever medium. As part of the transformation, photographers will be trained for all types of media.

---

[1] D. Gelernter (June 23, 2003), "The Next Great American Newspaper," *The Weekly Standard,* 8:40. Retrieved from: http://www.weeklystandard.com/content/public/articles/000/000/002/797bppbw.asp.

Figure 5.1 ■ The Telegraph newsroom in London is one of the largest converged newsrooms in the world. (Source: James Young [www.jbyoung.co.uk].)

- *Custom content.* Defining target audiences and then figuring out how to repurpose content to reach them, especially "magazine-like approaches to lifestyle and trends issues."
- *Public service.* Expanding the newsroom's First Amendment and watchdog role by getting the public involved through citizen journalism techniques such as *crowdsourcing,* where members of the public with differing expertise are invited to help tackle aspects of the researching and reporting. Searchable databases and interactive elements are also important.
- *Community conversation.* Expanding the editorial page using blogs and other online forms as well as traditional editorial columns. This includes getting the public involved and helping them create their own forums to discuss community issues.[2]

In early 2007, *The Atlanta Journal-Constitution,* the flagship newspaper of the Cox chain, announced a realignment of its newsroom similar to Gannett's, but the *AJC* said it would split the production of the newspaper from the gathering of the news and focus each newsgathering area on the medium to which it was best suited. So, for instance, the news and information desk—akin to the old metro desk—would focus on getting news out on the Web quickly and then to print. The enterprise desk, with its longer-form stories, would focus on print but use online to enhance its storytelling. Like Gannett, there would be a digital desk to aggregate information and create new information products with databases.

---

[2] J. Howe (November 2006), "Gannett: The Seven Desks," retrieved from http://crowdsourcing.typepad.com/cs/2006/11/gannett_the_sev.html.

But of most significance was splitting off a "print" desk to concentrate on putting out the paper. Editor Julia Wallace wrote the following in a memo to her staff.

> Much like the digital department, it will pull from news, enterprise and other sources, including Cox's Washington bureau. This department will focus on issues such as balance, story play, headlines, cutlines, photos and design—the many factors that determine a reader's experience with the paper. This structure places print and digital on equal footing, each taking what they need to satisfy their specific audiences.[3]

Other news organizations also are taking notice of the Journal Register Co., which fought its way back from bankruptcy by adopting a "digital-first, print-last" ethos and widespread experimentation, including creating a "Newsroom Cafe" at a Connecticut newspaper where people can wander in, keep tabs on what the paper is doing online, and even contribute to coverage.[4]

HOW NEW NEWSROOMS APPROACH THE NEW STORY

This new type of story takes a disciplined approach from conception. First, ask what is the absolute best way to tell the story. Then ask what can be done given the resources available (not just equipment and software but time, personnel, and skill levels).

For instance, perhaps you'd love to do some video. But do you have the time and someone with the necessary knowledge of what makes for good video? Even if you don't, you are apt to have a pretty good photographer with a digital camera, and more than likely someone has a digital audio recorder. So consider an audio slide show that can be assembled using just the video-editing programs available on most new computers (instead of video, you use the still photos as the individual "clips") or an inexpensive piece of software like Soundslides. There is a learning curve, but it is less steep than learning the basics of good videography and editing.

The Farmers Market Story

The farmers market has been a fixture in your community for years. But it sits on prime land, development is encroaching, and you've heard of plans to move it to a new complex south of town.

Traditionally, you'd write 500 or 600 words, maybe with a short sidebar on the market's denizens and their reaction to the news. On a good day, the design desk would create a small map to show the new and old locations.

---

[3] Wallace memo, retrieved Feb. 16, 2007, from Poynter.org, http://poynter.org/forum/view_post.asp?id=12316.

[4] R. Greenslade (June 9, 2010), "US Newspaper Boss Urges His Journalists to Experiment with Digital Tools," retrieved from http://www.guardian.co.uk/media/greenslade/2010/jun/09/digital-media-newspapers; K. Ackerman and D. H. Nenad (March 15, 2011), "10 Newspapers That Do It Right," *Editor and Publisher,* retrieved from http://www.editorandpublisher.com/Headlines/10-newspapers-that-do-it-right-64530-.aspx.

But people have fond memories of going to the market to pick out those special fixings for holiday meals or to get fresh fruit in the summer (along with a homemade ice cream cone from the market's dairy stand). The place is loaded with all sorts of colorful characters, like the guy who says he can teach you in a few minutes how to pick the best, ripest melon at any time of year. And it's a good illustration of how city and country keep running into each other as the city grows.

So let's stop a moment and think. Don't worry about resources yet. What can we do with this story both in print and online? You think for a bit and come up with these ideas:

- That main story and sidebar you were going to write.
- A video tour of the market.
- A diagram of the market's layout.
- Close-up photos of some of the more colorful characters.
- A map showing where the new market will be.

Even if your newsroom still tends to go to print first on anything other than breaking news, there are things you can do to invigorate your storytelling and make the transition to digital easier. Instead of 500 to 600 words, cut your main story in half. Move the number details and other quick facts into an "At-A-Glance" box that accompanies the story. Move most of your colorful quotes into a quote box. Use at least the map of the new location, but run the diagram as well, if you can. Use as many photos as you can, maybe linked to points on the market layout. At the bottom of the quote box, refer people to the Web to "hear the voices of the Farmers Market." On the map, invite them to go to the website to take a tour. And make sure you invite them to your website to post their reactions and memories.

Now let's consider some of the specifics:

- Your main story also will provide the intro for the online package, but it's short enough that time-pressed users can quickly digest it and get depth by following some of the links.
- With your digital recorder and accompanied by the photographer, you can gather material for your market tour slide show. It's much easier to edit sound and handle stills than video, and the stills can also be used in print. Combine the two in an inexpensive program like Soundslides or even the movie-creation software that comes with Mac and Windows machines, and you have a slideshow tour that hits maybe the top six to eight points of the market.
- Newer cameras designed primarily for still photos will also shoot some basic video. So if you find one of those characters who tend to hang out at the market, you can do a lively, quick interview. Video on the Web is best in tightly focused, short chunks, like having that guy show you how to pick a ripe melon.
- If you're having a really good day, the designer wants to try her hand at creating some interactive maps. So the static market diagram in your paper comes alive on the Web. Your users will be able to click on a part of the map and up will pop a photo and audio from one of the characters who hangs out there. But even if the designer is busy, Google's My Maps can be used

to show the old and new locations and some pop-up information for each. (Or you can create a map and then download the files onto your own server using a site such as click2map.com.)

- If you've used My Maps, you already have satellite view. If the designer is doing a more detailed map of the new location, make it clickable and link it to Google Earth—let your users see what the future site looks like now.
- Hopefully your sources were able to give you a copy of the study recommending the move, and you remembered to ask for a digital copy,. Put the file online. (If all you tend to get is paper, then get your bosses to invest in a good page-feed scanner for the newsroom, the type that can effortlessly turn multiple pages into a single PDF document.)
- See if the people who oversee your website can create a place where people can upload their old photos. You also can ask those with Flickr accounts to post them on that photo-sharing site with a Creative Commons license (so you can use them; see chapter 4 for details about Creative Commons) and tag them "Metropolis farmers market." You can then set up a link to that tag or have your digital experts create a small script that "scrapes" Flickr periodically for new photos with that tag.

What about some other new story forms? If you had the time and people, you could create an interactive database. How much are those Vidalia onions at the market compared with the grocery stores around town? Ideally, a user could type in "Vidalia onions" and get prices. That might be beyond the programming skills available in your newsroom, but at least a newspaper-style graphic showing the prices will bring depth to the overall story across media, far more than just including such information in text.

If you're having trouble getting started, try using the PCJ Story Grid for planning your multimedia and interactive elements (see figure 5.2). It is designed to let you consider all the interactive and multimedia possibilities for the key elements of your story, and you can then pick the approach for which you have the best resources.

Documents, Documents, Documents

We have all heard the admonition to follow the paper trail. Now, journalists who are digitally aware know it is more important than ever to remember to ask for "the documents"—and in digital form whenever possible. Online news sites give journalists an unprecedented opportunity to show the public the raw material on which their stories are based, enhancing both interactivity and credibility.

Services such as Scribd, Slideshare, and others make posting and linking to documents, PowerPoint presentations, spreadsheets, and other source material easy. But first you have to remember to ask for, and sometimes fight for, the material. It is not only common for many government agencies to resist releasing documents, but some also are providing data only in hard-to-parse PDF format instead of spreadsheet tables or comma-delimited formats that make analysis easier.

Even if you can get things only on paper, consider scanning and posting official releases and documents (city council meeting agendas, white papers, proposals, etc.) in order to add depth and context to stories involving government agencies. By regularly

"Adapting the Story"
Story organization and planning exercise

You have been assigned a story from today's news to refashion for interactive multimedia. Put a "1" in the box that's the best way to tell the story, and a "2" in the second-best. Is one of them doable given resources? Is there another way to do it? (For instance, video might be the best, but an audio slideshow might be an alternative.) Tx=text, Au=audio, Vd=video, Pho=stills, SS=slideshow, Gfx=graphics, Db=database, Mp=interactive map, Oth=other such as time line, quiz, survey. (Do again once you've started reporting. Have you found new ways to tell the story?)

Top points of story (one per line). Under "best told as," if you choose "oth," please indicate type (time line, quiz, etc.)		Best told as ("1" and "2")							
	Tx	Au	Vd	Pho	SS	Gfx	Db	Mp	Oth

Additional Content

Hyperlinks:

User-Generated:

Write a 100-unit "Twitter" headline to promote the initial follow-up:

Figure 5.2 ■ The PCJ Story Grid will help you plan the interactive/multimedia aspects of your story.

posting these materials and maintaining an archive of older material, you provide your viewers another reason to stay on your website.

Descriptions and contextual information are vitally important and should be included to prevent whipping up public furor over a relatively minor decision or burying an important item under jargon so no one notices. This problem might arise, for example, in a county council agenda with the following item: *Council will entertain a motion to change designation of county property XX-33-2-1 from agricultural (A) to multi-unit residential (R3).*

Although it may sound technical and unimportant, what's actually being considered is a request from a developer to put up condominiums or apartments on what is now a beautifully scenic area next to a lake. Simply posting raw information is not enough. As a journalist, you have an obligation to make its importance clear to your users.

HELPING THE USER

We are learning that business models online need to recognize that value comes from utility, not just content, which quickly falls to commodity value. A key skill in this new journalism will be helping users navigate and make connections among all the parts of a story, both on your site and throughout the community. Many will not come through the carefully crafted home page. With search engines and referrals from others, they may start at almost any element. The challenge is to provide enough context with each element but also to provide a navigational structure that allows users to find related elements and to share them with others

Website design has turned to simplification, and a premium is placed on graphics, sectioning of the page, and headlines that are clear but enticing and serve as links to get the user to click through. Shells, tags, and RSS feeds help us keep this coherence for the user at the same time new designs call for fewer elements on a page.

Shells

Also known as *microsites, evergreen packages, contextual navigation,* or *orbiting content, a Web shell* is a page or group of pages that centralizes all the online content on a particular topic. *The Washington Post,* for instance, uses a shell called "America at War" to centralize all its recent coverage of the Iraq war, Afghanistan, and national security. It includes a mix of special reports, current headlines, video, discussion transcripts, and other interactive elements. The page has its own RSS feed (see more details below) so that those with readers or RSS-equipped browsers can monitor any additions. Other sites use shells to consolidate things such as legislative coverage.

The editor whose memo opened this chapter worked with her Web developers to create a shell for that poverty series. A special graphic prominently displayed at the top of the home page helped readers easily find it. When they clicked through, they found a list of 16 stories, each with its own picture and short description. Readers also were invited to help shape the newspaper's and community's future response by answering three questions about how Sumter should attack the problem, what the person thought the root causes of poverty were and how they could be eliminated, and how the person would spend $10 million toward the elimination of poverty.

A shell (see figures 5.3a, b, and c) should provide both context and continuity of content. Jane Ellen Stevens, one of the major proponents of shells, compares them to Russian "nesting" dolls. An individual *story* shell can be placed within an *issue* shell. An *issue* shell, in turn, can be housed within a *beat* shell.[5] For example, a story shell about a new cancer-fighting treatment can hold three accounts: (1) the treatment itself and how it works, (2) the founder of the treatment or studies involving its development, and (3) a personal story about a survivor who is alive because of the treatment. The story shell can then be grouped with other story shells involving recent cancer breakthroughs. These and other similar medical-related story shells can all be placed under a "health" shell on the main page of the website.

Stevens also sees shells integrating not only stories and graphics but also wide ranges of data and other resources, including links to health providers, advocacy and support groups, government agencies, and relevant legislation. While relatively few sites have reached that level of sophistication, the shell might be seen as another new story form made possible by digitization. Shells bring with them the primary challenges of organization and updating because once the information is stored permanently online, it's always available. New information and updates are added, but the original reports may never go away.

Tags

You can use tags to categorize stories or even story elements (audio, video, still photo, text, etc.) so that you can find all other elements with similar tags. For instance, for the farmers market story, *farmers market* would be a unifying tag. If you clicked on that tag, you would see a listing of all other stories dealing with the market. *Farming* would be another possible tag; click on it and you would get a wider variety of stories. This can lead you to stories you might not otherwise see.

Tags can be used within your site to produce a *tag cloud,* a listing of tags that shows, by the size of the type, what are the most requested types of stories on your site. While shells impose an organizational structure, tags allow the user to create a structure of his or her own by browsing like-tagged items on your site. Tags are different from keywords, which are used to help search-engine optimization and generally go into the HTML header coding of a page.

The use of tags, always spotty among news sites, has been waning as they concentrate more on allowing users to share copy on social media sites. You are more likely to find them on blogs where the software makes it easier to create them and where one or a few people can more easily keep track of what tags are used. But tags properly used on a news site can also trigger formatting and other actions that can add interactivity, and news organizations should consider using them more. For instance, a story tagged "crime" could automatically call up a link that would navigate to a searchable map of all crimes in an area.

With many more journalists blogging these days, either independently or as part of their jobs, tags are something you should consider for those efforts, even if your news organization does not use them on its site.

---

[5] J. E. Stevens (n.d.), "A Health and Safety 'Shell'—or What a Health and Safety Section Looks Like on a News Organization's Web Site," retrieved from http://www.bmsg.org/h&s_shell.php.

(A) 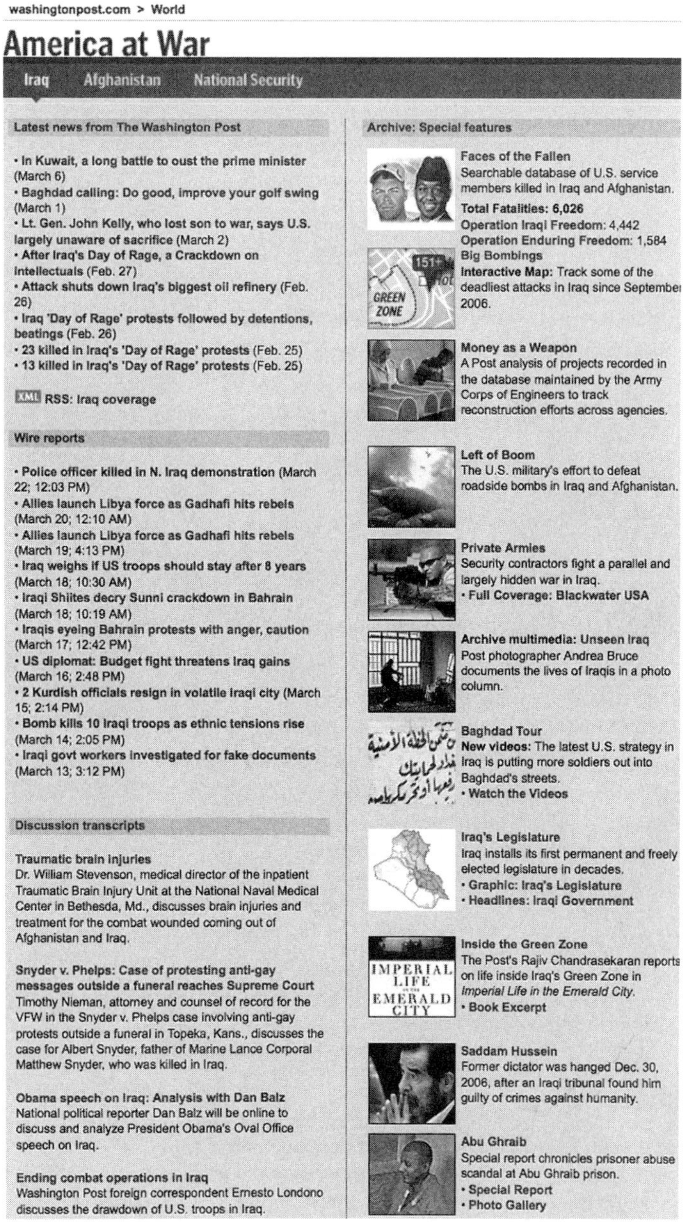 washingtonpost.com > World

America at War

Iraq Afghanistan National Security

Latest news from The Washington Post

- **In Kuwait, a long battle to oust the prime minister** (March 6)
- **Baghdad calling: Do good, improve your golf swing** (March 1)
- **Lt. Gen. John Kelly, who lost son to war, says U.S. largely unaware of sacrifice** (March 2)
- **After Iraq's Day of Rage, a Crackdown on Intellectuals** (Feb. 27)
- **Attack shuts down Iraq's biggest oil refinery** (Feb. 26)
- **Iraq 'Day of Rage' protests followed by detentions, beatings** (Feb. 26)
- **23 killed in Iraq's 'Day of Rage' protests** (Feb. 25)
- **13 killed in Iraq's 'Day of Rage' protests** (Feb. 25)

XML **RSS: Iraq coverage**

Wire reports

- **Police officer killed in N. Iraq demonstration** (March 22; 12:03 PM)
- **Allies launch Libya force as Gadhafi hits rebels** (March 20; 12:10 AM)
- **Allies launch Libya force as Gadhafi hits rebels** (March 19; 4:13 PM)
- **Iraq weighs if US troops should stay after 8 years** (March 18; 10:30 AM)
- **Iraqi Shiites decry Sunni crackdown in Bahrain** (March 18; 10:19 AM)
- **Iraqis eyeing Bahrain protests with anger, caution** (March 17; 12:42 PM)
- **US diplomat: Budget fight threatens Iraq gains** (March 16; 2:48 PM)
- **2 Kurdish officials resign in volatile Iraqi city** (March 15; 2:14 PM)
- **Bomb kills 10 Iraqi troops as ethnic tensions rise** (March 14; 2:05 PM)
- **Iraqi govt workers investigated for fake documents** (March 13; 3:12 PM)

Discussion transcripts

Traumatic brain injuries
Dr. William Stevenson, medical director of the inpatient Traumatic Brain Injury Unit at the National Naval Medical Center in Bethesda, Md., discusses brain injuries and treatment for the combat wounded coming out of Afghanistan and Iraq.

Snyder v. Phelps: Case of protesting anti-gay messages outside a funeral reaches Supreme Court
Timothy Nieman, attorney and counsel of record for the VFW in the Snyder v. Phelps case involving anti-gay protests outside a funeral in Topeka, Kans., discusses the case for Albert Snyder, father of Marine Lance Corporal Matthew Snyder, who was killed in Iraq.

Obama speech on Iraq: Analysis with Dan Balz
National political reporter Dan Balz will be online to discuss and analyze President Obama's Oval Office speech on Iraq.

Ending combat operations in Iraq
Washington Post foreign correspondent Ernesto Londono discusses the drawdown of U.S. troops in Iraq.

Archive: Special features

Faces of the Fallen
Searchable database of U.S. service members killed in Iraq and Afghanistan.
Total Fatalities: 6,026
Operation Iraqi Freedom: 4,442
Operation Enduring Freedom: 1,584

Big Bombings
Interactive Map: Track some of the deadliest attacks in Iraq since September 2006.

Money as a Weapon
A Post analysis of projects recorded in the database maintained by the Army Corps of Engineers to track reconstruction efforts across agencies.

Left of Boom
The U.S. military's effort to defeat roadside bombs in Iraq and Afghanistan.

Private Armies
Security contractors fight a parallel and largely hidden war in Iraq.
- **Full Coverage: Blackwater USA**

Archive multimedia: Unseen Iraq
Post photographer Andrea Bruce documents the lives of Iraqis in a photo column.

Baghdad Tour
New videos: The latest U.S. strategy in Iraq is putting more soldiers out into Baghdad's streets.
- **Watch the Videos**

Iraq's Legislature
Iraq installs its first permanent and freely elected legislature in decades.
- **Graphic: Iraq's Legislature**
- **Headlines: Iraqi Government**

Inside the Green Zone
The Post's Rajiv Chandrasekaran reports on life inside Iraq's Green Zone in *Imperial Life in the Emerald City.*
- **Book Excerpt**

Saddam Hussein
Former dictator was hanged Dec. 30, 2006, after an Iraqi tribunal found him guilty of crimes against humanity.

Abu Ghraib
Special report chronicles prisoner abuse scandal at Abu Ghraib prison.
- **Special Report**
- **Photo Gallery**

Figure 5.3 ■ A–C: Web shells help journalists organize and present information on complex and diverse issues such as terrorism, education, and politics. This was one version of the "America at War" shell on washingtonpost.com. Every time The Item in Sumter, S.C., published a new story on poverty in its area, it made sure a link to the special section on poverty appeared in the navigation bar on the left. The State newspaper in Columbia, S.C., has used a blog as its shell for political and legislative news.

(B)

TheItem.com

Current Temp 56°

High: 77° Low: 46°
Sunny and pleasant

Readers' Choice '07

Tuesday . April 17, 2007
Site Map | Subscribe | Contact Us | Advertise | E-mail

News Sports Entertainment Lifestyles Obituaries Classifieds Opinion Blotter

FRONT PAGE
SITE SEARCH
submit

FTC THE GREAT CONNECTION Old Friends. New Ideas.

NIE The Item NEWSPAPERS IN EDUCATION

SPECIAL SECTIONS
Auto Guide
24 Hours in Sumter
Poverty

What's in your TRASH CAN Click now to participate

PHOTO GALLERIES
Scottish Festival
Millwood Storybook
Signal Corps Band
Presidents Day Parade
Abbi Driggers

LOCAL NEWS
- 2 children die in house fire
- Clarendon 2 looks at '08 fiscal concerns
- Leventis: Arguments support consolidation
- Health care at heart of steel union strike
- Survivors pick up pieces after deadly twister
- Lawmaker: Bill could offer health insurance relief

ALSO AVAILABLE
Newspaper Ads
Lee County

Date Published: April 3, 2007

e-mail article print article

Educators talk poverty at conference

By MARY DOLAN
Item Staff Writer
mdolan@theitem.com

Greater family involvement is key to minimizing the effect of poverty on a child's education, according to former *Washington Post* columnist William Raspberry at a teacher conference at Coker College last week.

Raspberry, a Pulitzer Prize winner, was the keynote speaker at Friday's "Meeting the Challenge of Poverty" conference, the theme for the spring conference of the South Carolina Association of Colleges of Teacher Education and the South Carolina Association of Teacher Education.

Educators from across the state, including teachers, administrators, school board members and state Superintendent of Education Jim Rex gathered at Coker to

Most Viewed Articles
- Despite rumors, Lilfred's remains open
- 4 added to wanted list
- 82 years of wedded bliss
- Sumter makes mark in Columbia
- Obama: Rappers use same language as Imus
- Strawberries endure recent frost

View Today's Advertisements
- American Cancer Society
- Bank Of Clarendon

View ads from the last 7 days

TheItem.com page

Loos Change

Vernon P. Pate

Flowers & Baskets 778-1444

Seasons 803-905-5171

¡CONÉCTATE! Get Connected!

McLAUGHLIN Ford (803) 773-1481

Figure 5.3 ■ *(continued)*

The hierarchy of tags assigned by the journalist or organization is called a **taxonomy**. Even more opportunity for helping people find things on your site is by letting them create tags, called a **folksonomy**. For instance, you might tag something "cats," but a reader might use "felines" or the specific breed. Giving people as many ways as possible to find related information on your site is good business because it keeps them there looking at more of your content and ads.

(C) SC POLITICS TODAY

Haley: Added state money should go to taxpayers, not schools

Gov. Nikki Haley said Wednesday that she disagrees with a state Senate budget proposal that would adc $105 million to K-12 education spending, arguing the money instead should be used for tax cuts or to pay off state debt.

Senate OKs anti-copper theft bill

Haley vetoes borrowing by three school districts

SC Senate OKs new lines, tackles Congressional lines next

SC gov picks Public Safety chief as state top cop

Haley names a new inspector general

Budget negotiators weigh more money for schools or businesses

McConnell: Senators should vote on adding Haley agenda item to special session

Lexington GOP censures Knotts again

Romney leads in SC, new poll says

High court rules against Haley

State outlines plans for $125 million in new Medicaid cuts

SC Senate postpones illegal immigration changes

Summer school for lawmakers

Early voting in SC shot down for now

House agrees to amended tort reform bill

Amended bill would ban cash payments for copper

SC Politics Today
About this blog
A place to get fast updates on legislation and othe political news from the South Carolina State House.

For major news text alerts, **click here.**

For full stories and more politics news, see **our SC Politics page.**

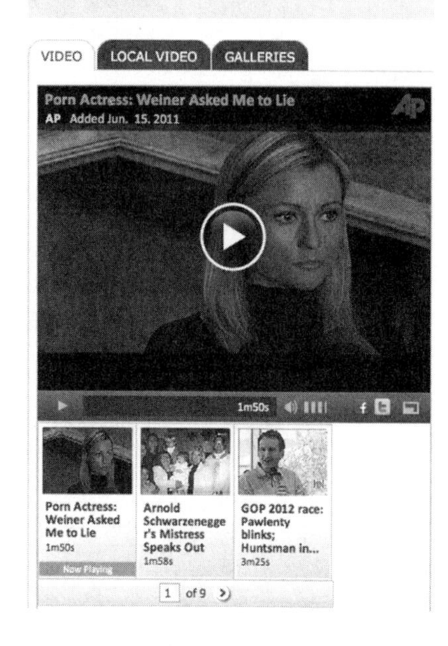

Figure 5.3 ■ *(continued)*

Instead of tags, some sites are using "search links" on key terms in their copy that, when clicked, bring up a screen of links to other stories containing that same term. The bottom line is that there is not one way, nor even a "best" way yet, to help users find related content, but finding ways to help people navigate your site more easily is important.

RSS feeds

RSS is known as "rich site summary," "really simple syndication," or, as one blogger put it, "ready for some stories." Another version is called "Atom." For the journalist, RSS provides a way to more widely distribute content and an easier way to monitor changes on Web sites. RSS is just a specially coded Web page designed to be parsed by

(A)

(B)

(C)

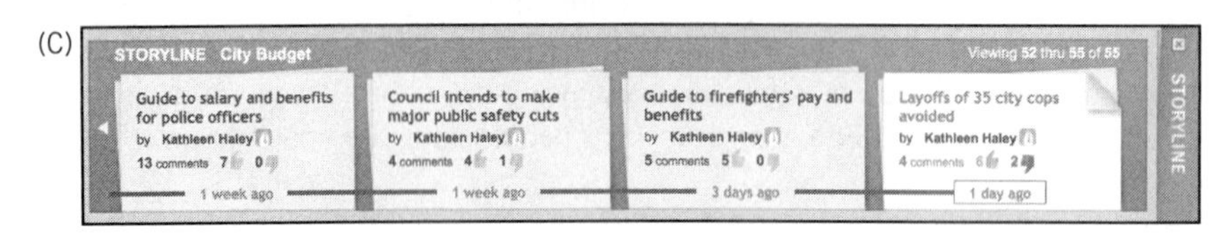

Figure 5.4 ■ News sites (A) continue to become more sophisticated in the way they are helping users navigate and find related material. At the Sacramento Press, for instance, a reader can call up a tag cloud (B) showing the most popular topics on the site at any time. And while reading a story, clicking on the "Storyline" tab calls up a visual timeline (C) of related stories.

specific software that produces a list of new items and lets you see all or part of each one without having to go to the originating site. There are Web-based feed readers or software you can download to your device, but many browsers also natively include the ability to manage RSS feeds.

Many early RSS proponents expected it to grow as people needed a way to easily and automatically draw content in from around the Internet. Some feed readers, such as Google's, also gave you the ability to share your items with others. Social media now seems to have taken over much of both roles, and some wonder whether RSS is dying. RSS has also been blamed partly for publishers' woes; not only does it allow people to consume content for free, it allows them to do it without ever going to the originating site.

The consensus seems to be that RSS will be used less as a consumer tool but that because it is used to tie so many parts of the Internet together, its chances of dying out are slim. RSS feeds, for instance, often power news tickers on digital signage, and they can allow one site to show another site's content. RSS feeds are discussed in more detail in chapter 13.

INVOLVING THE USER

News is now a conversation. The news editor is a guide, not a gatekeeper. Share your news. The new world of news should involve your readers, viewers, or users in some way. Entire books, manuscripts, and reports have been written about the rise of "citizen journalism," "participatory journalism," "user-generated content," and "shared media."[6] We will not attempt a comprehensive review; however, the modern journalist ignores the developments at his or her peril.

Steve Outing has proposed "The 11 Layers of Citizen Journalism,"[7] which range from allowing public comments on stories to "Wiki Journalism: Where the Readers Are Editors."

User participation in the process—and journalism has become a process, not a product—is now firmly established. At what levels users participate is now the subject of debate. What seems to be emerging is that users are less likely to be reporters unless they happen to be on the scene of breaking news, such as a fire, and can feed photos and initial details through their mobile devices. But they are likely to take on some of the roles of editing by providing feedback and by promoting stories through social media, for instance, or through sites such as Digg and Newsvine.

As noted in chapter 3, some news organizations are creating jobs specifically to manage user-generated content. Many news organizations invite user photos and other items; some have blogs written by those outside the newsroom. In most cases, however, the material is only lightly integrated, if at all, into the main news report (generally just by being displayed in a section of the home page).

---

[6] Two groundbreaking works are D. Gillmor, *We the Media—Grassroots Journalism by the People, for the People* (Sebastopol, Calif.: O'Reilly Media, 2004), available as an ebook at http://authorama.com/book/we-the-media.html; and C. Willis and S. Bowman, *We Media: How Audiences Are Shaping the Future of News and Information* (Reston, Va.: Media Center/American Press Institute, 2003). Available as a downloadable PDF at http://www.hypergene.net/wemedia/weblog.php.

[7] S. Outing (May 31, 2005), *The 11 Layers of Citizen Journalism,* Poynter Institute (updated March 2, 2011), http://www.poynter.org/uncategorized/69328/the-11-layers-of-citizen-journalism/.

Probably the most notable user-driven site is South Korea's *OhMyNews* (www.ohmynews.com). In the United States, some early attempts were South Carolina's *Bluffton Today* (www.blufftontoday.com) and the *Northwest Voice* of Bakersfield, California (now *The Bakersfield Voice* www.bakersfieldvoice.com). Many sites that are primarily user driven, however, have had an uneven history, and social media in some cases seem to have taken over some of the community-forming functions.

Nevertheless, the ubiquity of digital cameras and other tools integrated into cellphones, smartphones, and similar devices means nonjournalists will continue to perform acts of newsgathering, from transmitting pictures and sound of Middle East demonstrations globally to getting video of that 3 A.M. fire down the street. And that means that as a journalist you are likely to have to decide how, or if, you will integrate this material into your reporting and storytelling.

An analysis of *Bluffton Today (figure 5.5)*, for instance, found relatively few occurrences of user-generated content online making its way into print. However, the study concluded that such content added depth and perspective and that the real significance was not the number of stories but "the influence of readers' content on professional content. By reviewing citizen submissions online, professional journalists connect and communicate with the public in ways that were not available before."[8]

Journalists are being expected to pay attention to all of their environment, not just city hall, the Capitol, or the sports stadium. They are being expected to know how to monitor user-generated content, such as blogs, and when and how to incorporate it into their work. It may sometimes just be a tip to a story that needs more research; in other cases, such as Gannett's "crowdsourcing" initiative, it will mean learning how to lead and direct a corps of people who may not have formal journalism backgrounds.

Consider this ad for a national editor from the *Bakersfield Californian* that was posted to a national copy editors association jobs board:

Instead of depending solely on the usual services, the successful candidate will know how to scan leading blogs, the networks, talk radio and understand how to use the entire Internet to identify "Topic A" stories that will engage our readers.

And that engagement very heavily involves not just assembling information from a far wider variety of sources, but also *interactive multimedia.*

INTERACTIVITY, AN EVOLVING FRONTIER

The stress on "interactive" is important. Through much of the first two decades of wide public access to the Internet, multimedia largely meant doing audio and video the way they traditionally had been done and then just adding them as sidelights to a traditional text story.

They were interactive in a way, especially for newspapers, which had been constrained to static ink-on-paper words and still photos, in the sense that you had to click to watch them and then make the effort to sit through them.

The audio slide show was evolving during this time as probably the first interactive multimedia truly native to online. Unlike video, it had the advantage that the visuals and

[8] E. J. Storm, "The Endurance of Gatekeeping in an Evolving Newsroom: A Multi-Method Study of Web-Generated Citizen Content," unpublished master's thesis, University of South Carolina, 2006.

Figure 5.5 ■ Morris Communications' Bluffton Today in South Carolina was one of the first chain-owned news sites to not just experiment with incorporating user-generated content but also build part of the news report around it by prominently featuring community blogs.

audio did not have to occur together (quality news video usually also has good audio with it). It could be as powerful, sometimes more so, and it was quicker to assemble. Like video or audio, however, the interaction was largely constrained to hitting a start button.

Note that the audio slideshow is distinguished from the simple photo slideshow, a format often abused by websites seeking to artificially boost page views by making users click sequentially through photos that could just as easily be displayed in an interactive gallery where the user chooses which ones to click on for a closer look.

Many experiments were being done in more expansive and intensive projects. One of the earliest and most notable was the *Philadelphia Inquirer*'s *Blackhawk Down,* which combined text, audio, video, documents, and graphics into a comprehensive investigation of the ill-fated U.S. military rescue mission to Somalia. A user could literally spend days navigating through the multifaceted site (http://inquirer.philly.com/packages/somalia/sitemap.asp). A news organization could spend tens of thousands of dollars creating such a site.

Video and audio recorders shrunk; editing software became simpler and free; mapmaking resources that used to require expensive software and training became free online; data visualization tools cropped up. The push had begun toward *dynamic* interactive content, which is based on databases that contain all the story elements but respond differently based on user input (which the user may or may not be consciously making).

We have barely scratched the surface of interactivity in this section. We'll explore it in more detail in chapters 10 and 12. But the point for now is that if, as a journalist, you are to thrive in this interactive world, you have to think interactively starting from the moment of story concept. We've done a little bit of that with the planning grid earlier, but now let's examine a scenario.

BRINGING IT ALL TOGETHER: THE ACME WIDGET STRIKE

To illustrate this new concept of story, we use a scenario based on a strike at Acme Widget, your town's major employer. Your role (no matter the title) is "storybuilder," as explained in chapter 3, a new form of editor/producer who is a story specialist but media generalist. In other words, you might handle fewer stories, but you will handle them across all forms of media. We know that right now few people work in fully converged newsrooms like this, but with consolidations around the nation along with online startups not tethered to legacy media, that day may be edging closer. So play along.

11 P.M.: First Word

You've known for weeks of labor unrest at Acme and have been involved in the coverage. Now, you see a post on the union's Twitter feed: "Strike at midnight." Your legacy TV station has a newscast coming, and the newspaper presses roll soon after. There is one reporter. What to do?

- The reporter hits the phones and you pull together links (the company's and union's websites, company financial filings at the Securities and Exchange

Commission). *Interactivity: Maybe the newsroom has built a timeline or highlights box as the talks progressed (this attention to ongoing detail will be prized). If not, you have a few minutes to check your archives for a few key dates and developments and create one on Dipity.*

- The reporter confirms the strike and quickly files on Twitter using the **hashtag** #acmestrike. ("Acme Widget union to strike at midnight after talks break down. More than 2,500 workers. #acmestrike"). *Interactivity: The hashtag will let all the tweets with that tag be searched and grouped so they can be updated on your site as well as other sites.*
- You add a bit of background and ship it to the TV desk where the producer inserts it into the lineup with an over-the-shoulder graphic quickly pulled from the computer. You also file it online using the editor that allows you to quickly input text, create a link or two, and upload pictures, which you have pulled from the archives.
- In a few minutes, the reporter has interviewed a couple of key people on the phone and written about 350 words, partly using the background you found in the files. *Both of you knew interactive elements are important, so the reporter recorded the interviews (with the subjects' consent). While you edit the story, she's editing the audio.*
- You edit the story, making sure it has short, focused paragraphs and some of the other things that make it easy to scan (bulleted lists, subheads, etc.), and send it to the newspaper desk (the "printcast" format discussed in chapter 4 works pretty well in print too). You update the online story and file again on Twitter to point to the online link and ask people to use the "#acmestrike" hashtag for any related Tweets and the tag "acmestrike" for any photos they post on Flickr (so you can find those too). You also update the relevant Facebook pages to make the same pleas. (You might even put that information at the end of your online story.)
- If your newsroom is forward-looking, it also has an Evernote account (www.evernote.com) to which you have been uploading key pieces of information to be synchronized with all the other registered devices the reporters and producers carry.

Overnight

No one else is answering calls; the reporter, before heading home, added a little background to the timeline and then went to the plant and talked to one or two people outside, which was also added to the story (and tweeted). The audio has been edited, posted online, and linked to the stories. You've created an *Acme Widget Strike* shell on the website (it's easy with drag-and-drop editing tools, and your software creates an RSS feed for the page), and you've added links to all the material so far, including the archives. As you have been filing online, you also have been adding "tags" to the stories (e.g., *Acme Widget, strike, Teamsters*). You've also been monitoring the union's blog and Twitter feed, as well as that "#acmestrike" hashtag, and you've been looking for other blogs that might be plugged in using a search engine specializing in blogs, such as Icerocket or Google blog search.

At 3 A.M., a wire service story says Acme's plant workers in Ireland have walked out. It's not a lot, but it's fresh. The wire service story goes automatically online, but you also top your story and tweet the information. Now what do you do?

- There is no down time anymore. Just putting up a wire service story won't give you the beat as people start waking up and logging in. You track down someone at the *Irish Times* who covers Acme there.
- You could just have a phone conversation, maybe even do an audio recording. *But thinking interactively, you know video can be a draw. So you ask the reporter if you can use Skype to connect by video. You chat, and as you do, you use a video capture program like Snapz Pro or Camtasia. Conversation over, you quickly edit and post chunks of the video.*
- Your newsroom also has a *geotagged feed* (see chapter 10) set up for traffic problems. You'll load strike information into that so drivers can avoid picket lines.

Morning

The morning crew rolls in (but you're pulling a double shift—too good a story to leave, and besides, we need you here for the simulation). TV is headed out to the plant, but you make sure the feed is set up to go live online as well as on the air and that it's recorded so it can be edited for online replays. (If you are really pushing it, you make sure one camera is live at all times and set up a continuous video feed online using Livestream or a similar service.) Your Acme beat reporter also heads out with a photographer, but she also has a smartphone with a decent camera, just in case she sees something the photographer doesn't. She also has an audio recorder, or she can record sound on the smartphone.

- You've reminded them to *coordinate on a slide show.*
- You've got the basics in place—shell, timeline, story, audio, video—but before the fresh copy comes in you're already looking ahead to midday interactivity. *You'll work on lining up an independent labor lawyer to explain, during an online chat, what the issues and stakes are.* (You might do the chat through something like Cover It Live.)
- As other reporters and producers come in, they'll work on various aspects, such as getting more from the company, the mood at union headquarters, and the possible economic effects. *You've talked with everyone about the need for not only audio or video (with their mobile devices or small handheld cameras) but also about the need to get documents in electronic form for uploading.* If the city says it's been projecting the police overtime costs, for instance, ask for the spreadsheet or word-processing document.

The TV reporter, after her live shot, has written about 300 words focusing on the interviews she did with union and management officials. That tops the main story already online. You also have provocative, emotional video from the union leader and protesters. Is the text story really your "story," or is it the video? A possible solution might be to allow the video to front your Web page but also to provide a clear link to any response from the company (with luck, you have video from Acme too). You are dealing with a generation familiar with YouTube and similar devices, and the video images, not the words, convey the main story.

The challenge throughout the day is to keep information flowing, but not to bog down the reporters with constant posting and reporting. They need time to delve deeply into a story that has major ramifications for your community. You'll spend lots of time as traffic cop and editor as material comes in as well as coordinating with the TV and newspaper folks to make sure what's being produced meets their needs.

Early Afternoon

Your ace Acme reporter has been given a database of all the striking workers' addresses, incomes, and seniority. The standard response might be to do some sorting, get some basic parameters, do some interviews, and write a several-hundred-word "river of text." But is that really your story?

- You could create a database searchable by worker. But what about privacy? Just because we can do something doesn't mean we should. Besides, the "knowledge" value here is showing how the strike, in aggregate, could affect various neighborhoods.
- *The interactive solution is working with your technical experts to create a map driven by the interactive database. You should realize this is now your "story," not some river of text. Users can query the database and see, for instance, how many Acme workers live in an area, the average salary, maybe even the average seniority.*
- Meanwhile, you dispatch crews to those areas to interview people. Armed with the specific information, they can report with more depth and authority. *If your users roll their mouse over (or, on a mobile device, touch) each neighborhood, up pop options to read the stories and see the videos from that area. The notion of story has been converged.*

This is not some entirely futuristic vision. Rather, it represents one vision of the complexity of the resources you can apply to a story. There are even more ways you can attack the story online; these are discussed in chapter 10.

SUMMARY

The Internet affords exciting new opportunities for convergent journalists to play an active role in their community. News is now a conversation, and the emphasis is on interactivity. Newspapers have had to rethink traditional approaches to stories, newsrooms, and ways of reporting community events.

The key is to think interactive multimedia from the beginning. Just trying to bolt on multimedia after the story is written is too late. It's also important to give your users *utility* because that is becoming the basis for online business models.

Consumers have a variety of tools to access news reports, including shells, tags, and RSS feeds. All of these are simply ways to engage the consumers of news and help journalists better fulfill their role in the community.

Box 5.1 Good Web Content: Questions to Ask

- Is text the best way to tell this story, or are there other, better ways?
- Is the headline or link to the content a clear and complete thought? Does it shun "headlinese" (nix, mull, tab, etc.) and use common words, especially verbs?
- Can the reader easily scan the content and pick out key information?
- What role will each element play in providing a complete package?
  - Do the items link to each other so the reader can easily follow the path? (This includes photos, which may be reached by a search engine. Consider putting a link in the caption so the user can at least get back to the accompanying story.)
  - Are there links to related material, current and past, so the reader can learn the historical context? (These links might be provided through labels and tags or through placement in an overall Web shell.)
  - Are there links to relevant outside material so the reader can understand the story's wider context?
- Does each item have enough information by itself so that readers coming to it through a search engine need not read or view something else to understand the basics of what you are talking about?
- Are multimedia elements appropriate and in the right format?
  - Web video works best with close-ups and medium shots because of the small viewing screen. It also seems to work better when it can focus on one topic and be kept to less than two minutes (although longer, compelling pieces certainly do work). Natural sound and the voices of people generally have been preferred to narration.
  - Stills fashioned into slide shows with audio can work better for showing the broad sweep of things.
  - Short (no more than 45 seconds in most cases) audio clips can be a way to quickly add multimedia. As you would when quoting someone in a story, avoid purely "informational" sound bites and use those that encapsulate the moment's emotion.
  - Web graphics work best when kept simple and layered through linking.
- Is there a way for someone to interact with the story?
  - Is there at least a way to mail a copy to someone else?
  - Can someone comment? Will you respond?
  - Will you, under a Creative Commons license, allow some reuse of the material so that your users can create their own works (mashups) with credit to you?
  - Will you have more complicated interactive elements, such as games or searchable databases?
  - Will you solicit user-generated content to complement what you have done?

Box 5.2 Tips for Compelling Web Content

Recommendations for Video and Audio on the Web:

Video and audio work best online when they are tightly focused and short. (This is why just throwing a typical TV story online often does not produce the best results; it is produced for TV, which is a different medium for a different attention span.)

As general rules, try to keep video under two minutes and audio under 45 seconds (of course, if you have more powerful audio or video, let it run).

Treat video and audio as you would quotes: Avoid the purely informational, bland stuff, such as a sheriff droning on at a news conference about a crime. Pick just the best two or three sentences that come together. (Don't splice to make them appear to come together; that's not ethical.) Don't use video or audio just because you have it. Both convey emotion as well as information. Like spice, use too much and it throws off the recipe.

Recommendations for Graphics:

The typical photo or graphic file size should be no larger than about 40kb to ensure quick downloading for high-speed, dial-up, and mobile users. If you are saving from a photo-editing program, this usually means a resolution of 72 dpi and a JPEG quality of about 60 (medium-high).

Print graphics will have to be reformatted, often enlarging the text and converting the color from CMYK (for printing) to RGB (for the Web).

Newspaper graphics often do not do well on a small computer screen. Online requires simplicity, and that can mean a different version of a graphic.

Online, try to match a photo to where the person or object appears in the story. If the reader must scroll, try to make sure that another graphical element appears from the bottom as one moves out the top.

The Acme Widget Strike suggests how journalists can use all the tools at their disposal to tell stories. These stories can take different forms, with different emphases, that will reach different audiences. In this way, the news organization can best draw consumers into public discussion and help bring to light the numerous ways an event can resonate throughout a community.

EXERCISES

1. Either you or your instructor choose two stories from the front page of today's newspaper. Complete the PCJ Story Grid (see fig. 5.2) to identify the dimensions of the story and which elements will work best for online presentation.
2. Take these stories and examine how your local newspaper treated them on its website.
3. Visit the website of a national newspaper and observe how it treated comparable stories.
4. Take the same three stories and propose four relevant tags for each. Show the story, but not the tags, to another person and ask him or her to pick out four terms he or she would use if looking for the story in the future. How closely did you match? Discuss with the

person what went into his or her thinking so that you can improve on your tagging. After adjusting your tags, try it with a second person and maybe a third. Is agreement improving?

5. Visit Twitter or Delicious, a social bookmarking site, and put in the name of your hometown. See what the conversation is about. Are you surprised?

CHAPTER 6

FROM BROADCAST TO INTERNET: REPURPOSING CONTENT

This chapter builds upon the basics in the previous chapters using a broadcast perspective. The most important point is that broadcast news is no longer limited to the airwaves. Modern broadcast news operations must maintain a prominent Web presence to stay competitive. The printcast product (combining print- and broadcast-style content) is as important as the broadcast product.

Audiences expect news on demand. Because of work schedules and leisure time, people will seek out news when it's convenient for them, and news organizations have learned to accommodate that. This means presenting top-quality news content in both broadcast and Internet forms so as to build audience share and brand identification.

Here's how the two work together: Let's say there is a high-profile murder trial in your community. Your station has a satellite truck outside the courthouse, and you are scheduled for live broadcast reports at noon, 5 P.M., and as soon as possible after the verdict announcement. The case comes to a close around noon, and after two hours of deliberations, a "not guilty" verdict is announced at roughly 2:10 P.M.

First you would send a short message to those who have subscribed to your site's news updates. It might be on Twitter, it might be a text message, or it might be on email; in many newsrooms now it is all three. Next, you might upload photos as well as call the station with the details so the news anchor can break into programming with the result.

Next, you and your videographer go back and collect interviews and prepare for the 3 P.M. live report. Sometime around 2:45 you would stop gathering content in order to prepare for that report. In this way, Internet and broadcast point toward each other and attain the goal of establishing your news organization as an important brand in your community.

For other examples you can go to any of the award-winning websites listed in figure 6.1 to see how news is presented in various forms involving text, still images, video, audio, and interactive feedback solicited from the viewer/reader.

Rather than create all new online stories, stations have found it effective to repurpose the stories they air. *Repurposing* is taking what has been produced for one medium and tailoring it for another; the tailoring differentiates it from the often-derided "shovelware." This goes beyond just streaming the newscast online to include text versions reworked from the broadcast script or even raw, unedited video of an event. The key is to decide what makes the most compelling version for each medium. Television is linear—each element follows the previous, with no chance to go backward—and relies heavily on visual images and personality. Being online allows you to write effective text-only versions or quickly record audio accounts as well as include still images or animations, post complete interviews with newsmakers, or even link to other online pages or sites with relevant documents or information.

Repurposing content has become increasingly simple for some stories. Many stations use one of a handful of website providers, and these companies make it exceedingly easy to copy the text from a script in the newsroom computer system (ENPS, for example) and paste it into a form that allows quick reformatting (including adding links, still photos, and, in many cases, the embedded video) and publishing to a preset area on the station's website.

WHY REPURPOSE?

Online combines strengths of both print and electronic media. Text lets readers quickly scan or thoughtfully digest passages, and stories can be as short or as long as needed.

Television Network/Syndication Service, CNN ***CNN.com***
Radio Network/Syndication Service, National Public Radio ***NPR.org***
Online News Operation—National, The Tyee ***thetyee.ca***
Online News Operation—Local, TBD.*com*—Washington, D.C.
Television: Large Market, KING-TV—Seattle, WA **king5.com**
Radio: Large Market, WBUR-FM—Boston, MA ***wbur.org***
Television: Small Market, KTVB-TV—Boise, ID ***KTVB.COM***
Radio: Small Market, Rubber City Radio Group—Akron, OH ***AkronNewsNow.com***

Figure 6.1 ■ Each year the RTDNA recognizes excellence in electronic journalism with the Murrow Awards. In 2011, 62 organizations received 95 different awards for excellence. Here are organizations recognized in one category, Outstanding Websites. Retrieved from http://www.rtdna.org/.

Unlike newspapers, where the news hole is limited by advertising constraints, or broadcast, where there are strict time limits, writers, editors, and producers can determine the optimum length, as well as any additional elements such as photos or video, needed to tell a story.

Audio and video are experientially rich and have a home on the Web. A long-standing criticism of TV news has been the viewers' inability to rewatch stories or video clips, but the Internet has changed expectations. Now, news and information consumers want to be able to choose among quick summaries or comprehensive text-based accounts as well as video on demand. The result is a drive among news organizations to provide the most up-to-date, comprehensive accounts of important and interesting events with actual video of the most compelling moments.

The video might be the broadcast news "package" report uploaded online, video clips edited from the full package, some of the unedited video used to produce the package, or something entirely new prepared specifically for the Web. Online live reports are still rare but will increase as technology improves and websites continue to gain importance.

Repurposing allows a broadcast station to expand the reach and shelf life of its journalism. News consumers can watch live broadcasts at scheduled times, or they can actively access the website content and update it themselves. The website is the virtual storefront for the broadcast news station, extending its brand in the community at relatively little additional cost. It is open at all times and delivers desired information into the home, office, or mobile device when the consumer wants it. Repurposing stories is both good journalism and good business, although some critics still deride the practice as not taking full advantage of all the new possibilities the digital frontier offers.

RADIO VERSUS TELEVISION

In this time of media convergence, news websites increasingly look the same, whether the organization (and the orientation) is television, radio, or newspaper. Websites perform the same basic functions, providing up-to-the-minute news, sports, and weather information in a variety of formats. Video is no longer just the province of the TV station site; radio station websites also offer video news reports, although these are mostly limited to national video feeds, primarily from the networks or wire services. Otherwise, website content reflects differences in staff size and organization goals. Newspapers tend to have the largest reporting staff, followed by TV stations, cable news channels (depending on the market), and radio stations.

Radio has been considered the "sound-only" medium. But transmitted online, radio news can offer the same services and information as other media. In addition, those stations playing primarily music may have the edge on others in terms of personalities and interactivity with the local audience through contests, giveaways, promotions, music events, and so on.

The most popular format on American radio stations continues to be News and Talk, numbering more than 1,500.[1] Since many broadcast on lesser-quality AM frequencies, online delivery improves their fidelity. Despite these overall numbers, radio news does

[1] State of the Media 2011. Traditional Broadcast: Audio. Retrieved from http://stateofthemedia.org/2010/audio-summary-essay/traditional-broadcast/

not hold as much opportunity for employment or content creation. For national network news, it seems only National Public Radio has shown an increase in listeners. According to *State of the Media 2011*, NPR's news audience increased 3 percent in 2010 to 27.2 million weekly listeners.[2]

According to Bob Papper's 2010 Radio Television Digital News Association (RTDNA)/Hofstra University survey, the average radio newsroom only has about two people.[3] Depending on the market and management support, some station clusters may have five or six full-time staff positions and larger markets may have more than a dozen. The overall trend for radio news continues to be to maintain employment numbers but serve more stations because of ownership concentration. For this reason, the average news/talk station may find it hard to compete with television or newspaper websites in breadth of local video news content. But radio reporters carrying digital cameras and advanced cellphones and smartphones also are finding it easier to provide some rich online content. Augmented by *user-generated content,* radio news may be able to compete for a piece of the online pie in larger markets. In smaller towns, the radio station's website may be one of the area's primary news sources.

THE BASICS OF TELEVISION NEWS WEBSITES

Television news staffs are smaller than those of newspapers, but they compete vigorously. Local news is vital for broadcast stations to survive because local news drives traffic to the station websites.

Television websites are typically created and maintained either in-house or by contract. Several companies compete for this business such as Internet Broadcasting, whose clients include Cox Media Group, Meredith, Hearst Television, Post-Newsweek Stations, and Telemundo; Inergize Digital, whose clients include Newport Television, Gray Television, and Fisher Communications; Broadcast Interactive Media, which manages websites for stations from Belo Television Group, Fisher Communications, Granite Broadcasting, and others; and WorldNow, which counts among its clients stations owned by ABC, Cox, Raycom Media, and Barrington Broadcasting Group.

Television websites rely on posting content—lots of it—and replenishing it as often as possible. The synergy between the broadcast station and online delivery of video content is continuing to evolve. At first, websites were designed primarily to promote the broadcast brand, but now the Web is key for delivering news content and in many stations has dedicated staff and resources.

The Look of News Websites

Careful attention must be given to the site's overall design. Websites are often criticized for having a cluttered look, with banners, headlines, video, interactive elements, blogs, personality features, marketing information, and other items that can overwhelm a visitor.

---

[2] State of the Media 2011. Audio: Medium on the brink of major change. Retrieved from http://stateofthemedia.org/2011/audio-essay/

[3] Kevin Finch, (2011, March 23). Radio news on more than just a shoestring. Communicator, retrieved from http://www.rtnda.org/pages/posts/radio-news-on-more-than-just-a-shoestring1303.php.

Most news websites look similar for at least three reasons. First, a relatively small number of people design them, and they use tried-and-true formulas for presenting information online and follow the conventions of effective Web design (for example, the site index runs vertically along the left side, words are read left to right, etc.). Some of this has changed, however, toward a more minimalist design with headlines, graphics, navigation bars that pop up or expand when the cursor is over them, and subject tabs carrying more of the navigation. This approach tends to avoid the long and awkward left-side "rail" site index.

Second, the nature of news is also relatively standardized. Journalists have traditionally presented news items according to geography (international, national, regional, and local) and by category (government, crime, health, sports, entertainment, business, etc.). The Web enables new categories, and we now see text-only versus video report sections as well as "interactives" (see chapter 12 for more on interactives) that include things like blogs, time lines, instant polls, chat rooms, comments, ratings, and other means by which visitors can give their views and opinions or fashion their own reports.

The third reason most news websites look alike is the competitive environment. In the hypercompetitive world of journalism, everyone closely watches what others are doing. Anytime someone experiments or finds a way to do something new and different, competing organizations usually copy it and adopt it themselves, and sometimes even announce that *they* thought of it first.

While software such as Dreamweaver is often used to build websites for teaching purposes because it allows changes to be made easily, the systems you will use in many professional operations are not engineered so that the typical user can easily change the design elements. Nevertheless, website design can be a valuable skill for those with the talent and inclination. If you are interested, you should look into Web development and content management system courses at your local college or technical school or online.

Similar Content

For branding and internal consistency, the news organization's website content and design elements (such as the logo) should match the on-air product. Obviously, news and sports stories will be found both on-air and online. But, for instance, if the station also has a contract to broadcast weekly health reports (courtesy of a well-known HMO), the corresponding information should also be on the website. This cross-promotion often is contractual, but it has also been found to help bring people to the website and enhance the overall branding of both organizations. This cross-promotional element is standard for all news organizations and includes routine local promotions and sales events.

Uploading Scripts

At most stations, the reporters and producers refashion their scripts to more of a print style and then post that onto the website. The process becomes easier with each new generation of software, but the basic steps generally don't change:

- The story is opened in the broadcast editorial system, such as ENPS.
- In another screen, the website management system is opened and a new page is requested.

Figure 6.2 ■ This is a typical TV station Web site (WVEC-TV 13, Virginia Beach, Va.; http://www.wvec. com). Notice the use of branding elements in the top left corner. Stations may also place photos of the news team here or move them to the station Facebook page. Notice that most of the page is text—there is more text than video on most TV stations' home pages. Navigation bars across the top help the user find specific information on the site. The most important stories—and the weather—have prominence in the center of the screen. Finally, the display ads and text ads provide revenue from the website.

- The text is copied from the editorial system to the appropriate box in the website management page and any formatting changes, such as adding bulleted lists and writing out the quotes, are done.
- Other boxes are filled in with headline and summary information that will be used on the home page and other pages to get users to click through to the story.
- Links are added, either by filling in more blanks for those that will go alongside the story or by highlighting text in the story and filling in a form to create an in-text link.
- Pictures are uploaded and captions are written, also in specified places on the input form.
- If there is video, it usually will have been uploaded to the site's servers separately, but there will be a box or button that has to be checked to associate the video with the story and embed the video player.

- Any tags are added, social media options are selected, and the story is assigned to various categories (news, sports, breaking news, etc.) on the site.
- The story is published. As part of publishing, the system takes care of putting all the referring links on other parts of the site, creating the story page with appropriate embedded elements.

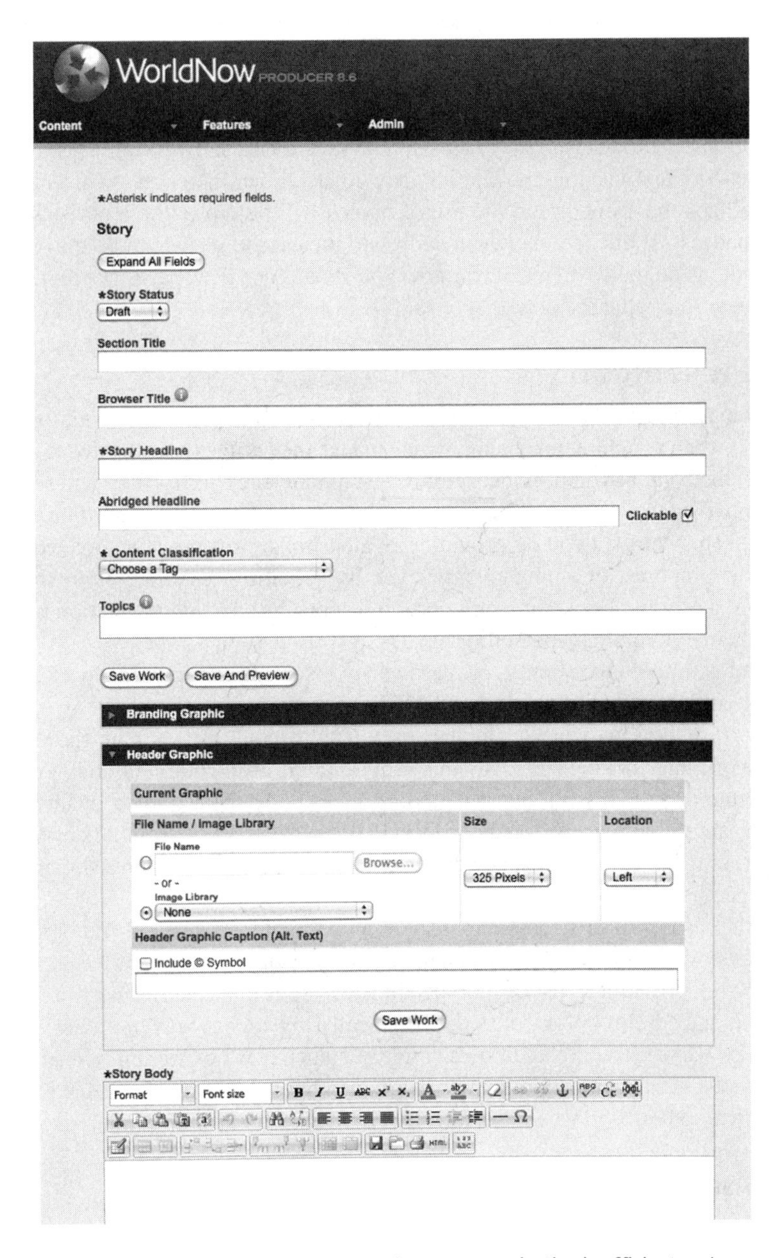

Figure 6.3 ■ Uploading material to the website of a news organization is efficient and easy with templates like this one used by WorldNow.

BROADCAST STORIES ONLINE

The stories on the website can be essentially the same as those broadcast. Length is not as constrained as it is for on-air broadcasts, but the rule for the Web remains "keep it short and get to the point."

A few important changes must be made for online. Although the conversational style should remain, the writer will have to remove all self-references and descriptors that come from ad-libbing and injecting personality ("as we see here," "this is happening right now," "here on your news channel," "our Action News exclusive," "Eyewitness News has learned," etc.). Although these expressions and phrases may be standard procedure for on-air broadcasts, they can seem awkward and self-serving in text formats. For online story text versions, attribution may go last rather than first (as in a newspaper story). Perhaps most important, the use of quotes will be more like a newspaper story than a broadcast. While we may eventually find it easier to post sound bites online and place a link inside the written text, for now you should use newspaper style and provide short quotes from what the newsmaker said.

Story Presentation

A key element in crafting a Web story is interactivity. People online tend to be more active than when watching television, which means they will expect to have to *do* something with the content you provide. If the Web content is text-only, they will scan it and quickly move on to something else, so you must present them with opportunities to stay interested. This can be done by providing related links; offering story-related images, informative graphics, or animations; or even by soliciting responses with short polls or opinion questions. Depending on your job responsibilities and the station resources, you'll either be doing this yourself or have help.

If the featured Web content is primarily visual (such as an individual package, news headlines, or the entire 5 o'clock show), think of ways to help the user stay interested. Get away from thinking that Web audiences will sit through a 30-minute show. Instead, aim for short, interlocking segments that require the user to routinely click or respond every minute or so. This can mean including a link to a photo gallery or insta-poll or asking for an opinion (in 50 words or less) that can be referred to in a later television broadcast. In many cases, this is now being done by linking to tools on a station's social media page on Facebook.

Another aspect of presentation has to do with the physical layout and organization of the story online. Stations will post all the top stories together on a main page (index or primary page), providing a list of short headlines or slugs that describe each story. These may be organized chronologically, geographically, by topic, or some other way. Top stories may also be accompanied by a single-sentence tease or summary lead to pique reader interest. An accompanying photo is optional but helpful. The headline will be the Web link to another page where the full story or story versions are available.

Web Shells

As noted in chapter 5, an increasingly common feature of news websites is the use of Web shells—dedicated space on a site to hold the reports, multimedia elements, and related information generated over time on a specific topic.

Television stations' smaller staffs make it harder to "drill into" a particular topic, so while stations often have a "special reports" section on their website, these are more of a compilation of investigative reports on a variety of topics rather than multiple stories and other elements about a single topic. However, smaller staffs don't have to be an impediment. If there is a big local story, members of the community are likely to be posting photos on a photo-sharing service like Flickr, for instance, or short messages on Twitter. Using tags on the photos and hashtags from Twitter (see chapter 11 for more), this content can be pulled into a shell to provide more material.

Standardized newsroom system software makes uploading content to shells relatively easy. Stations should provide new employees a cookbook set of instructions at some point in an orientation. Even a custom-designed website should follow a standard format and organization structure. The templates are supposed to make it simple to post material and designed with standard newsroom software in mind. With a bit of practice, the entire posting procedure can take only a few moments.

HANDLING MULTIMEDIA CONTENT

It seems that each year creating multimedia content—things like audio, video, photos, graphics, and animations—and distributing it online becomes faster and easier. Only the basic principles and processes are covered here, but there are plenty of free and low-cost online sites that go into greater depth if you want to plunge into a particular skill.

Audio Only (Podcasts, MP3)

Editing and processing audio tends to be faster and easier than video. Audio files have less information, which means smaller file sizes and quicker handling (see box 6.1).

In some cases, especially where processing time is a constraint, audio alone will be the best choice, even if it is quickly stripped from a video segment. Creating audio-only content is reasonable and by providing some interactivity adds value to the news organization's brand (and in the branding of the news worker). In addition to simply posting links to sound bites, those audio tracks can be gathered into a podcast, which can involve a little more production effort. The simplest podcasts may be nothing more than recording an extended interview or gathering sound bites and stitching them together with a little narration, then posting the MP3 (compressed audio) file with the appropriate coding so that users with software like iTunes can find it automatically. The most elaborate and popular podcasts, like NPR's *Wait Wait... Don't Tell Me*, are full-fledged programs, highly produced and mixing several elements including music and multiple voices. But simple podcasts can be produced quickly and provide rich content for breaking news events or an undated feature offering commentary and analysis.

A small digital recorder to use along with the video camera and microphone should be a standard part of any reporter's toolkit. When conducting an interview or attending a news conference, the reporter can put it on the lectern or plug it into an audio feed box separately. A number of audio recorders now can produce MP3 files that can be directly loaded online (though you should avoid this option if you plan on editing the file since MP3, as a "lossy" format, loses quality quickly with editing). Because there are no moving parts, the audio picked up by the built-in microphone can be almost as clear as that gathered through an external microphone. Even when shooting video, reporters should

Box 6.1 From Bytes to Yottabytes: Comparative File Sizes

Note that we've rounded off for ease of understanding; file sizes are relative and vary greatly depending on format. In addition, it is important to remember that one kilobyte is actually 1,024 bytes, and so on.

Byte (8 bits)	
1 byte	A single character
10 bytes	A single word
100 bytes	A telegram, punched card, or short SMS
Kilobyte (1,000 bytes)	
1 kilobyte	A few paragraphs
2 kilobytes	Typewritten page
10 kilobytes	Encyclopedia page or static Webpage
50 kilobytes	Compressed document image page
100 kilobytes	Low-resolution photograph
300 kilobytes	Average-resolution photograph (JPG) or 20 seconds of 8-bit mono audio
500 kilobytes	30-second audio/radio commercial announcement
Megabyte (1,000 kilobytes or 1 million bytes)	
1 megabyte	A small novel, 1 minute of 8-bit mono audio, or 1-minute stereo MP3
2 megabytes	High-resolution photograph, 7 megapixel, 2,832 x 2,128
5 megabytes	Complete works of Shakespeare, 30 seconds of TV-quality video, or 5-minute podcast
10 megabytes	One minute of uncompressed, CD-quality sound or 25 seconds of smartphone mp4 video
100 megabytes	One meter of shelved books or a two-volume encyclopedia
216 megabytes	Standard digital video, 720 x 480, 5:1 compression, 1 minute
650 megabytes	CD-ROM capacity, audio or data
Gigabyte (1,000 megabytes or 1 trillion bytes)	
1 gigabyte	Pick-up truck filled with paper, 10 meters of shelved books, or a CD-quality symphony
5 gigabytes	One standard DVD (digital video disc or digital versatile disc)
6.5 gigabytes	Half-hour show, standard DV, 720 x 480, 5:1 compression
15 gigabytes	High-definition DVD (holds 4 hours of HD video)
50 gigabytes	Floor of books
300 gigabytes	A full broadcast day, standard DV, 720 x 480, 5:1 compression

Box 6.1 (continued)

Terabyte (1,000 gigabytes)

1 terabyte	50,000 trees made into paper and printed
2 terabytes	Entire contents of an academic research library
20 terabytes	Printed collection of the U.S. Library of Congress

Petabyte (1,000 Terabytes)

3 petabytes	Total holdings, all media, U.S. Library of Congress
20 petabytes	Total production of hard-disk drives in 1995
200 petabytes	All printed material or production of digital magnetic tape in 1995

Exabyte (1,000 petabytes or 1 billion gigabytes)

5 exabytes	All words ever spoken by human beings up to the year 2000
12 exabytes	Total volume of information generated worldwide 1999
500 exabytes	Total digital content in 2009

Zettabyte (1,000 exabytes)

1.2 zettabytes	Estimated total amount of data produced in 2010

Yottabyte (1,000 zettabytes)

1.0 yottabytes	Estimated storage capacity of one million data centers filling Rhode Island and Delaware

use the audio recorder when it would not be obtrusive. It will give you an audio backup and allow you to log your audio cuts in all sorts of locations without the hassle of having to use a video unit just to listen to what you've got.

Audio's greatest strength has always been its portability—one can listen and at the same time drive, paint, juggle, or watch television. Therefore, a website visitor can listen to a live debate, sample individual audio cuts, or tune in to a more highly produced podcast while at the same time looking at your photo essay or answering your online poll.

Video

Visual images tend to be more demanding, more complex, and generally perceived as having more value than simple text or audio. Video also takes longer to process, digitize, edit, and package.

Some news organizations still use video cameras that record to digital tape, but most are switching to cameras that record direct to memory and to removable storage like flash memory cards. The disadvantage of tape is that it takes almost as long to play the tape and transfer the material (called "capturing") to the computer for editing as it took to shoot the video. With "tapeless" cameras, the file can be transferred much quicker from the flash memory card or, in some cases, from the camera using a FireWire (IEEE1394) cable.

Once the digital file is in the computer, the procedure for processing and editing is fairly straightforward (detailed in box 6.2). Editing software such as Avid, Final Cut Pro, Adobe Premiere, or Sony Vegas is used to extract and reassemble the video in the order you want it and then export the new file, often compressed to a smaller size than the raw data so that it is easy to use on the Web. How long it will take depends on the degree of editing, the type of compression, the speed of the machine, and the software being used. If you have learned to edit in the camera—shooting your shots in the basic order and length in which they will be used in the final story—such editing can be fairly simple. Experienced videographers, with that innate sense of story flow, can produce video that needs little editing and can be moved online more quickly in its raw form (although it still has to be compressed and encoded for Web delivery).

One complaint in the digital community is that the Web has no video standard. Windows Media Player, Adobe Flash Player, or QuickTime are the most common formats. Flash is the most common because it allows streaming, where software reads an incoming digital stream of information but does not store it on your computer. The Flash player is compatible across operating systems and is largely ubiquitous as a plug-in to today's Web browsers. Converting video to play on an iPod or similar portable player takes yet another codec, however.

After the video has been processed, it depends on server access and station policies on who actually uploads the video. At some stations, the reporter will post the material; other stations will put this task in the hands of the editor, the assignment desk, or the online department.

Box 6.2 Procedure for Processing and Editing a Video Clip

Step 1: Set up the project using standard video editing software.

Step 2: Import the video footage.

- A. If the material is on disc, from inside the editing application, select File > Import. Find the file and bring it in to the computer's hard drive.
- B. If the material is on tape or DVCam hard drive, you'll need to sync the camera to the software (as with Final Cut Pro or Adobe Premiere) or set up the project, manually start the camera, and record when you want. For more details, consult the appropriate manual.

Step 3: Watch the video clips or segments.

Step 4: Use drag-and-drop editing to drag individual segments to the timeline and create a sequence.

Step 5: Save the edited file using a name you can remember or associate with the content.

Step 6: Export the video in the appropriate format and with the necessary compression compatible with how it will be viewed (streaming, downloaded file from online, from a DVD, etc.)

Figure 6.4 ■ The revolution in portable audio and video has been led by Apple's iPad, which has created a number of opportunities for journalists to distribute news and other information. Millions of iPads have been sold since the product was introduced, and the podcasts and other content created for it can be played on almost any computer or portable media device.

WEB SITE MANAGEMENT

When to Update

News organizations are being pushed to provide the latest news and information 24 hours a day, seven days a week. This schedule presents problems in terms of allocating resources. Since it is not so important to have *all* the latest news *all* the time, news still operates with peak times and down times. However, the peak times can vary by medium. While TV gets its heaviest use at night when people are home, for instance, online use tends to peak during the day when people are at their offices and want quick hits of information (however, there is some peaking in traffic at night—as people download digital movies). The governing rule still is to allocate staff and resources as common sense and time allow.

Each station should provide guidelines on how often Web content is expected to be updated. Generally, the broadcast versions of stories still get greater priority than filing to the Web because on-air deadlines have no flexibility. National and international updates can be automatic (through wire service or network feeds).

Breaking news usually is immediately placed on the website. Any story important enough to break into programming should be posted to the website as soon as information is received, with updates as new information arrives. The problem is making the judgment regarding stories that are not urgent enough to break into programming but for which your audience would have enough interest to visit your Web page for an update. Again, common sense, combined with good news judgment, is the best barometer.

Box 6.3 Electronic Journalism and Ethics

Bias: Passion versus Protection

The way video can be edited to introduce bias or slant has always been a concern among electronic journalists. Examples abound on the Web. Whether it's "ethicsalarms" or "Foxnotnews," there are plenty of places to find critics who present examples of network news stories that have misreported or misrepresented an event through careful (or sloppy) editing.

In teaching electronic journalism, we've often spent just enough time on editing to get the buttons right. We focus more on good writing and accurate reporting. It is even more difficult to teach or come to a consensus on the aesthetics of video editing.

Editing video to reinforce a given political or social agenda has a long history. A rally we sympathize with will be shot tight to give the impression of a full house. A speaker with whom we disagree can be shot wide to imply no one is listening. The famous "Howard Dean scream" in January 2004 demonstrated the power of audio and video presented out-of-context. What was natural and normal in the moment was presented as scary and unstable; the result was that a presidential candidate's campaign quickly ended.

Even a well-meaning slant is still a slant, and the probable beginning of the slippery slope. Saving the whales may be a good thing, but we give away the moral high ground whenever we refuse to entertain the notion we could be wrong. The *Rashomon effect* warns us that perception is subjective. Observers of an event can produce surprisingly different accounts. Journalists in particular must strive for accuracy in order to minimize such an effect. Liberals dislike conservative views and vice-versa. Each admittedly gravitates toward news and information that confirms their position. But in so doing, we can inadvertently jump to a wrong conclusion. It happens in our everyday life—that's why we make bad stock picks or buy cars that are clunkers.

Therefore journalists have to know their bias and check against themselves. We are in the truth-telling business. This demands fact-checking and fact-verification even when it comes from our favorite reliable source. But fact-checking takes time. It slows us down. And we have an equally fierce competing imperative for speed. Deadlines race to us and we in turn race to them. But speed kills. Speed kills accuracy. Broadcast journalists know and love the excitement of the live report. They learn to love the adrenaline rush of being "*Live*!" But critics note that this energy and excitement comes at the cost of measured analysis and fact-checking. Going live is exciting and feels good. But you can say things that haven't been verified. You can get caught up in the moment and say something because it sounds good. Now with the Web, your video report can go global. So slow down. Check your facts. Unverified, unvetted, unprotected information can cost you. Check your facts BEFORE posting.

Special Sections

The previous section dealt primarily with local news. Sports, weather, and interactive sections of the website are handled a bit differently.

Weather

Every television station has a staff of "weathercasters." Increasingly, they are certified meteorologists also trained in professional on-air performance. They generate the weather maps and present updates through concise and often enthusiastic reports. Many stations present short weather updates throughout the day that can be recorded and uploaded onto the website. Especially when the weather turns bad, this type of news and information becomes a priority for the community and a boon to the website.

Because it is commonly accepted that "bad weather trumps everything," these reports must be updated on the Web quickly and often. During severe weather (a tornado or hurricane) or a disaster such as an earthquake, the website may need to be updated as often as new information arrives until the greatest danger passes. Stations are also finding that social networking sites are convenient for this kind of updating.[4]

Sports

Sports can be as important as any other category of news and information. Whether it involves professional, college, or high school sports, TV stations (and their websites) compete to be the primary provider for news and information about the local teams. This includes promotions, ticket giveaways, contests, player interviews, paraphernalia, live broadcast of games, exclusive player interviews, game analysis from coaches, and any and all other means of building hype in the community. Many stations have set up separate websites that focus solely on college or professional sports in their area, and some do the same thing for high school sports (see figure 6.5).

Sports departments must play two conflicting roles in order to survive. Most of the time, they are expected to be active, enthusiastic boosters of the home team. They are routinely criticized for lack of objectivity. But when the news is unpleasant (such as a scandal involving a star player or coach), the reporting must be fair and balanced, and fans will be just as outraged because of a perceived lack of support. Despite these conflicts, there is no disagreement that sports news and information are crucial to the station brand and must be actively cultivated.

Traditionally, broadcast coverage of local teams has been limited because of time constraints. Within a newscast, sports may take up only three to five minutes of the 30-minute program. But on the Web, the sports staff is only limited by its imagination and contractual agreements with teams. Getting people involved through the website also helps generate traffic (figure 6.5). The key to a good sports site is to remember the basics: report the scores, analyze the games, and let your audience know who the next opponent is.

Multiple Versions of the Same Story

Since the beginning of electronic journalism, the practice of creating multiple story versions has been common. Because of audience turnover and research findings that people tune out if they hear or see something they've already experienced earlier, newsrooms have worked hard to keep audience interest by providing multiple versions of news events. For example, a television reporter is typically required to provide a packaged report for the 5 o'clock show, a live report for the 6 o'clock show, and then a VO/SOT

[4] J. L. Reeves (May 24, 2011), "Newsroom, Community Use Facebook as Key Hub After Joplin tornado, *Mediashift*, http://www.pbs.org/mediashift/2011/05/newsroom-community-use-facebook-as-key-hub-after-joplin-tornado144.html.

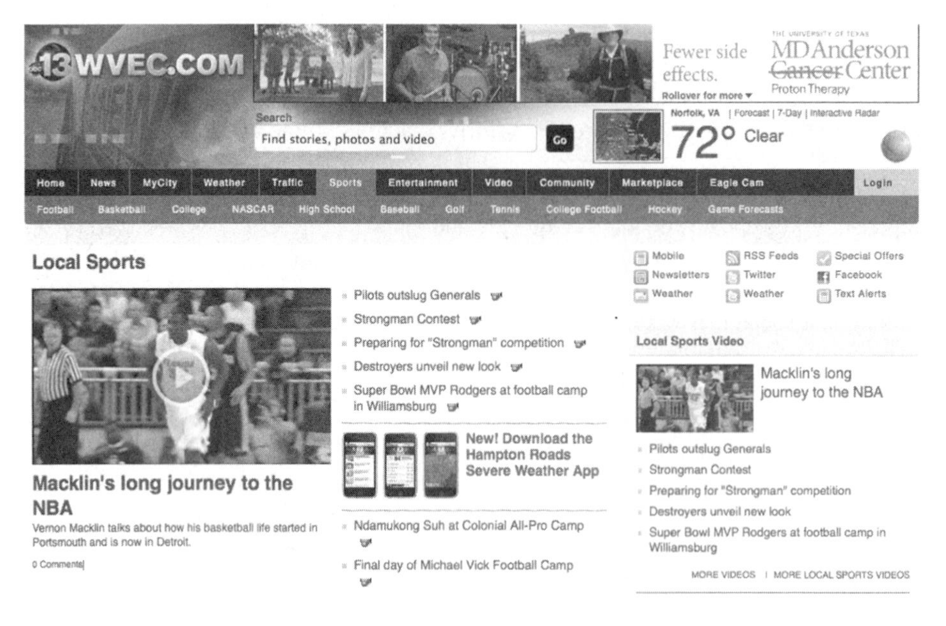

Figure 6.5 ■ Local sports pages frequently allow viewers to contribute content to a television station's website.

(voice-over/sound on tape) report for the 11 o'clock show. Depending on the newsroom and the news of the day, a reporter may have to cover more than one story—and provide multiple versions of each.

The way producers traditionally determined which version went where depended upon a host of factors, including when the event took place, whether it was a slow news day, the ability of the reporter to sell the story, whether something more important broke that afternoon, and what the competition was leading with ("exclusives" were given greater prominence than something everyone else was airing).

Because the Web provides a new degree of flexibility for storytelling, it actually raises some of the most basic and important questions of the craft.

Broadcasters have been constrained by time in that all video must be presented in sequence (beginning, middle, and then end). Viewers could not jump to the end and watch the report backward or even jump around to key segments within the report.

But the Web enables professional storytellers to finally give thought to what seems most obvious—they can decide the best way to tell a story. This includes all elements of story content and presentation. The amount of content that can be posted on the Web is not limited in terms of time or space as opposed to newscasts, which have to put everything the newsroom produces inside the 30-, 60-, or 90-minute box we call a "program" (including commercials, promos, teases, sports, and weather).

Broadcast reporters now face the same challenges faced by print reporters that were outlined in chapter 5—that the best way to tell a story may not be the usual way—either text-based or relying on video. It might be a database or matrix of video clips (e.g., see the website http://tenbyten.org); or it might be a graphic, like a map, that allows the user to mouse over various markers and pull up video clips or full reporter packages. Now that television has converted to digital transmission, the "television" as people now know it is more likely to transform into a digital appliance that blends TV with some of the functions now used on computers. Modern game-playing units already are doing that, and more and more TVs have digital networking inputs. The broadcast reporter who assumes the "newscast" will remain the primary way of delivering video and audio information does so at his or her peril. Some stations already allow Web users to pick and choose video segments to create their own newscast, and some news organizations use a Creative Commons license that allows freer sharing of the material (depending on the license, users may also be allowed to remix some of the material into their own creations). Some of those issues will be examined in the next chapter.

SUMMARY

This chapter provided an understanding of how broadcast script and video is repurposed for the Internet. The focus included step-by-step procedures for posting broadcast news scripts online as well as taking video content and placing it on a station's website. Some ongoing issues include content format and presentation; editing; providing multiple versions; and meeting audience expectations of having all possible points of view, analysis, and detail about a given news event. According to the annual survey of journalism and mass communication graduates, entry-level salaries in print and broadcast in 2009 and 2010 were around $25,000 per year.[5] At that level of compensation, you have to love what you do!

EXERCISES

1. Record the 6 o'clock news from a local station in your area. Choose a story where it appeared there was a spontaneous question-and-answer exchange between the anchor and a reporter. Compare the broadcast version with the print version that appears on the station website. Is the Web version a transcription of the broadcast version? In what ways are they alike and in what ways do they differ?
2. Take a look at the TV news websites of stations in your area. What types of broadcast material can you find repurposed for the Web? How is video presented and organized online? Is it separate or combined with text-only versions? Would you describe the menu of stories as being organized by story or event, by relative importance, by relative timeliness, or by some other criterion?
3. After getting the appropriate permissions and passwords from your instructor, digitize a ten- to twenty-second clip of video and post it to the Web. Be careful about naming protocols, and use the appropriate compression format for your school or organization.
4. Write and produce a broadcast (video-based) news package, around 1:15 to 1:30 in length. Then write a text-only version as complete and comprehensive as possible.

---

[5] L. B. Becker, T. Vlad, and P. Desnoes, "Job Market Goes from Bad to Worse," *AEJMC News* 44, no. 1 (November 2011): 1, 4–8; aejmc.com/home/2010/07/aejmc-news-issues.

Which do you think would be of greater interest to an online audience, and why? What could be done to make the text-only version more interesting?

5. Choose a story of interest and record an interview with an appropriate source. Then produce a broadcast news package and a VO/SOT (voice-over/sound on tape). Which version do you think an online audience would prefer: the package, the VO/SOT, or the unedited recorded interview? Why? Weigh the pros and cons of posting all three.

CHAPTER 7

FROM BROADCAST TO INTERNET: NEW TYPES OF CONTENT

The Internet not only represents an additional outlet for traditional content, such as real-time newscasts and updates, but also enables broadcast news operations to integrate new forms of content to reach audiences. In earlier chapters, we examined how convergence has changed the way we think about what stories are and how newsrooms (and journalists) should cover them. The same changes are also occurring in broadcast news operations, giving journalists exciting opportunities.

For example, suppose your station has arranged to cover a sporting event such as a high school football championship (this is always possible, no matter the market size). The broadcast will have an announcing team providing play-by-play and color commentary. Someone will provide statistics, background information, and updates of other games. Finally, a reporter and videographer are likely to be assigned to each team for interviews and features.

But with online, the website now provides real-time updates on the action and statistics throughout the game, which also may be streamed live, based on what the league or team allows. Recorded material, such as interviews with coaches, players, and parents, can be featured, and there should be links—lots of links—to other related online material and to what the fans are saying on social media.

Liveblogging invites reader comments at any time, adding to the conversational nature of the Web. A postgame podcast takes only a few minutes to record and upload, highlighting the good, the bad, and the ugliest parts of the game.

During the game or immediately afterward, interactive polls can be put up to start a conversation or keep it going: "Which team seems the most prepared? Which player was most valuable in the game?" Pictures of players, their families, the fans, and the coaches can be taken and uploaded quickly. These online photo galleries can be expanded with additional photos taken by others who attended the game.

Game blogs are standard today, and the possibilities for advertisers to sponsor any and all of these are endless. The most exciting part is that all of this is done without any great effect on the traditional broadcast. Those wanting that experience can enjoy the televised game in the living room, increasingly in high-definition on their 60-inch plasma screen with surround sound. But as figure 7.1 shows, the material online allows that viewer to dip into a richer experience along with (or before or after) the broadcast. In addition, it also opens your site to a whole new set of users, those on the go with mobile devices who often are among advertisers' most desired demographics.

OPPORTUNITIES FOR NEW CONTENT

A starting point is to clarify what we mean by new content. What is new today is likely to be old tomorrow, so it is important you stay up to date by reading blogs, industry newsletters, and other publications that track change. Broadcasters continue to experiment with the changing technology and seek ways to meet the audience demands for news. Survey results announced in 2010 from Hofstra University and the Radio Television Digital News Association provide a glimpse of the changes going on in broadcast journalism[1].

Television

First, it's good to know that journalism fundamentals work well. Show people and tell people what's happening. In 2010 almost all the stations surveyed (above 95 percent in most markets) reported they used the staples of still images, text, and video online. This is a useful benchmark for comparing the relative success of other online practices. Practices become universally adopted because they work and are the right thing to do. In terms of journalism, they are useful, efficient, profitable, and a benefit to society.

Likewise, if more people are doing something—or doing something more—it's also on the way to becoming a standard. TV stations are noticeably increasing their adoption online of livecams (such as traffic or weather cameras), posting audio clips, posting recorded newscasts, and hosting staff blogs. In 2010 roughly two-thirds of TV stations report they are doing all these things.

Meanwhile, some practices have leveled off or are decreasing: streaming audio (TV newscasts without the visuals), doing podcasts on TV websites, and letting viewers assemble their own news program from a menu of video segments. It may just be the wrong time or the wrong application, or the audience doesn't see the value yet of these practices.

---

[1] Bob Papper (2010), "TV and Radio News Staffing and Profitability Survey," RTDNA.org, Retrieved from http://www.rtdna.org/pages/media_items/2010-tv-and-radio-news-staffing-and-profitability-survey1943.php?id=1943.

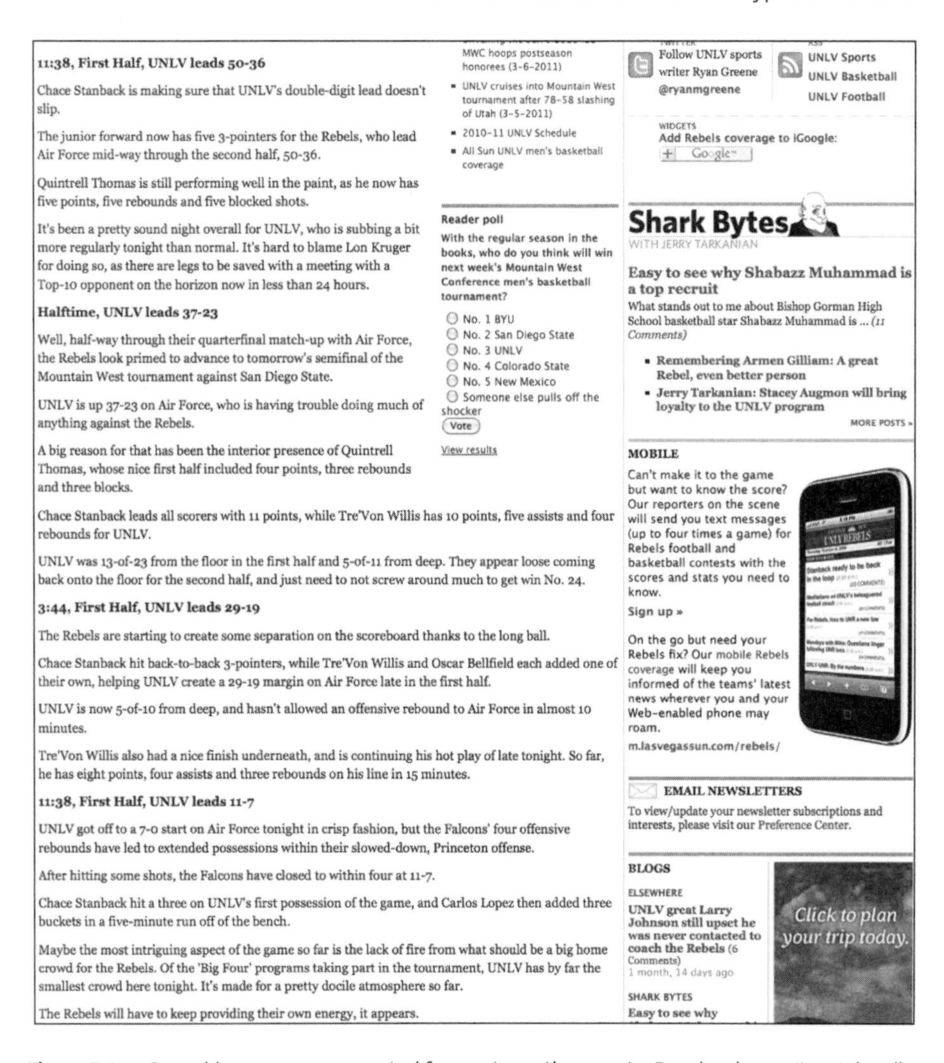

11:38, First Half, UNLV leads 50-36

Chace Stanback is making sure that UNLV's double-digit lead doesn't slip.

The junior forward now has five 3-pointers for the Rebels, who lead Air Force mid-way through the second half, 50-36.

Quintrell Thomas is still performing well in the paint, as he now has five points, five rebounds and five blocked shots.

It's been a pretty sound night overall for UNLV, who is subbing a bit more regularly tonight than normal. It's hard to blame Lon Kruger for doing so, as there are legs to be saved with a meeting with a Top-10 opponent on the horizon now in less than 24 hours.

Halftime, UNLV leads 37-23

Well, half-way through their quarterfinal match-up with Air Force, the Rebels look primed to advance to tomorrow's semifinal of the Mountain West tournament against San Diego State.

UNLV is up 37-23 on Air Force, who is having trouble doing much of anything against the Rebels.

A big reason for that has been the interior presence of Quintrell Thomas, whose nice first half included four points, three rebounds and three blocks.

Chace Stanback leads all scorers with 11 points, while Tre'Von Willis has 10 points, five assists and four rebounds for UNLV.

UNLV was 13-of-23 from the floor in the first half and 5-of-11 from deep. They appear loose coming back onto the floor for the second half, and just need to not screw around much to get win No. 24.

3:44, First Half, UNLV leads 29-19

The Rebels are starting to create some separation on the scoreboard thanks to the long ball.

Chace Stanback hit back-to-back 3-pointers, while Tre'Von Willis and Oscar Bellfield each added one of their own, helping UNLV create a 29-19 margin on Air Force late in the first half.

UNLV is now 5-of-10 from deep, and hasn't allowed an offensive rebound to Air Force in almost 10 minutes.

Tre'Von Willis also had a nice finish underneath, and is continuing his hot play of late tonight. So far, he has eight points, four assists and three rebounds on his line in 15 minutes.

11:38, First Half, UNLV leads 11-7

UNLV got off to a 7-0 start on Air Force tonight in crisp fashion, but the Falcons' four offensive rebounds have led to extended possessions within their slowed-down, Princeton offense.

After hitting some shots, the Falcons have closed to within four at 11-7.

Chace Stanback hit a three on UNLV's first possession of the game, and Carlos Lopez then added three buckets in a five-minute run off of the bench.

Maybe the most intriguing aspect of the game so far is the lack of fire from what should be a big home crowd for the Rebels. Of the 'Big Four' programs taking part in the tournament, UNLV has by far the smallest crowd here tonight. It's made for a pretty docile atmosphere so far.

The Rebels will have to keep providing their own energy, it appears.

MWC hoops postseason honorees (3-6-2011)

- UNLV cruises into Mountain West tournament after 78-58 slashing of Utah (3-5-2011)
- 2010-11 UNLV Schedule
- All Sun UNLV men's basketball coverage

Reader poll

With the regular season in the books, who do you think will win next week's Mountain West Conference men's basketball tournament?

- No. 1 BYU
- No. 2 San Diego State
- No. 3 UNLV
- No. 4 Colorado State
- No. 5 New Mexico
- Someone else pulls off the shocker

Vote

View results

Follow UNLV sports writer Ryan Greene @ryanmgreene

UNLV Sports
UNLV Basketball
UNLV Football

WIDGETS
Add Rebels coverage to iGoogle:
+ Google

Shark Bytes
WITH JERRY TARKANIAN

Easy to see why Shabazz Muhammad is a top recruit

What stands out to me about Bishop Gorman High School basketball star Shabazz Muhammad is ... (11 Comments)

- Remembering Armen Gilliam: A great Rebel, even better person
- Jerry Tarkanian: Stacey Augmon will bring loyalty to the UNLV program

MORE POSTS »

MOBILE

Can't make it to the game but want to know the score? Our reporters on the scene will send you text messages (up to four times a game) for Rebels football and basketball contests with the scores and stats you need to know.

Sign up »

On the go but need your Rebels fix? Our mobile Rebels coverage will keep you informed of the teams' latest news wherever you and your Web-enabled phone may roam.

m.lasvegassun.com/rebels/

EMAIL NEWSLETTERS

To view/update your newsletter subscriptions and interests, please visit our Preference Center.

BLOGS

ELSEWHERE

UNLV great Larry Johnson still upset he was never contacted to coach the Rebels (6 Comments)
1 month, 14 days ago

SHARK BYTES

Easy to see why

Figure 7.1 ■ Game blogs are now expected for most sporting events. People who can't watch or listen rely on the game blog for regular updates while they may be busy doing something else online.

As a case in point, broadcasters have spoken hopefully since the Web's beginning about allowing viewers to create or assemble their own newscasts online, a TV-centric view of "personalized news." The idea was that TV stations would put all the segments up and people could watch what they wanted, when they wanted, in the order they wanted. But while a number of stations tried this, the practice peaked at around 10 percent of those surveyed. By the end of 2009, fewer than 5 percent reported doing it because it was too resource-intensive or user interest was not there.[2]

[2] B. Papper (2010), "TV and radio on the Web," RTDNA, Retrieved from http://www.rtdna.org/pages/media_items/2010-rtdnahofstra-staffing-profability-survey--full-data1944.php.

Radio

Radio is also embracing the Web's promise. Traditionally, radio stations focused on sound-only content. Talk and radio news were all about writing and editing content to be heard, not seen. For generations, radio was called the "theater of the mind" because it relied so heavily upon the spoken word. In a converged world, radio broadcasters have to compete with online radio, online music services, satellite radio, and all other media that compete for people's attention and advertising dollars.

As radio adapts to convergence, stations are also exploring what online content works for them. Not surprisingly, radio stations are relying on core content—all things audio—to put on their websites. Recorded and streaming audio and blogs are all becoming increasingly common on their Web pages. Podcasting is relatively common in large markets (53 percent reported doing podcasts) compared with smaller markets (less than 25 percent). Only 10 percent of all TV stations reported doing podcasts.

One of the better predictors of radio website development is staff size. Radio stations with three or more people working in news were able to create a noticeably more complex Web environment with video and livecams, especially in larger markets. Around 10 percent of radio stations overall were posting video online by 2010, with livecams less common. But the Web's blurring of the lines between legacy platforms is important. That radio online can become more like television opens up opportunities for content and revenue that never existed before the Internet.

Therefore, we see the rate of change in society and in media technologies makes it difficult to anticipate every new technology or application. It may perhaps be more useful to consider broad categories of what might be considered "new" and where change might come from. Such a framework enables us to consider broad changes and find specific technologies and applications that fit into them. There are at least four areas from where we might expect new material—new content—to emerge:

- The news events themselves.
- The reporter's or individual's opinion about an issue or topic.
- Promoting either the organization's "brand" or the people working there.
- Public involvement in the newsgathering and editing process, often termed *user-generated content* or *UGC*.

THE NEWS EVENTS

The first category of new content forces us to consider how we attend, gather, and record news events as they happen for electronic media, such as radio and broadcast TV, or their cousin, the 24-hour cable news channel. As mentioned in chapter 2, some of it depends on whether the event is scheduled or unplanned.

How we discover or are informed about breaking news can include news releases from a government or organization (these days usually by email, Twitter, or text message), police or other emergency calls on a scanner, a tip from a source, or notification from an ordinary person witnessing an event. While those witness tips used to come mostly by phone, now they can come via a tweet, a post on social media, a clip on a video-sharing service, or a photo on a photo-sharing service.

Example: Coach Kaye Goes Away. The extremely popular and successful basketball coach at your local university, Coach Kaye, announces he's moving to another school across the state. It's huge news. The important points for today's broadcast journalist are (a) how did *you* hear about it, (b) how fast is the story moving, (c) who and what are your sources, and (d) what are your resources.

A. How did *you* hear about it? Most of the time journalists are notified through standard channels (phone, email, Twitter, or text messages). As mentioned in earlier chapters, you should have enough advance notice to be part of the pack who will attend the pending media circus. But also consider whether you were either the first or last to know. If the coach called you personally before it was announced, congratulations. If a university PR person let you know, at least you're on the call list. If you were the last to know—maybe you found out by a tweet from a fan who heard it elsewhere—or missed the announcement entirely, that says something too. As mentioned in chapter 2, you're only as good as your sources. Tweets are good for tips. Having a coaching staff member notify you on your cellphone "Coach has major announcement @ 3 conference room" is good.

B. How fast is the story moving? Having been tipped, you need to think how you're going to break the story. Without specifics, you can't just go live and say he's suspected to be leaving. In broadcast journalism, you'll need to work with your team. Make phone calls and coordinate. Someone can prepare to break in live as soon as you get that confirmation or begin writing something for the Web. Someone else needs to find photos or file video of the coach. If you're the reporter and it's 2:45P.M., the news conference is 3 P.M., and you're across town, you have to be resourceful. You could just grab your gear, jump in your car, and be only a few minutes late. But better to stop, think, plan. You might first send a brief text to either the coach or a spokesperson asking (a) to confirm what the announcement will be or (b) if you can arrange an exclusive interview as soon as possible after the announcement. Depending on the answer, you will have to decide what you will post or tweet for your audience. And be careful about your wording!

C. Who and what are your sources? You need to get video and sound-on-tape. If you can't speak directly to the coach (who is now very busy), trusted assistants, staff, or family or friends must be sought. Think about who you need to get information from. Use the telephone first, even if it's just to call your friend at a competing newsroom to confirm what everyone's doing and where everyone is going. Get connected. And in a pinch, don't forget to ask if you can use the audio or video of the announcement from the competition (with credit to them). Or check to see whether the school is recording the news conference and will make a copy for you or whether it is streaming the announcement live. In that case, someone at the station might use screen capture software (many programs also record video) to record it. If the school won't provide a copy or is not streaming it, urge the PR folks to put a copy on YouTube quickly. You can use services such as Keep Vid (http://keepvid.com) to grab the video in a way that you can download a copy.

D. What are your resources? Reporters now have a range of tools, but video and images are still central to broadcasting. We can scour social media sites for hints, tips, and reactions—and images. We can search the long tail of the Internet for archived information—and images. We can look through whatever archived rich media (audio and video) is in our library. Did we mention the need for images? Other possibilities include something like a Skype-to-Skype call (as also mentioned in chapter 5) that can allow you to capture an image of someone at the place where the coach is going. The goal as always is to reach primary rather than secondary sources, have something for others to see or hear, and keep the conversation going. And for goodness' sake, make sure you have a picture!

The key point is that, as described throughout this textbook, all journalism—print, online, and broadcast—is a conversation in our networked world. Journalists rely heavily on information that can take many forms. Information can be dated or just released; it can be official or unofficial and must be treated differently according to privacy and other related laws. If visual, it may have images that are still or moving (photo or video) or be in a form that is relatively permanent or difficult to manipulate or edit (paper or PDF). Not all of these are new, but they all must be considered in a converged environment where each can be used across platforms. In this context, creating new content means collecting, sifting through the old, and coming up with new and interesting ways to keep the dialogue moving forward.

Mobile Posting: Moblogs

Mobile Web logs, or *moblogs,* allow almost instantaneous event coverage, combining text and images. Moblogs allow you to build a story in real time in the form of a blog and include images captured from your cellphone or other camera-equipped portable device. The steps are simple: (1) take a photo, (2) post the image, (3) write the caption, and (4) fill in the proper hyperlinks. There are many promises in the technique, which can be thought of as creating a larger mosaic of an event through many smaller image tiles—from dozens of intimate moments captured digitally comes a greater understanding.

Several free or low-cost sites (Camblog, Ourmedia, Posterous, Tumblr) allow you to easily set up a moblog (sometimes called "livestreaming") and integrate it into your main Web site. A site called "Cover It Live" lets you do something similar, but you can more easily integrate user comments and embed the window that shows the running discussion into your website.

One of the early examples of a moblog for news coverage was the 2004 Wireless Election Connection, which used college students from around the country to cover political conventions and elections. More recent election moblogs can be found at moblog.net.

Critics say you can miss the meaning because you're so busy chronicling the moment that the captured content can be trivial and uninteresting. Moblogging seems best suited for reporting on something that happens in real time, can be captured as it happens, and is an event where video is not practical or allowed. Conceptually, it may be something breaking someplace with limited access to online capacity, or something where there is no means for editing video so only still images are practical. It lends itself well as a fallback means of catching something unexpected as it happens or of getting the first words and pictures out until video crews can get there. This kind of reporting can come from journalists as well as the community.

To successfully moblog, you must be skilled at using a camera phone or similar camera-equipped wireless device, at creating short captions using texting, and at sending both those and the photos back to the news center. If a true mosaic is to be created, more than one person should be covering the event from different angles and locations. At the news center, at least one person will have to monitor the incoming flow to create coherence in the mosaic and to augment the information with relevant links or other information. Thought will have to be given ahead of time to standard formats, but there also must be willingness to modify those as circumstances dictate. (During the Wireless Election Connection, for instance, every time a convention delegate was interviewed, two links were added to the caption—one to the person's hometown website and one to a MapQuest map showing where the town was located.)

One person (the storybuilder during the Wireless Election Connection) can handle this task, but the person must be a fast editor and skilled in tracking down online information. It is easy for the material to get backed up. Wireless Election Connection storybuilders were backed up by "news resourcers"—skilled journalists who researched additional links and other relevant online material. There also was a newsflow editor who operated the same as an executive producer in a broadcast newsroom and oversaw the process.

If you have only one or two persons available, what does this mean for the moblog, for the division of labor, and for quality? In fact, these are questions news managers must address when it comes to creating much of the richer, multifaceted content for online.

We are closing in on a time when wideband wireless will let us regularly send video in real time to bloggers or storybuilders. The next generation of converged journalists might use videophones to send wireless feeds directly to the news center. One version could be "live and uncut," while the other would be processed and edited by the storybuilder. The packaged account will offer added value because it will be edited, and sound bites and detailed text information will give users the context for the event and its meaning. It is important to anticipate these changes and equip ourselves for tomorrow's jobs.

Extended Audio or Video Interviews

A second area of new content is the greatly expanded news hole online. The Web allows you to provide raw, unedited, or partially edited interviews with newsmakers. In deciding whether to post, how much, and in what form, the journalist must consider (1) audio-only versus video and audio; (2) unedited, edited, or partially edited; (3) news value (timeliness, prominence of interviewee, conflict, etc.); and (4) time and resources needed to package and post the information.

There is no easy formula for making these decisions. As mentioned earlier, both radio and television news operations have experimented with different forms of content with varying success. The ultimate test will be seeing how many times the segment is accessed once it is posted. If no one clicks on your carefully crafted 20-minute interview with a student leader complaining about a school policy, you've not spent your time wisely. In fact, you have instead essentially performed public relations work because he or she now has a 20-minute video news release promoting the protest of a school policy. Perhaps you could at least get paid for that?

Video files are much larger compared to audio files (see box 6.1 for relative file sizes) and are more complicated to package and post online. But the historical success of television news suggests that people prefer to both see and hear newsmakers. Unedited video gives a feeling of spontaneity but the content must be compelling. Talking heads are only good for 30 seconds or so unless it's a major news event like a presidential speech. To keep viewer interest you may need to consider editing, but editing takes precious time. Current approaches to Web posting do not favor investing more than a few simple, quick cuts at best. This practice may change as Web video use and expectations increase.

In the example of the just-announced departure of the popular basketball coach, unedited video of the announcement should go online right away. Just give it a headline and provide as much text as possible. Then provide the added value by hyperlinking to other sources (covered in chapter 4) or perhaps providing images of relevant scanned documents.

Basic Rules for Posting Unedited Online Audio or Video:

a. Make sure you have the legal right and that nothing could get you into legal trouble. That's why it's important for you (or your partner) to record the event rather than getting it from someone else or simply downloading from the Internet.

b. Decide the length and content. For audio, critically listen first and judge the content. What do you want your listeners to *hear*? Be specific and critically decide the beginning and end. *Do not* cut or sweeten anything in the middle unless you have time and it doesn't editorially change the clip. The main point is, don't make people sit through a three-minute clip just to hear the exciting minute at the end. Give them just the part that commands your attention.

c. Do the same for video. What do you want viewers to *see*? Decide on the most appropriate beginning and end points. Try not to editorialize by eliminating one side. But don't waste the viewers' time; give them only what's necessary.

d. Listen and look for recorded quality. There is a threshold where content becomes unusable. With audio, if there's noise, a hiss, or pops and crackles, or if the speaker mumbles, you need to judge harshly whether to even post it. Software can lessen and even fix some of the problems (if you know how), but if they can't be adequately fixed, don't post it. Better just to paraphrase and do better next time.

e. For video, if people are the wrong color, if it's too dark or too light, if it's too shaky or out of focus, judge whether to go with just the audio. Bad video can be too distracting.

f. Clearly label and provide enough text information for the listener to know what to listen for and better understand what the story is about.

Box 7.1 Plagiarism, Permission, and Fair Use

With the Web, getting permission to use the words or ideas of others isn't just a good idea. It's the law. Violating this is done at your own risk. As journalists and creators of original content, we are constantly being given things that others say, do, design, publish, aver, insist, believe, and take credit for. In the oldest days of journalism we could simply quote the source and be done with it. But with electronic means of creating exact records of what was said and done, the idea of permission and reproduction has become much more sensitive.

Plagiarism is taking another's work and publishing it as your own. How much or how little is allowed is continually argued and debated. Published research by Norman Lewis (2008) in *Journalism & Mass Communication Quarterly* examined 10 years of plagiarism cases and found that journalists blame such lapses on overwork, depression, and problematic techniques such as "blending" press release information with reporters' notes without attribution.

In addition, there are also problems in the legal and working definition of plagiarism. Some feel it is okay as long as there is no malice; others think it's okay if you're just "fixing quotes." Still others wonder if it is just a matter of counting words (so, for example, copying 20 is okay, but copying 30 is plagiarism). If you're artful in your paraphrasing, can you get around being accused of being a plagiarist?

For better or for worse, all of these can and will be fireable offenses. Most newsrooms have a zero-tolerance approach. And just in case you didn't know, yes, you can be fired for plagiarizing yourself. Any column, story, or article that was previously published with your name on it cannot simply be resubmitted or even lightly edited and submitted as "new."

Thanks to the Internet, others also have ways of checking up on you and what you publish. For example, bloggers and other online outlets have been sued by companies specializing in pursuing copyright infringement on behalf of the owners. As in movie rights, the Internet is an easy place to mine for unauthorized use of copyrighted material. The limits of how far companies can pursue you is still under debate and will undoubtedly continue for years to come.

N. Lewis (2008). Plagiarism Antecedents and Situational Influences, Journalism and Mass Communication Quarterly, 85(2), 353–370.

Quality vs. Content vs. "Local"

There was a time when broadcasters would only run video that was shot at the highest resolution. But digital cameras and the diffusion of sufficient-quality video formats (MP4 on Android phones, for example) have resulted in an explosion in what broadcasters now consider to be acceptable for air.

Whether it's consumer-grade shaky grainy video of a tsunami or an on-campus shooting, the key has always been the compelling content. The Zapruder film of the Kennedy assassination was famously shown repeatedly because viewers demanded to watch it repeatedly.

A networked world also means we have to change our definition of "local." Many news organizations already know much of their Web traffic comes from outside the market. "Home is where the heart is," and for many of us, we develop connections with at least a few cities and towns over the years. Even though we don't live there anymore, we are separated only by geography.

In the case of Coach Kaye, wherever he is going, you should begin to connect with people there. Best will be the ones from your locale who will be excited to know he's coming to "their town." Maybe you already know someone, but you can also put up an invitation on your website and your news organization's social media pages for anyone in the new city to comment, express thoughts, or volunteer information on this event.

You also now have a golden opportunity to create synergy with news organizations in that area. They will want to know all about the coach. As soon as possible, make connections via telephone or email to share information and materials. You have everything to gain and nothing to lose.

OPINION, ANALYSIS ABOUT AN ISSUE OR TOPIC

New content reflecting staff opinion or analysis is also being experimented with online. The rise of talk radio and cable news network programs has helped blur the lines between news analysis and punditry. It may be difficult for some to tell the journalistic difference between Bill O'Reilly, Anderson Cooper, Rachel Maddow, or Wolf Blitzer. Regardless whether this reflects audience acceptance or expectation, it is increasingly common for broadcast journalists to find venues for expressing opinions on various matters.

But every famous name had to begin somewhere and you also have to consider how to enhance your personal brand as a converged journalist and media personality. While this is covered in greater depth in chapter 15, it bears noting here because one of the freedoms you gain as a media personality is being able to share your own thoughts and ideas on a number of topics. But as always, be reasonable and know your limits. Editorializing can be done appropriately to push issues forward. Editorializing can also turn around and bite you, making you or your newsroom an object of derision or even protest. Pick your battles, be smart, and ask for input from others before you post an online rant.

Blogs

Blogs were one of the first forms of online publication that created the shift into convergence. Instapundit, BoingBoing, Gawker, kuro5hin, and Engadget remain some of the better-known blog sites. Numerous political blogs began making a mark for the form during the 2004 elections, when a debate raged about whether bloggers were truly journalists (especially after the Democratic Convention issued credentials giving bloggers access to cover the proceedings). Today, blogs are mainstream and serve a variety of functions for broadcast journalists to connect with people.

Blogs are more common in television. In 2010 around 70 percent of TV stations reported they had staff blogs. But in radio, again reflecting staffing issues, only around 20 percent of radio stations report having blogs. A related cousin is the Facebook page, and many news organizations have made updating that a routine part of the job as well.

While it's still tempting to think of broadcast journalism as primarily visual- and performance-oriented, written communication will always be an integral part. The sheer act of writing regular blog entries will make you a better writer. You will continually improve whether you craft 100-word daily posts or 500 to 1,000 words once or twice a week. Regular writing trains you to be quick at putting words together and to be able to tackle and explain complex issues. You also learn how to locate and acknowledge the value of diverse outside sources, including those that do not agree with you. This process hones critical thinking and sharpens your analytical abilities. Over time, you can build a track record of creating content and putting forth ideas in your own words. Pioneer bloggers including Dan Gillmor (box 7.2) have been able to shape the discussion on a number of important social issues.

Blogging is so widespread and fulfills so many roles it is best to consider the practice both conceptually and practically (see chapters 4 and 11). In relation to new content, the blog ethos, when it comes to news or issues blogs (as opposed to personal diaries), generally encompasses three things: regular posting, copious linking to outside sources, and substantive ideas that encourage others to link to your postings and, as a result, refer other readers to them. Regular posting does not necessarily mean daily, but it usually means at least once per week (although your news organization, if you are blogging for one, may specify generally how often you should post).

After that, arrange for a set time each day or week to write, depending on your time and commitment. Some entries are no more than a few dozen words with numerous links to other sources; you are trying to point out other interesting things online and provide some context. Other times, an entry may run several hundred words to get your point across. If it's too long, you're likely to bore readers, so be tenacious and merciless in your self-editing.

Finally, put some thought into how you are going to respond to reader comments. As said before, with all criticism, pick your battles and think long and hard before you respond. Because your blog or Facebook account is linked to the news organization,

Box 7.2 Blogging Pioneer Dan Gillmor

Dan Gillmor is one of the most prominent journalists to make the transition from traditional journalist to blogger. After more than 20 years as a journalist, Gillmor was one of the first to realize the potential of blogging. He was a columnist for the *San Jose Mercury News* during the explosive growth of the Internet in the late 1990s, and his work in technology led him to become one of the first journalists to add a blog to his repertoire. Gillmor's blog explored journalism and the world of technology, and his insight and reporting resulted in his becoming one of the most widely read journalists in the blogosphere. In 2004 Gillmor left the *Mercury News* to become director of the Center for Citizen Media at the University of California–Berkeley. Currently he is the founding director of the Knight Center for Digital Media Entrepreneurship at Arizona State University's Walter Cronkite School of Journalism and Mass Communication. He continues to write, speak, and blog about journalism, technology, and other topics.

you are in the best position to shape the dialogue. You can always turn negative comments aside by responding instead to what aspect of an issue can be most beneficial to the community.

Podcasts

Podcasting, being audio-oriented, continues to look increasingly like the domain of radio broadcasters. As mentioned earlier, podcasting on TV websites has leveled off to around 10 percent. But in the larger market for radio around half the stations routinely produce and post podcasts, extending their brand and that of their personalities.

Podcasts are audio feeds distributed through the Web via RSS and made popular by Apple's iPod. For examples, go to sites such as http://www.podcast.net/. One is the regularly produced online newscast that is highly polished and has high production elements. A second is kind of an audio equivalent to the blog. Yet another is like the sit-down public affairs conversations on Sunday-morning radio and TV.

Basic Podcast. Creating the most basic kind of podcast can be remarkably simple. Such an audioblog should be short, sweet, and to the point. You should initially decide whether you want to try to "capture life's moments" unscripted or have something to read aloud. Lighthearted observations may work well off-the-cuff, but for more serious content, you will almost certainly need a script.

Factor in things like recording location. Indoors you have more control over ambient noise, but outdoors will have a warm feel to it. Will you sit or stand (or walk)? Sitting allows you to read but moving around will demand a card with notes on it. Finally, consider the means of recording what you want. Some sort of audio recorder should be handy and ready. There are numerous devices (iPod, MP3 player, DVcam, 4G cameraphone) now available at reasonable prices.

Make sure you make your point and support it with evidence. You should consider your oratory style, but generally we find that speakers are most effective when they are conversational yet succinct. In chapter 8 we note some styles and tips to keep your speaking delivery interesting (if not entertaining).

When using a script, practice by reading it out loud as if you are talking to someone. This rehearsal should identify tongue-twisters and awkward words (e.g., "thwarted" sounds odd to the ear, "foiled" or "stopped" sounds better). Rewrite the script to eliminate tricky passages, and underline words that should be emphasized. Also note where it is best to take a breath.

When you're ready to begin, simply click the "record" button in your software control and speak. Listen to your podcast for flow, pacing, tone, and overall sound. If you're happy with it, save it and send it out by RSS.

But also consider that, like radio, few people want to listen to more than a minute or two of someone just reading a script. Think about the production values you are capable of. Those might include music; sound effects; crazy, exaggerated pacing or enunciation; or, if you team up with another person, a sense of timing. Like all performance media, the most successful podcasts generally involve a bit of showmanship. Be careful with music; don't run afoul of copyright law. However, it is easy to search for "podcast-safe" or "Web-safe" music. Many artists, to promote themselves and their work, have put tracks online that anyone can use.

Weekly public affairs podcast. A more serious commitment to launching a podcast involves planning, thought, and all the things that go into good journalism. Many successful podcasters have found the lighter touch useful, but you don't have to be humorous if your content is compelling. A regular public affairs podcast, for instance, might not be humorous, but it might use music, natural sound, and other production elements to help illustrate what is being talked about. Since our focus is on the journalistically oriented podcast, we can recommend the following steps in planning and execution:

1. ***Have something to say.*** There should be a coherent beginning, middle, and end. Make each roughly the same length.
2. ***Decide how long it should be.*** You are not under the artificial constraints of broadcasting, but people generally don't want to listen for hours, either. Think in terms of the standard jog or the standard drive to work—from five to 15 minutes. Be honest about your material; don't try to stretch it.
3. ***Record your interviews as needed.*** If you are going to include other people's views, arrange and get permission to do so. Remember to ask open-ended questions in the best journalistic tradition so the focus is on the person being interviewed and his or her answers. And *be conversational.* Podcasts generally have a more relaxed tone.
4. ***Gather your other production elements.*** If appropriate, music and natural sound can enhance your work. If you are narrating some parts, record those. Use your natural speaking voice with some inflexion and expression (but avoid false and exaggerated voicing). To record, just try to find a quiet place without a lot of hard surfaces (that echo). Keep the microphone about 12 inches from your mouth. Some people use headset microphones instead because they shut out almost all noise.
5. ***Assemble the podcast using your editing software.*** Basic audio recording software like Audacity (figure 7.2) is easily found online. After mixing your sound sources, save and export as an MP3 file to the site where your podcasts are stored, and, if necessary, create the feed file notifying those monitoring your site that a new podcast is available and can automatically be downloaded.
6. ***Plan a regular schedule.*** Like blogging, if you are not filing regularly, your audience will drift away.

If the newsmaker you are interviewing is an outstanding or famous personality, you're hardly going to need all the other production elements to keep people interested. The content alone may be sufficient. Or maybe you'll find you are a talented interviewer and your interplay with newsmakers will carry the day. There is no one formula to a great podcast. Just keep it interesting and at a length appropriate for the topic.

Podcasts can take a bit more technical skill, but they are worth it. The magic of creating and distributing podcasts can come from capturing interesting segments of your life or your reporting and the aural presentation of your thoughts, dreams, and insights about virtually anything. Putting together a podcast can be as fun as the early days of radio. You're limited only by your creativity and your time.

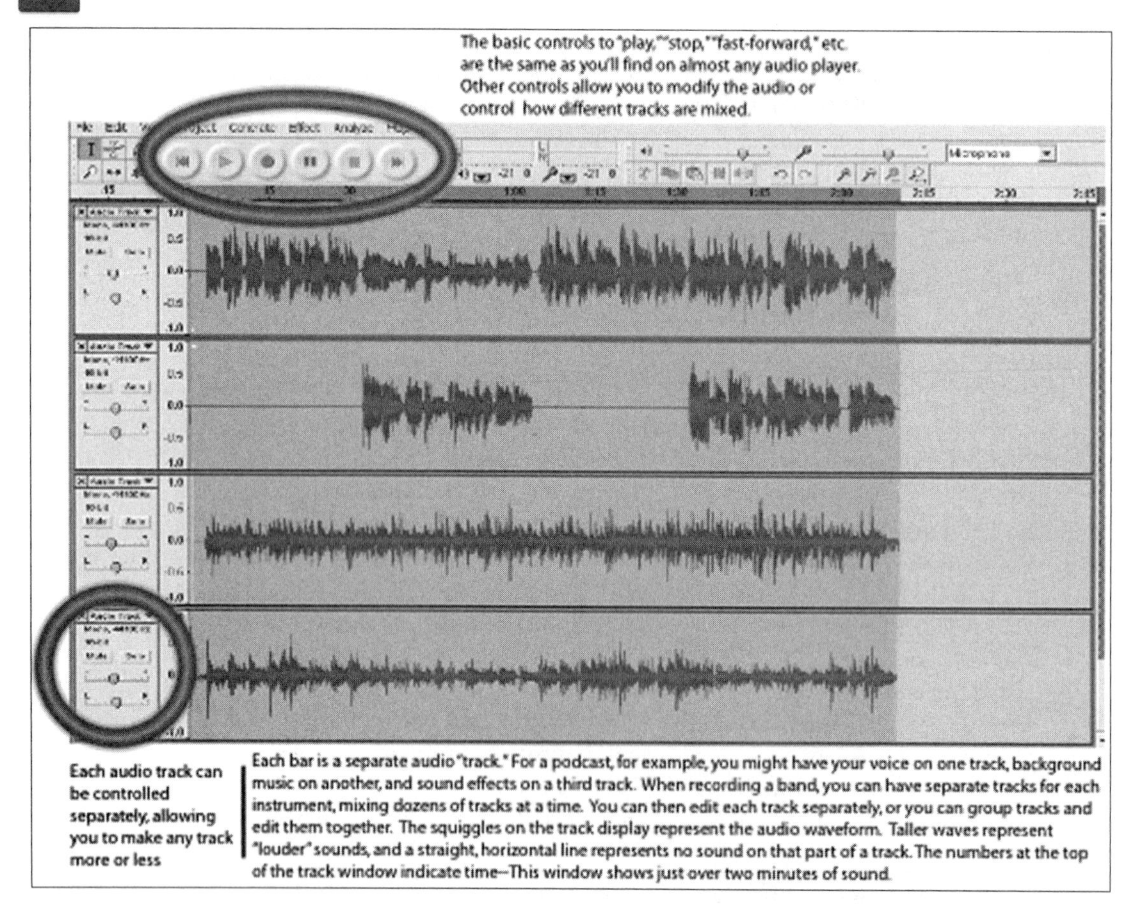

The basic controls to "play," "stop," "fast-forward," etc. are the same as you'll find on almost any audio player. Other controls allow you to modify the audio or control how different tracks are mixed.
Each audio track can be controlled separately, allowing you to make any track more or less
Each bar is a separate audio "track." For a podcast, for example, you might have your voice on one track, background music on another, and sound effects on a third track. When recording a band, you can have separate tracks for each instrument, mixing dozens of tracks at a time. You can then edit each track separately, or you can group tracks and edit them together. The squiggles on the track display represent the audio waveform. Taller waves represent "louder" sounds, and a straight, horizontal line represents no sound on that part of a track. The numbers at the top of the track window indicate time—This window shows just over two minutes of sound.

Figure 7.2 ■ Audacity is a simple audio editing program that allows you to easily edit and layer voices, music, and sound effects

CONTENT PROMOTING THE WORKER OR THE ORGANIZATION

News organizations in an age of convergence must promote themselves as well as their people. Audiences can get news and information from almost anywhere at any time. To rise above the noise and clutter of the media marketplace, news organizations have to work at staying atop people's "go to" list. But it's not enough just to do a great job providing news and information. You have to repeatedly announce it, and announce it in ways that enhance the reputation of the organization and the individuals who work there.

Related to all this, journalists must consider when and how to promote themselves (see chapter 15 for more on personal branding). The relative fame that broadcasters traditionally received from being on television has become magnified in a modern age of celebrity and branding. It can be the edge that helps us survive in a competitive and uncertain marketplace. Although few news workers like this side of the business, more are acknowledging the wall between news and promotion is down for good (read more about this in chapter 14). The course now is to understand and embrace the potential benefits while avoiding ethical or legal mistakes.

Promotions

News organizations must promote their content, which includes not only the news-related content they create but also the staff who gather and produce it. Television has embraced self-promotion over the years because TV audiences could be tracked and the "face" of a TV news program mattered.

The resulting "star system" in network and local news was rewarded with greater ratings, revenues, and loyalty. Even though television viewing is evolving, there is evidence that the benefit of celebrity and name recognition may actually be increasing in other sectors.

As the marketplace for news continues to change, broadcasters continue to experiment with ways to involve the audience in order to survive. In some markets, local TV stations may give up local news altogether or simply broadcast the top-rated news show from another station in the market. This type of uncertainty means all newsrooms have to maximize any strength they have. And the best resource in every newsroom is the people who work there.

Those who work in the newsroom are not only content gatherers and creators but also marketable brands that are part of the overall station brand. Promoting those personalities is in the best interest of both the organization and the individual.

In a society often jaded to hyperbole and insincerity, modern promotion techniques work best when they are sincere and honest. Understatement sells, so promotional materials must not appear as simply hype. Presenting "exclusive news you won't want to miss" will probably drive more people away because audiences are becoming increasingly sophisticated—and jaded—to such ploys. The essence of good public relations is accurately identifying the unique thing you're offering and providing it. If you say you've got exclusive video featuring a man biting a dog, then show it. At least the viewers who show up won't be disappointed.

Branding and the Journalist

You can do some things to help promote your organization, your content, and you. First is to understand brands. Viacom, Disney, Belo, Clear Channel, and others are all corporate brands. Stations also have their own organizational branding, such as "AM-850," "Newschannel 3," or "Eyewitness News."

Another type of branding is with labels such as "special reports," "live and late-breaking," "family-friendly," or "news you can use." All of these position an organization to be the leader in a particular type of news content.

You and the others who work on-air are commonly known as "talent," and talent is a promotable commodity. The more you can develop and promote interest in you and those with whom you appear on-air, the more you will extend the brand.

Due to staff limitations, broadcast journalists often started as general assignment reporters who then moved to an area of specialization. The result was that every broadcast newsroom had its own consumer reporter, science expert, education specialist, or the equivalent. This has not been a bad thing because it's how the community recognizes the news organization has experts on staff and also how the organization promotes itself to the community. So whether you do consumer features, investigate crimes, or special reports on science and health, over time you build a reputation for both you and your company.

News organizations are a part of the community, and another way to make yourself promotable is to be recognized in your particular area. The most common means is certification or community service. Developing expertise through coursework or volunteer activity can take time but it benefits everyone. For example, it is now common for weather journalists to have studied and gained certification in meteorology. For crime reporters, a night class in paralegal studies or criminal justice can get you contacts, story ideas, and, of course, expertise.

Finally, to become a journalist that is a promotable, recognized brand you can help to organize special events—community forums—where you can be a moderator or discussant. This enables you to be a part of the community conversation while avoiding accusations of personal favoritism or bias.

The power and effect of celebrity can make a difference between similar brands. As shown in figure 7.3, broadcast organizations continue to seek out people who can assume the role of local celebrity with grace and professionalism. There are countless stories of how a TV station was second or third in a market until a new hire seemed to capture the imagination, and the ratings, of the local audience.

In an age of media convergence, organizations actively seek people who can have this effect on viewers, and both are constantly seeking new and creative ways to capture audience attention.

There remains the question of "how much is too much" in terms of intrusion into the lives of the branded journalist. Some newsrooms have webcams inside the newsroom, and some are being placed in television studios and control rooms. We're waiting to see how long before news personalities experiment with webcams in their home. This will be yet another item for negotiation between the individual news worker and the parent organization, including rights and limitations.

INVOLVING THE PUBLIC AND USER-GENERATED CONTENT

Finally, new content comes from the vast array of group, network, and syndicated material of which all stations are a part. No news organization operates in isolation. All have ready access to special reports and ongoing features from any part of the state, the nation, and the world. This material helps cross-promote the broadcaster and its website as a one-stop provider of all the information needs for a given community. Whether it is the latest in health news, travel advisories, or sports, if the local community thinks you have what it wants, people will come to you when that need arises.

So many people have entered the conversation on community issues and events that news websites increasingly accommodate and solicit their contributions as in figure 7.4 below. As mentioned in chapter 3, newsrooms need someone to coordinate and oversee these contributions. The *user-generated content coordinator* helps keep the discussion online from getting out of hand or moving into inappropriate areas. Another position we discussed, the *digital rights manager*, is needed to make sure that content ownership issues are kept clear.

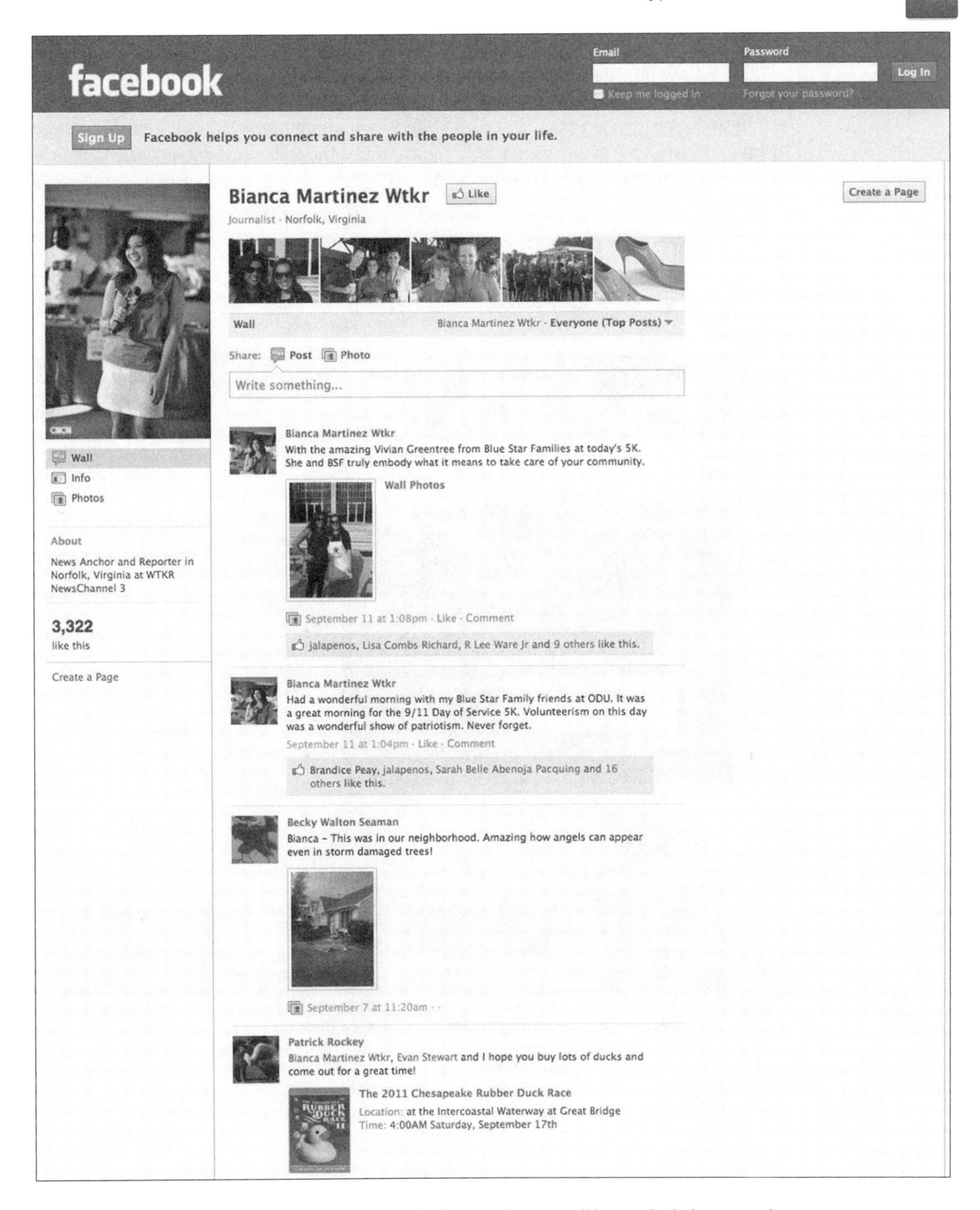

Figure 7.3 ■ Journalists can often be seen as public figures who are well-known in their community. By establishing their presence on the organization's Facebook page they personalize stories and help bring attention to important local issues.

Literally millions of people are now media content creators who perform so-called random acts of journalism. Increasing numbers of people have basic skills in digital photography and video. This increases the likelihood that spontaneous news events are caught and can then be posted for all. Many people can now say they have been an "iReporter" or "citizen journalist" or "community blogger" and have posted photos, video, commentary, or information to propel a news event forward in the collective mind of the community. This trend will continue, if not increase.

(A)

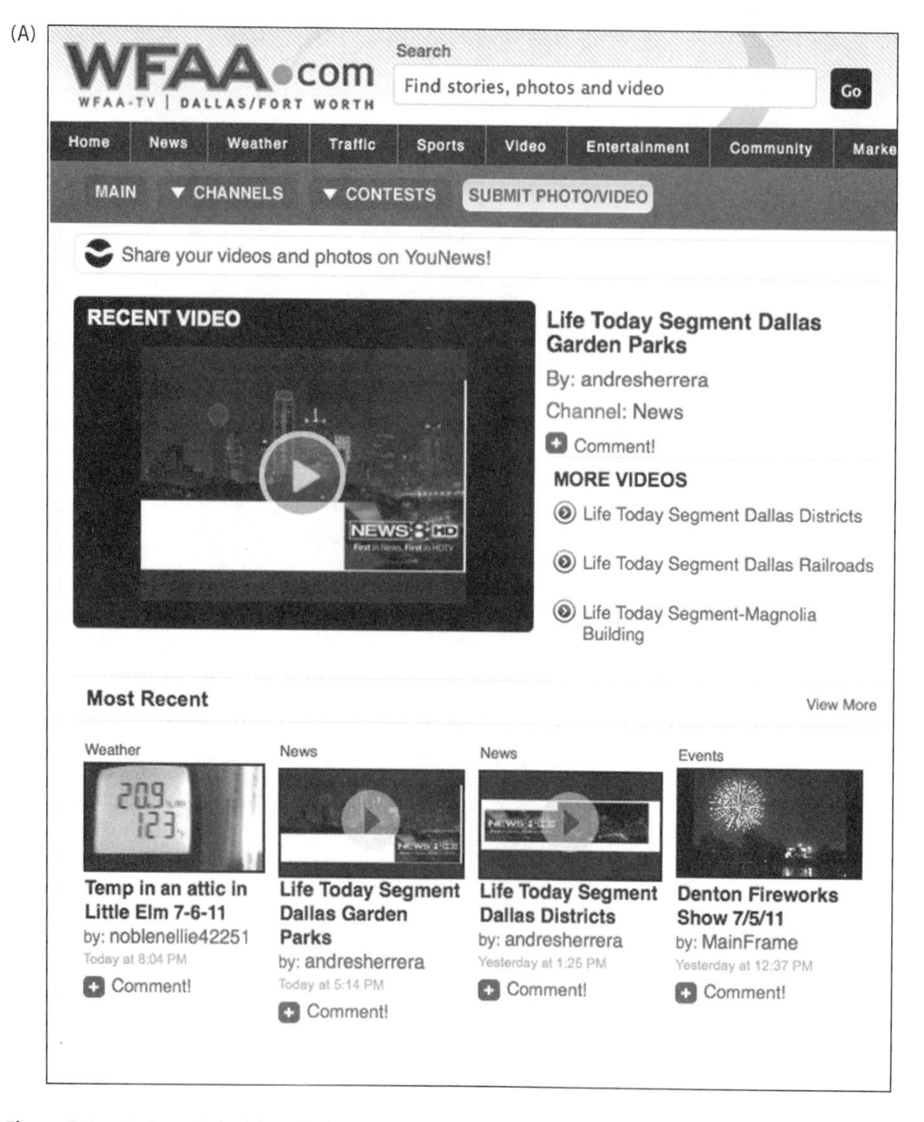

Figure 7.4 ■ A: Some television stations are using their websites to provide a range of information that goes well beyond what they offer on the air. In this example, WFAA-TV (Dallas, Texas) has added interactive pages that emphasize the theme of "Life Today." B: Television stations can increase viewer involvement on their websites by allowing users to contribute stories, pictures or video.

(B)

Figure 7.4 ■ *(continued)*

SUMMARY

This chapter provides examples of new types of online content that can easily be provided by broadcasters in some form or capacity. One category includes all content that relates directly to the news event. This content can include photographs and video as well as interviews with newsmakers. A second category is content that is more editorial in nature; this includes blogs, podcasts, and means by which a news worker can provide insight, opinion, critical commentary, and analysis of a news event or issue facing the community. The third category involves content that directly or indirectly promotes the organization or an individual. This includes promotional information that emphasizes the branding of the journalist as well as that which promotes celebrity and personality. The final area of new content is user-generated content. This material comes from the community and may take a variety of forms including website postings, photos, and video of a breaking news event. Newsrooms will need people to coordinate and appreciate all these ways that broadcast journalism is evolving. Students of convergent journalism must begin planning and considering the most appropriate ways to promote themselves and their organization.

EXERCISES

1. Plan and execute a moblog. Pick an event (e.g., a public meeting or even a campus organization), get needed permission, and work with one or two others to cover it in real time. Roles may switch or remain static throughout, but agree in advance. Afterward, assess and evaluate the final product.
2. Create your own two-minute podcast. Critically analyze and assess technical quality and content. What worked and what didn't? Usually, people hate the sound of their own voice—what are your thoughts? Watch diction, grammar, and breathing, and write conversationally.
3. Design a once-a-month plan for promoting yourself or those you work with. Think in terms of visual layout and design, script elements (copy), and scheduling that may attract favorable attention. How far in advance do you need to plan and pull the information together each month? Where will you actually post these promotional elements? Considering you may have no budget to work with, how much time will you allocate for this ongoing activity? Who should execute this service?
4. Go to any television news station's website or Facebook page. Take a look at the type of discussions and comments posted by the community on a particular issue. Are the journalists leading or following the dialogue? Why or why not?

CHAPTER 8

BASICS OF BROADCASTING

One of the good things to come out of convergence is the end of the artificial distinctions that journalists used to align themselves by medium. For generations, society was the loser as print and electronic journalists put each other down as either inferior or jealous. Today news and information washes over us 24/7, so no one has time to worry about whether it's inherently better or more interesting in either print or broadcast. The important thing is for news organizations to gather, verify, and present information in a way that enables the consumer to make decisions on how to live.

What has emerged is what Kovach and Rosenstiel call "sense-making journalism,"[1] and it is found at any time, in any medium. Thus, the basics of good television journalism are the same as for any type of journalism. This chapter briefly explores the similarities between television journalism and other types, then explores the differences. You'll learn how television newsrooms are organized, how broadcast writing differs from other types of writing, and how visuals and words flow together in a television news story.

WHAT'S THE SAME

In a converged media environment, all journalists need some common skill-sets because the basics of good journalism remain the same: accuracy, attention to detail, compelling information, solid attribution, and great writing. Together they make for good factual storytelling and are the foundation for the practices presented throughout this book.

[1] B. Kovach and T. Rosenstiel, *The Elements of Journalism: What Newspeople Should Know and the Public Should Expect* (New York: Three Rivers Press, 2001).

Accuracy

There is no substitute for accuracy in all elements of newsgathering. You still need to get the names, titles, dates, times, and actions correct; but increasingly we find the need for accuracy extends beyond these mechanical elements. The *perception of being biased or misinformed* can be just as damaging as committing the journalistic sin of not getting the basic facts correct.

In an age of "spin," these perceptions can result from the choice of a single word. Saying a source "claimed he was innocent" comes across as if the claim is not true. These subtleties of wording—whether "saying," "insisting," "blaming," "claiming," "arguing," or "agreeing"—are an important factor in shaping reader perceptions of a story.

Attention to Detail

Strong writing uses details for their full effect. For instance, after talking generally about a "fund-raising concert," you might mention a telling detail, like "white plastic buckets filled with quarters and dollar bills lined the front of the stage." As you will learn in the next chapter, having those details in your notebook will be extra important if you have to write primarily text-based stories for online or print. You must use words to make people "see" and experience the story. Just because you have a camera to capture the scene, don't let that dull your senses. Remember to write down what you smell, feel, and hear as well as what you see because the camera and microphone can't capture everything.

Compelling Information

Careful presentation of information creates meaning for viewers and helps move them toward some universal human truth. It's the difference between regurgitating a series of facts and painting a vivid picture in the mind of the reader that can result in tears, laughter, and even a resolve to change.

This can be called the "why" behind a story or event that journalists strive to answer. In an age when "facts" fly around the Internet at lightning speed, usually available for free, journalists are finding that digging behind the facts to get that compelling information is where their viewers and readers find value. One of the things about social media, for instance, is that even when people find out initially about something through those channels, they go to more established media for confirmation, explanation, and analysis.

Appropriate and Solid Attribution

Electronic journalists have the benefit of video that captures and presents quotes as they are spoken. Still, the Internet has also increased the necessity for solid attribution. Careful attribution may be the biggest factor differentiating the amateur blogger from the professional journalist. In a world where credibility increasingly has to be earned and is not conferred just by institutional status, attribution helps transparency, which can be important in gaining trust.

A related practice is searching out and contacting the appropriate sources for a story. Good reporting is talking to those with firsthand knowledge or who can provide some important insights into a given story or event.

Great Writing

Short, compelling sentences with proper word order remain the cornerstone of good journalism. You should know how to avoid dangling participles and other misplaced modifiers, how to make verb tenses and moods consistent, and how to avoid using imprecise or wrong wording (e.g., "expired" rather than "died," or saying "less people" when you mean "fewer people"). You should know correct idiom (e.g., someone is "prohibited from" but "forbidden to") and proper punctuation, although broadcast writing does use some nonstandard punctuation conventions to aid in speaking the copy aloud (covered later in this chapter).

The essentials of reporting and writing have not changed regardless of whether you work for a newspaper, radio or television station, cable news channel, or online news site or you simply participate in acts of journalism because you care. All of us must embrace the practices that stem from these principles that are even more important in a time of converged media.

Box 8.1 Ethics: Codes of Ethics and Humor

Both SPJ and RTDNA codes of ethics focus on the basics. They both agree that journalists must accurately tell the truth as well as be independent, fair, accountable, and minimize harm whenever possible. One of the slippery slopes is where these journalistic values collide with humor. Journalists and the audience actually have an awkward and uncertain view of humor. Basically we like it unless it crosses an invisible line.

In an age of comedy news, journalists are also offering mixed messages. For years news anchors have been rewarded for being lighthearted, witty, and able to engage in light banter. This informal style of presenting the news is being adopted across the globe because people like it. There is rarely a problem because in the scripted, controlled world of the television studio, it's pretty obvious when we have to be serious and a story touches on a sensitive topic.

But reporters in the field have fewer guidelines and the cues are not so clear. So we teach the default approach, which is to be serious and professional when dealing with the public. But in actual practice, we discover that during the course of human interactions there is a lot of give and take. City council meetings can go on for hours. Public officials start joking around. Even at crime scenes police and firefighters engage in "gallows humor" (the phenomenon of joking about a serious subject as a means of strengthening morale). While it may be okay to laugh, we have to resist the urge to participate or lead in the joke-telling. We may even be told to lighten up, but the problem comes when the line is crossed. Once a journalist becomes a clown it's hard to cross back. Not impossible, but hard. And you may not even know you've crossed the line because no one will tell you until it's too late (if people complain about you later, you can be reprimanded or even fired for unprofessional and inappropriate behavior).

It is important to remember that lighthearted events can suddenly turn serious, and reporters must also quickly change to the appropriate mood while continuing to engage in information gathering, getting the facts right, and trying to convey the truth of an event. The need for personality and "high-EQ" has increased in the Facebook-Twitter-Google+ age, because afterward we chat, blog, or tweet to keep the dialogue moving forward. And keep that appropriate mood and level of intellectual discourse. If you slip up and make a bad joke at the wrong time, the results could be disastrous. Over time we all get better at finding the right balance, but none of us are impervious to bad humor.

WHAT'S DIFFERENT

Having looked at what's common, we now look at three principles where television news is unique in how it does journalism with a capital "J"—gathering, verifying, and presenting information in a way that best equips the public to make decisions.

Stress the Visual

Television is a visual medium, and regardless of what the reporter wants to emphasize, the pictures generally dominate. Viewers expect exciting and interesting images, and entire textbooks have been devoted to explaining the aesthetics of video images. The best stories weave sight and sound into a unified whole.

The reporter or narrator is like a guide who takes the viewer into an event and provides a series of images and interview comments that let the viewer make sense of developments and somehow become a better person for the experience. But be careful about what grabs attention. The story might be an important one about safety or traffic concerns during spring break, but too much video of bikini-clad students on the beach can visually drown out those potentially lifesaving details.

Stress the Moment

It's no accident that the slogan for some broadcast newsrooms is "live and late-breaking." The strength of broadcast news has always been timeliness—the notion "this just happened!" Most television station news departments are on-air more than a dozen times each day. This frequency provides ample opportunity to bring the latest happenings and updates for viewers.

In addition, bringing an event live always holds an element of the unexpected and brings a certain level of excitement no matter how dull the event. But be careful to deliver the goods! Going live to a reporter who essentially says, "I don't know," or "I'm standing where something happened three hours ago," can breed viewer resentment.

Stress the Simple

Broadcast's linearity is a constraint on storytelling. When we read text on a page, we can return to earlier passages in order to understand the overall account. In video news storytelling, the viewer can process the information only in the way and the order in which it is presented.

Linear presentation has some benefits; for instance, most narrative storytelling (the natural way in which we process information) is chronological. It forces us to tell the story as simply as possible and to pay attention to structure, such as making sure we present concepts in more general terms before presenting specifics.

HOW THESE PRINCIPLES AFFECT PRACTICES

The principles just described influence the business and practices of broadcast news in five interlocking and sometimes overlapping areas: the tendency toward smaller staffs, greater reliance on visuals, different reliance on and use of time, an emphasis on personality, and a more conversational writing style.

Smaller Staffs

As TV stations have fallen in status and influence, news departments have also trimmed staff positions while increasing their expectations. In 2010 the average TV news department added an additional half hour of programming—to five hours per weekday—without adding staff.[2] Since TV news positions have always been fewer than those in print newsrooms, stations have tended to operate in a daily "crisis mode," with just enough people on staff to meet the normal demands of happenings in the area. Any breaking news item will pull people away from their typical tasks in order to accommodate the new development.

The impact of smaller news staffs is reflected in fewer beats and more general assignment positions. As fewer staff members really know an area's history, geography, and personalities, the danger is that news coverage will tend toward the superficial and the sensational.

Radio Staffing: Radio news staffs are typically much smaller than television or cable news operations, and less work space is needed (see figure 8.1). Although some larger operations may still allow specialization as a producer, writer, or editor, most positions are generally one of three broad categories:

1. *News director.* He or she oversees news operations and the budget and typically delivers morning or afternoon newscasts. In smaller markets, the news director may also take on reporting duties.
2. *Anchor.* The anchor makes beat calls, rewrites stories, and produces and delivers newscasts. At some stations, the news anchor is encouraged to be a "personality" who engages in on-air banter with music announcers and talk show hosts.
3. *Reporter.* The reporter gathers, researches, and presents news stories from the field. The reporter will also provide stories and actualities (recorded sound bites and interview snippets) for the anchor to integrate into the newscasts.

Television Staffing: Television newsroom staffs, as illustrated in figure 8.3, are much larger and more task-specific, and they rely more on teamwork among reporters, producers, and anchors. In smaller markets you see smaller staffs and more of the "one-man band" position, where individual staff members have to do it all—gather information, shoot and edit video, and even anchor. The most common television news positions are:

1. *News director.* This is the top person in the news department, responsible for hiring, firing, promoting, budgeting, and working with other department heads.
2. *Producer.* The producer is the newscast architect, determining what stories will be included as well as their placement. The producer also decides story packaging—whether it will be a reader, anchor voice-over, VO/SOT/VO (voice-over with sound-on-tape interview in the middle), edited package,

---

[2] Bob Papper (2010), "TV and Radio News Staffing and Profitability Survey," RTDNA.org, Retrieved from http://www.rtdna.org/pages/media_items/2010-tv-and-radio-news-staffing-and-profitability-survey1943.php?id=1943.

Figure 8.1 ■ Radio newsrooms are smaller than most newsrooms. They are usually configured for one person to gather information from wire services, online sources, and telephone; to edit and mix the audio; and to write scripts for the newscast.

Figure 8.2 ■ Television newsrooms are dominated by the assignments desk. Except for the logos and TV lights, these newsrooms look about the same as newspaper newsrooms.

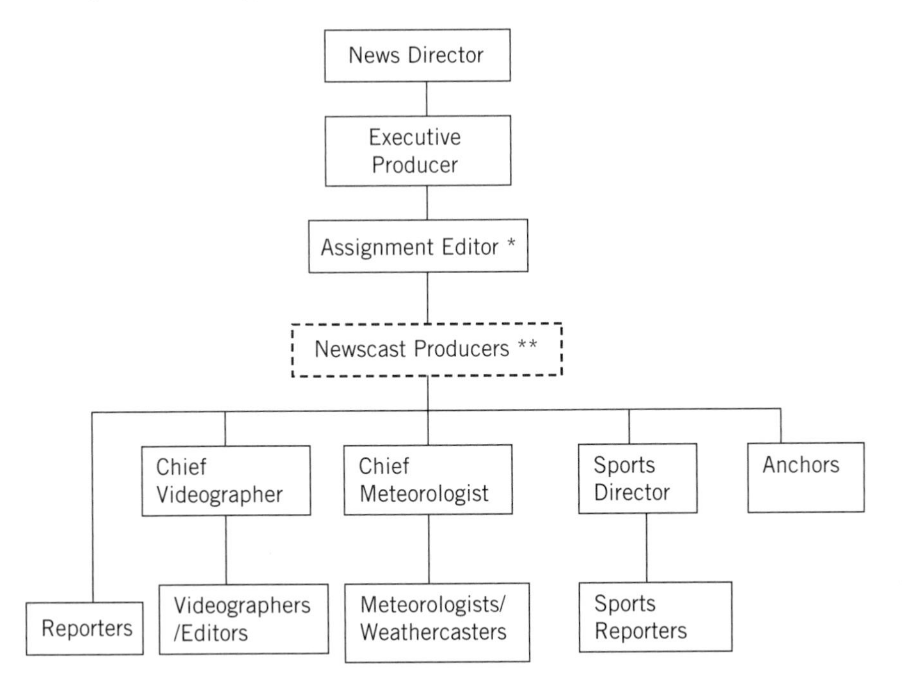

Figure 8.3 ■ This chart illustrates the structure of a typical newsroom. Note that the staff is organized by skill set, with almost all reporters serving as general assignment reporters.

* In smaller newsrooms, the news director may serve as executive producer and assignment editor; in larger newsrooms, multiple assignment editors may work at different times during the day.

** Each newscast will have a different producer who coordinates with the assignment editor, anchors, and production team to put together each newscast.

or live shot with the reporter in the field. The producer uses newsroom software to keep track of time, in terms of both deadlines and show segments. The producer also often acts as a copy editor and ensures that stories are complete, accurate, and easy to read.

3. *Assignment editor* (sometimes known as "assignment manager"). As newsroom "traffic cop," this person (persons in a major-market newsroom) maintains futures files; monitors police, fire, and emergency services scanners; coordinates field crews with show producers; and performs a host of other tasks—sometimes even updating the news department website.
4. *Anchor* (also called "talent"). The anchor is the newscast host and often spends a lot of time editing and rewriting copy in order to improve readability. Anchors, especially of the morning, midday, and weekend newscasts, also often double as reporters.
5. *Reporter.* The field reporter is at the heart of the news organization as the daily neutral witness or observer of significant local events. Reporters put events or decisions in context and explain how they will affect people. Each

day they may be assigned to cover an important activity or event or pursue something they have heard about or observed. Not every story must be weighty; a good, entertaining human interest story can be just as valuable in providing insight into your city or town. Reporters, because they are in the field more than other staff members, are the public representatives of the media organization and the face of the business.

6. *Photographer.* Photographers call themselves many things (photog, cameraman, videographer, shooter, photojournalist), but they are the ones who record video in the field. They also drive the satellite truck, run the equipment, set up lights, make the live shot work, and otherwise make the reporter look calm, cool, and in control. Photographers are creative and approach their craft as art, and accomplished ones sometimes get to produce "video essays" for certain spectacles and events.

   In addition to the video shown on TV, sometimes photographers produce additional video for use online as a package or as sound bites. In smaller newsrooms without separate video editors, photographers also edit their own video in the field or back in the newsroom as time and assignments allow.
7. *Video editor.* At many stations, the editor also works as a photographer. Where staffing allows, video editors also are responsible for handling all news video sent by the network outside of newscasts (called a "feed") as well as that shot locally by the photographer. Editors must work fast and on deadline.
8. *Graphic artist.* This position often does double duty with news and production (traffic, promotions) in designing materials for promotions as well as for news programs. The graphic artist is skilled in image, animation, and multimedia software and production techniques.
9. *Studio production staff.* Live news still demands positions such as director, technical director, audio technician, and floor manager. Many studios now have robotic cameras run from the control room, leaving only a floor director in the studio to relay instructions from the director or producer. These are not typically considered news personnel but come under programming and production.
10. *Field producer/editor.* Generally found only at the largest stations, this combination of producer and editor works in the field with a reporter, helping to gather and edit information and then ensuring that completed stories are sent back to the newsroom for broadcast or for uploading to the website.

Some stations also used to have a librarian-archivist to help research information and keep track of film or videotapes of significant events for use in future news stories. Computerized, digital storage systems now save and log most video automatically, and reporters can do most research from their computers using online databases, so such positions have generally disappeared except for a few at the networks and the very largest stations.

Reliance on Visuals

Each medium has its own strengths and weaknesses. Print allows readers to scan, pause, and reread segments, making it easier to follow and understand a complicated story.

Television is a dramatic medium that best conveys information through emotion and action, especially events unfolding before the viewer. Because of TV's reliance on images and sound, reporters and editors have a responsibility to present information in a clear, linear fashion that won't confuse the viewer.

Basic Visual Principles: Of all the principles for shooting and recording video, framing is probably most basic and essential. Framing is the idea that the object you wish to focus on should dominate the screen. The object generally is near the center, but when doing interviews, photographers often use the "rule of thirds" that places the subject in the left or right third of the screen so the person is looking into the wider area. This ensures "look room" or "nose room" so the person is not directly facing the camera. The extra screen space focuses attention on the person's gaze or motion and is especially important when following action.

With cameras getting smaller, it is tempting to simply hold them in your hands as you record the scene or an interview. But experienced videographers use a tripod whenever possible. Few people find it pleasant to watch news video shot in a shaky, handheld style. Steady shots help the viewer focus on the action, not the technique. If you must hold the camera, reduce the shakiness that is accentuated by lens magnification. Zoom out, and get close-ups by physically getting as close to the subject as possible.

You should know four basic shots: WS (wide shot, also known as LS or long shot), MS (medium shot), CU (close-up), and ECU (extreme close-up). Close-ups and extreme close-ups work better with online video because of the smaller screen, and wider shots work better on widescreen high-definition television (close-ups can work too, but extreme close-ups of a face can be unsettling on a big screen).

Try to get as many close-ups as possible. It's hard to get too many. Emotionally, CUs are like exclamation points, with the greatest emotional and informational content. Medium shots transition between close-ups and wide shots.

Try to have action or movement in every shot. Our brains are wired so that motion captures our attention.

People like to see people, so include them in every shot if possible. When shooting a person in close-up or a medium shot, try to frame the subject so you see both eyes.

Signs and empty buildings are boring (and signs are hard to read in online video). Shoot them for insurance and hope you don't need them.

Except for the rare case of artistic effect (the iconic shot of someone walking into the sunset, for instance), avoid "butt shots"—shooting video of people from behind as they walk away—and any angle that is unflattering to your subject (up into someone's nose, for example).

When shooting video, record each shot for at least five seconds, and ten seconds is better. You will use a shorter segment of each clip when editing, so having the extra seconds will save you many cases of heartburn. Movement shots such as zooms, pans, or tilts tend to be a bit longer. Tracking a rocket launch or ice dancing performance can be beautiful for a full 20 or 30 seconds.

Packaged reports are created using a computer-based nonlinear editor (NLE) such as Avid Media Composer (for journalists there's a stripped-down version called Newscutter) or Apple's Final Cut Pro. Increasingly a third editing program, Adobe Premiere, is being adopted as well. Premiere is the cheapest and easiest for students to learn basic video editing techniques. Video capture, editing, transitions and effects, and rendering for broadcast or the Web are standard.

For the most advanced video productions, many people are trained on Avid. It's a high-powered professional editor that can do multiple edits with effects very quickly. Final Cut Pro on the Mac has also been extremely popular with multimedia enthusiasts since it was launched in the 1990s. Many people advocate being knowledgeable of both Avid and Apple because they are comparable. More recently, Premiere is gaining respect because of improvements and the added bonus of being an integrated part of the Adobe CS Suite of multimedia programs.

On the horizon, Sony now offers a high-definition 3D stereoscopic video editor called Vegas. It may be a long time before journalism moves in this direction because so far there's little demand for 3D news; but it's always good to see what's going on in the rest of the world of video production.

Editing Basics: The shot you use to introduce your package is also called the ES, or establishing shot, because it establishes for the viewer where the story is taking place. It is usually a wide shot (or a medium shot online, since wide shots do not translate so well to a small screen), although in some rare and more artistic cases, editors might start with a close-up and then come back to a wider shot. When editing video, it is important to think in terms of "sequence," not "series." When we look at something, our eyes and brains work together to establish a sequence: We take in the entire scene, then we move a little closer visually, and finally we focus in on something. We might look at it from several angles, pulling back to a medium view, then darting back in for a close-up, before we pull out to a wide shot again to seek the next thing of interest.

In terms of video sequencing, then, avoid going from wide shot to wide shot. Instead, strive for a visual sequence (LS-MS or MS-CU), and never edit together motion-to-motion shots (a pan to a tilt or a zoom to another zoom, for example). Put a static shot between the two, preferably a medium or medium close-up (by static, we mean the camera is not moving; people might be moving in the shot).

Maintain a line of action (the 180-degree rule); if you're shooting a parade from the left side, stay on the left side. You'll sometimes also hear this as the admonition, "don't cross the plane of view."

Avoid jump cuts that come when scenes that are too similar are edited together or when you have to cross the plane of view. The result is what looks like an impossible jump by whomever or whatever is on screen or a jarring visual reorientation. You avoid this by placing a neutral third shot in between. These shots are often called cut-ins (an overused classic is a close-up of someone's hands while they talk) or cutaways (for instance, the reporter listening to the person speak). When crossing a visual plane, take special care that the neutral cover shot has as little discernible orientation as possible (which is why a CU or ECU is often used in such cases). Whenever there's a jump cut, the blame falls on the editor.

As you might have guessed, the time to start thinking about editing is when you are in the field shooting the video. Make sure you have the shots you need (preferably more than you think you need), in roughly the same sequence.

Television often has difficulty with complicated stories or those without compelling visuals (e.g., a story about reassessing property values). This problem underscores the notion that one medium is not necessarily better than another but that some stories are best told in a specific medium.

Broadcast journalism has different emphases that audiences have come to expect. Television is neither inferior nor superior to other media, but it is different. Some stories are told better with video (like a dramatic car chase), while others work best using only text (perhaps describing the effects of new legislation).

The history of TV news suggests the best product is not always rewarded with the highest viewership. In fact, the lurid and sensational are often rewarded by the society that so quickly condemns the practice.

Besides video, television news also depends heavily on graphical elements to bring a show together. Several times during a show, viewers are likely to see maps, charts, lists, still images, animations, or other contextual information. These materials can consist of statistics, facts, highlighted document text, weather developments, and the names of everyone who appears on screen. All stations have a graphics package that includes a number of station logos with music to help promote branding, and, as noted above, some have graphic artists to create material as needed.

Writing Visually: Writing to visuals is not intuitive but learned. We can provide a simple demonstration or exercise, but one becomes better and faster only with practice.

To demonstrate how to think visually, let's take an example of a city council meeting and a discussion of the police budget. The basic facts include the names of politicians and police representatives, who said what, the final vote (if there was one), whether the budget would go up or down, and the effect of the changes on the number of officers, patrols, response times, pay, equipment, and so on. If you focus only on the meeting and its action, the story will not have much visual interest. So you have to *think ahead* as much as possible about the images or pictures you need to better present the story. In this case, you might begin with visuals of the meeting itself and consider sound bites and close-up shots of the key speakers. Next, you must think of specific kinds of visuals needed to demonstrate the points you'll make in the script. For example, if you're talking about police, you need video or images of officers in various activities (on the street, talking with pedestrians, giving talks in schools, chatting with each other at the station); shots of equipment including police cars, police dogs, practice facilities, holding cells, jackets, weapons; and anything else related to equipment. Whether the budget goes up or down can be conveyed in a number of ways with charts and animated graphics.

In actually writing the story, remember to think about the visuals you have and then write the script first, placing the sound bites in their appropriate places. When you talk about the decision, use the complementary video of the meeting. When describing the budget needs of the department, show officers, equipment, or facilities. If the budget is going up or down, show a chart or animation. Then, provide a reaction to the decision by someone at the meeting who was affected by the vote—a sound bite from a police official, police union spokesperson, or city official.

Thinking in terms of visuals and using images to tell a story have long separated print and broadcast journalists. But in the age of media convergence, with equipment that is simpler and quicker but still can produce and edit professional-quality audio and video, these differences are being moved aside so all journalists can focus on the story itself and what's needed to tell it best.

Notion and Use of Time

In broadcast news, all processes and content production issues revolve around time. Except for the cable all-news channels, broadcast news serves an audience with certain expectations in terms of when and how news will be presented. Morning shows tend to focus on short headlines and generally lighter stories. Midday shows are typically geared toward those in the home. The early evening show (often done in several segments starting as early as 4:30 p.m. and going as late as 7:30 p.m.) aims for the largest ratings and broadest demographics, presenting the day's top stories as well as special reports. The 10 or 11 p.m. newscast tries to wrap up the day's events for those getting ready to sleep. Even in these days when people increasingly use digital video recorders to time-shift their viewing, the basic formula still is generally followed (if nothing else, so people know when to record the shows).

Television is time-sensitive, and timeliness is often a key consideration for determining what makes good television news. Television operates around the clock, and updates on an important story may air at any time. A new deadline may come up every 30 minutes or less when news is breaking.

As with much of journalism in the age of convergence, the differences between broadcast and print newsrooms are narrowing on this point as well. While the physical newspaper's publishing deadlines remain important to print newsrooms, newspapers increasingly are breaking news on their websites and updating it online as quickly as their broadcast competition.

The Live Newscast: Many broadcast news programs are aired live, which means the anchors appear in real time to present the news. This lets the newsroom bring viewers the latest news and information, including stories still in progress. Many television news shows feature at least a couple of live shots, where a field reporter can introduce a story as it occurs with the help of the TV news van (figure 8.4).

Local TV stations are still routinely criticized for going live simply because they can, giving us a lonely reporter talking about things that happened sometimes hours earlier. A second downside to live broadcast is the potential loss of control. There are countless stories of anchors' faux pas, reporters' meltdowns—even arguments between reporters and those they were interviewing—that erupted unexpectedly in the middle of a live broadcast. When you go live, there are no second takes.

Each news show has hundreds of elements that must come together sequentially for the program to run seamlessly. Producers need scripts and graphics ready well before airtime (typically 30 minutes). Live field reports have to be set up as far in advance as possible, with edited portions prepped and ready. Anchors have to be in place having preread their scripts and ready to go because once the show rolls, there's no going back.

Writing Stories to Time: Besides meeting deadlines, the stories themselves must adhere to constraints related to time. Newsroom software such as ENPS automatically calculates the time it takes to read a script, so writing to time is a skill that can be learned.

Broadcast stories are far shorter than a typical print story, but having audio and visual elements can make a story richer as it's processed through multiple senses simultaneously. TV news stories tend to take one of a handful of forms:

1. *Reader.* The most basic form is the reader or script-only story with no pictures. A reader tends to be about 20 seconds maximum.

Figure 8.4 ■ TV news vans are a critical component of live reporting. These vehicles contain everything needed to capture and edit video, along with a transmitter and antenna used to send the signal back to the station for broadcast.

2. *Voice-over (VO).* The VO is a staple of TV news. The news anchor introduces a story, and after the first sentence or two the viewer will see video of the story while the anchor continues reading. VOs tend to run 20 to 30 seconds.
3. *Voice-over/sound on tape (VO/SOT).* The VO/SOT is the same as the VO with the addition of a sound bite from someone involved with the story. A VO/SOT can also be called a "VO-bite." Related to the VO/SOT is the VO/SOT/VO, which simply adds more anchor voice-over video after the sound bite. This type of story generally runs 25 seconds to a minute.
4. *Package.* The *package* is a reporter's recorded story. The anchor introduces the story and includes the reporter's name ("TV 3's Bob Smith has been at the beach all day and gives us this story…"). Packages typically run from 1:15 to 1:45 but can go as long as three minutes. Packages usually include seeing the reporter on camera in either a stand-up open, stand-up close, or bridge.

   Part of news program branding is to emphasize the personalities presenting the information, so reporters should appear at least once in the story, in the beginning, middle, or end. The stand-up open is effective when the anchor introduces, or "tosses," the attention to the reporter and viewers immediately see him or her. The *bridge* is a transition in the middle of the package between two locations, two thoughts or ideas, or two sound bites. A typical bridge has the reporter appearing on camera to sum up a point or perspective before moving on to another point. The stand-up close is used by the reporter to appear on camera and sum up the story for the viewer. It typically ends with a standard out-cue (SOQ or SOC, also sometimes called a sig-out or a lock-out) in which the reporter gives his or her name followed by the station ID ("I'm Jane Kirker, Channel 8 News").

5. *Telling stories with pictures—the video essay.* Although most stories rely on a reporter and the spoken word, television news can also offer viewers a video essay, or montage. For example, in the aftermath of Hurricane Katrina, a number of stations showed the devastation with no reporter commentary, just the scenes and sounds of those who had been affected. Because television is foremost a visual medium, sometimes powerful images alone are sufficient.

On paper (or in the computer), the newscast comes together in the *rundown,* the document that integrates all the stories in various forms plus graphics, commercials, teases, tosses, and music stings (see figure 8.5). Every news program has a producer who takes all these components and weaves them into a coherent whole. All newsroom systems have flexible templates that allow producers to add, delete, and shift program elements throughout the day as some items become dated and are discarded while others develop and increase in importance.

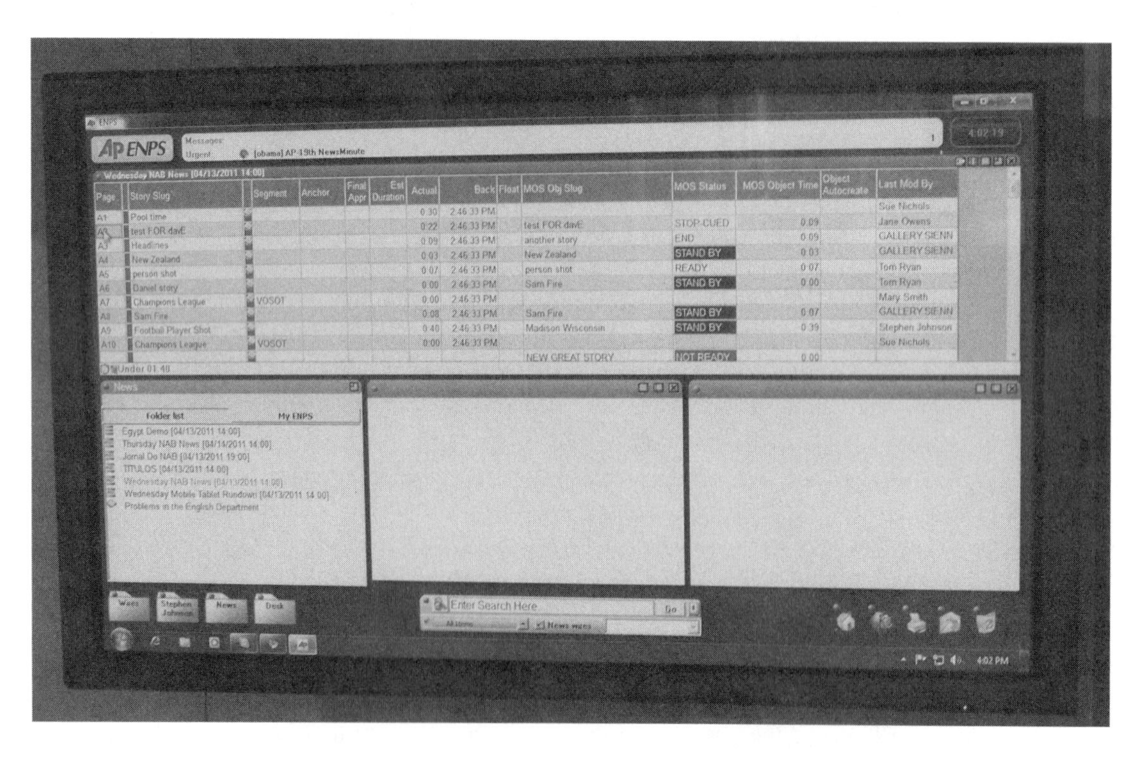

Figure 8.5 ■ The "rundown" organizes a television newscast. Each line on the rundown is a separate story, tease, commercial break, or other element of a television newscast. Separate columns list the start time, end time, running time, description of the element, and source. Editing a rundown moves elements within a newscast.

Personality: The Reporter Is Talent

For generations, reporters could sit in the back of the room and quietly take notes. They could be unobtrusive—a watcher, an observer, a lurker. This was a great benefit and gave us the notion that news is the "first rough draft of history" and that the reporter was simply chronicling events as they transpired.

But first with radio, then television, and now the Web, we have entered the age of celebrity. The reporter must be prepared to be at least a minor participant in events, and in the digital age there is much talk about all journalists, not just broadcasters, managing their "personal brand."[3]

It is not unusual for the arrival of the news media to coincide with a change in the atmosphere of an event or activity. Participants who had been civil may abruptly change and grandstand for the camera. Obviously, the general principle is to avoid and discourage such displays, but the reality is that a reporter is a member of the media, and media figures have a degree of celebrity. Accept it for what it is and find ways to use it (and discourage it from getting out of hand).

For example, print reporters and editors who think they can avoid appearing on camera are finding their employment handbook may require them to appear in any other medium the news organization designates. Often, these are question-and-answer sessions (sometimes called "debriefs") done during a cooperating TV station's news or on one of the national news or sports networks, especially on cable television. In other cases, both print and broadcast reporters are being enlisted to hold live online "chats."

You should cultivate some characteristics of your public or on-camera persona. Practice in front of a mirror, and use a voice recorder or camcorder to critique your performance. You should strive to be as natural as possible. Some basic vocal skill is expected and can be developed as follows:

1. Start with a good script. If a sentence is longer than 10 seconds, you'll have to take multiple breaths.
2. Speak in a monotone, and then vary it to add emphasis. There are three ways to vary a monotone:
   a. Inflection or changing the pitch of your voice. This technique is often overused by people starting out, and leads to what we call a "sing-song delivery." By emphasizing the same elements in each sentence, we develop an odd-sounding rhythm that is noticeable.
   b. Amplitude or volume, where we speak louder or softer to emphasize specific words or phrases. Good public speakers know how to alternate shouts and whispers to keep an audience and make their points.
   c. Pauses, or silence. A pause in an appropriate place will rivet attention to the very next thing you say.

---

[3] See, for instance, the *Brand me a journalist* blog written by Jennifer Gaie Hellum, http://brandmeajournalist.com/. See also: V. Lavrusik (May 2011), *Vadim Lavrusik: How Journalists Can Make Use of Facebook Pages,* Nieman Journalism Lab blog, http://www.niemanlab.org/2011/05/vadim-lavrusik-how-journalists-can-make-use-of-facebook-pages/.

3. The format of the script is important. You want it:
   a. Written to time. People tend to speak at roughly 180 to 200 words per minute. Newsroom software automatically provides reasonably accurate times.
   b. Easy to read. Use double- or triple-spacing and an appropriate font (Arial, Times New Roman). TV stations use Teleprompters to take care of many issues related to this (see figure 8.6).
   c. Broadcast-Ready. This means difficult-to-pronounce words are spelled out as they sound. Don't use complicated phonetic symbols; use common words or syllables to spell out names and other words that are difficult to pronounce. (For instance, the Delaware River tributary that separates West Philadelphia from Center City is the Schuylkill. In broadcast copy, that would be written as SCHOOL-kill.)

Once you have the basic voice training as well as appearance (professional wardrobe, trimmed hair, and conservative jewelry and facial hair), work on your overall presentation. Viewers have certain expectations of reporters and anchors to go along with a slick and professionally designed set (figure 8.7).

1. *Authoritative.* This doesn't mean you need the "voice of God" or the appearance of a matinee idol. It means you're generally serious and neutral. Avoid extremes in emotions, but do not come across as distant or aloof. You should speak in measured tones and not get caught up in the moment, no matter how crazy things may be around you.

Figure 8.6 ■ Although a paper version of a television news script is always printed, the most important output is the teleprompter, which has to scroll through the script as the anchor reads it.

Figure 8.7 ■ A television news set is an important part of how the news is "packaged," with great care going into every element, from the size and placement of the logo to the color of wood used on the set. Many sets also change the background image of the city, using a night shot for late news and a daytime shot for daytime newscasts.

2. *Friendly.* Unless you intentionally want to try marketing your persona as a "sour, dour curmudgeon," you will need to be somewhat friendly. We're not talking about obnoxious and excessive hand-shaking or telling jokes and guffawing. You should not be unnatural or fake but instead convey the impression you are a sober and mildly positive "people person."
3. *Folksy.* Off the air, you'll spend lots of time with people like farmers, housewives, clerks, taxi drivers, and police. If you've spent your entire life with upper-middle-class success stories, you'll need to adjust. You're trying to tell the stories of people who need an advocate—oftentimes poor, downtrodden, uneducated, and underprivileged. Most important, be natural and genuine. Don't be pretentious, and don't use your credentials like a club.
4. *Energetic.* Public presentation rules are now fairly standardized, regardless of whether one is in media or public service. When appearing in an official capacity, the audience expects you not to be dull or to lack confidence. Practicing in front of a mirror is not uncommon for anyone going into the public eye. You should appear energetic and confident without coming across as hyperactive, nervous, or arrogant.
5. *Sincere.* As the saying goes: "The secret to life is sincerity. Once you can fake that you can do anything." Just kidding. If you're not sincere, you should do something else. Most of us don't like phony people and some react to insincerity with hostility.

Broadcast Writing Style

Broadcast writing is more conversational, but it's possible to be conversational and grammatically correct without loading your script with poor word order, poor usage, and slang. Just listen to any of the major network newscasts, especially a show like CBS's *Sunday Morning*. Good usage and grammar are even more critical in broadcast because your listener or viewer doesn't get a second chance to try to figure out what you are saying.

Broadcast style differs from print primarily in the need to make the copy easier to read, say, and understand. We mentioned earlier, for instance, that hard-to-pronounce words are spelled out using common syllables or shorter words. This is not a stylebook, so we won't attempt to cover all the intricacies. There are many good stylebooks and references for that. However, there are a handful of key points for anyone used to writing "print" who now is being asked to write for broadcast (or podcast).

1. Listeners can't go back and relisten, and even with something like a podcast, they are unlikely to want to.
   a. Generally put titles before names: *State Corrections Director Joe Smith*, not *Joe Smith, the state's corrections director*. (If it is a long, unfamiliar title (Deputy City Manager for Economic Development Marie Jones), we'll avoid it in favor of a more descriptive term (the city's economic development director, Marie Jones).
   b. To help the reporter or anchor, avoid abbreviations such as "St." and "Ave." Also avoid symbols, such as the ampersand (&), even if it is part of a company's name. And avoid the dollar sign. We write "26 dollars" for broadcast, not "$26."
2. To aid in speaking, numbers are almost always written out from one through eleven (eleven because on the old teletype machines the two ones looked like a double lowercase letter "l"). From 12 to 999, the numerals will almost always be used.
   a. Numbers greater than 999 use terms, not strings of zeros: "25-hundred," "64-thousand."
   b. Avoid hard-to-digest forms like "three-point-seven million." Say "close to four (m) million" (the "m" in parentheses helps signal the news reader to clearly pronounce the word "million").
   c. Sometimes for ease of reading, a number like a street address is hyphenated: "The fire at 64-10 Old Wide River Avenue did 50-thousand dollars in damage." (Note, by the way, the correct use of "damage." The singular is used in this case. "Damages" is what you win in a lawsuit.)
3. Avoid quoting someone in text. Let the sound bites handle that heavy lifting. If you absolutely must quote someone, avoid the "quote/unquote" method. Try to find other ways to signal a quote.
   a. The prosecutor says—in her words—"The Statehouse is a cesspool, and we will clean it up."
   b. As one witness put it, "It was the most amazing thing I've seen in my life."
4. Broadcast is a medium of the moment, so you will write with a lot more present-tense verbs, especially "says."

Box 8.2 Shooting, Writing, Editing, and Producing a Story

Here are some basics steps to creating a video news story.

I. Preproduction and reporting issues

1. Pick the topic or be assigned the topic

a. Read whatever you can about it; use a variety of media sources.
b. Plan whom to interview and locations to visit (for B-roll).
c. Make appointments and get permissions, as needed.
d. Get equipment, make sure you've got batteries, lights, and other necessary items and whatever you use to record on· memory stick, hard drive, tape, or some other medium.

II. Field production issues

2. Go to the interview location(s)

a. Arrive on time or a few minutes early.
b. Make introductions, icebreaking.
c. Set up camera while reporter gets background information (not recorded).

3. Record interview

a. Keep it short; record your best three questions (some places say two questions or even ask your best question).
b. Shoot cutaways; reporter finishes up and gets follow-up information.
c. Make sure you have the interview, be friendly and polite, say goodbye.

4. Go to location to shoot B-roll (while on the way, reporter writes stand-up)

a. Be careful about public versus private property, check first, get permission if needed.
b. Be mindful about privacy concerns; use a preventive strategy whenever possible.
c. Shoot bridge or stand-up or MOS/MOTS (man-on-the-street).

5. Repeat steps 3 and 4 until finished

a. Make sure you have good audio quotes.
b. Make sure you have lots of B-roll (at least 20 usable shots combining sequences of long shots, medium shots, and close-ups, each 5 to 10 seconds long; avoid excessive motion shots like pans or zooms).

6. Write up script, pick sound bites (may be done in the field or back at the station/ studio)

a. Choose sound bites based on emotion, opinion.
b. Pack facts, information into your script (paraphrase the interviewee).

III. Post-production issues

7. Lay down (record) voice track

a. Typical sequence may be
Script part A
Sound bite 1
Bridge
Sound bite 2
Script part B
Stand-up close and/or standard out-cue

Box 8.2 (continued)

8. **Lay B-roll**
    a. First scene is establishing shot and is usually wide, providing context.
    b. Match script wherever possible.
    c. Keep pacing consistent (each shot :03–:05).
    d. Keep out bad composition, unnecessary movement, poor lighting, etc.
9. **Export to tape, DVD, Web server, etc.**

These four points will cover most of the broadcast style issues you will face in coming from a print-oriented environment.

Finally, on the production side, there are a series of basic steps to help you produce a TV news story package (box 8.2). While entire courses are built around learning these skills through repetition, this guide proivdes the basic steps in field reporting.

SUMMARY

This chapter highlights the differences and commonalities between print and broadcast reporting. Radio news staffs are small and continuing to shrink, and television is learning to adjust in a converged media environment. But the basic skills of broadcast reporting are now being applied to a host of emerging media. The basics of good reporting have not changed, and it is important for journalists working in all media to realize they are all working together to "shine light in the dark places." Accuracy, attention to detail, and clear communication of thoughts and ideas are paramount to being a good journalist. To work in broadcasting, specifically television, however, there are some additional considerations.

Television is an emotional and active medium. It emphasizes the visual and dramatic aspects of stories. In addition, the reporter is an integral part of the presentation and must act appropriately. Developing a pleasing persona is a fact of life for all modern journalists.

EXERCISES

1. Choose one television station in your area and record a morning, midday, and afternoon news program. Find a local story, topic, or event that was reported on throughout the day and analyze the coverage for that story from three perspectives: First, look at the type of story coverage used in each newscast—VO, VO/SOT, package, or live report? Second, what types of visuals were used each time, and what images were different? Third, what meaning or perspective did the reporter provide the viewer? What sound bites were selected and did they change throughout the day? In addition to the reporting, how did the talent present this information? Was the story presented by an anchor or reporter on the set or with a live shot from the field? What characteristic or quality do you think

the personality was able to inject into the report? As a news consumer, did you feel the journalist injected too much, too little, or just the right amount of personality?

2. Record an afternoon and evening of a television station's news programs. List all the local stories. The next morning, take a copy of your local newspaper and compare your list. Note where each of the TV stories appears in the newspaper. What stories do you think were given more coverage than they deserved in each medium, and why? What stories do you think were not given enough coverage, and why?
3. Practice visual thinking by providing three to five visual images or graphics to demonstrate the following concepts. Some are easier than others, and not all lend themselves to the task (if it was easy, it wouldn't be an exercise). Then rank each list according to most to least effective.
   a. Music is important to civilized society.
   b. Obesity among children is increasing.
   c. Home property values are increasing.
   d. Violent crime rates are going down even as white-collar crime is going up.
   e. Every year, thousands try to avoid paying taxes.
4. Practice an on-air persona. From the newspaper or Web, write up about two minutes of copy using broadcast news script style guidelines. Next, record yourself using a variety of personalities (serious, energetic, upbeat, etc.). Do enough takes of each to figure out which ones you're most comfortable with. Wait 24 hours to review them (it helps eliminate bias). In viewing each of them, which personality do you think communicates most effectively, and why? Which one would you say is the second best, and why?

CHAPTER 9

BASICS OF PRINT

Good storytelling has one goal: to create a picture in the viewer's or reader's mind as a way to impart information clearly and effectively. The challenge for the "print" writer is how to take words, which exist in one dimension, and assemble them in a way that creates a multidimensional experience in the reader's mind.

Although it is used extensively in both the industry and academia, the term "print" is misleading and easily misconstrued if you think of it as referring only to how information is delivered to the reader. No longer is the print writer confined to ink on paper; in fact, much of online news is primarily text-based and relies on many of the conventions that grew up around newspapers and magazines. So, perhaps, "text" would be the better term, except digital media also allow the text writer to augment his or her writing with video, audio, photos, slide shows, data visualizations, and so forth. New technologies allow such transformation, recombination, augmentation, and reconceptualization. It is not glib to suggest current medium- or form-based labels have a built-in inadequacy. But they are what we have to work with, so keep in mind that when we use the term "print," we are talking about a concept that is more than a physical dimension.

This chapter is aimed partly at those primarily trained in electronic media who might already be aware of all the nonverbal means of communication that convey information, such as gestures, tonal inflections, and the visuals themselves—things that a print writer must instead re-create and transmit in words. It is not a deep analysis of how to improve your print writing. There are many fine readings for that. This chapter is designed to help those whose primary experience or training is in another form master the basics of print writing so they can easily post stories online and, perhaps, create something for the more traditional paper format (after all, *multimedia* means being able to navigate across all media, including the legacy models).

We will start with a broadcast story and then examine how the information traditionally would be augmented and what differences exist in a print story. We also look at different story forms, one of which broadcasters already commonly use and which, when fleshed out in more of the print style, can be an excellent form for online.

DETAILS HELP CREATE WORD PICTURES

When writing for broadcast, we have the *help* of pictures and sound, but broadcast journalists also know the most effective reporting and writing goes beyond the images to allow the viewer to imagine smelling, tasting, and feeling the story—in short, to experience it.

Good print writing—whether on paper or the Internet's "printcast" version we discussed in chapter 4—seeks to do no less. In traditional newspapers and magazines, pictures and graphics may accompany the words, but they are static. Online, you can add dimensions through interactivity and multimedia, but those items generally are not bound as tightly to the work as they are in broadcast and they usually require the extra effort, however slight, of the reader to click through. As long as online remains primarily text-based, the journalist has one main tool to engage readers so they do click through to the other parts—the storyteller's craft of using the right words, which means getting the right details.

To see how this might translate from a television story to print, let's start with a broadcast package illustrated in box 9.1, a story that, sadly, is a common one for some farmers every year.

This TV news script gives you the high points. Seeing the anguish on Ackerman's face during the interviews helps you emotionally understand what Framingham County farmers are going through, and in that way it more efficiently and effectively conveys the information. The reporter was able to give you some specifics: more than 100,000 head of cattle and about 300,000 bales of hay. But there just isn't time to fit in much more.

So you know farmers are in deep trouble. You can see Ackerman's pain and feel his anguish. But you lack context: Is 300,000 bales of hay very much? If 100,000 head of cattle come to market, will the price for steak drop? How much help can the state afford relative to the possible harm?

While the tradition of broadcast is to capture the emotion, print emphasizes powerful details and context. Even the most skilled writers will have trouble competing with the raw emotion displayed from Ackerman's squinting eyes and sun-baked brow. But with the right details they can still create an effective word picture that extends the story to answer deeper questions that readers might have.

Handling Quotes

Although this script and the newspaper story that follow are based on real stories, they were created for this text and not broadcast or printed. So we will allow ourselves the

Box 9.1 Example of a Broadcast TV News Story Script

ANCHOR: ONCAM :09	LITTLE RAIN AND SCORCHING TEMPERATURES ARE THREATENING AREA FARMERS' LIVELIHOODS. JANE KIRKER SAYS ONE FRAMINGHAM COUNTY FARMER IS ABOUT TO TAKE SOME DRASTIC ACTION:
NAT/SOT FULL :04 CU Feet crunching corn stalks	Video—NAT :04
VO/SOT :20 NAT under Super: Framingham County	THAT'S THE SOUND OF FARMER JACK ACKERMAN'S CORN CROP BURNING UP IN THE FIELDS.
(CU continues :03. MS from back of Ackerman walking, front shot, then cover shots of him examining shriveled ear and stalk.)	WE'VE HAD LESS THAN AN INCH OF RAIN IN THE PAST MONTH. DAYTIME TEMPERATURES ARE RARELY BELOW 100. EARS ARE BAKING ON THE STALKS. THE STATE'S CLIMATOLOGIST SAYS IT'S A "SEVERE DROUGHT." ACKERMAN SAYS IT'S A DISASTER:
SOT :06 "I'd be lucky to get a couple hundred bushels out of this. You can't hardly feed a herd of cattle on that." Super: Jack Ackerman	*SOT :06... herd of cattle on that.*
VO/SOT :13 (NAT under) Cattle in field and being worked in feedlot.	SO ACKERMAN—AND A LOT OF HIS NEIGHBORS—ARE THINKING OF SELLING OFF MOST OF THEIR HERDS. THE STATE AGRICULTURE DEPARTMENT SAYS THE AREA HAS MORE THAN A HUNDRED-THOUSAND HEAD OF CATTLE. EXPERTS SAY IF THOSE HIT THE MARKET ALL AT ONCE, IT WOULD SHATTER PRICES:
SOT :08 "Prices could drop to below 30 cents a pound here. The last time this happened—1962—it took ten years for the area to recover." Super: Mary Holman, agricultural economist, State U.	*SOT :08... area to recover.*
SOT :07 Ackerman: "I don't know what else I'm supposed to do. I don't have enough hay to feed them through the winter, and I can't afford to buy much more."	*SOT :07... afford to buy much more.*
VO/SOT :08 (Cattle eating.)	THE AGRICULTURE DEPARTMENT IS TRYING TO ORGANIZE HAY SHIPMENTS. SPOKESWOMAN BETTY RAPP SAYS 300-THOUSAND BALES ARE AVAILABLE.
SOT :12 Super: Kirker	**[STAND-UP at feedlot]** BUT FARMERS SAY IT'S TOO LITTLE TOO LATE. IF THEY DON'T GET AT LEAST AN INCH OF RAIN IN THE NEXT WEEK, THESE CATTLE ARE HEADED TO MARKET. IN FRAMINGHAM COUNTY, I'M JANE KIRKER, CHANNEL 8 NEWS.

luxury of having sources that are quotable and concise. As any experienced reporter knows, that is a rare thing to be cherished.

One of the things broadcast reporters discover when trying to transcribe their on-air sound bites into text quotes is that sometimes what works on TV doesn't work well otherwise. The quotes may be too short, or they may be fragments. The speech may be filled with stops, starts, and other affectations people take on when a microphone is thrust in front of them. The quotes may make perfect sense in the context of a broadcast package where the lead-in is visual and we can see the person while he or she is speaking (remember, nonverbal communication is a powerful additional channel), but without that context in print, the words may seem odd or incomplete.

Print also tends to avoid "information" quotes that may work better in broadcast when coupled with visuals. For instance, it's not unusual in a broadcast story to hear the fire chief solemnly describing something like this: "We found the woman's body in the bedroom, near the door, and a second body, that of a man, in the kitchen. They may have been trying to crawl to safety but were quickly overcome by smoke."

A good broadcast journalist is going to "cover" at least part of that with pictures of the fire scene. Put that all in print, however, and it's too dull. A print journalist might write: *The woman's body was near a bedroom door and the man's was in the kitchen, the chief said. "They may have been trying to crawl to safety but were quickly overcome by smoke," he said.*

Print reporters spend time talking to sources not only to get the facts, depth, and context but also to get the quotes "right" (thus, the same question sometimes asked several ways). They often must think a bit differently about how to structure parts of a story to make sure material flows into and out of a quote and helps it make sense. They try to avoid situations where the quotation has to be followed by "said of" or "said about" to explain more fully what the quotation was about. That generally means the quotation was not set up correctly. Such things can make a story momentarily lose momentum or, worse, make readers have to backtrack to get the full meaning.

So broadcast reporters who also have to write for print or online might need to spend a few additional moments getting "print" quotes in their notebooks.

Getting Details

Let's look at box 9.2 to see how a "print" writer might handle Ackerman's tale. In this case, we'll say it's a writer for a local paper. (A national writer would have to do some additional things, such as give a better geographic fix on Framingham County's location.)

In the example, words in bold indicate specific ways the print reporter builds the mind's picture and expands on or extends the broadcast report. The story runs about 480 words, about two screens' worth online and about 13 inches in print, which is average. Notice how the broadcast script uses "we," while the print story takes a more neutral tone. *USA Today* is notable for its use of "we," but many editors still think it sounds a bit patronizing.

We used only quotes from the broadcast story; however, our "print" reporter would be expected to interview several other farmers, local businesspeople, the climatologist, people who were around in 1962 and can remember that time, or perhaps even Ackerman's wife to get a better idea of how she and her husband were handling

Box 9.2 Example of a Print Version of a Story

Step. Crunch. Step. Crunch.

As Framingham County farmer Jack Ackerman walks through his rows of corn, the **sickening crunch underfoot** is the sound of his crop baking and burning up in the field.

The six-county metro area has had less than an inch of rain the past month. The temperature **has dropped below 100 just four days out of 30,** and the state climatologist's office says the area is in a "severe drought." Dozens of area farmers like Ackerman are struggling, and if history is a guide, their troubles could spread to the area's economy.

It's barely 9 a.m. Tuesday and already the temperature is 95. Ackerman takes out the red bandanna his wife says he always carries and wipes his brow. The bandanna's already soaked.

Ackerman said he's about ready to plow his **260 acres** of corn under.

"I'd be lucky to get a couple hundred bushels out of this. You can't hardly feed a herd of cattle on that," he said.

In a normal year, Ackerman said, he would get almost 40,000 bushels.

Unable to adequately feed his **280 head** of cattle, Ackerman, like many of his neighbors, says he's ready to sell off all but a few animals, **which he will keep for family use. His daughter, for instance, is raising one of the animals for the county fair.**

Framingham and its two neighboring counties, Chatham and Prescott, have **112,163** head of cattle, the state Agriculture Department says. Were all those to hit the market within a few weeks, prices could drop to below 30 cents a pound, said Mary Holman, an agricultural economist at State University.

"The last time this happened—1962—it took 10 years for the area to recover," she said.

However, don't expect steak to get much cheaper, said Jim Abbott of the National Cattlemen's Association. The cattle in this area still represent only about a quarter of the state's production, according to Agriculture Department statistics. Nationwide, more than 14 million cattle were held in feedlots for slaughter this year, according to the National Agricultural Statistics Service Web site.

Growing conditions are normal in most of the country, the agency says.

Area farmers say that if it doesn't rain at least an inch in the next week, they will start the sales.

"I don't know what else I'm supposed to do," Ackerman said. "I don't have enough hay to feed them through the winter, and I can't afford to buy much more."

About 300,000 bales of hay are available **from Georgia and South Carolina,** and the state Agriculture Department is trying to have them shipped in, department spokeswoman Betty Rapp said. **She did not know how much it would cost.**

But area farmers say such a shipment **would last for only about three months. Normally, hay is used to tide the animals over until the corn crop can be harvested and made ready for feed.**

the pressure. This contextual information enables "writing with authority"—for instance, the little but telling detail from Ackerman's wife that he always carries the bandanna with him, plus the reporter's observation that the bandanna is red and that it's barely 9 A.M. and the bandanna is already soaked. From that you can practically feel how hot it is.

The broadcast reporter might well have wanted to do the same, but the added time needed to shoot video and then edit the video into a package often makes that more difficult. Getting those multiple voices and details can pose a challenge for broadcasters called on to write "print style."

Notice also how the print story is very precise on where the information came from. The reporter has also sought out state and national statistics for context to help you judge how serious a problem it is. (For online distribution, we might further augment that by linking to the actual sources from which the statistics came.)

As you compare these stories, keep in mind that one is not "better" than the other—each one is created for a specific medium, with a special set of considerations and opportunities. It is the journalist's job to be aware of the strengths of each medium and work to get the material necessary to work best in each one.

PRINT WRITING

> A sentence should have a fact in it. If it doesn't, it must be there to explain something, elaborate on something or substantiate something.
>
> —Advice to contributors on South Africa's www.reporter.co.za, a now-closed citizen-journalism website

In broadcasting, if the producer and reporter decide in advance that a story will be a two-minute packaged report, there is rarely enough time to trim it significantly. In print, however, the reporter and editor are always mindful that the story slated early on for about 500 words (15 inches in a newspaper, about two screens online) could be cut to 350 words (about 10 inches) or fewer as other priorities take over. The same things can happen to a broadcast story; but once the package is edited and slated into the show, it is more likely to be bumped than completely re-edited. (That process can be different at the 24-hour cable networks or large TV newsrooms, but we're talking about the average midmarket TV operation.)

That means a print story must be written with an eye toward how it can be cut. This practice is one of the foundations of the "inverted pyramid" writing style, in which all the key information—the who, what, when, where, and how—is presented in the story's lead (print folks spell that "lede" to distinguish it from the actual word, "lead"). But it does not mean the inverted pyramid is the only—or necessarily the best—answer. Let's look at two common print writing styles: the inverted pyramid and the hourglass.

Story Forms: Inverted Pyramid

Writers have long criticized the inverted pyramid as formulaic and stifling storytelling. It is easy to make a mess of it by trying to cram everything at the top. Yet it remains one of the most efficient styles for quickly summarizing and delivering information and can be cut easily from the bottom. For online scanners primarily seeking information, it is ideal.[1]

However, the "classic" inverted pyramid is more lore than reality in most modern news writing. It has evolved in many cases to a "Christmas tree"—a series of smaller inverted pyramids, each designed to summarize a part of the story, stacked one on the other. At the bottom tip of each is a turn, something designed to engage the reader and push him or her forward to the next bit of information. It might be a pithy quote, a memorable detail, or a foreshadowing sentence.

---

[1] J. Nielsen (1996), "Inverted Pyramids in Cyberspace," http://www.useit.com/alertbox/9606.html.

This might be an older-style lead:

> *Two people, a man and a woman whom the fire chief said were apparently overcome by smoke as they tried to crawl to safety, were found dead by firefighters who needed two hours Monday to bring a fire in a west-side house at 5126 Oak Lane under control.*

That monstrosity is 48 words, but don't laugh. One of this book's authors, a former AP news editor, once was handed a 52-word lead by a writer, and it won't take long looking through microfilm of papers from the 1950s, '60s, and '70s to find similar specimens, even among those papers considered to be the most well-written.

Here's how we'd probably approach it today:

> *Two people were found dead in a west-side house Monday after a fire gutted the brick bungalow that was supposed to have been empty.*
>
> *The body of an unidentified woman was near a bedroom door in the house at 5126 Oak Lane, and an unidentified man's body was in the kitchen, Fire Chief Blake Smith said.*
>
> *"They may have been trying to crawl to safety but were quickly overcome by smoke," he said.*
>
> *The house was engulfed when firefighters arrived, Smith said. It took two hours to put out the fire, and a cause was under investigation, the chief said. According to city records, the family that had lived in the house moved out in December, he said. . . .*

The lead is actually three paragraphs long, the first inverted pyramid in the "Christmas tree." It ends with the chief's quote, which is the "turn," that little literary device that the writer hopes keeps you reading (They were trying to escape? How do we know that? Tell me more.). The second inverted pyramid begins with a paragraph that summarizes what happened and the mystery of people in a supposedly abandoned house—in essence, a sort of secondary lead. This section would probably then go on to explain details about the bodies and why it looked like they were crawling.

If there were space, there might be a third inverted pyramid detailing the firefighting and why it took so long to bring the flames under control, and so forth.

In that way, it is much like some good broadcast stories that move along in a series of info-chunks between the great sound bites that help propel the reader along at each juncture.

The Nut Graf

In the example above, the lead serves as the "nut" paragraph—the reason you are reading the story (there was a fire and two bodies, and a mystery about how they died and what started it). But we're always looking for wider meanings in stories, for that's how information becomes knowledge. The nut graf summarizes the story, tells readers why it's important to read the rest of it, and often provides a broader perspective on the news.

In the inverted pyramid, it often is the lead graf. In stories with more anecdotal leads, it may be several paragraphs into the story, just as the reader is asking, "So why is this important?" In more narrative forms, such as the hourglass (discussed below), it may mark the turn where the story moves from an inverted pyramid style into a more chronological form.

For instance, suppose there had been a series of fatal fires in the area. The writer might fashion a fourth paragraph like this: *Four fires within a mile of this one during the past two months have killed a total of nine people, including a family of four. Smith says investigators are still searching for some common thread to explain the outbreak, but he wonders if the age of the homes, many of them built in the 1920s and needing maintenance, is a factor.*

Figure 9.1 provides another example of a story that has an inverted pyramid lead but still benefits from having a nut graf not long after. If you are writing a print story that's longer than a couple of hundred words (a brief), you should expect that editors will usually look for a nut graf, ask for it, or fashion one themselves and put it in your story.

The nut graf also exists in broadcast but often is less prominent. Look back at the TV story that began this chapter. The reporter wrote: *We've had less than an inch of rain in the past month. Daytime temperatures are rarely below 100. Ears are baking on the stalks. The state's climatologist says it's a "severe drought." Ackerman says it's a disaster.*

That neatly summarizes things, but it's not really a nut graf. Compare it with the print story: *The six-county metro area has had less than an inch of rain the past month. The temperature has dropped below 100 just four days out of 30, and the state climatologist's office says the area is in a "severe drought." Dozens of area farmers like Ackerman are struggling, and if history is a guide, their troubles could spread to the area's economy.*

That paragraph not only summarizes but also gives the reader a larger reason to continue reading—the entire area economy could be jeopardized. Both the print and broadcast stories explain farther on; but while the print story tends to foreshadow what is coming with the nut graf, the broadcast story gets to it in more linear fashion.

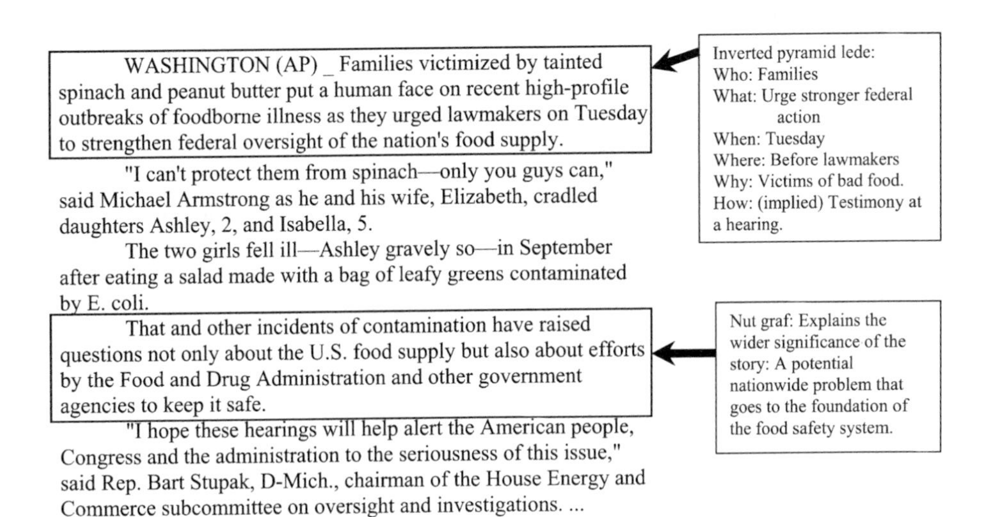
WASHINGTON (AP) _ Families victimized by tainted spinach and peanut butter put a human face on recent high-profile outbreaks of foodborne illness as they urged lawmakers on Tuesday to strengthen federal oversight of the nation's food supply.

"I can't protect them from spinach—only you guys can," said Michael Armstrong as he and his wife, Elizabeth, cradled daughters Ashley, 2, and Isabella, 5.

The two girls fell ill—Ashley gravely so—in September after eating a salad made with a bag of leafy greens contaminated by E. coli.

That and other incidents of contamination have raised questions not only about the U.S. food supply but also about efforts by the Food and Drug Administration and other government agencies to keep it safe.

"I hope these hearings will help alert the American people, Congress and the administration to the seriousness of this issue," said Rep. Bart Stupak, D-Mich., chairman of the House Energy and Commerce subcommittee on oversight and investigations. ...

Inverted pyramid lede:
Who: Families
What: Urge stronger federal action
When: Tuesday
Where: Before lawmakers
Why: Victims of bad food.
How: (implied) Testimony at a hearing.
Nut graf: Explains the wider significance of the story: A potential nationwide problem that goes to the foundation of the food safety system.

Figure 9.1 ■ Inverted pyramid story with nut graf.

Sometimes smaller "nuts" introduce specific sections. In the print story, consider the lower paragraph that tells us not to expect lower steak prices, even if all those cattle go to market. Its form is very similar to that of a nut graf.

Story Forms: The "Hourglass"

The "hourglass" combines the inverted pyramid and the more narrative, linear style of broadcast. As illustrated in figure 9.2, it starts with a summary of the story—usually

One minute, Melissa Broan was sitting down, preparing to order lunch. The next, she was dodging the 1996 Toyota Corolla that hurtled through the front of Tony's Deli on Wednesday.

Broan was one of five people slightly hurt when the car smashed the plate-glass window, ran through the 40-foot-long dining room and came to rest against the back wall of the restaurant at 225 Senate St. No one was killed.

The driver got out of the car, picked his way through the wreckage and ran, police said. He has not been identified. The car had been stolen about three hours earlier and was being chased by police – for the second time – when the accident happened.

"There was no warning, no screeching of tires or anything," Broan said. "It was just, bam! I saw this car coming at me and I just jumped."

Broan said she landed on a table nearby, which broke her fall. She suffered a gash on her leg and numerous bruises, but said she did not want to go to the hospital. Medics treated her at the scene.

"It's amazing no one was killed," she said. "I saw one man, he had to have been thrown five feet up and 15 feet across the room."

Three of the five people were taken to Mercy General Hospital where they were treated and later released, police Sgt. James Ready said.

Restaurant owner Antonio Shila estimated the damage at $120,000 and said the deli would be closed for two to three weeks.

The events that led to the car's ending up in the middle of his dining room began three hours earlier in the Kensington neighborhood when a neighborhood patrolman spotted the stolen Corolla and called in a patrol car.

The car took off when it spotted the patrol unit, beginning a chase that lasted about 20 minutes through the neighborhood's narrow, twisting streets. At times the Corolla veered across the sidewalk and through front yards, knocking over fences and lawn ornaments, to get around the traffic, Ready said.

Police cars did not follow, but enough patrol cars were in the area that they were able to pick up the trail, he said, until the driver made a particularly dangerous maneuver around a tie-up on Winsley Road, dodging an oncoming trolley in the process, and disappeared, the sergeant said.

At about 11:20, the Corolla was spotted again, this time about five blocks from Tony's ...

The typical hourglass story form. Even though this story starts with a softer lead, the first eight paragraphs form an inverted pyramid giving you the basics. You could cut the copy after that and still have the essentials of the complete story.

Then comes the "turn" (boxed), a transition paragraph that shifts the story into a more narrative, chronological form. The hourglass often is used in broadcast reports, too, as it combines the hard news and the more chronological form common to broadcast.

Figure 9.2 ■ Hourglass Story Form.

an inverted pyramid that plays out over several paragraphs—then reaches a turn, and finishes out with a longer narrative.

Sometimes the turn is a nut graf. In other cases, it is a transition phrase that also provides overall attribution for the following narrative that usually is written in a chronological style. The overall attribution allows the writer to jettison some of the sentence-by-sentence attribution that can bog down traditional print writing.

The hourglass has become more popular as "print" writers are urged to think about more narrative writing, plus it has utility for broadcast because it summarizes things and then turns to a linear form. It can be especially useful for crime stories where the narrative follows a sequence of events. Often, the anchor lead serves as the summary for the story, and the turn happens when the anchor throws it to the reporter's package.

Story Forms: The Dollar Sign

Let's go back to farmer Jack Ackerman's story and, instead of a quick 480 words, your editors want you to spend several days in that county and produce 1,500 words explaining how the drought is affecting famers not only there but also throughout a five-state region. You can't get to five states in the time allotted and there's no way to get extensive details from all five in the space available. So you'll do what good writers have done for centuries—tell the story through the experiences of a few people (Ackerman and his fellow farmers) and draw parallels to and differences from what is happening elsewhere. You can do this through some phone calls or through dispatches from other reporters on staff.

The story might start out with the same three paragraphs, but then you'd add more about how the problem extends to the entire five-state region and how thousands of farmers face ruin and so on. But that can quickly become boring, so you have to get back to Ackerman wiping his brow and ruminating about possibly plowing his fields under.

Then you might talk about crop insurance and similar things, come back to Ackerman possibly selling his cattle, talk in more depth about the effect on the multistate market, and finally finish with some pithy observation from Ackerman. If you plot it out, the story starts out going down the original center line with Ackerman, then wanders off left a bit to take in a wider perspective. Then it crosses back over that center line (Ackerman) to keep us grounded and then veers off right to talk about some wider issues before coming back to the center. Plotted in its simplest form—starting on the center line, coming back to cross it once, then finishing back on the center—it looks like a dollar sign. The *Wall Street Journal* perfected this form to tell complicated stories, so perhaps the dollar sign is appropriate. But there are also dangers in anecdotal writing:

- *The anecdote must be exactly right:* Good writers seeking to use anecdotes spend a great deal of time making sure they have one that not only illustrates what they want to show but also is something people care about. There are plenty of scenes that can be written about from our daily lives, but how many do you truly want to read about?
- *Beware the "Zimmerman"*: A common mistake is to lead with an anecdote (too often a lame one) and then never bring the person back into an otherwise turgid narrative. The "Zimmerman lead" comes from the mythical "George Zimmerman" that editors and writing teachers have used for years to illustrate

the anecdote's perils. (*George Zimmerman searched frantically for his car keys. Where could he have put them? Panic. Only then did he realize, as have millions of drivers, that he no longer needs a key to start his car.*)

- *Avoid "bookending"*: A companion mistake is throwing George back into the story at the end, almost as an afterthought. (*Zimmerman is still getting used to the keyless ignition, but is relieved. "I'll never have to worry about those stupid keys again," he said.*) "Bookending" a boring story with two halves of a lame anecdote just leaves you with a boring, lame story.

STYLE

Most print newsrooms will use the *Associated Press (AP) Stylebook* for their overall guide, but they are also likely to have their own local style manuals. Because print is "seen," while broadcast is read but rarely seen, print style is detailed and intricate.

Much of style has its history in trying to save space, and thus money. But online news distribution, where anyone from around the world can look at your stories, is forcing news organizations to reconsider some of their longstanding rules of style. For instance, the Associated Press has considered dropping the state abbreviations that generations of journalists have had to know in favor of spelling the state names out. It is doubtful, for example, that someone in India looking at your story knows what "Calif." means.

Likewise, the old guide that "print" stories largely used past tense is being rethought. When stories go online, they are more immediate, like broadcast, so why not use "says" instead of "said" more often? Even in print, some newspapers are bending on that, realizing that in today's world, the past tense can too often signal to readers that they are getting yesterday's news tomorrow.

Style Differences

A few quick pointers on differences between print and broadcast style:

1. *Spelling.* Broadcasters spell out many words to more easily read them ("12-thousand dollars"), or they may spell them phonetically or separate the letters to emphasize pronunciation ("F-B-I"). Print follows the common conventions of spelling found in the dictionary and, where there are conflicts, the stylebook. So it's "$12,000" and "FBI" or "F.B.I.," depending on local style.
2. *Numbers.* Print puts more emphasis on look, not pronunciation. Print would write "March 9" (not "9th") while a broadcaster would write "March ninth." Print tends to spell out "one" through "nine," as opposed to "one" through "eleven" for broadcast. But there are many idiosyncrasies, such as ages, percents, and millions/billions, so check the stylebook.
3. *Punctuation.* Broadcasters should follow traditional punctuation, but they sometimes use nontraditional punctuation to signal pauses or emphasis (e.g., a dash where you would not normally find one in print copy, or perhaps an ellipsis). Print style uses punctuation in traditional ways, although the trend has been toward minimizing some marks, such as commas and hyphens.

4. *Identification.* Print newsrooms often use a person's age and middle initial in identification. Whether they are always necessary or even relevant is a discussion for another text. But since print stories tend to carry more of this information than broadcast, if you plan to turn a broadcast story into one for print or online, remember to get the person's age (preferably their date of birth) and middle name or initial in your notebook.

ACCURACY

As our comparison shows, both print and broadcast try to convey an accurate picture of the world, in their own way, in the viewer's or reader's mind. This means they share the basics of good journalism: accuracy in fact, tone, and display.

Fact: This means more than just getting the names, dates, places, details, and other facts correct. It includes getting the facts of language correct—the grammar, style, usage, spelling, and punctuation. Many broadcast reporters have discovered to their chagrin when their copy was shoveled onto the Internet that their nonstandard spelling and punctuation won't work in standard written English. "Cite" means something entirely different from "sight" or "site," for instance. Simple use of commas around a person's name in a sentence, depending on how it is constructed, can signify whether he or she is an only child or has other brothers or sisters. A close reading of the *AP Stylebook* will probably give you most of what you need to know, but it doesn't hurt to have a good language and usage guide on your desk too.

Tone: Words have the same potential benefit or harm whether spoken or written. Saying someone "claims" something still casts aspersions in broadcast, print, or online. Calling someone a "murderer" (or a "suspected" or "accused murderer") still effectively convicts him or her. The ephemeral nature of broadcast news sometimes meant such issues received less attention in TV and radio newsrooms. But with the Internet, broadcasters are finding what print reporters and editors have known for a long time—written words can come back to haunt you when you least expect it. Although Internet stories can be corrected quickly, once a wrong version gets into a search engine cache, it can live forever.

Display: Accuracy in display is certainly the goal of any broadcast reporter, producer, or videographer in assembling a visual story. In print or online, the goal is similar: How to make the myriad elements on a printed or Web page work together and avoid improper juxtapositions, hard-to-follow text, and so forth. Here is one of those little checklist things for those working across media: If you are being asked to shoot stills (as well as video), try to get the shots in the camera with an eye as to how they will display on a page, not just in a video report. You may someday have a frantic designer coming to you begging for a photo that "looks" left instead of right so that it looks "into" the page from where the designer wants to put it. ("Flipping" the direction of the photo looking right so that it now looked left would be ethically dishonest.)

OTHER ISSUES

It used to be easy to delineate other issues between print and broadcast: writing style, headlines, and news cycles, for instance. But the economics of the news business and the exigencies of online are pushing aside or muting those differences in newsrooms large and small. Traditional "print" newsrooms have had to take on more broadcast characteristics, such as frequent deadlines, and broadcast newsrooms have taken on print aspects, such as getting more details in the notebook and learning to write enticing headlines.

It used to be common to say that print was different from broadcast because those reading a print story could reread it to make connections or review anything unclear. But with an audience more conditioned to scanning online, even in print every effort must be made to continually move the reader *forward*, not backward. As has often been said, the easiest thing for a reader to do is to stop reading, and making the reader backtrack in a story is a quick way to invite the reader to do something else. Print stories may not be as linear as broadcast, but they must be as easy to follow.

Headlines used to be high art on print copy desks, but now broadcasters filing online as well as community managers and editors overseeing online sites have to write them too. Even within newspaper newsrooms, writing headlines is no longer confined to the copy desk as reporters are pressed into writing their own blog items. The discussion now is whether the art of writing bright, witty headlines that tell the story accurately in limited space is dying as more headlines are written to be search engine optimized.[2]

Even the news cycle, which used to be the clear demarcation between print and broadcast, has collapsed in the push to get news online first and fast. Broadcast reporters increasingly are being called on to do short print-style stories for online, and traditional print reporters are being handed point-and-shoot cameras that can take both stills and video.

Another clear line of demarcation, the amount of editorial scrutiny a story is likely to receive in a traditional print versus a traditional broadcast newsroom, is also becoming blurred as the number of editors looking at a story has been cut drastically in many newsrooms.[3] Many writers now file stories, especially breaking news, to the Internet with much less, or no, editorial scrutiny.[4] (See more on the typical editorial process below.)

The biggest differences remaining may be in the orientation toward detail and the types of stories handled in print versus broadcast.

As the scripts at the beginning of this chapter and the ensuing discussion show, print does require more attention to detail than the average broadcast story. As long as online remains a heavily text-oriented medium, getting that detail will be important to make the story come alive in the reader's mind. This isn't to say good broadcast reporters don't also gather and present facts about a story. The power of video to show the anguish on a victim's face is not the same as providing the context and detail found in a print report.

---

[2] D. Wheeler (May 2011), "'Google Doesn't laugh': Saving Witty Headlines in the Age of SEO," *The Atlantic*, http://www.theatlantic.com/technology/archive/2011/05/google-doesnt-laugh-saving-witty-headlines-in-the-age-of-seo/238656/.

[3] A. Alexander (January 15, 2010), "Why You're Seeing More Copy-Editing Errors in The Post," *The Washington Post*, http://www.washingtonpost.com/wp-dyn/content/article/2010/01/15/AR2010011502419.html. Also J. Shafer (March 2008), "From Assembly Line to Network at the Post," *Slate*, http://www.slate.com/id/2186624/.

[4] J. Russial, "Copy Editing Not Great Priority for Online Stories," *Newspaper Research Journal* 30, no. 2 (Spring 2009): 6–15.

Whether you are doing a print-style piece for your station's Web site or working with a traditionally print newsroom, you'll probably need to augment the details and sources you normally get in your notebook for a broadcast story.

It's also a reality that TV newsrooms are not as inclined to do that in-depth look at the city budget's winners and losers unless there are good visuals to go with it. The print side, armed with a good graphics program, can produce an array of static visuals that probably won't work so well on TV but can provide a comprehensive, in-depth, interactive story online. The debate is far from settled, but the future place of newspapers is often projected to be as analytical complements to the emotional, in-the-moment newsgathering of broadcast and the Internet's ability to inundate the user with data and information.

THE PRINT NEWSROOM

Compared to other media in a typical midsize market, print-oriented newsrooms (circulations of about 50,000 to 150,000) still generally have more people, a greater division of labor, and more sets of eyes looking at a story as you can see in figure 9.3. That contrasts with a broadcast newsroom, where a handful of producers and the assignment desk all generally work together in a less-hierarchical way.

But while those broad statements generally hold true, the Internet is forcing newsrooms to rethink everything they do. As a result, broadcast and print newsrooms are less differentiated than they were.

The newspaper's focus on just a handful of daily deadlines to produce the paper is waning. As detailed in chapter 5, many newsrooms are going to a continuous news flow, where stories are posted online first and then expanded for the newspaper. Broadcast newsrooms, which traditionally have had faster news cycles because their newscasts are spread throughout the day, also are moving to continuous news flows.

The struggle for both print and broadcast is how to balance the demands of the paper or newscast, which still brings in more of the money, while adjusting to online, which continues to grow as a share of the business.

Without the luxury of just a few deadlines, and with broad cutbacks in their copy desks, many newspapers are also giving stories less scrutiny before they are posted online. This is moving closer to broadcast newsrooms, where a story might be seen by a producer or two and perhaps be read by the anchor before air, but not at the level of detail required on a newspaper copy desk. In contrast to broadcast, however, in all but the smallest traditional print newsrooms, at least two people still will see the story at a greater level of detail—the assigning editor and the copy editor—and often there will be more before it goes in the paper.

But in the quest for speed, more reporters in both print and broadcast are also filing directly online, with editors or producers looking at the story afterward. This puts new pressure on reporters, print or broadcast, to think about missing elements, poor phrasing, logical construction, factual presentation, and questions readers might have that should be answered with alacrity. Broadcast reporters whose jobs now include posting online are also being expected to learn techniques closer to those traditional in print newsrooms because, for now, online remains more of a text-oriented medium.

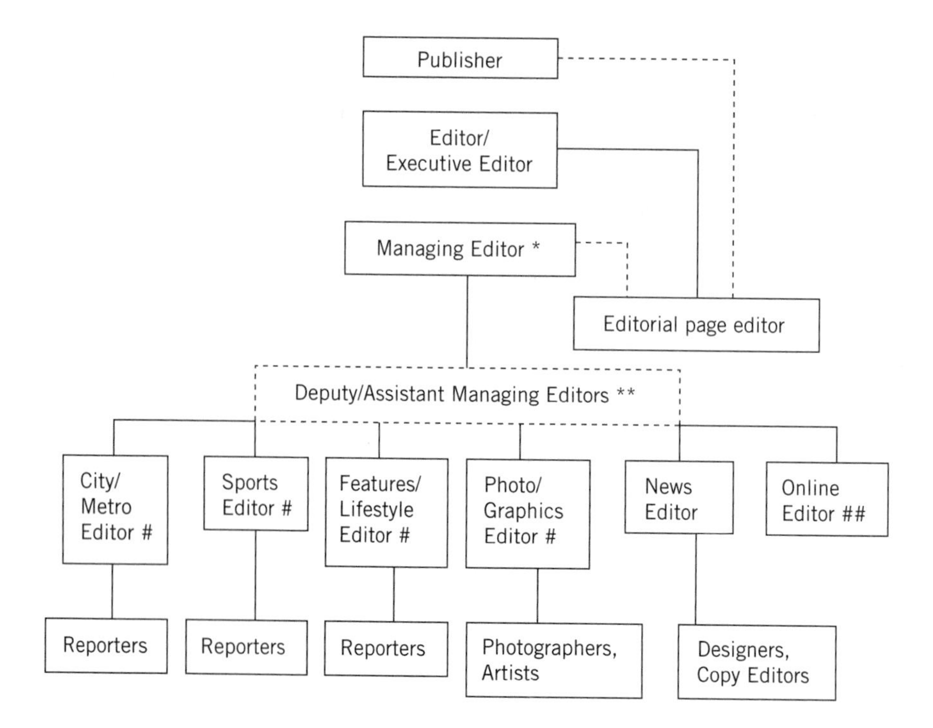

* Larger newsrooms may have multiple managing editors, such as one for news and one for administration, while smaller ones may do away with the position.
** Larger newsrooms may have many deputy and assistant managing editors responsible for various positions. For instance, some have an assistant managing editor in charge of copy desks and others have an AME in charge of "presentation," under which come designers, photographers and graphic artists.
# Each of these positions often has one or more assistant editors who work directly with reporters on developing stories and shaping copy while the overall editor handles planning, direction and administrative chores.
The online editor's position can occur under any of several other editors, as well as reporting directly to the managing editor. Sometimes the position falls under the news editor. Sometimes the position is actually that of the head of a separate subsidiary away from the newsroom.

Figure 9.3 ■ This is a typical newspaper organizational chart. Note how much larger and more complex it is than the TV newsroom organizational chart in Figure 8.3. Note that there are enough reporters to divide them by specialty (or "beat").

Box. 9.3 shows how jobs in print and broadcast newsrooms compare. Unlike broadcast newsrooms with central assignment desks, assigning editors in print newsrooms generally are divided by specialty (e.g., health, governing, public safety, business, sports) or section (Metro, Lifestyle, Sports, Business, Neighbors). In smaller newsrooms, like that seen in figure 9.4a, a reporter or freelancer is likely to deal with the editor directly in charge of that area or section; in larger ones, like that in figure 9.4b, the reporter may deal with an assistant, such as an assistant metro editor.

The managing editor leads the newsroom, and in larger ones, assistant managing editors—now called "content editors" in some newsrooms—may oversee the assigning editors and often help edit major stories and projects.

Box 9.3 Newspaper and Broadcast Roles Compared

PRINT NEWSROOM ROLE

Publisher: In charge of the newsroom, all other departments, and budgeting.

Editor/Executive Editor: Oversees the entire newsroom, including hiring, firing, and meeting budget, and in many cases serves as the lead person who determines the paper's editorials.

Managing Editor: Oversees the day-to-day operation of the newsroom.

Assigning/Line Editors: The city/metro, sports, lifestyle, online, etc., editors who run those particular desks. They may work directly with reporters to develop stories or, in larger newsrooms, have assistants who do most of that. They have great input into the content of newspaper or online sections but may have to defer to other editors and designers on the final product.

Reporters: Specialists in getting the story, they are being called on more and more to file not just a "print" story but also to blog, post on social media sites, etc.

Copy Editors: Examine stories for consistency, fact errors or missing information, libel, etc., as well as for grammar, style, punctuation, and similar requirements.

Photographers: Especially with more video on the Web, they are tending to shoot stills *and* video.

BROADCAST NEWSROOM ROLE

Station Manager: Ultimately in charge of all station operations and budgeting.

News Director: In charge of all newsroom operations, hiring, firing, and meeting budget. In stations where there is no executive producer, may oversee the day-to-day operation.

Executive Producer: Oversees the daily newsroom operations.

Newscast Producers: Similar to assigning or line editors of print but with more latitude in setting the look and feel of their newscasts. They also may write more copy ("readers," "teases," "bumpers," and "lead-ins") than print editors, but they often have less interaction with the reporter in directly shaping the story.

Assignment Editor: Works directly with reporters and videographers to plan or assign coverage. In print, part of the assigning editor's job.

Producers, Reporter/Producers: Their focus tends to be more on getting the story, video, and audio. They are generally expected to do their own word editing, often without any position equal to that of a print copy editor.

Videographers: Same as newspaper photographers but less likely to shoot any stills.

The Editing Process

A reporter or freelancer typically deals with a "line," or assigning, editor or assistant from the moment a story idea is proposed (see figure 9.5). Line editors oversee reporters, and once the story is complete, the line editor also gets the first look at it, focusing on structure and completeness. If the story is one of the major ones of the day, the managing editor or an assistant managing editor might also read it.

Depending on how the newsroom is organized, the story might also have been sent to the newsroom's online desk or copydesk (which in many newsrooms also handles online), where it is quickly checked and posted. In some newsrooms, reporters might file some stories directly, with editors looking at the stories once they are online.

Once a line editor has cleared the print version of a story, it usually goes to the copy desk, where it will be read by a copy editor whose job is to serve as a surrogate

(A)

(B)

Figure 9.4 ■ These two figures show the contrast between a small (A) and a large (B) newspaper newsroom. Note that the general structure of these newsrooms is similar to the TV newsroom illustrated in chapter 8—cubicles with telephones, computers, and centralized printing.

for the reader. A copy editor is supposed to bring a detached eye to spot logical and potential legal problems in the story and to anticipate readers' questions and make sure they are answered. Style, grammar, and other technical details are also the copy editor's specialty, as are writing headlines and, in some cases, photo captions. The copy editor may send questions back to the line editor or may ask the reporter directly (and since copy editors tend to work nights, this is the source of the infamous 9 or 10 P.M. call to a reporter that begins something like, "Hi. Jane on the copy desk. I have a couple of questions...").

Once the copy editor finishes the story (including the headline, which in print is based on the space allowed in the page design, and online is determined by the

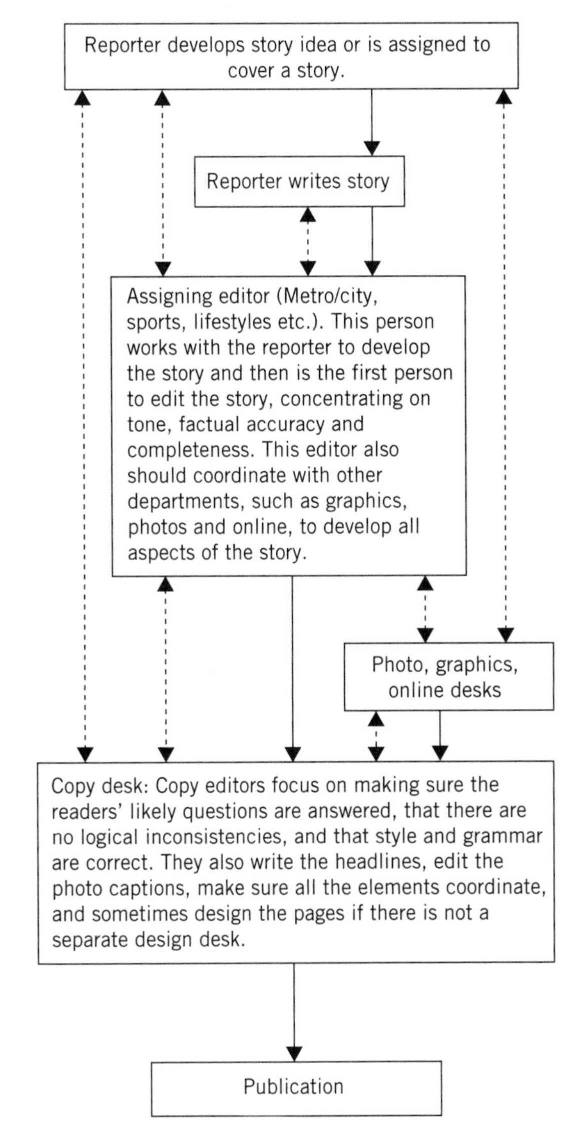

Figure 9.5 ■ A print story is processed by many people once a reporter has finished writing it. Note that it may be shortened at many of these stages, but it is almost never lengthened. Dashed arrows are conversations; solid arrows are story flow.

requirements of search engine optimization), the work may then be reviewed by a supervisor (the "slot"), who may make or request further changes. In some cases, yet more changes can be suggested or ordered by the news editor (sometimes now called the "content editor"), who is in charge of getting the pages produced and often supervising the paper's designers and copy desks. Finally, even once the story is laid out on a page, that page is "proofed." While major changes are not supposed to be made, any glaring errors or inconsistencies should be addressed at that time. Increasingly, and especially in media chains, copy editing is being centralized in a few locations, with each "hub" handling numerous newsrooms.[5] This is a controversial shift, but it means you might have to deal with questions from a copy editor far away and with little knowledge of the local scene.[6] (Freelance writers for many magazines have dealt with this for years, fielding the intensive questions of a fact-checker from afar.) Copy editors are gaining new skills and desks are evolving in order to better deal with stories filed to the Internet. Editing standards will change to meet the needs of the evolving media audience.

SUMMARY

This chapter provides an overview of how newspaper operations typically work. They tend to have built into their workflows more checks on a story than in broadcast newsrooms. As these traditional print organizations embrace convergence, some elements are changing, but a broadcast reporter working with a print partner or even filing a print-style story online should be familiar with the level of detail the form typically requires. As long as online remains largely text-based, the broadcaster also needs to be comfortable with the style differences of print.

It is vital for modern journalists to understand and take advantage of the strengths of producing print-style content if they want to truly be able to work across media. By understanding and applying the strengths of each medium, a reporter gains the ability to tell a more complete story, which provides a greater service to the public and demonstrates a wider range of skills to potential employers.

EXERCISES

1. Look at your local newspaper either in print or online. Can you find stories written in the inverted pyramid style? In the hourglass style? What type of story (harder news or feature) tends to be written in each style? Do you see any other styles?
2. Record a local evening newscast, then look at the local paper (either the print version or online if the paper just dumps its print stories online) and find two stories covered by both (avoid wire service stories, where each newsroom is likely to get the same or similar versions). What kind of differences do you notice in things such as names, titles, attribution, and other details? (For broadcast, you might want to pay attention to the "lower third," where people's names and titles briefly appear during the story.)

---

[5] D. Sullivan (July 2010), "Copy Editing, a Hub-Bub from Gannett," http://davisullblog.blogspot.com/2010/07/copy-editing-hub-bub-from-gannett.html.

[6] T. Tomlinson (December 2010), "Bagpipes for the Copy Desk," *Tommy's Table blog, The Charlotte Observer*, http://ttomlinson.blogspot.com/2010/12/bagpipes-for-copy-desk.html.

3. Looking at those same stories, how is the lead handled differently in print versus broadcast? Can you find a nut graf in either one?
4. Go on the TV station's and newspaper's websites and compare how those same stories are written.
5. Find the "Contact Us," "Staff," or similar links on the local newspaper and TV station Web sites. Try to find the list of reporters and editors for the newspaper and of anchors and other staff for the station. Many stations list only their on-air talent, but even if you doubled that number to include producers and other staff, how does it compare with the newspaper? Does either list include positions you can identify as working specifically for the newspaper or TV station's website? How do the staffs compare?
6. Find a local news blogging site or an individual blogger who covers the community. Did he or she choose any of the same stories? What were the differences in coverage and writing?

CHAPTER 10

ONLINE NEWS

The Internet provides one of the most incredible opportunities for journalists since the introduction of television news. You can deliver not only the same text, pictures, audio, and video that have traditionally been distributed through newspapers, radio stations, or television stations but also new types of interactive content that respond to user input or to input from the user's environment. These new types of content include:

- *Hyperlinks,* which allow users to immediately get more information on any story component or to plot their own paths through story elements.
- *True multimedia,* which combines video, audio, text, graphics, photos, and other elements powered by dynamic databases that display elements based on user input or even recombine elements into what is called a "mashup." This is distinguished from simply delivering typical broadcast or print content through what effectively are separate digital channels or websites.
- *Geolocative,* which uses global positioning or other sensors to detect a user's location and tailor or suggest content based on that location.
- *Recommendational,* which tailors content or recommends other elements based on information the user provides or on the user's interactive behavior that includes searching, viewing, and clicking through links.
- *Data visualizations,* which take vast quantities of information and reduce them to easier-to-understand graphical representations, often changing based on user input or additional time-series data.
- *Archives* of previous content, including news, photos, features, and editorials.

And, of course, there could be combinations of types. For instance, a motorist who subscribed to your newsroom's driving dangers information system might be alerted to an upcoming dangerous pothole when his or her mobile device, equipped with positioning sensors, automatically and periodically queried the database you uploaded with geocoded information from the city road department. The database might also be augmented by other drivers who, having run into the pothole, file a report on their mobile devices that automatically transmit the geolocative information with the report.

Meanwhile, your computers build a Web page with a map where people can search for the worst potholes. And you are using all this information combined with traditional journalistic methods to create a series of stories and other multimedia elements, especially video and audio, detailing how the city's streets are crumbling because there is little money to repair them. This series can include links to stories in your digital archives about how the city was warned five years ago this would be a problem if money was not budgeted.

Besides allowing access to and distribution of these new kinds of content, the Internet does not have time and space limitations that constrain traditional media. The news hole of a newspaper has always been limited by the amount of advertising space sold and the press capacity. Radio and television newscasts are always assigned a fixed length, regardless of the amount of news (except during rare and extreme events, such as 9/11).

Conversely, there is virtually no limit to the number of words you can use in an Internet story or to the amount of audio or video that might be used to tell the story. The practical limit thus becomes a trade-off between the resources the news staff wants to devote to a story and the amount of time individual audience members are willing to devote to consuming it.

The Internet also is a distribution system that serves content to a variety of media, including websites, mobile apps, social media, and email—just to name the most common. This chapter focuses on websites as the delivery vehicle, with later chapters addressing social media, apps, and other technologies. All these forms use interactivity to varying degrees, along with traditional text, video, audio, and images, to get news to the public. But for now, websites are the most ubiquitous way to deliver content over the Internet.

In addition to content, a journalist must consider audiences, technical issues, and ethics to better understand the context of Internet journalism. These factors will then be applied to the discussion of stories and information, including both traditional forms and the new content types listed above.

It is tempting to begin this discussion by exploring these new content types and the Internet's immediacy. But the continuing rapid digital evolution will generate additional opportunities as well. You'll be better able to take advantage of these new capabilities if you start with an understanding of the Internet's fundamentals. The most fundamental consideration of any medium is the audience.

AUDIENCE CONSIDERATIONS

The nature of the audience and its members' wants and demands are the most basic things that must be addressed when delivering news over the Internet. In many cases, the people visiting your website for news may be the same as those reading your newspaper or watching your television newscast. The fastest-growing group is made up of people who get news from only online sources. They are also likely to be younger, yet also more affluent.

In addition to considering who will be using your website as a source of news, you need to consider where and when they will be accessing the news, as well as how much depth you need to provide.

WHERE AND WHEN THE PUBLIC ACCESSES NEWS ON THE INTERNET

One of the Internet's advantages over traditional media is that the public can access news from your site almost any time of day or night. Because of this advantage, early website editors tended to update their sites whenever new information or new stories became available.

But human beings are truly creatures of habit. User studies reaffirm that Internet news is consumed much the same as other media. So a person who checks your site for the latest news at noon today is likely to visit your site at the same time tomorrow. Thus, with the exception of breaking news, it may be preferred to update on a regular schedule. Developing such a routine allows people to build reading patterns around the schedule you use to update pages. It also allows you to set routines within the newsroom and run the operation more efficiently.

Breaking news is different and must be posted online as quickly as possible. People who visit your site regularly will be looking to you first when something noteworthy happens. Depending upon the story's importance, it can also be posted in pieces, starting with a headline or one-paragraph summary and then adding information as you gather and verify it. In this respect, breaking news becomes a "flow" that builds over time rather than a single story that must be completed and packaged before anyone can read it. In the competitive news landscape, the *only* thing more important than being fast is being accurate.

As illustrated in figure 10.1, the increasing availability of wireless networking allows anyone with a laptop or other mobile device to access your site from a variety of locations, including airports, parks, offices, homes, restaurants, bookstores, libraries, and schools. Excessive noise is usually not tolerated at many of these locations. Therefore, take care when designing the site to avoid, for example, audio that starts as soon as a page is opened. Users should always have control over the playback of any form of audio and video so that they can avoid embarrassing themselves or disrupting others.

The key point to underscore is that the time and place that information is accessed from your website will vary by person, by type of story, by importance of the news story, and so on. As discussed later in this chapter, one major advantage of distributing news over the Internet is that you have an exact measure for each story (or group of stories) of when and where people accessed the story and how long they spent with it.

Need for Depth

The manner in which Web pages are created, stored, linked, and transmitted allows an almost unlimited amount of information to be relayed for any story. From the newsroom perspective, the only limitation might seem to be the amount of time a reporting team

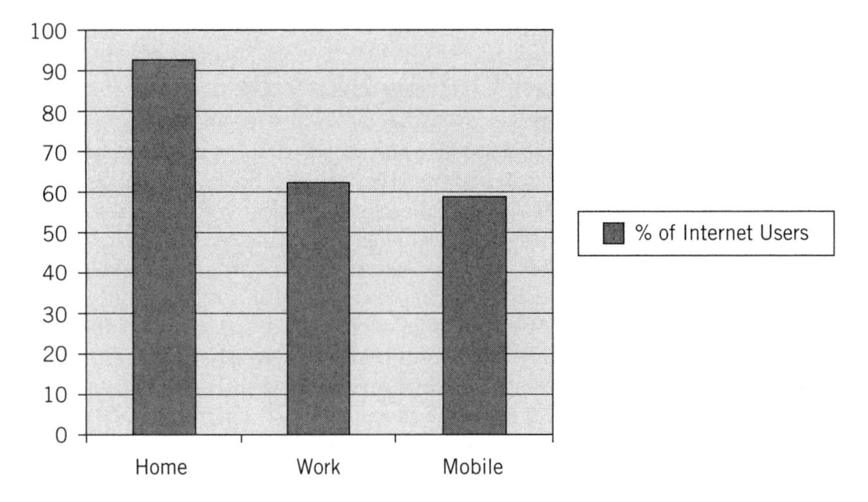

Figure 10.1 ■ Internet Access Locations
One thing that makes the Internet different from other media is the wide range of places where people access it. Only radio is more pervasive, and devices that allow mobile Internet access are becoming more prevalent each month. (Source: Pew Internet & American Life Project Surveys, 2008-2010.)

is willing to invest in writing stories; creating graphics, databases, or other interactive elements; or uploading photographs, video, or audio.

But there is a more important limitation: the amount of time your users want to spend reading a story. (Consider Tom Klipstine's suggestion in box 10.1 that stories on the Internet should be shorter than those published in print.) Stories on arcane topics such as land use zoning ordinances need background information and context, but the depth of coverage must be proportional to the number of times the information is accessed by the public. As discussed later in this chapter, news organizations now can know how many times every element in a story is accessed—every photograph, every sidebar, every database, and, of course, every piece of the story itself.

You will have to consistently decide how much attention to pay to these measures. It is tempting to look at the stories, photos, and sidebars that get the greatest number of page views and conclude that more stories and related information of this type should be provided because that's what people have demonstrated they want to see. On the other hand, a basic principle of journalism is that the public must be given the news it needs along with the news it wants. The key question is how to balance these two, and the answer is more complicated today than ever because we have such accurate measures of the public's consumption of every element of a story we publish online.

TECHNICAL CONSIDERATIONS

Sharing news and information through your website is complicated by the tools you can use to share multimedia content with the public. For now, many types of content require the installation of special software on each user's computer (although changes in the specifications for HTML, the markup language that dictates how browsers display information, may standardize more of this). This is usually done through "plug-ins" that

Box 10.1 How Long Should an Online Story Be?

Research by Tom Klipstine suggests that online stories should actually be far shorter than they are. Klipstine noted that because several studies have shown users read electronic material slower than paper-based text, some 25 percent slower, electronic-based stories should contain less material for enhanced user readability and satisfaction. According to Klipstine, users today do not read electronic material word for word but skim and scan the information, searching for specific words or phrases. While newspaper stories and features can run to 500 words or more, Klipstine suggests that 200 to 250 words, or one screenful of text, may be more effective. In addition, for increased readability electronic material should be developed in a more user-friendly style, incorporating textual highlights, such as headings, bold print, bullet points, and hypertext, allowing the user to easily scan the information presented. Klipstine noted that developing electronic text is simply different from writing for a paper-based medium and, for more effective communication, the focus needs to be on the user, not the sender.

Source: T. Klipstine *Writing For The Electronic Media: Using A Receiver Based Model To Improve Communication Effectiveness.* Paper presented to Convergence and Society Conference, October 2006, Columbia, SC.

the browser calls on when it encounters a specific file type. These enable the multimedia content to be displayed inside the browser in most cases, without the computer opening a separate program.

The most common plug-in is Adobe's Flash Player. Flash allows you to build interactive graphics and animations to convey complex information and to play back video. According to Adobe, as of 2011, the Flash Player was installed on 98 percent of desktop computers in "mature markets" like the United States, Canada, the United Kingdom, France, Germany, Japan, Australia, and New Zealand.[1] One of the problems, however, is that Apple would not support Flash in the early versions of its popular iPad tablet. (Microsoft has a similar product, Silverlight, that was introduced years after Flash and remains well behind in number of users.)

Apple's QuickTime Player and Microsoft's Windows Media Player commonly handle audio (usually MP3 files) and video, which comes in various file types. There are numerous other players such as iTunes, which if installed primarily handles audio on Apple's devices; Real, which used to be one of the most popular but has dropped off; Winamp, an audio and video player for Windows machines; and VLC, an "open-source" player that handles multiple formats.

As noted, audio is pretty simple—almost all audio content is encoded these days as an MP3, and almost any player can play that format back. Video is much more

[1] http://www.adobe.com/products/player_census/flashplayer/.

complicated (the technical details are far beyond the scope of this book) and requires making some judgments about what players your audience is likely to be using. Not surprisingly, a large number of organizations choose Flash and, perhaps, one other container format that can be played by QuickTime or Windows Media. One way to make things easier for users is to insert code in the Web page that checks whether the correct plug-in is installed on the user's computer. If not, an offer to download and install the needed component is made.

Unless you are directly involved in Web development, however, those decisions are likely to have been made for you. Once that is done, the software and online interfaces used to upload audio and video files, usually for streaming, are fairly simple and intuitive.

Fully interactive Flash animations, on the other hand, usually must be created in that program, which takes some time-consuming programming skill. As often happens, however, some companies are developing tools that simplify the Flash design and scripting process, so someday creating such interactive content may become much easier.

Likewise, putting a database online through a Web page so users can interact with it usually takes some knowledge of SQL (a database language) and PHP (which controls the interactions with the database). Some things you see Web pages do (such as drop-down menus or photos that enlarge when clicked on) also require JavaScript. Don't panic! While gaining some experience in one of these (PHP/SQL or JavaScript) is admirable, it's more critical that you are aware they exist and the limitations they put on your journalism so you can discuss things with the technical experts. For instance, it would be useless to get critical information from City Hall in a database format if you didn't have someone with expertise to build the database queries. In that case, you'd be smarter to request the information be converted to a spreadsheet format that can easily be opened with programs such as Microsoft Excel. (But you would also have to remember to ask how many items are in the database. Most databases can handle huge amounts of data while spreadsheets are more limited; you might have to ask that the big file be split into pieces that your spreadsheet program can digest.)

Although this is changing with new design standards, for now the fonts you select for text, headlines, and other content must also be installed on a user's computer; otherwise, the browser will select a substitute font that may look very different from what you intended. Displaying type in a nonstandard font usually means converting the text to a graphic file—essentially a picture–that is inserted into the Web page by the browser. Many newspapers, for example, do this with their mastheads. But graphic files are generally larger and take longer to transmit and display.

Web pages may also display differently on different types of computer operating systems So if you are designing a site, you should check to see how it looks and behaves on several computers (usually Mac and Windows operating systems, although the Linux operating system is also used by some), using operating systems and in different browsers as well.

Mobile devices present yet another challenge. Because the displays are so much smaller than regular computer screens, many news organizations create special pages formatted for readability on the small screen. A new development is the application, or "app," designed specifically for mobile devices and discussed in chapter 13.

Just because more and more people in the United States (and other developed countries) have high-speed Internet connections doesn't mean you can move huge files to their browsers. Plus, about a third of online users still have slower dial-up. You have more control over the file size of photos and graphics than any other element.

When preparing a photo or graphic for a Web page, you can reduce the file size by reducing the image to 72 dpi (dots per inch, the optimum resolution for display on a computer screen). Since most images are generated with a higher resolution (as high as 300 dpi) to facilitate print quality, reducing that will reduce the file size and result in a page that loads more quickly.

AESTHETIC CONSIDERATIONS

It is a Western convention that we read text from left to right. If you find yourself dealing across cultures or in other languages, keep in mind that some culturesread right to left or top to bottom. In addition, some Eastern cultures lean toward swirls and waves as opposed to straight and rigid lines. And even among individuals, color can alter the perception of a website. Some people prefer earth tones, while others like bright primary colors.

Some research in video aesthetics suggests that Westerners scan pages in the shape of a "Z," starting from the upper left, then moving to the upper right, then lower left to lower right. Other eye-tracking research shows that people tend to read most online pages first across the top and then by scanning down the left "rail" (where the navigation is on many sites), occasionally darting over to the right until they see something to click on. This is called the "F" heatmap or pattern, although it has been criticized as applying more to text-heavy pages than those with more graphics and focal points.[2]

Common to both is that layouts should include the most important information (headlines, menu bars, etc.) across the top of the page, with the least important information displayed at the bottom right.

Many of the basic considerations used for print page layouts are also relevant to Web pages. Empty sections of a Web page are similar to "white space" in a print publication, attracting attention to the information in the center of the empty space. Only a few fonts should be used throughout a website, with particular fonts reserved for headlines, body copy, sidebars, and other items, and they should be limited to those commonly available on most computers.

Color is a powerful tool to use in Web design, but its overuse can be worse than using no color at all. As with fonts, a limited palette of colors should be chosen for a website, with a preference for those that reinforce the news organization's logo or branding. When used sparingly, color is a powerful tool for drawing attention to specific content.

ETHICAL CONSIDERATIONS

The strengths of the Internet can also become great weaknesses for news organizations. The most important ethical considerations regarding Internet news content are

[2] S. Bradley (February 7, 2011), "3 Design Layouts: Gutenberg Diagram, Z-Pattern, and F-Pattern," retrieved from http://www.vanseodesign.com/web-design/3-design-layouts/.

(1) plagiarism in the form of unauthorized republishing of someone else's content; and (2) accuracy and verifiability of information derived from Web sources.

Plagiarism Online

Online, there is the ever-present temptation to copy material without giving proper credit. It takes only a moment to copy a picture or paragraph from another site; the critical decisions are how much rewriting or editing is needed before the material can be inserted, whether to credit the site, and whether to simply insert a link to the original material. Some of these decisions can seem complicated, but the resolution of these ethical dilemmas is actually comparatively simple: If the content is good enough to use, the source of the content deserves credit. For short excerpts (such as a phrase or a sentence or two), most problems will be avoided by inserting quotation marks, citations, or hyperlinks. Longer excerpts of text and all photographs and graphics should be used only with permission granted by the original site. Otherwise, as noted in chapter 4, consider linking to the photo or information rather than "stealing" it.

Some organizations are obtaining copyright assignments from publishers and then aggressively suing websites that post that copyrighted content without permission.[3] (While many of those suits have been dismissed on technical issues, there is no reason to think some publishers won't look for new ways to pursue such aggressive tactics.) The Associated Press has also developed a system that can put electronic markers in stories and then track how and where they are used, and it has worked with a company that can track misuse of its stories on other sites.[4]

The first 20 years of general public access to the Internet were notable for the widespread movement toward free content. But many organizations are now rethinking that (see chapter 14 for a deeper discussion), and as more move their content behind paywalls, you can also expect they will be more aggressive in pursuing those who violate their copyrights.

Accuracy of Web Sources

As mentioned in other chapters, the Internet makes it much easier to find sources. One way is through websites such as Zabasearch.com, which searches various telephone listings and other databases. You can also use reverse telephone directories. A second means is to look into archives of news stories and legal documents through services such as LexisNexis and NewsBank. These types of services can be searched and charged as needed and no longer require expensive annual subscriptions. A third option is to access online compilations of information, such as Google Scholar, Google's specialized search tool of scholarly articles, or Wikipedia. (But be careful: Wikipedia can be a good place to find sources of information, but its articles are sometimes full of errors.)

---

[3] S. Green (May 6, 2011), "Despite Setbacks, Righthaven Forges Ahead with New Copyright Lawsuits," retrieved from http://www.vegasinc.com/news/2011/may/06/despite-setbacks-righthaven-forges-ahead-new-copyr/.

[4] M. Taylor (August 3, 2009), "How the AP's News Registry Will (and Won't) Work," retrieved from http://www.poynter.org/how-tos/digital-strategies/e-media-tidbits/97578/how-aps-news-registry-will-and-wont-work/.

Finally, there is an ever-changing and improving array of search engines. Box 10.2 provides a useful list of sites that can help you evaluate information found online.

But just as Alice easily slid down the rabbit hole into Wonderland, so you too can slide into the wonderland of the Internet. Time better spent talking and interacting with people can be crowded out with endless Web searches and links to other links. Even electronic interviewing (sending questions via email) is a poor substitute. You can't truth-test a computer by listening to the tremor in a voice or watching the nonverbal cues that a good interviewer will use to size up a source and the veracity of the source's information.

The Internet offers an opportunity for anonymity, and some sources may seek to hide behind fake names or email addresses or spoofed websites that prevent you from knowing who they are. These sources should be treated with skepticism—one of your jobs as a reporter is to develop trusted sources so you can verify information before it is published. This also means not quoting unsubstantiated or anonymously sourced information from blogs, email, and personal Web pages.

Box 10.2 Checking Online Information

There is a lot of bad information online, but there also is a lot of good information about how to evaluate what you find. Here are some resources:

University of California–Berkeley Library

Evaluating Web Pages: Techniques to Apply and Questions to Ask, http://www.lib.berkeley.edu/TeachingLib/Guides/Internet/Evaluate.html. An excellent five-point guide to things such as what the Web address (URL) can tell you and how to find other information about the page's author.

Johns Hopkins University Library

Evaluating Information Found on the Internet, by Elizabeth E. Kirk, http://guides.library.jhu.edu/evaluatinginformation. Covers many of the same points as Berkeley's page but with a little different approach. Also talks about how the ranking on a search engine page may not be an indicator of quality.

Ithaca College

John R. Henderson's "A Guide to Critical Thinking about What You See on the Web," http://www.ithaca.edu/library/training/think.html. This site includes an excellent "quiz" on women and AIDS sites that starkly illustrates differing quality and why search engines can lead you astray.

Cornell University

Evaluating Web Sites: Criteria and Tools, http://olinuris.library.cornell.edu/ref/research/webeval.html. This site has links to the above sites and to many others.

Health Information

The reliability of online health information can be especially troubling. The National Institutes of Health has an extensive guide to evaluating such information at http://www.nlm.nih.gov/medlineplus/evaluatinghealthinformation.html.

The basic standards of verifying information and sources are the same, no matter what the journalism platform. But because you don't have those nonverbal cues, you have to develop skills for verifying online information: When was the page updated? Is the website's suffix (.gov, .org, .com, .biz, .mil, .edu, .info, for instance) among those with a history of abuse? (For example, .com, .biz, and .info have more notorious histories as homes for scam artists.) Does the organization behind the page provide complete contact information online, including names, phone numbers, and a street address, not just a post office box? Does the information match up with a search of the online "Whois" databases of those who register websites? (This means of verification is not infallible as more registration services allow the cloaking of identifying information, but it still is a good check.) Above all, does the information violate two of the journalist's key questions: How do we know this? Does this make sense? As discussed in box 10.3, an editor usually asks even more questions before accepting a story.

Jonathan Dube, publisher of CyberJournalist.net, has led online news efforts at MSNBC, the Canadian Broadcasting Corp., ABC, and AOL. He lists five criteria for judging an online source.

1. *Authority.* Who wrote it, and what are their credentials? Who published it? What affiliations (if any) are there?
2. *Objectivity.* What are the biases (and are they expressed), and again, are there any affiliations (sponsors) that might create bias?
3. *Timeliness.* Is it an old site, out of date, or has it been recently updated?
4. *Sourcing.* What sources are quoted, cited, and/or presented? Are they reliable?
5. *Verification.* Can you find at least one other reputable source that provides the same information?[5]

At times, however, the Internet can be a valuable source on its own. For instance, let's say you check the railroad company's site after the train wreck discussed in chapter 1, and it has a statement boasting about the company's safety record. You probably want to save an image of that page (a list of useful tools for doing this is at http://freenuts.com/save-web-pages-for-reading-later/). If you come back to the railroad's site and that page is gone, that in itself might be a story; and you will have an earlier copy of the site as evidence.

The Hidden Web

A vast part of the Internet is hidden from search engines or difficult for them to reach but is filled with treasures for a journalist: databases and Web pages that for numerous reasons are not easily indexed by search engines. It has come to be called the "hidden," "deep," or "invisible" Web, and experts say it makes up a significant portion of the digital information out there, even though estimating its true dimensions seems impossible.

A website or page might be hidden from search engines for several reasons, such as being password-protected. It might be a "dynamic" page generated from a database with a search engine–unfriendly URL consisting mostly of letters and numbers, or it might be a page that is not generated until a person puts information into a form. It might also

[5] J. Dube (July 27, 2002), "Internet IQ for Journalists," retrieved from http://www.poynter.org/column.asp?id=32&aid=3086.

Box 10.3 Six Basic Questions for Editors

Editors should ask six basic questions about every element that goes in their publications, no matter what the medium. The first three—*Who cares? So what? What does it mean?*—deal primarily with thinking about your readers. But the last three are valuable in evaluating any kind of information, especially that from the Internet:

- *Do I understand what is being said?* Don't rationalize past this. Just because it is on some fancy website and sounds erudite doesn't mean it's any good. If you can't understand it, how can you evaluate it? And how will your readers understand it?
- *How do we know this?* "We found it on the Web" is not a good answer. What do you *know* about the source—and its sources? Have you done any of your own reporting? This is why many news sites were embarrassed when they relayed bad information in 2007 that Democratic presidential candidate John Edwards was suspending his campaign after his wife announced her cancer had returned.
- *Does this make sense?* Many of our embarrassments can be traced to failing to ask this simple question. Sometimes things don't make sense initially, and good journalism eventually does make sense of them. But more often than not, if it doesn't make sense, it's nonsense. The life experiences of you and those around you—and common sense—can be your best defense.

Source: D. Fisher (2002). "Six Questions for Editors," *Common Sense Journalism*. Retrieved Oct. 30, 2007, from http://www.jour.sc.edu/news/csj/CSJ01Feb02.htm.

be a non-HTML resource, such as a PDF document, or the site's owner might be blocking search engine "spiders" from indexing the site. (Search engines generally respect these requests and do not try to force their way in.) Search engines have been improving and are discovering and indexing more of the Web. PDF documents, for instance, now routinely show up in many searches, as do more databases. But there still is hidden gold out there, and one of the best places to go for help in how to search for them is run by Marcus Zillman, who puts out periodic papers with long lists of resources.[6]

Databases can be among the most valuable resources for journalists, but even if they are being indexed, few will show up on the front page of most search engine queries unless you take a minute to fashion the query correctly. For instance, let's say you wanted to check some background and other details in connection with the train accident mentioned earlier in this book. If you just put "train accidents" into the search engine, you'll get a lot of irrelevant stories about accidents. Even if you put in your specific location, the results probably won't be relevant because (1) you're likely to see your own story first and (2) you are looking for a way to develop a wider context.

The best strategy is to put in "railroad accidents database" (we could have used "train," but part of effective searching is thinking how the person creating the information might label it, and "railroad" is a more formal term). As you can see in figure 10.2,

---

[6] M. Zillman (2011), "Deep Web Research 2011" [PDF], retrieved from http://DeepWeb.us. Zillman's main site, the Virtual Private Library at http://virtualprivatelibrary.com/, is a cornucopia of useful resources for doing Internet research.

SELECTION: Railroad - All Railroads
All Regions
State - SOUTH CAROLINA County - All Counties
January To December, 2010

```
        TOTAL ACCIDENTS/INCIDENTS:      113  Number of fatal accidents/incidents 9  7.96%
                 Total fatalities:        9  Total nonfatal conditions:        64

Total accidents/incidents is the sum of train accidents, highway-rail incidents, and other incidents.

            TOTAL TRAIN ACCIDENTS:     10      Number of fatal train accidents 0       . %
                 Total fatalities:     0       Total nonfatal conditions:        0
                       Collisions:     0        . %
                      Derailments:     6      60.00%
                  Other accidents:     4      40.00%

          ---------------------------Primary causes---------------------------
          Human factors:   30.00%      3        Track defects:         3   30.00%
      Equipment defects:   20.00%      2       Signal defects:         0      . %
   Miscellaneous causes:   20.00%      2

 Number of accidents on yard track:        5    50.00% of all train accidents.

Train accidents represent  8.85% of all reported events.

Number of train accidents involving passenger trains   0    . %

Number of train accidents that resulted in a release of hazardous material 1   10.00% of total
Number of persons evacuated    471  Number of rail cars releasing hazmat      5

A train accident is an event involving ontrack rail equipment that results in monetary damage to the equipment
and track above a certain threshold.  Lading, clearing costs, environmental damage is not included.

                      HIGHWAY-RAIL INCIDENTS                  TRESPASSING INCIDENTS(not at crossings)
Crossings:   3,927       Incidents:          50
                 Total fatalities:            4                       Total fatalities:          5
        Total nonfatal conditions:           16               Total nonfatal conditions:         7
     Number of fatal crossing incidents 4        8.00%
```

Figure 10.2 ■ Screenshot of Railroad Database
Hidden databases such as this railroad safety report can provide a wealth of background information to add depth and context to a story.

right at the top will be the Federal Railroad Administration's searchable online safety database site (http://safetydata.fra.dot.gov/officeofsafety/). From that you can generate reports on all sorts of safety information by railroad, state, region, and so on.

Even better, now on the first page of the search results, you can see there are some other agency databases. The government's watchdog arm, the Government Accountability Office, has put out a critical report on a Federal Transit Administration accident database, and someone has referred to an NTSB database, reminding you that it is the National Transportation Safety Board that actually investigates the causes of major accidents. A little refining of the search, and you can find its accident reports online (http://www.ntsb.gov/investigations/reports.html).

Some data sets are stored in spreadsheet file formats, so search for the file extension .xls on Google, for instance, using "filetype": *railroad accidents filetype:xls.* Google puts out a list of tips and what files it indexes (http://www.google.com/help/faq_filetypes.html). In Bing, another popular search engine, you use "contains" instead of "filetype." Some of these databases can be difficult to use, however, and a good place to check for insight into how others have used them is Investigative Reporters and Editors (www.ire.org).

The Internet also can be useful for tracking down people to interview. Putting "conductors union" into a search engine, for instance, will show you that the union now is part of the United Transportation Union and will give you some leads on tracking down a union official. Put in "railroad engineers union" and you will find the Brotherhood of Locomotive Engineers and Trainmen. If you need to track down a specific name and phone number for someone, Zabasearch can be an especially helpful site. If you know the wreck's approximate location, you can use a reverse directory site to allow you to find addresses so you can start doing telephone interviews while others (reporter, photographer, producer) head to the site. (And don't forget Google Maps and MapQuest can help you pinpoint the location.)

But the use of computers goes well beyond looking for background information or identifying sources. Complex quantitative information, such as budgets, standardized test scores, and even sports scores, can be input into a spreadsheet or database file to help you find patterns or identify trends. Although not every reporter needs to be expert with every database and spreadsheet program, you should be familiar enough with one or two programs so you can identify patterns in complex numerical information as well as create graphs and charts that easily communicate information to your readers.

INTERACTIVE CONTENT: ELEMENTS OF MULTIMEDIA STORYTELLING

Good multimedia storytelling starts with the same basic tools used in all journalism—good reporting. But for the modern journalist, good reporting also means recognizing when multimedia content is available and can be captured or created, edited, and integrated into the final product.

Regardless of the type of multimedia content, a reliable and authoritative source must be found. In the case of graphics or video, the content is created by the story team, but the raw information that goes into producing the graphics or video must be acquired using standard reporting techniques that include verifying content and finding multiple sources of information when possible.

Writing the Basic Story

Before writing—and even better, before beginning your reporting—the digital journalist whose mandate is online first must decide what elements will constitute the story and how they will be arranged. As mentioned in chapter 1, will the online story appear as text-only, a multimedia or video package, or a combination? How will the parts be linked? The Internet and multimedia tools allow you to organize information in such a way that individuals can pick and choose any desired elements of a story to read or watch, in whatever order they want to read or watch them. And you have to consider whether there may be a more traditional "linear" presentation as well for legacy media, such as a video package or newspaper article.

A linear story makes the user read, watch, or hear the information in the order you present it, but the user also can stop viewing at any point—usually the point at which he or she loses interest in the story. An interactive, nonlinear format, on the other hand, allows users to select which elements (text blocks, pictures, graphics, or video bites) they will see and the order in which they will see them. This interactivity results in greater attention to those individual story elements that draw the greatest interest, but users also are free to completely skip the parts that you thought were important.

The easiest thing to do for online news would be to duplicate the format of print or broadcast stories. But eye-tracking studies demonstrate that most people don't read text on a computer screen the same way they read it on paper. As was explained more extensively in box 10.1, text should be written so they can scan it, with extensive use of bullets, lists, and headings to organize information. The information must be broken into meaningful chunks, then organized to help the users put the story together in their minds. The order in which information is presented is important, as is an understanding of what users probably already know about the subject (remember, background can be provided by linking).

Sentences and paragraphs should be short and not loaded with clauses. They should be written directly—subject-verb-object—as verbs and nouns convey more meaningful information more quickly than adverbs and adjectives. As noted earlier, this blended form, which combines many of the techniques of broadcast with some of the conventions of print, has been labeled "printcast."

Readers should be able to see the parts of a story at a glance so they can choose what to read first and then follow the details of the story in the fashion that best satisfies their curiosity. How the story is organized is just as important as how well individual sentences are written.

Hyperlinking

In chapter 4 we discussed at length how linking was an important part of repurposing traditional news content for online to take advantage of the ability to provide background and context without the need to write lengthy sections as you might in a linear newspaper or broadcast story. Hyperlinks allow users to jump to another Web page or site with one click and have become an expected part of online material.

But hyperlinks also open an entirely new way to "write" a story where the reader becomes the author's collaborator, choosing various paths through the work. Some theorists have suggested hyperlinking might totally change the way we present story information online. The introduction of multimedia and interactivity allows journalists to consider how to use links to help tell stories in ways that increase user engagement and understanding.

This ability to link content across the Internet helps give "the Web" its name and one of the most powerful features for delivering news via the Internet. By its very nature, it introduces interactivity. But as with any resource, the power of the hyperlink is a function of how it is used.

One of the basic ways hyperlinking should be used is to tie all related parts of a story together. Every story element should have a clear path to get to the others, whether it is through linking back to a "shell" (as explained in chapter 5) from which the user can pursue links to other elements, or whether each element carries a full set of links that lets the user reach other parts. Too often, the user is left with one-way linking and has to use the browser's back button to return to the main story in order to reach other parts.

Perhaps returning to a previous page will become less onerous with the spread of touch screens that let a user simply swipe a finger across the screen to go backward. The architecture of those screens also is promoting more displays where multiple elements are visible and can be enlarged and made smaller by a few gestures, which could replace linking. For now, however, proper linking ties all elements together.

Another consideration is the degree to which you link to pages inside your website versus linking to other websites. Any link off your website offers the potential for losing the attention of the user to another website and, thus, losing the ability to deliver other news or advertising that supports your organization. On the other hand, some external sites may be able to provide more detailed or more authoritative information than yours—or these sites may have information that can't be found on your site at all.

It is possible to add a hyperlink to virtually any person or organization mentioned in your story so that, by clicking on the word, the user is connected to more information about that word. For example, one mention of the President of the United States could link to the President's official White House biography.

The Web is plagued with "link rot" where links no longer work because the pages they point to have been taken down, moved, or put behind a paywall, so you have to use some judgment. Government and educational sites tend to be a bit more stable, but there's no guarantee. You're unlikely to be able to monitor all your previous links for expiration, but a "report dead links" button allows the public to help you do your job.

A story peppered with hyperlinks can be distracting. Each is a momentary decision: Do I or don't I click? The editing load also increases because, as with phone numbers, all links should be checked to make sure they work. One mistype and you could take your users to a pornographic site or to one that downloads a computer virus. The most common practice seems to be to avoid links in the first paragraph but use the first mention of a term, name, or concept outside of the lead. You'll find plenty of exceptions, however.

The best words to use as links are nouns describing the destination page. Verbs invite actions, such as going to watch an animation. But links to multimedia elements and other parts of the story trail, because they are likely to require more engagement, are often put outside the text you are reading. And allowing someone to click on a thumbnail-sized image to see the full-sized version has become a widespread practice.

Setting Hyperlinks

Many content management systems or Web-filing programs have a create-link button that looks like the link in a chain or a globe with a chain link.

1. *Copy the Web address.* There is less chance of error if you go to the site you want to link to, highlight the URL (uniform resource locator) from the browser's address bar, and then electronically copy it.
2. *Highlight the text you want to be the link.* Then click on the create-link icon and a drop-down menu usually appears. Put your cursor in the line for the URL and paste what you just copied.
3. *Click OK or Submit.* The text you highlighted automatically turns into a link.

If you are not using a content management or Web-filing program, you might have to insert the link manually. Here is the coding:

```
<a href = "link URL">Text to become link</a>
```

The quote marks around the URL are important, and the URL should include the "http://" or "https://" at the beginning. If you want the link to open in a separate window, add "target" as shown here:

<a href = "link URL" target = "_blank">Text to become link</a>

The "_blank" with quotation marks is exactly what you type. Depending on how the user has set his or her browser, the links will open in new windows or new tabs. As a courtesy to users, put language at the top saying stating that links will open in new pages or tabs.

The link URL need not be a Web page on your site or elsewhere. It also can be a file path that points to any number of file types, such as an image, a document, or a video, on your servers. But remember to warn the user if it is a file type likely to start another program on the computer to view the material or if it will trigger a download box. Different styles of linking are illustrated in figures 10.3 and 10.4.

Linking is not the same as *embedding*, which you often see done with videos, such as those from YouTube, that show up on other sites. Embedding uses the <embed> and <object> tags and is beyond the scope of this discussion, but it allows you to, for instance, put the YouTube player, and not just a text link, on your site. That practice is increasingly common with multimedia elements reposted on blog sites.

Occasionally, the argument resurfaces that linking to a specific page deep in another site, called *deep linking,* is stealing. The contention is that you should not be guiding people to bypass the site's home page, which might be set up to show specific ads and other content. This practice was challenged in the late 1990s and early 2000s; but the courts generally have allowed it so long as you do not frame the linked information with ads or items that make the other site's material look as if it is your own.

Adding (True) Multimedia

When considering multimedia to tell a story—be it more traditional audio and video, or new forms, such as animations, data visualizations, or dynamic databases—you must consider the most effective format for communication. Some stories, especially breaking news involving accidents or natural disasters, are highly visual. If you are lucky enough to have a reporter on the scene or members of the public have video or audio they can share with you, that can be some of the most compelling content on your website. Even if audio and video do not exist, extensive reporting could provide material to produce animations, map mashups, and so on. On the other hand, 10 years of experience with online news has taught us there are limitations. Even if we have compelling video footage of an interview with a public figure, most people will choose to scan a text story summarizing the interview rather than sitting through the video.

The most common video format has remained the broadcast-style "package" that tells a story in an edited one- to three-minute linear presentation. One of the authors of this text has been conducting experiments measuring the impact of multimedia formats on how much people remember and how long people spend on a site. Significantly, the format that leads to the greatest recall and time spent is raw video rather than the package.[7] Although these results are preliminary, they suggest more needs to be known about story formats and what type of multimedia presentations are most effective for online news.

---

[7] J. Karlis, D. Guerazzi, and A. E. Grant, "The Effects of Video Formats in Online News: A Study of Recall and Stickiness," Paper presented to the Convergence and Society: Journalism, Sustainability, and Media Regeneration conference, October 2011, Columbia, South Carolina.

Adding multimedia content to a story requires a number of decisions:

- Will the content include video and audio only, or will it also include graphics and other text?
- Will the information be presented in a linear package or as a set of pieces, giving the user control over which parts of a story to see and in what order?
- How long should the multimedia package be? How much time will users devote to watching a multimedia presentation?

(A)

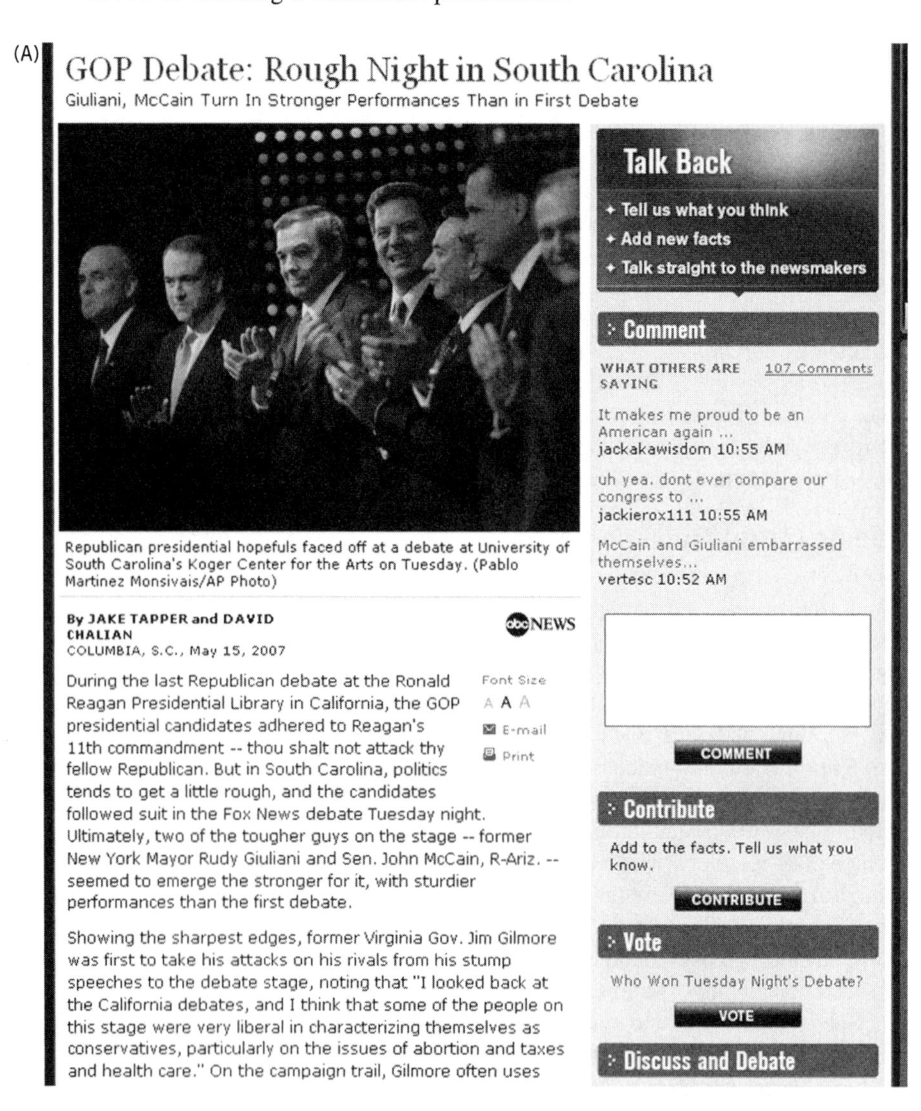

GOP Debate: Rough Night in South Carolina

Giuliani, McCain Turn In Stronger Performances Than in First Debate

Republican presidential hopefuls faced off at a debate at University of South Carolina's Koger Center for the Arts on Tuesday. (Pablo Martinez Monsivais/AP Photo)

By JAKE TAPPER and DAVID CHALIAN

abcNEWS

COLUMBIA, S.C., May 15, 2007

Font Size

A A A

E-mail

Print

During the last Republican debate at the Ronald Reagan Presidential Library in California, the GOP presidential candidates adhered to Reagan's 11th commandment -- thou shalt not attack thy fellow Republican. But in South Carolina, politics tends to get a little rough, and the candidates followed suit in the Fox News debate Tuesday night. Ultimately, two of the tougher guys on the stage -- former New York Mayor Rudy Giuliani and Sen. John McCain, R-Ariz. -- seemed to emerge the stronger for it, with sturdier performances than the first debate.

Showing the sharpest edges, former Virginia Gov. Jim Gilmore was first to take his attacks on his rivals from his stump speeches to the debate stage, noting that "I looked back at the California debates, and I think that some of the people on this stage were very liberal in characterizing themselves as conservatives, particularly on the issues of abortion and taxes and health care." On the campaign trail, Gilmore often uses

Talk Back

+ Tell us what you think

+ Add new facts

+ Talk straight to the newsmakers

Comment

WHAT OTHERS ARE SAYING

107 Comments

It makes me proud to be an American again ...
jackakawisdom 10:55 AM

uh yea. dont ever compare our congress to ...
jackierox111 10:55 AM

McCain and Giuliani embarrassed themselves...
vertesc 10:52 AM

COMMENT

Contribute

Add to the facts. Tell us what you know.

CONTRIBUTE

Vote

Who Won Tuesday Night's Debate?

VOTE

Discuss and Debate

Figure 10.3 ■ These two sites illustrate the extremes in the use of hyperlinks. **A**: This page contains almost no hyperlinks, limiting the reader to the information in the article but keeping the reader on the site. **B**: This page has a large number of hyperlinks, allowing interested readers to get as much information as they would like but also sending them to other sites.

(B) washingtonpost.com > Politics > Elections

Print This Article
E-Mail This Article

MOST VIEWED ARTICLES

Updated 1:30 a.m. ET

- Republicans Debate Their Conservative Bona Fides
- Gonzales Hospital Episode Detailed
- Bush Taps Skeptic of Buildup as 'War Czar'
- Lawmakers Find $21 a Week Doesn't Buy a Lot of Groceries
- Clinton, Obama to Back Vote to Cut Off Funding for Troops in Iraq

E-MAIL NEWSLETTERS

View a Sample and Sign Up

- **Daily Politics News & Analysis**
- **Federal Insider**
- **Breaking News Alerts**

Manage Your Newsletters

TODAY IN SLATE

What Was Gonzales Doing At Ashcroft's Sickbed?

Republicans Debate Their Conservative Bona Fides

Divisions on Display In Second Face-Off

By Michael D. Shear
Washington Post Staff Writer
Wednesday, May 16, 2007; Page A01

COLUMBIA, S.C., May 15 -- The leading Republican presidential candidates parried accusations from their rivals that they have strayed too far from their party's conservative philosophies on abortion, taxes and immigration in a debate that featured some of the most direct exchanges of the 2008 battle for the GOP nomination.

The debate included sharp jabs as the candidates pledged tax cuts and all but one reaffirmed their support for the war in Iraq. The contenders also further exposed their party's divisions over social issues, including abortion and stem cell research, on a day when the Rev. Jerry Falwell's death cast a shadow over the campaign.

The entire group appeared more relaxed and at ease than they were in their first meeting in Simi Valley, Calif., two weeks ago. And some of the most memorable moments were the lighter ones, as when former Arkansas governor Mike Huckabee joked that the Congress had "spent money like John Edwards at a beauty shop," an allusion to reports that the Democratic candidate had paid $400 for a haircut.

But the Republican candidates, who have to date reserved their toughest rhetoric for Democrats, engaged one another directly in ways they had not in the earlier debate or on the stump.

The most aggressive was former Virginia governor

Enlarge This Photo

Supporters Sen. John McCain of Arizona and former Massachusetts governor Mitt Romney greet motorists near the debate site in Columbia, S.C. (By Pablo Martinez Monsivais -- Associated Press)

RELATED STORY

Harnessed The Political Power of Evangelicals

Jerry Falwell, 73, a Southern Baptist preacher who as founder and president of the Moral Majority presided over a marriage of Christian beliefs and conservative political values -- a bond that bore prodigious fruit for the Republican Party during the past quarter-century -- died May 15 of congestive...

Figure 10.3 ■ (continued)

Carolina
Reporter & News
CAROLINA REPORTER NEWS
CAROLINA NEWS
USC, School Of Journalism and Mass Communications

Email Share Print A A A Text Size

Feature

Arcade artists bring Main Street building more life

Recommend Be the first of your friends to recommend this.

Posted: Oct 12, 2011 1:54 PM EDT
Updated: Oct 27, 2011 8:45 AM EDT

Equitable Arcade building on the National Register of Historic Places

FACEBOOK: Art Studios in the Arcade

First Thursdays on Main Street blog

Free-Times report on plans for Assembly Street

SEE: Jan Swanson at work

SEE: Suzy Shealy in her studio

The State newspaper report on plans for Assembly Street

Timeline of the Equitable Arcade building

By Sarah Peterman
Edited by Brett Weisband

Walk into the Equitable Arcade on Main Street, and it's hard to figure out the almost 100-year-old building's purpose. There are several salons, a boutique, a deli and a cobbler. The smells of incense, bacon, hair products and grandma's basement linger and mingle.

Then you turn the corner of the L-shaped building and find a row of artists' galleries lining both sides of the two-story main hall.

While much of the focus of Columbia's arts scene has been on the trendy Vista and its galleries, 15 artists have made their home about six blocks northeast in what was Columbia's first indoor shopping center. The Arcade, on the National Register of Historic Places since 1982, is unique in Columbia.

Art Studios in the Arcade, a group formed by the artists, has called the space home for about a year. The artists have participated in Open Studios and First Thursday, events that encourage people to see art in Columbia and rediscover Main Street.

Jan Swanson, who was looking for a studio for her oil paintings, discovered the Arcade because her son owns Swanson's Deli, which is in the building. She noticed the many unoccupied shops and offices and saw potential for studio space.

"We came into a building that didn't have a lot going on and helped to bring a variety of different artists in," Swanson says.

Eric Stockard, owner of S&S Art Supply three blocks north on Main Street, is glad to have more artists nearby.

"Professional artists are about 50 percent of my clientele," he says. "And having the art studios there helps make Main Street more whole. It brings a cultural aspect, not just a financial one."

Eileen Blyth, a mixed media artist, says the building inspires her.

"There's something in here that's very conducive to creating. It's got good bones," she says.

The Arcade, which wraps around the Barringer Building, was built in 1912. Terra cotta panels with urns and cherubs line the walls. A skylight illuminates the wide corridors. The building's entrances on Main and Washington streets, have identical recessed facades with marble columns.

Figure 10.4 ■ In addition to embedding hyperlinks in a story, a separate list of links like those in the left column can be posted with a story to provide readers with access to additional information.

In chapter 12 more discussion is provided on the steps needed to upload multimedia content to your website.

Since interactive multimedia elements can be complex and driven by dynamic databases, you need to first assess whether you have the technical expertise readily available. But just as important may be deciding exactly what information is needed and in what format.

For instance, in our pothole example, the reporter had to know to ask the city whether geocoordinate data existed for the potholes and make sure it was included in the database. If not, did the news organization have the resources to get it? Citywide, that would probably be a daunting task. But for a hyperlocal site covering a few neighborhoods, a few people armed with a GPS tracker might, over a few days, get all the information needed themselves.

ARCHIVES

Only a few years ago, someone who wanted to see a newspaper from last month or last year had to find a library that stored the newspapers or microfilm copies. These archives were cumbersome to search and cost newspapers for maintenance and cataloging. For broadcast content it was worse—newscast recordings were saved in an internal tape library, accessible only to staff members who knew exactly when and where to search to find an old video clip.

But now the cost of digital media storage has fallen to where any content that ever appeared on your website can be saved, along with photos, video, and other content that may have never been published. In most cases, the information is easily searchable through a title or description attached to the content (called "metadata") or, in the case of text, through searching the content itself.

Newsrooms typically limit access to nonpublished content to their own organization, but published content has become a mainstay of Internet news sites. Some companies make money by charging for access or including advertising on pages that display archived content.

The public might get to such content in multiple ways. Your site could have a keyword archive search. As discussed above, hyperlinks to archived content from newer stories can be used to provide greater context and depth for a story. External search engines such as Google, Bing, and Yahoo might send users to specific older pages based upon their search terms. Finally, some sites, such as the Internet Archive (www.archive.org), actually download and store Web content to preserve it for future generations.

These archives are important to you for three reasons:

1. They represent a new outlet for your work and a possible new source of revenue for your employer.
2. Everything you write—good and bad—will be saved somewhere for someone to look at in the future.
3. If you ever make a mistake in your reporting, a correction is not as simple as running a sentence or two the next day. To the extent that you can update online content with corrections, you should do so.

The combination of hyperlinks, multimedia, various other interactive technologies, and archives provides reporters with new tools that have the potential to revolutionize journalism. But keep in mind they will never be a substitute for good reporting.

A converged news organization that provides these materials and follows these principles will have the best chance of surviving in today's hypercompetitive news environment. Consumers more than ever want their news and information immediately, in the form they want it. If they want more information, they will seek more. Don't give them enough—or give them too much that is poorly presented—and they'll look elsewhere, perhaps to come back another day, perhaps not.

But the Internet is truly interactive, and even as the consumer has maximum choice, every page, every image, every story that is accessed and clicked through leaves a trail. This has yielded yet another new set of tools for converged journalists: Web measurement.

MEASURING WEB AUDIENCES

Just as newspapers can estimate the number of readers by looking at copies sold (and multiplying by the average number of readers per copy), and television stations can subscribe to ratings services that estimate the number of viewers for their newscasts, specific tools measure the size of Web audiences.

Unlike traditional media measurements, Internet audience size can be measured almost instantaneously. Additionally, a great deal more detail is available than for other media.

More newsrooms are using such real-time online measurement, but the ability remains to be exploited in most organizations. There is a reluctance among journalists to pay too much attention to customers' preferences for fear that celebrity news and unusual events will crowd out coverage of business and economic issues that may not be as interesting but have a much greater impact on people's lives.

While these metrics should not become the absolute measure of what stories to cover or follow up, they can provide insight that helps you meld your news judgment with the needs or wants of your audience. The servers that deliver your Web content to the public can record a great deal of information about every user, including:

- Number of pages viewed.
- Total time spent on your site.
- Average time spent on each page.
- Type of computer, operating system, and browser.
- Day and time of use.
- Where the user was when he or she looked at your page—not just at home or at the office but the specific Internet address of the computer.
- Geographical location of users.

Web servers store so much information about each visitor and visit that it is not possible to look at the raw data files and understand use patterns. But special computer programs analyze these files to create automatic, periodic reports that summarize the full range of factors regarding your website, from number of users and time spent to the most popular pages and referring sites that led someone to your website.

You need to decide how frequently to view these reports. Is weekly enough, or with breaking news do you need to know right away what pages have been visited? If you let them, these reports could end up taking most of your time. Keep in mind that they are just one of many tools that inform story selection; your news judgment is much more important.

MORE IMMEDIATE THAN BROADCAST OR PRINT

The last difference between distributing a story through the Internet and traditional media is the immediacy. Any story can be posted on your website as quickly as information is gathered, and updates can be posted as often as new information is obtained. Television news operations have the potential to be almost as immediate, but in order to do that, a station must interrupt its scheduled programming and commercial announcements. As a result, TV stations interrupt programming for only the most important breaking stories.

There is one other important difference. When a person hears about a breaking story and wants more information, he or she is increasingly likely to turn to the Internet rather than traditional media because of the wide range of sites and information available. This is especially true as tablets and smartphones become ubiquitous information appliances. As discussed earlier in the chapter, if a person visits your site regularly, he or she is more likely to visit during breaking news. Thus, it becomes more important to provide as much depth as possible for breaking news stories so that users won't be tempted to look elsewhere for details.

As noted several times in this book, however, immediacy also has its downside—less editing, more chance that rumors will be published, and more chance the information is wrong. The pressure will remain to post things more quickly; our job as journalists is to find ways to maintain the principles of truth, fact, care, and fairness in the new workflows.

SUMMARY

We are still exploring the most effective ways to use the Internet to distribute news. The first news websites simply repeated news stories found on traditional media. A newspaper's website had long stories that looked like those in print, and a TV station's website was more likely to have short broadcast scripts and video. Many still do.

But as the Internet evolves as a news medium, it is developing its own differentiating character. The most exciting aspect is that you have the opportunity to experiment with format, multimedia, and interactivity to help discover new ways to distribute news and information.

As of this writing, multimedia is the most pervasive form of new content distributed on news websites. Chapter 12 discusses production of multimedia news stories in detail.

EXERCISES

1. Compare a website for a national news organization with that of a local one. How does the content differ? How much national content is on the "local" website? How much local content is on the "national" website?
2. Compare television and newspaper websites in your community, asking the same questions about content origination as in exercise 1.
3. Choose a story from today's newspaper and rewrite it in a format that works better on the Web. Then compare your rewrite with what the newspaper put on its website. Did the paper rewrite the story or simply reprint it?

4. Repeat exercise 3, only this time include as many hyperlinks as possible. How do hyperlinks alter the news-packaging process? In what ways do they improve your story, and in what ways can hyperlinks become a distraction?
5. Analyze a local website for a television station or newspaper, looking at aesthetic and ethical issues. Make two lists: What does the site do well, and what would you do differently based upon what you've learned from this chapter?
6. Select a recent event or news story in your community. Use online search tools to find out more about persons, places, or things involved in the event. How does your new information change your view of the story? What aspects or elements do you think "traditional media" may have missed?

CHAPTER 11

SOCIAL MEDIA AND JOURNALISM

It was late in the evening of May 1, 2011, hours before U.S. President Barack Obama would announce the death of terrorist leader Osama bin Laden, and the world already was—unknowingly—getting a live account of the action leading to bin Laden's death as Navy SEALs invaded his compound in Pakistan. A Pakistani, Sohaib Athar (with the Twitter handle "ReallyVirtual"), had noticed helicopters buzzing above his home in Abbottabad (figure 11.1).

"Helicopter hovering above Abbottabad at 1AM (is a rare event)," he put onto the short-message social media service. Shortly thereafter: "A huge window shaking bang here in Abbottabad Cantt. I hope its not the start of something nasty."

A little later, Keith Urbahn, a former aide to Donald Rumsfeld when Rumsfeld was U.S. defense secretary, put this message on Twitter: "So I'm told by a reputable person they have killed Osama Bin Laden. Hot Damn." It would still be more than an hour before the president would tell the world "justice has been done," but while Athar's tweets had gone largely unnoticed, Urbahn's, especially in the echo chamber that is Washington, D.C., did not (figure 11.2). Twitter exploded with tweets and retweets.[1] Soon, the *New York Times* and U.S. TV networks were confirming that bin Laden was, indeed, dead.

[1] M. Glaser (May 2011), "Timeline of Tweets Around Death of Osama bin Laden," retrieved from http://storify.com/mediatwit/timeline-of-tweets-around-death-of-osama-bin-laden.

@ReallyVirtual
Sohaib Athar

Helicopter hovering above Abbottabad at 1AM (is a rare event).

1 May via TweetDeck

Retweeted by RodolfoHARamos and 100+ others

Figure 11.1 ■ Sohaib Athar's first tweet unknowingly alerting the world to the raid on Osama bin Laden's compound.

The virtual world soon discovered Athar as well. His Twitter followers shot up into the thousands, his phone began ringing (prompting later plaintive tweets to leave him alone), and he made this wry observation: "Uh oh, now I'm the guy who liveblogged the Osama raid without knowing it."

CHANGING JOURNALISM'S FORMULA

Digital publishing changed the underpinnings of journalism. Social media has changed its practice.

For more than a century, the journalistic formula had been almost unchanged. Something big happened and journalists got the word out, which, before broadcasting, could be a day or more delayed. They tracked down survivors, eyewitnesses, and official sources and stitched together the first draft of history. Invariably, the reports had flaws—people have faulty memories; things are embellished and spun; the quotes filtered through the journalists' reporting may have been cleaned up and not exactly what was said; and the scene, by the time the journalists arrived, might be far different from what had happened.

Days or even weeks later, journalists stepped back and tried to make sense of it all with further reporting, analysis, and commentary.

The telephone made getting the first word out easier and quicker. Broadcasting, then 24-hour cable news channels, sped up the news cycle further and brought us the quotes and pictures relatively unvarnished. As officials and even ordinary people learned to play to the camera, that authenticity diminished.

But with social media, the journalist is increasingly not the first witness to history. The "second day" story that allowed journalists to analyze and reflect upon the event is now the "second hour" story. The blogger or tweeter is just as likely to be an accidental witness and the world's first portal to what is happening in unpolished prose and graphics. The video and photos that eyewitnesses capture are as likely to be shared on Facebook or YouTube as to be on the evening news.

(A)

So I'm told by a reputable person they have killed Osama Bin Laden. Hot damn.

1 May via Twitter for BlackBerry®

Retweeted by arturart and 100+ others

(B)

@ReallyVirtual
Sohaib Athar

Uh oh, now I'm the guy who liveblogged the Osama raid without knowing it.

2 May via TweetDeck

Retweeted by inevitablygrey and 100+ others

Figure 11.2 ■ Keith Urbahn's tweet (A) bringing first word that Osama bin Laden might have been killed. Sohaib Athar's tweet (B) a few hours later when he realized he had first alerted the world to the raid on bin Laden's compound.

Stacey Higginbotham, reflecting on how the bin Laden story unfolded, has identified seven stages of how news now develops on social media:[2]

1. Excitement over being potentially first to report big news.
2. Uncertainty over whether the early word is legitimate.
3. Searching for validation. At this point, people tend to turn to traditional media, though there also are those scornful of the doubters.
4. Confirmation. "The search for meaning, data and tasteless jokes will begin in earnest."
5. Jokes, profits, and platitudes. This is when fake sites trying to profit from the event proliferate, a dangerous time for journalists.

---

[2] S. Higginbotham (May 1, 2011), "The 7 Stages of News in a Twitter and Facebook Era," retrieved from http://gigaom.com/2011/05/01/the-stages-of-news-in-a-twitter-and-facebook-era/.

6. Action. People seek more information from friends and begin to act, such as organizing relief drives or creating meet-ups. "This is where Facebook and social media really shine," Higginbotham wrote.
7. Real analysis, usually in longer-form media.

Debate will continue about how journalists are pressured by social media to speed up their reporting and, as a result, increase the chance of errors. Many said that even before the tweet storm began, they were digging heavily to confirm bin Laden's death. But clearly the journalist, having earlier lost control of the monopoly on distribution, now has lost the monopoly on observation. As Rory Clellan-Jones, a BBC reporter who blogs about how technology changes our lives, observed in the hours after the bin Laden raid by U.S. forces, "Such is the power of this network that it has become the key resource for older media trying to stay ahead of events—a journalist who does not use Twitter is now like one who abjures the mobile phone."[3]

THE TECHNOLOGY IS NEW, "SOCIAL" IS NOT

Technology has enabled instant sharing and has turned journalism into a conversation, not one-way delivery. Yet even in journalism's early days when two-way communication was not the norm, newspapers were "social" and started conversations in their communities. And many still are—just ask the publisher or editor of a small community newspaper whether people wait for the weekly edition, pass it around, and quickly make known any disagreements they have with it.

Many newspapers in the 19th century, and into the 20th, were only part of their proprietors' printing businesses. Breaking news was posted in their storefront windows for all to gather around, read, and discuss (figure 11.3). Newsboys shouted the headlines on street corners to attract a crowd, sell papers, and get the conversations started.

In broadcasting, local radio stations routinely did, and many still do, "remotes" from advertisers' stores or car lots. Aside from being an advertising vehicle, they encourage interaction and conversation, whether about the news or, more likely, the music of the day. Talk radio embodies many of those same aspects of conversation and interaction.

TV and the suburbs changed things, however. Television production equipment, by its nature, was difficult to set up and move. Going "mobile" could involve one or more tractor-trailers and, even for a local station, a small army of technicians. So most interaction meant you had to come to the TV stations' fortress-like buildings.

As suburban growth spread, the media also started leaving downtown for campuses closer to highways and surrounded by parking lots and tighter security. Major metro newspapers increasingly were unable to cover neighborhoods in the close-up, personal way that encouraged social interaction. Circulation began sliding but was masked by mergers and acquisitions that led to record profits.

This estrangement was captured presciently and succinctly in the first episode (1977) of *Lou Grant*, a TV series about a Los Angeles newspaper that captured the

---

[3] R. Clellan-Jones (May 2011), "Twitter Captures the Osama bin Laden Raid," retrieved from http://www.bbc.co.uk/blogs/thereporters/rorycellanjones/2011/05/ tweeting_the_osama_raid.html.

Figure 11.3 ■ **Brockton Photo.**
"Social" media on Christmas Eve 1940 as people look at the headlines posted in the window of the *Brockton* (Mass.) *Enterprise*. Library of Congress archives, by Jack Delano for the U.S. Office of War Information..

essence of so many newsrooms. In the episode, Grant, played by Ed Asner, arrives in the lobby of the *Los Angeles Tribune* to be hired as city editor by an old friend. But to the security guard, Grant is a nobody and is summarily ignored while the guard exchanges pleasantries with all the employees coming in and out. Once Grant demands the—rather annoyed—guard's attention and announces his business, he is given a floor pass and admonished to go straight there and nowhere else. Grant, once hired, later summons the guard and, although we never see the interaction, we can assume that since Grant was from the old school, the guard was admonished to treat the public with respect.

The newsroom was not only insulated from the public. The lucrative flow of advertising dollars allowed news organizations to create "firewalls" between those who reported the news, the editorial side, and those who brought in revenue, the business side. Journalists mistakenly thought they were safely isolated to focus on "just the news." But with the emergence of widespread digital technologies in the 1990s, many journalists began to realize with shock and horror how estranged their audiences had become. The Great Recession of the mid-2000s turned the estrangement into a rout, both by audiences and advertisers.

Yet the public's desire for "social media" never left. As noted earlier, many small town or neighborhood editors, publishers, or broadcasters say they have done relatively better economically than their larger counterparts. A 2008 ethnographic and anthropological study of young adult news users underwritten by The Associated Press found that "[t]he enlightened consumers turned news into 'units' of social currency that could be used in a variety of interpersonal situations—to look smart, connect with friends and family and even move up the socio-economic ladder."[4]

Further, the study said, when they did not find the depth they wanted behind the headlines:

> "Several participants sought help, not from the media, but from their own networks of friends, family and co-workers. Not surprisingly, sports and entertainment news was quickly shared and transmitted, checked and re-shared over varieties of media and platforms. Sharable information was the key. In this study, people were observed in constant communication with their extended social networks. Following a particular news story was in large part dependent on whether the news was worth sharing with a trusted member of the network. As one member of the study said, 'News helps me maintain relationships.' "

News organizations' failure to position themselves as social networks for their communities may have been a missed opportunity, though given the fractious nature of the business, it might have been difficult to achieve the scale necessary. Still, many were slow to adopt and adapt the available social media tools; according to one report the surge in adoption did not occur until the 2006–2008 period.[5] Looking forward, the challenge now is how you will incorporate social media into your career as a journalist.

---

[4] Associated Press (June 2008), *A new model for news: Studying the deep structure of young-adult news consumption,* retrieved from http://www.ap.org/newmodel.pdf.

[5] Bivings Group (December 2008), "The Use of the Internet by America's Largest Newspapers," retrieved from http://www.bivingsreport.com/2008/the-use-of-the-internet-by-americas-largest-newspapers-2008-edition/.

In this chapter, we'll start by defining what we mean by social media and then explore a variety of ways that you can use the concept in the practice of journalism. (You may notice "social media" is referred to in this chapter as both singular and plural. Much as "data" is now used in both forms, as a singular, "social media" refers to the overall concept; as a plural, it refers to the universe of tools and platforms that enable sharing and propagation across nodes and networks.)

DEFINING SOCIAL MEDIA

The restraints of a physical and industrial model limit mass media's "social" characteristics, but digitization encourages the social characteristics of communication to propagate across networks.

Social media can be defined a number of ways. We will use a functional model that embodies what seem to be the most common aspects:

- The ability to easily share content with individuals and networks.
- The ability to receive feedback.
- On open loop that allows others to interact with that content and feedback.

Social networks like Facebook have become the icon of social media, but they are only a subset. Most media these days have some kind of sharing function, if nothing more than a Facebook "like" or a "tweet this" button, and they have RSS feeds that can be injected into other platforms and further shared. Many also allow commenting on items. In those rudimentary ways, they fulfill the basic conditions for social media.

A social network, however, has additional key properties:

- The ability to create, upload, or remix content (that can then be shared).
- The ability to easily manage whom you connect with, the terms on which you engage with them, and the personal information you reveal to them. (Some experts also say one of the defining attributes is that those you seek to connect with can easily reciprocate.)
- The ability of others, known or unknown to you, to take the shared content, including any feedback, and send it to other nodes on the network.

Evolution of Social Media

Media started moving toward those more recent concepts of social media almost as soon as information could be digitized, but there has been an evolutionary path. Most if not all news or information sites engage in this kind of sharing, as do many sites for businesses and other nonmedia organizations.

Email

It was relatively easy to share content by forwarding a link, cutting and pasting, or attaching a copy, and those receiving it could propagate it to their contacts (thus the infamous and annoying chain letters). Feedback was also possible and at least open to those to whom the original message had been sent. Management of connections was difficult, however.

Discussion Boards or Forums

Discussion boards or forums allow people to post their views on a topic and respond to others. They were among the earliest interactive areas online, many through a service called Usenet that later became part of Google. The "groups" function of Facebook and discussion boards on LinkedIn, for instance, are similar. Forums also remain popular as technical support sites, where a person can post a question and others can answer. Some news organizations created discussion boards as part of their early online sites, but most eventually shut them down as they became infested with off-topic, incendiary, and often profane comments. Most boards were not moderated because of the amount of time and number of people involved. Section 230 of the Communications Decency Act of 1996 protects those providing such forums from legal action for others' posts.

Blogs

With the ability to create and publish content for anyone to see and to solicit comments and respond, blogs have many aspects of social media. But blogs lack the ability to control one's connections or generally cannot easily propagate the content across networks without links from others or the use of helper programs.

Crowdsourced Editing

Digg, Reddit, StumbleUpon, and others were created to share online items and let the community decide which would be perceived as most important or popular. Delicious started as a bookmark-saving service but made it easy to search the community's lists and share those you found interesting. These are not networks, but they contain communities. Any sharing to other Web nodes has to be done by linking, RSS feed, and so on.

Document, File and Video Sharing

Services like Scribd, SlideShare, Flickr, and Photobucket are dedicated to allowing easy sharing of documents, graphic presentations, or photos. YouTube, Vimeo and Blip.tv are among the most well known for video sharing. Posting items does not automatically propagate them to others' nodes. There still must be linking (or embedding of the material) on others' websites, blogs, and pages on Facebook and similar sites.

Geolocative

Services like FourSquare and Gowalla are based on the idea of sharing your location and related information. There is also an element of "gamification"—the introduction of aspects of gaming to nongame functions—because you can earn badges and other recognition as you use the services. Geolocative functions are being built into many online services, including social network.

Social Networks

As a social network, Facebook facilitates the "social" aspects of other media channels and adds utility by consolidating creation, sharing, and feedback tools with those that allow you to manage members of your social network or "graph." (While people refer to their social "networks," the more correct term is "social graph," which describes interrelationships. We will use them interchangeably, though you may find some experts insisting the term "network" be limited to describing the technology infrastructure.) Facebook also makes it easy for information to jump between network nodes because each person is a bridge to others (sometimes called "friend of a friend," or FOAF, a concept designed to make descriptions of social graphs machine-readable, eventually allowing interconnections without the need for centralized databases).

Text messaging, a one-to-one medium, led to sites allowing the sharing of messages. Twitter followed and added social networking attributes to what previously had been the closed system of text messaging. There is some debate over whether it should be called a "social network" because it does not automatically propagate content without "retweeting." Much of Twitter's power has come from an open architecture that has spawned dozens of other services to create, track, manage, and share tweets.

It is easy to focus on Twitter and Facebook (with its hundreds of millions of users). But journalists do better to recognize and capitalize on the larger issues, opportunities, and challenges social media represents.

Remember that Facebook is the technological innovation of today. Whether it's more like the telegraph (that became obsolete) or television (that continues to change) remains to be seen. Alternatives are being created, and researchers are working on ways to create computer-to-computer networks using things like FOAF. This is part of the vision by Tim Berners-Lee, often credited as founder of the World Wide Web, of a "Semantic Web," where metadata like FOAF allow machines to make inferences and connections. That kind of distributed world is likely to be a more challenging place for journalists who can now simply troll Facebook and find tremendous amounts of information on most people.

Specialized social networks already are proliferating, such as LinkedIn, which is aimed more at businesspeople, allowing them to set up discussion groups and share content. In the face of widespread criticism of Facebook's privacy policies, we are seeing a rise in services, most focused on mobile devices, to allow creation of private social networks.[6]

Facebook is trying to remain at the center and be the arbiter of much of the world's conversation. For instance, it has created a message service and a system that allows comments and responses made through the Facebook plug-in on other sites to automatically propagate on Facebook.

These developments have prompted warnings that publishers risk becoming beholden to a third-party site that does not have their best interests in mind. As one writer observed:

> *Everything that journalists are doing on Facebook today—engaging readers in conversation, soliciting sources, polling users, posting "behind the story" material—is stuff they could just as easily do on their own websites. So why are they doing it on Facebook?*
>
> *One answer is obvious: That's where the people are!*[7]

---

[6] L. Sydell (December 1, 2010), "New Networks Target Discomfort With Facebook," http://www.npr.org/2010/12/01/131700947/new-networks-target-discomfort-with-facebook.

[7] S. Rosenberg (May 3, 2011), "Why Journalists Should Think Twice About Facebook," http://www.wordyard.com/2011/05/03/why-journalists-should-think-twice-about-facebook/.

Still, media have gone social, whether in allowing—and responding to—comments, having a "share this" button, or trying to create their own community online (such as the *St. Louis Post-Dispatch*'s my.stltoday.com).

TACTICAL VS. STRATEGIC THINKING

To effectively use social media, you must determine what you are trying to accomplish and how you will get there. Social media has tactical and strategic aspects. [8] While they are related, each requires different approaches, management, and commitment.

If you are thinking tactically, for instance, you generally are thinking how to get your material in front of others. That means understanding how the community or communities you want to reach generally receive their information.

For instance, the desktop computer is giving way to the smartphone and tablet, and mobile devices require different thinking about how news and information are displayed and the speed at which it is disseminated. Mobile is built on the concept of sharing and being social (for instance, most people use text messaging to alert others about what's happening, where they will be, etc.) and the user no longer thinks about sharing or content creation as a separate function—it all becomes part of the conversation. But assuming your audience is "mobile" could be entirely wrong. Many may not have smartphones. And if a phone is "smart," what kind is it? There are two or three major operating systems.

To what extent do they use social media and which networks? What are their social graphs? Are key demographics migrating to some of the private social networks instead of spending the bulk of their time on Facebook or Twitter?

As an example, Web usability expert Jakob Nielsen says his testing shows it's a myth that college students "are enraptured by social media"; they associate Facebook with private discussions, and if they want more information about an organization they are less likely to go to its Facebook page than a search engine to find the organization's official site.[9] So for that demographic, allowing the sharing of content through Facebook by widgets on your site might be more effective than having a separate, branded Facebook page.

As the rise of digital media and networks blew apart the old monopoly media business models, we have learned that one size does not fit all, and this applies even more so to social media. It is imperative that modern journalists and publishers research their audiences as deeply as they would research a story—and keep researching, because things change quickly in the digital age.

If you just pay attention to the devices the people around you are using and simply ask them how they get various types of information, you'll get a good idea of how to reach people. Since our social views tend to be myopic, however, we should try to reach those beyond our social circle.

---

[8] Parts are adapted from D. Fisher (January 2011), "Social media: Tactical vs. strategic thinking, *Common Sense Journalism,* retrieved from http://www.jour.sc.edu/news/csj/CSJJan11.html.

[9] J. Nielsen (December 2010), "College Students on the Web," retrieved from http://www.useit.com/alertbox/students.html.

Tactical Aspects

The idea of social media is appealing to journalists, reflecting the old mass distribution model where, by seeding links to stories, those links will magically propagate across networks.

Many newsrooms now have a Facebook page, Twitter feed, or both on which they post stories and links. It's also increasingly common to have an email link, a Facebook or Twitter button, possibly a Digg or StumbleUpon button, and maybe an "Add This" or "Shareomatic" dropdown box that allows the user to post a link to dozens of sites. But pushing out news requires relatively minimal effort by the journalist. Someone who has had to post on a blog, Facebook, or Twitter—or all three—while covering a sporting event or breaking news might disagree, as might one who has had to craft a 140-character tweet about a complex story. But much of this "push" tactic is now handled by automation, such as pushing RSS feeds, discussed in chapter 13, onto Twitter and Facebook.

Using Twitter and Facebook, however, is like firing a shotgun and hoping to hit something. Because of Facebook's size, the assumption is that's where the audience is. But is your key audience there? You need things like surveys to find where your audience hangs out, tracking cookies to see where people are sharing your stories, and metrics to see where your online traffic is coming from. You also have to stay alert to shifts in user preferences. Remember, at one time Friendster and Myspace were the online gathering places (for some of your audience they still might be), and the dramatic rise of Pinterest in early 2012 shows how quickly users can embrace new platforms.

Journalists are also finding social media to be a valuable reporting tool in developing background information and finding sources. When news breaks, many newsrooms now not only routinely post it on Twitter and Facebook to gather an audience, they also commonly turn to Facebook to find the pages of those involved or, in the case of a company, to find the personal pages of key executives, or they Tweet a message asking for help in locating information.

Let's say there is a major shooting at a mall in which several people are killed or injured, including the gunman, a recent high school graduate. Before Facebook, you might have sent someone to the local high school or college to look for a yearbook picture and maybe the names of people who knew the shooter and the victims. Now, if you can find the person's Facebook page, you are likely to find pictures, you will find a list of friends, and you may even find incriminating or enlightening messages the person has posted.

So far, news media don't seem to have had many ethical qualms in using the information, but this raises ethical questions we will discuss in detail later.

Social media also can aid in locating sources. Journalists are finding that posing a question on Facebook, Twitter, or LinkedIn looking for topic experts or first-person accounts of an event can connect with people who before might have been overlooked or hard to find. Reporters might also find angles they had not thought about.

The danger is in sitting at a computer all day doing only that. Even if you are writing strictly for an online community, it's still important to make personal contact so you can gather all those nonverbal cues that come from a conversation and are important to evaluating information and seeking out truth.

Because the tools and tactics are evolving, smart journalists will take advantage of the sites (like allfacebook.com) and tutorials that can keep them abreast of new ideas.[10]

Strategic Aspects

The social media world was abuzz when, in mid-2011, the *New York Times* replaced its automated Twitter feed with two people actually deciding what to post and fashioning the tweets. For a few days, the newspaper was experimenting with crossing from the tactical side of social media to the strategic side.

But the strategic side is harder. It requires committing to a long-term engagement with your audience, and that takes planning and resources. Joy Mayer has identified three areas of engagement for journalists in social networks:[11]

- *Outreach:* finding people and then inviting them to interact.
- *Conversation:* not only talking, but also listening.
- *Collaboration:* letting your audience help you.

Newsrooms formerly walled off from their communities are learning how to re-engage the public. In many cases, without adequate management guidance and planning to allow journalists the time to handle the change, the result has been that messages are sometimes ignored or the replies are hasty and canned. The feedback loop that helps define social media is at least two-way and often is multiparticipant. One-way feedback, from audience to media (with little in return), is antiquated in the digital age. Many of the world's largest companies realize such social media conversations are critical to satisfying customers and improving their reputations. Journalism has become, at its core, a service rather than a particular product like a newspaper or broadcast (the best journalism flows across multiple media).

Bloggers steeped in the ethos of conversation understood this early on. They responded to comments, which encouraged others, and which thus made blogs more personal and helped to turn the Web into "a sort of conversational water cooler and confessional."[12] That helped make them the disruptive force they became for established media. Most newsrooms of any size now have some kind of staff blogging. Some understand the idea of conversation, but a cursory inspection shows some still have minimal engagement.

The stakes increase with a Facebook page or Twitter account. While many people posting comments on a blog remain anonymous or use pseudonyms, Facebook requires

---

[10] S. Buttry (November 23, 2010), "Entrepreneurial Journalists Need to Master Social Media," retrieved from http://stevebuttry.wordpress.com/2010/11/23/entrepreneurial-journalists-need-to-master-social-media/ and A. Rushbridger (November 19, 2010), "Why Twitter Matters for News Organisations," retrieved from http://www.guardian.co.uk/media/2010/nov/19/alan-rusbridger-twitter.

[11] As cited in M. McLellan (May 2, 2011), "Terms of Engagement," Knight Digital Media Center, retrieved from http://www.knightdigitalmediacenter.org/leadership_blog/20110502_terms_of_engagement.

[12] S. Rosenberg, *Say everything: How blogging began, what it's becoming and why it matters.* (New York: Crown, 2010), p. 12.

real identities and, as a result, the interactions are more personal. Readers who post questions expect an answer. Some news organizations have found that leaving questions unanswered on Facebook pages is a bad strategy because the readers will turn the silence into that day's posted conversation.

Managing Social Media

If you are a solo journalist, it might be easier to pick one or two social media channels and concentrate your efforts, but you will still have to budget time for it. Using email notifications of new comments or monitoring tools such as Netvibes, an RSS reader with the added ability to monitor and file your Twitter and Facebook streams, can help. In a larger organization, however, this demands effort and raises new management challenges:

Who will monitor your social media channels? How should they respond? Do you have guidelines, and if so, are they strict or do they allow the employee to exercise some judgment in dealing with dynamic situations?

Who will monitor the responses and how? Someone has to have management oversight.

Will you allow employees to have their own accounts on various services, or will you use institutional accounts? Who will keep the passwords and what protocol is in place to update them if a key employee leaves?

If employees are blogging or posting on Twitter or social networking sites, will there be any editing and will it be before or after posting? Who will monitor their posts, especially on fast-moving services such as Twitter, or will you not monitor them and just hope for the best?

Should you have rules regarding what employees are allowed to post on their personal sites? Some argue that everything a journalist does reflects on his or her employer.

And finally, what do you hope to accomplish by doing all this? How will you measure if you have been successful? If not, then what? And if so, what's the next step?

Who knew social media could have so many issues and questions?

Figure 11.4 is a form used to help news organizations that also can help structure your thinking in this area. As you fill it out, remember that the "why" for doing something need not be simply sales or profit. Gaining experience in an area or experimenting are equally noble reasons, as long as you know why you are doing it, what you hope to accomplish, and how you will measure whether it's a success.

Recent years have seen the emergence of jobs such as "social media manager." Some businesses and nonprofits have made social media and creating communities of interest a central part of their marketing. Some of the efforts have become iconic, such as the Old Spice Man of 2010. Some newsrooms have encouraged their social media managers to become deeply involved in the online community and to serve as coaches for other journalists. In others, however, the role has been merely to shovel headlines and stories onto Facebook, Twitter, and the organization's website.

Throughout the newsroom, reporters and managers must understand social media and be willing to monitor and engage with it. The time has passed for letting someone else do it or throwing something out there to see what happens.

<table>
<tr><td colspan="3">What are you proposing? (Please make any mobile component a separate project.)</td><td>Start date:

End date:</td></tr>
<tr><td colspan="4">Why should we do this (include details on target audience, if relevant)?</td></tr>
<tr><td colspan="4">What are our goals (be specific)?</td></tr>
<tr><td colspan="4">How will we measure those goals (be specific)?</td></tr>
<tr><td colspan="2">What will be considered success?</td><td colspan="2">Not a success?</td></tr>
<tr><td colspan="2">If successful, what will be the follow-up?</td><td colspan="2">If not successful, what do we do?</td></tr>
<tr><td>Who will manage?</td><td>When progress reports due?</td><td colspan="2">Estimated total cost (provide time frame). Please attach a detailed budget.</td></tr>
<tr><td colspan="2">If monitoring is necessary, who will monitor and how?</td><td>In-house resources needed (attach sheet, if necessary)</td><td>Outide resources needed (include any software, shareware or freeware; attach sheet, if necessary)</td></tr>
<tr><td colspan="2">Do we need a separate URL? yes no</td><td colspan="2">If so. what name do you propose?</td></tr>
<tr><td colspan="2">(Circle one)Will we use a:
Resource a/c (companywide logon and p/w)
Personal a/c Both (please detail):</td><td colspan="2">If a resource a/c, who controls the master logon?</td></tr>
<tr><td colspan="4">If a resource a/c, how will security be maintained (when staffers leave, etc.) and who is in charge of that?</td></tr>
<tr><td colspan="2">Submitted by:</td><td>Phone:</td><td>e-mail:</td></tr>
</table>

Figure 11.4 ■ Project evaluation form
This form can help you cover all the things that need to be considered in proposing a digital project.

SOCIAL MEDIA TOOLS AND PRACTICES

Social media applications are constantly being developed. Twitter, for instance, created few tools of its own, but opened its system to developers who quickly created several utilities that moved beyond Twitter's basic functionality. Facebook has developed an extensive guide to plug-ins and apps as well as its application programming interface (API).

There are good lists of Twitter tools online,[13] and searching for "Twitter tools" or "Facebook Strategies" will find new ones that seem to pop up weekly. But we can talk about some specific aspects of social media and the best ways to use them.

Blogging

The "granddaddy" of social media still has some vitality, though there are questions about its continued usefulness as a mass publishing platform.[14] But journalists still find it useful as a personal publishing platform. Sports journalists, for instance, say blogging has dramatically increased their engagement with readers.[15] Some blogging programs also can be used to create entire websites.

There is a more extensive discussion of blogging in chapter 4, but in terms of social media, the three key concepts are:

Regularity: You don't have to post every day, but if you have a community of followers, they've come to expect a regular dose of your wit or wisdom.

Linking: Often called the "currency of the Web,"[16] linking helps get your material across the network, along with providing context for readers to explore. Those you link to are likely to link to you, and some systems show who has linked to a post, inviting readers to go to those linking sites for more.

Commenting: Blogs that don't have commenting enabled are just simple publishing systems. You have to be willing to accept comments and to respond (although you have no obligation to respond to trolls and flamers).

Blogging is also advancing from older platforms like TypePad, Blogger, and WordPress to "livestream" platforms such as Posterous and Tumblr that are tuned more for quick posting of multimedia and distribution of those posts to social media sites. Tumblr, in particular, has become popular among the media[17] for its Twitter-like functions such as "reblogging," following, and designating favorites and its integration with mobile devices.

Texting/Twitter

Strictly speaking, texting is more point to point. However, since it and Twitter are so closely related, it's worth discussing both here.

The International Telecommunications Union estimates 6.1 trillion text messages were sent in 2010, triple those in 2007.[18] Obviously, texting, more formally known as SMS (short message service), remains a valuable channel for journalists to reach readers.

---

[13] Smashing Magazine (March 2009), "99 Essential Twitter Tools and Applications," retrieved from http://www.smashingmagazine.com/2009/03/17/99-essential-twitter-tools-and-applications/.

[14] D. Duray (February 2011), "The End of Blogging," *New York Observer,* retrieved from http://www.observer.com/2011/tech/end-blogging.

[15] B. Moritz , " 'The First Draft of Journalism:' How Blogging Has Affected Sports Reporters' Roles and Routines," *The Convergence Newsletter* 8, no. 7 (October 2011), retrieved from http://sc.edu/cmcis/news/convergence/v8no7.html.

[16] M. Ingram (September 6, 2010), "Links: Not Just the Currency of the Web, But the Soul," retrieved from http://gigaom.com/2010/09/06/links-not-just-the-currency-of-the-web-but-the-soul/.

[17] C. Cameron (June 2010), "Traditional Media Outlets Flocking to Tumblr," retrieved from http://www.readwriteweb.com/archives/traditional_media_outlets_flocking_to_tumblr.php.

[18] International Telecommunications Union (n.d.), *The world in 2010: ICT facts and figures,* retrieved from http://www.itu.int/ITU-D/ict/material/FactsFigures2010.pdf

While Twitter limits messages to 120 characters, including punctuation and spacing, some text systems allow up to 160. With Twitter's popularity, however, it's probably best to learn how to express yourself in 120 (or fewer so you have room for a shortened link)—it's always easier to add information than delete it.

An effective message is more than a headline. It should be broad enough and contain enough context to allow the user to take action, if necessary, or to make an informed decision about whether to seek more details.

For instance, what would you do if you got this message on your cellphone:

> *Crash blocks I-26 westbound*

Where, you might ask? How can I get around it? Is there much of a backup? But what about this, as in figure 11.5:

> *Traffic backed up 3 miles after truck crash blocks I-26 at mile 103. Alternate routes: St, Andrews Road, Lake Murray Boulevard.*

Now you have information you can use—in 127 characters and spaces, well within the limits for texting. But what if you also wanted to simultaneously file the message on Twitter? It's OK to use some abbreviations that might not conform to Associated Press or other longstanding newsroom styles. Try this:

> *I-26 traffic backed up 3 miles, truck crash mile 103. Alternates: St. Andrews Rd., Lake Murray Blvd.*

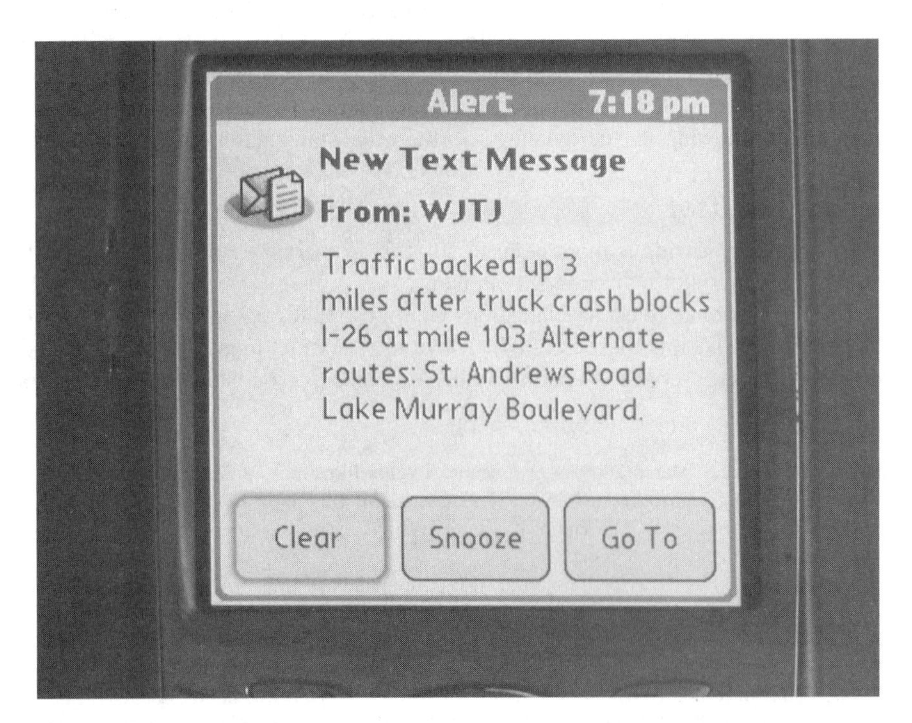

Figure 11.5 ■ As telephone display screens become larger and capable of displaying more information, they will be used more often to convey news and information of immediate concern to the public.

Box 11.1 Link-shortening Services

Services to create short Web links, or URLs, from long ones have been around for many years, but Twitter's need for brevity has made them more prominent. Some companies have built link shorteners into their websites to make it even easier to share material.

One of the oldest services is tinyurl.com, but its long name made it less favored for Twitter's constraints. Bit.ly is probably the most widely seen now, but people use many others like tr.im, ow.ly, is.gd, and notlong.com. When looking for a link-shortening service, consider these things:

- Will the links stay active? Some expire if not clicked on, so that could be a problem if you want traffic from the Web's "long tail."
- Is there an optional "bookmarklet," a snippet of script you drag to your browser's toolbar? While on a page, click on the bookmarklet and the link is automatically shortened.
- Do you want to track click-throughs on your links? Some services, like bit.ly, show traffic statistics for each shortened link.
- Can you to use a "plain English" link? Most services create a sequence of letters and numbers as the new link. You might want to sacrifice some brevity for a more "branded" approach with a named link that's easier to remember.
- You should experiment with several link-shortening services and probably have two or three in your bookmarks for various uses.

At 100 characters and spaces, that leaves room for a shortened link using services like bit.ly or is.gd, or Twitter's built-in shortener, t.co, that can send users to a longer story and visuals on your site (see box 11.1 for more information on such services).

Some websites use something similar to a tweet or text message atop a story to summarize it for scanners:

> *City Council raises property taxes 5%. Average $50 yearly per home, but raises $30 million for sewer repairs.*

That gives the reader the news and context—in 109 characters and spaces.

If you've learned how to sell a story at a morning news meeting or to summarize an investigative piece in a paragraph or two for the news budget, you know how to squeeze information, and the basics of SMS and Twitter should be easy.

Twitter's power over text messaging comes from several things:

- The ability to "retweet" others' messages, thus adding a social networking dimension.
- The ability to reply to others tweets publicly, by using @ and their username, thus creating a conversation thread, or to reply privately with a direct message using "D" or "DM" and the username.

- The ability to "follow" others' tweets and to have other people follow yours.
- The ability to use "hashtags" to provide an on-the-fly way of aggregating tweets on the same subject from multiple sources. The hashtag is a word or phrase preceded by a "#." For instance, a hashtag for *Principles of Convergent Journalism* might be #pcj. Anyone wanting just those tweets could then search for the hashtag.

Twitter also allows you to follow an RSS feed of anyone's tweets, and several tools let you organize and categorize tweets, write a tweet now and schedule it for delivery later, or attach a photo. Among the most popular tools are TweetDeck and HootSuite, but as noted earlier, there are many others, and you should explore to find what works best for you. For instance, Twitaholic provides a convenient way to find the top Twitter members in your city based on their number of followers from that area.

As with blogging and other forms of online media, there is an ethic in the Twitter community. Here are some of the top points:

- Don't use "@" replies for routine comments that don't really add to the conversation; use a direct reply instead.
- Remember that many of your followers on mobile devices can be inundated and become annoyed if you let go with a rapid-fire stream of tweets from, for instance, a live event The same problem arises if you have linked your Twitter accounts to LinkedIn or Facebook—all your friends may not appreciate having their walls monopolized. At least put out a Tweet warning them the stream is coming.
- Follow a good proportion of the people who follow you. If you have many followers but follow few people, it could get you labeled as a spammer.
- Keep private conversations private. Remember, the world can see everything you post, so if you reply using "@" you may be spreading some embarrassing details the original sender might not want out in the world.

Social Networks

"Facebook" has become the shorthand for social networks, with more than 600 million users worldwide in 2011, but it is just one of many social networks. LinkedIn is a popular social network for business users with more than 100 million users, for instance, and other networks have substantial user bases in other regions like Orkut (India and Brazil), Hyves (Netherlands), and Sina Weibo (China). There are invitation-only networks, such as A Small World.

Each network has its own protocols, tools, and functions. For instance, LinkedIn, because it is business oriented, allows you to provide recommendations for other members, just as you might if a potential employer asked for one. There are so many networks that any journalist can only be familiar with a handful. But since Facebook is the behemoth in much of the world and the first place many journalists are likely to turn, some guidelines are helpful:

- Remember that not only may your "friends" see something but also the friends of your friends can view items with a simple click over to that person's page. Be judicious, especially if you are breathlessly promoting that latest sewer commission story.
- As with Twitter, don't bombard your friends with messages.
- Be careful when "tagging" people. Facebook allows you to insert an "@" before a person's name to link either a text post or a photo back to their account. But watch those embarrassing moments, poses, and so on. When you propagate something, it goes places you might not expect. The person can remove the tag, but why tempt fate?
- Use first-person voice. This may be controversial for some journalists taught since college that "while there's an I in journalism, it's not about U." But this is social media and the very term "friends" suggests people want to interact with you as a person, not some distant entity.
- Create a page to go along with your personal profile (pages must be linked to a profile unless you create a business page, but those pages have limited functions and engagement). You can have unlimited connections with a page versus 5,000 with a profile.
- Explore the applications that Facebook and developers provide. (For a list, see http://www.facebook.com/apps/directory.php). Many can be useful, such as importing RSS feeds to your page. Remember, though, don't overdo it.
- Consider adding Facebook comments to your blog or website pages as a way to further expand the conversation. Many content management software packages also now include options to put Facebook "like" (and Twitter "tweet this") buttons on your pages, but if not, consider adding them. Most services provide instructions (they require a little bit of programming savvy, so you may want some help).

Facebook has become such an important tool for journalists that it has created a set of pages devoted specifically to best practices for journalists and media (www.facebook.com/journalist and www.facebook.com/media). Other sites (such as allfacebook.com) also have helpful advice, such as using Facebook's markup language to customize parts of your page. Facebook requires journalists to craft posts that stand out from the crowd and to engage with others. But the potential payoff is also greater.

Other Tools

A class of tools is emerging that allows journalists to pull together posts from across the Internet's social networks and social media sites to create a seamless story thread (see, for example, Mark Glaser's *Timeline of Tweets Around Death of Osama bin Laden* referenced at the beginning of this chapter).

Storify (storify.com) allows you to pull all the stories, Facebook comments, tweets, and Flickr photos on a topic together in one place. Chirpstory (chirpstory.com), another tool, aggregates Twitter posts. Still others are sure to emerge.

With such tools, it can be easy to think that journalism can be practiced merely by sitting at a computer and curating the world's social media streams. But as a Storify reviewer wrote:

> *Ultimately, while using Storify, one word kept on popping into my head: Why? Why was I using this instead of going out and finding real people to interview? That's still what journalism is about—telling the stories of real people and what matters to them.*[19]

ETHICS

Much of the practice and discussion about social media ethics is evolving. Entire books on digital ethics are being written and revised[20] as new technology presents new challenges and gives old problems new dimensions. It is not possible to present an extensive discussion here, but we can suggest some questions and issues that go beyond the etiquette or ethos discussed above.

What expectation of privacy should someone who posts on a social network have? Currently, journalists rummage around anyone's information available online, much as they might page through a high school yearbook. They take profile pictures to use online, in print, or on-air when someone gains attention or notoriety. But a Facebook profile has far more information than a yearbook entry, and the networking nature means one can more easily track down relatives and friends. Is everything public just because it sits on a social networking platform?

Some have argued for a new perspective, that a post intended for a limited circle should be presumed private. Others project a society where we will be less sensitive to privacy, but visible to a wider sphere—a tough argument to make at a time when the push seems to be for transparency, where reputation management will become paramount and the media will be expected to play a role in helping people do that. Either way, it's clear our concepts of privacy are changing and that social media will continue to press this issue.[21]

In this "always on" world, when is it still appropriate to put away the iPhone or Blackberry and refrain from bringing the world an event in "real time"? Despite the changing landscape, some things still make many people recoil. A backlash ensued when a *Rocky Mountain News* reporter tweeted the funeral of a boy killed by a vehicle that crashed into an ice cream shop.[22] Tweeting trials while they are in progress is

---

[19] E. Zak (May 2011), "Storify: The Pros and Cons," retrieved from http://www.mediabistro.com/10000words/storify-pros-and-cons_b3712.

[20] C. Friend and J.B. Singer, *Online Journalism Ethics* (Armonk, N.Y.: M.E. Sharpe, 2007). R.I. Berkman and C.A. Shumway, *Digital Dilemmas: Ethical Issues for Online Media Professionals* (Hoboken, N.J: Wiley-Blackwell, 2003).

[21] "The Evolution of Privacy, Identity and Forgiveness," in J.Q. Anderson and L. Rainie (December 14, 2008), *The future of the Internet III,* Pew Internet and American Life Project, retrieved from http://www.pewinternet.org/~/media//Files/Reports/2008/PIP_FutureInternet3.pdf.pdf.

[22] C. Degette (September 10, 2008), "RMN 'Tweets' the Funeral of 3-year-old Boy Killed in Ice Cream Shop," *Colorado Independent,* retrieved from http://coloradoindependent.com/7717/rmn-tweets-the-funeral-of-3-year-old-boy.

becoming more widespread, raising questions about the effects on fair trials (especially since the legal system is struggling with the issue of jurors tweeting during trials). Are there some things that should not be shared with the world as they happen? Where are the new boundaries? And if you are assigned to tweet as part of your coverage, what should be the decorum and protocols?

What should be the limits, if any, for journalists who engage their audiences using social networks? As noted earlier, many news organizations and journalists are struggling to find new norms and boundaries. In one informal online poll at PBS's MediaShift, "engage audience and break news on social media sites" was far and away the leader, followed by "common sense; be fair."[23] That might be easier for a journalist running his or her own site, or for a small group of like-minded journalists, but it is likely to run into problems at larger organizations that view information as their proprietary product. Do the benefits of drawing a larger audience and staying financially viable outweigh the damage that might be done to the organization's traditional way of making money by selling scarcity of access? What about any potential damage to the subjects of those stories by premature release of bits and pieces?

Journalists have long done "work for hire"—whatever they produced for the company belonged to the company. But can the same be said for their online social network followers? Should their employer "own" their followers' information the same way the company owns its subscriber list?

How transparent should journalists be? Should they admit they have biases and points of view as they try to be more conversational and open with readers on social networks?

How should we handle "real time" errors in a world where journalists increasingly are expected to file live and make sense of it all later? Should we ignore them, knowing we are likely to update the material quickly, and hope no one notices? Should we put a notice at the top of the item detailing what was changed? Should we have a separate corrections area? Who will be in charge of making sure corrections are made and handled properly?

How will we handle trolls, flamers, and other rogue commenters? Do we have the resources to do it in-house, or should we consider outsourcing comment moderation? Are there cases where we would close—or maybe not open at all—comments? How can we justify that if we are promoting transparency? What kinds of comments are so harmful they outweigh the benefits of robust discussion?

One of the things we have learned from various online experiments is that the traditional journalistic reaction to expose ne'er-do-wells like trolls, flamers, and "sock puppets" (people who set up multiple false identities to make it seem like there is more support or opposition for a position) can backfire. In a conversation environment, an attempt to cut someone off from the conversation can portray you, the moderator, as heavy-handed and leave others wondering whether you will use the same power against them. It takes a new set of skills, and patience, to moderate online communities.

---

[23] M. Glaser (May 3, 2011), "What's the Best Social Media Policy for News Organizations?" Media Shift, retrieved from http://www.pbs.org/mediashift/2011/05/whats-the-best-social-media-policy-for-news-organizations123.html.

The discussions will be ongoing, and journalists grappling with all the changes of the digital age would do well to stay plugged into the dialogue and think about the ongoing questions. Having thought about one's ethical compass is even more critical now; if there was little time before, there is even less time now in the current news cycles.

CONCLUSION

Social media continue the reshaping of journalism that began with blogging and easy digital publishing platforms. Combined with the growing ubiquity of mobile devices, we continue to a time when creation, sharing, and discovery of content will become just part of our regular routine of interacting with our digital information environment. More of what we do will move from node to node, and network to network, using machine-readable, semantic clues, dubbed by some as "Web 3.0" and by others the "Semantic Web."

The journalist's role will be transforming and challenging—how to maintain the old practices of confirmation, verification, clarity, and completeness while being able to productively tap into the ever-changing world of social media.

We can take heart that, while social media may have broken the practical monopoly that news organizations had on observing events and distributing information about them, ultimately people seem to want journalists to help explain world events and provide the context. Journalism, at its core has always been "social," and now it finally has the tools to enter that conversation.

EXERCISES

1. Pick 10 friends outside of journalism and identify all the social media platforms they use. Twitter? Facebook? Tumblr? Plaxo? LinkedIn? Following the concepts of uses and gratifications, find out why they specifically use each one. Are there some people they link with on one system, but avoid on others? Why?
2. Map a quick social graph among you and the 10 and try to figure out who is the most influential within each network and across networks based on number of connections.
3. Inventory all your social media accounts as though you were a journalist looking for dirt on you. What do you see that might be of concern regarding your privacy? Don't just stop at your sites—follow the links to the sites of your first-level friends. What kind of overall impression do you think a journalist—or an employer—would get? (Even better, see if your teacher is amenable to having his or her online presence dissected; it might surprise everyone.)
4. Using services like Twitaholic, Klout, and Twittercounter, try to identify the top Twitter users in your area and their influencer or "clout" scores. Imagine you have access to a big computer monitor that will be used to show the entire newsroom the key tweets of a day in your area in a live stream. Which 10 of these would you include in that and why? Are there others not on that list (such as government agencies, police, fire, etc.) that you would include and why?

5. Go to the websites of the newspapers and broadcast stations in your area and examine what kinds of "social media" things each is doing. Can you comment on stories or email a story to a friend? Are there many interactive elements? Are there staff blogs? Community blogs? A place to submit your own stories or photos? Using a scale you develop, pick a day and rate each site on how much it seems to engage with users. Be prepared to explain your ratings and justify your scale.

CHAPTER 12

ADDING MULTIMEDIA TO THE WEB

The phrase "interactive multimedia" can frighten a nontechnical person. Since the mid-1990s, journalists have sat through presentations showing us the future through multimedia—spinning globes, dancing hamsters, and crashing browsers. Journalists shivered. Thankfully, times have changed. We don't have to choose a color using HTML, and we don't have to spend hours to create a five-second animated butterfly. The tools have become much simpler, much quicker, and more powerful. Interactive multimedia have become a useful and indispensable part of convergent journalism. But they are only a means to help us reach people with news and information they both want and need. This chapter will offer some instruction about what multimedia is and how it is used in journalism.

DEFINING MULTIMEDIA

Multimedia, short for "multiple media," describes using various forms and combinations of media—sound, text, video, animations, and dynamic databases that respond to user input (and anything else that may come along)—to allow us to experience that content. Digital tools have made gathering and presenting that content progressively easier. Multimedia content is both a means and an end. As a means, there are suites of software to create dynamic Web pages, mobile apps, exploding planets, and interactive soundscapes. We will discuss some of these later in this chapter. But more importantly, we use multimedia as an end, to do good journalism and help create community.

HOW TO BUILD COMMUNITY: A LOCAL LANDMARK CLOSES ITS DOORS

Here is an example that happens almost everywhere: The owner of a restaurant that's a local landmark announces it is time to close after decades of business. Everyone has a story to tell or an experience they remember there. Think of this event, this story, as an opportunity for you to build community. In so doing, you will not only honor people's memories of special events, you can even generate revenue (not a bad thing for a modern newsroom). The issue becomes how you can use multiple media to create synergies that build the story into something that forever ties your coverage to the collective memories of the event.

Traditionally, a newspaper would do a retrospective, possibly a package of several stories, that might be published the Sunday before the closing (because Sundays traditionally have the most readers) or on the morning of the closing day. Television would arrange for the usual live report on the final night, perhaps including a reporter package that contains an interview with the owner and a few customers, B-roll of the interior and exterior, and file footage of the restaurant's heyday a generation ago. These angles are good and should still be done, but now there's so much more you can do to explore the story.

Today you approach this not only in purely journalistic terms but also as an opportunity for marketing your brand—all while building a sense of community. You can quickly use your website to put together a multipart series recounting the history of the business and its place in the community. You can also provide video accounts, including both fully produced features and unedited interviews with key people. You can invite others to share their memories online, especially inviting stories and photos from events such as engagements or parties that happened there, plus you will want to monitor social media sites like Facebook where people are likely to share other interesting material. Some of those items could be included in an interactive timeline.

You can provide Web space for a montage of images over the years and invite patrons to submit their own photos—what they looked like when they went to the restaurant. Animations might show how the neighborhood has changed, with specific benchmarks (the end of World War II in 1945, 1969 moon landing, the aftermath of September 11, 2001) to jog people's memories. Taking a page from radio, you can create podcasts with customers and workers sharing their stories and invite others to submit their own. Sponsors can be solicited to come up with appropriate contests and giveaways. The final day could be turned into a farewell concert with prizes for people who show up to say goodbye—and we've not even spoken about ways to raise awareness through text alerts or social media.

By inviting participation, local events can become a new level of integrated, interactive community journalism that pulls people together. Multimedia can provide the cues to trigger people's memories related to that particular business and, in the process, foster a sense of community through the sharing of common experiences. But it takes foresight to anticipate and plan, plus the will to allocate enough resources to do it.

People's greater needs include sense-making and assigning meaning to seemingly random events. But since the opportunity to transform experiences from the private and individual to the public and communal applies to tragedies as well as celebrations, journalists must use care and discernment with these new capabilities.

In many cases, text remains the glue that sticks the content together, but multimedia—those forms of news and information where text is of secondary or shared importance—are common and popular. There are roughly six categories of media that we will deal with in this chapter: still images, sound, moving images, animations and graphics, other interactive items, and combinations thereof.

STILL IMAGES

We've already discussed the basics of taking good photos. Here, we'll explore ways you can help the reader interact with them to create an experience online. The threshold question is what kind of experience you want to create and from that how to display them. For instance, if you want the user to be able to wander around numerous photos, finding her own way, and rediscovering her own memories, then a **photo gallery** is best. If you want to use the photos to emphasize how the restaurant and the community evolved, you might put them in a **timeline**. If you want to combine the powerful ability still photos have to stir memories along with the emotional effect that audio has—especially former customers, workers, and neighbors telling their stories—then a **slide show** might be the choice.

But first you must think about what images you will need to help relate the story your research tells you is out there. What General Dwight Eisenhower once said about war is also true about journalism: "In preparing for battle, I have always found that plans are useless, but planning is indispensable."

Finding and Capturing Memorable Images

The best photos become forever linked with an event. Iconic images often seem the result of luck or serendipity, but good luck often results from professional practice and forethought. As the examples in figure 12.1 illustrate, photographs can summarize an entire complex event in a single image (9/11, the smoking towers; Super Bowl XXXVIII, Janet Jackson's "wardrobe malfunction"; World War II, Marines planting the flag atop Mount Suribachi on Iwo Jima).

For the local landmark closing, what images might you want? It might be an elderly patron hugging the owner or perhaps a piece of distinctive furniture, decoration, or architecture. It could be one of the little rituals that made the place unique (a small bell rung at closing time); certainly there will be some "characters" on the staff and among the customers (maybe someone, for instance, wears a tuxedo to the closing night).

There is likely to be lots of emotion, hugging, crying among the staff and customers. Are crowds likely to be lined up outside? Is the inside brightly lit or full of shadows and dark wood? If you consider the possibilities, you will also be looking for them and thinking about how to position yourself to get them.

Preparation means having the gear. Camera, lights, batteries, cables, microphones, filters, tripod, duct tape, a marker—there is almost no end to the things accomplished photographers will bring with them based on experience. Preparation also means getting there early, walking around, mentally framing shots. It also means doing research, chatting with people and soaking up the ambience in order to get a better sense of what you're looking for.

The first few pictures let you judge your instincts. As the event builds into the evening, you'll get a clearer view of your own success. At the end of the night, the owner rises to ring the bell for the very last time. You know where you'll stand and how you'll snap the series of pictures. The moment comes, you do your job, you get the images.

At the end of this section, we'll talk more about what to do with the images technically once they are in the camera. But first, let's talk about your plans for displaying them.

(A)

Figure 12.1 ■ A single photograph can capture an event that resonates across time. A: New York City, September 11, 2001. B: Super Bowl XXXVIII—Janet Jackson and Justin Timberlake, February 1, 2004. C: Iwo Jima, February 1945. (Source: A: AP Photos/Jim Collins; B: AP Photos/David Phillip; C: AP Photos/Joe Rosenthal.)

(B)

(C)

Figure 12.1 ■ (continued)

Photo Galleries

Photo galleries are best when you have large numbers of images and want users to be able to find their own path through them. In other words, a gallery leaves the user in control.

If you use a photo-sharing service like Flickr or Photobucket, or you create "albums" on Facebook, you know what a gallery is. Most of them give you the option of choosing to look at the photos as a slide show, but this is far different than some news sites that put what should be galleries into slide shows just to make people click through so the site can increase its page views.

There are four general steps to creating a gallery:

1. Creating smaller versions, called "thumbnails," that become the preview images you see in the gallery. Click on one and the larger version appears.
2. Sizing the photos so they properly fit in the main display window (the one that comes up when you click on one of the thumbnails).
3. Creating any necessary captions.
4. Uploading the photos.

The sizes for the main and thumbnail photos will be specified by the program you are using. If you use a photo-sharing service like Flickr or Photobucket, the photos will be resized and the thumbnails created automatically when you upload your images.

Many content management systems used by news organizations have slide show capabilities built in. Or you can use something like Simple Viewer (http://www.simpleviewer.net) that lets you load a group of photos and thumbnails and then provides the necessary Flash files to display them. You take the finished files and put them on a "host" server to be displayed when users click on the link you create, wherever (and however many times) you want to link to that content.

Timelines

Interactive timelines are perfect when putting your photos in chronological order helps produce a natural narrative. You generally will have to work with someone who knows how to create them in Flash or the newer display options of HTML5, or you can use an online service like Dipity (www.dipity.com).

Interactive timelines can display not just text but also photos, video, audio, and links to other things like maps. So, for instance, if you had a point on the restaurant timeline keyed to the moon landing, you might be able to upload an archive shot of the spacecraft. (However, there are legal and ethical considerations that we'll talk about later in the chapter.) Even bettesr would be a picture from your archives or the files of the owner or a customer showing people crowded around a TV set in the restaurant watching the landing (thus the need for planning—you need to find out ahead of time what old photos people will share).

When doing a timeline, there are two major considerations:

1. Pick a span of time that will adequately encompass what you are trying to illustrate without being too long (and making the user scroll left and right excessively). With the restaurant, this is easy, from its opening to its closing. But some things, such as a long-running battle over paving county roads, don't have definite starting points and need some judgment.
2. Pick divisions that position key points without their piling up on each other, but not with so many that the timeline becomes unwieldy and creates large gaps. If that restaurant has been open 80 years and you create a timeline divided by years, that's 80 divisions, and there are likely to be gaps between the images

you can get from years ago. Likewise, if you tried to put a point in for every year or two to cover the gaps, the amount of work is unreasonable and is likely to look jammed in and overwhelm the user. But if you picked every five years, for instance, that's 16 divisions, a reasonable number to work with.

Slide Shows

Slide shows can be a powerful way to combine images and audio, sometimes more powerful than video. They are better than video when the images and the audio happen at different times (for instance, a customer talking about the old days at the restaurant while you show photos from that era). They also are quicker to assemble than video, but they require just as much planning.

First, you are going to be working in two dimensions—audio and video—not just one. The question often arises, which should I do first? The answer is both. The images aren't always going to wait for you to collect audio—you'll have to do that afterward to get an explanation of what you just saw and got in your camera. Other times, you can get the audio first and then plan your shots around that.

Programs like Soundslides (http://soundslides.com) have made creating slide shows easy. In general, there are these key things:

1. Using an average of 12 to 15 shots per minute of slide show, shoot double what you think you will need. You will thank yourself later.
2. Shoot plenty of close-up shots that can be used for transitions. Also, shoot in sequence (long, medium, close), not just randomly. Like video, you will be grouping sequences of shots.
3. Make sure the audio is clear. Nothing ruins good visuals like bad audio. Listen before you leave.
4. Edit your audio first and export it, usually as an MP3, using the instructions for your slide show program (not all MP3 sampling rates are accepted, for instance). The audio will determine the slide show's length and how you arrange your photos.
5. Do any photo editing and make sure all the photos have been saved using Web parameters (usually density of 72 dpi, red-green-blue color space, "jpg" format, medium or medium-high quality).
6. Put all the photos you want to work with in a folder. Then upload the photos following the program's instructions (usually, you just point to the folder) and the audio (usually just point to the audio file).
7. You will see a screen with all the photos laid out along the timeline that corresponds to the length of the video. Some programs also show you a gallery. Now you start deleting some photos, moving others around, adjusting timing. It's important you vary the timing and pay attention to the audio (if the person is saying "cow," we don't want to see "horse"). Many of the same techniques of good video editing apply.
8. When finished, you save, then export the slide show. The program provides a folder with the necessary files to go on a server from where you can link to it.

Archives and Ethics

With the maturing of digital photography, images are ubiquitous online. But as explained in chapter 4, just because it is on the Web doesn't mean it is there for your taking.

All images in digital form are owned by someone (or some organization), and you need permission to use them. Often, you have to pay. Content creators have increasingly turned to legal means to protect their work.

Many news organizations subscribe to at least one wire service (Associated Press, Reuters, AFP) for access to images and at least one video service (ABC, Fox News, CBS, MSNBC, CNN, AP, Reuters). Even then, archive images usually have to be bought separately. Permissions contracts are fairly standard, setting out a specific way an image can be used and for how long.

There are some free and low-cost alternatives, if you are careful. Some photographers license their images using Creative Commons (explained in chapter 4). You can use those as long as you give complete and clear credit. Flickr, for instance, allows you to search for images posted with a Creative Commons license. There also are websites that allow you to use free "stock" photos (generally not tied to a specific news event—think things like sunsets, mountains, pictures of historic buildings, sometimes well-known people), but be very careful to (1) read the terms of use and give credit as requested (have a legal expert review them if you are not sure) and (2) make sure each file you download is scanned by a virus checker. One of the original sites is FreeStock-Photos.com, which also has an extensive list of other free sites. Finally, because of the competition, some photo agencies like Getty will sell you the rights to use a photo for much more reasonable terms than they used to.

Every news organization should also have a rich archive of the images it has taken (part of the library shown in figure 12.2). Even as newsroom libraries and photo editors have been cut, this resource has become more important not just as a newsroom resource but as a way to generate traffic and even make additional money. Why shouldn't every photo on your website have a "buy this" link under it to capitalize on impulse purchases? And by making their archives searchable and available to the public, newsrooms become part of the conversation again.

Editing and Processing Photos

As with video, the editing of photos begins when you are shooting them. First, make sure your camera settings are correct. Some photographers shoot in a "raw" mode that produces very large, uncompressed files. Unless you plan to sell shots for high-quality magazine or reprint work, in most cases a "high" or "medium jpg" setting will produce photos with plenty of information for online as well as basic print.

Try to frame every shot you take to minimize the need to "crop" (removing the unwanted parts of a photo so the final image displays what is most important). Every extra step you can save in editing helps.

Transfer the photos to the computer using the camera's instructions (usually by a USB cord that plugs into the camera and computer or by a chip that comes from the camera and goes into the computer). *Be very careful to turn the camera off and on in the exact sequence required, or you could damage your files.*

The photos usually have arcane file names, but most computers now have an option to look at files as images, not just names, so you can pick the ones you want.

Figure 12.2 ■ Large news organizations such as newspapers maintain libraries that include copies of the publication, reference books, unpublished photos, and other archival information that can assist reporters in preparing the story. Many libraries are moving to electronic storage, but a designated "library" is still found in most newspaper newsrooms.

Make copies. Pros rarely work with the original so they can go back to it if something goes wrong. *Back up all your work.* There is a saying there are two kinds of computer users: Those who have backed up their work, and those who *will* (after they've lost everything.)

Open your editing software. Photoshop is the most common, and expensive, program, but there are less expensive (such as Photoshop Elements) and free alternatives (such as Irfanview, PhotoFiltre, and GIMP). Open the files in the program to size the images, crop them, and correct any mistakes in color. Ethically, you can fix certain technical problems but not content or aesthetics. The most important thing is not to change the reality or meaning of an image. (For instance, your final photo shows the restaurant owner laughing with a wealthy but notoriously single socialite, but you cropped out the owner's wife, who was also standing there.)

If you have to write a caption, make sure it is not misleading, doesn't tell us what we can already see in the photo, *gets the names spelled right*, and follows correct grammar and style. Here are some of the things you might do in editing software.

- *Cropping.* If you don't like what you've just done, you usually can hit "undo" (Ctrl+Z in Windows or Command+Z in Mac) *and try again.* Cropping in most programs is done by starting somewhere in the upper left, holding down the left mouse key, and dragging to the lower right. A crop box of your desired dimensions is drawn around the picture. You then tell the program to actually "crop" and discard the unwanted parts.

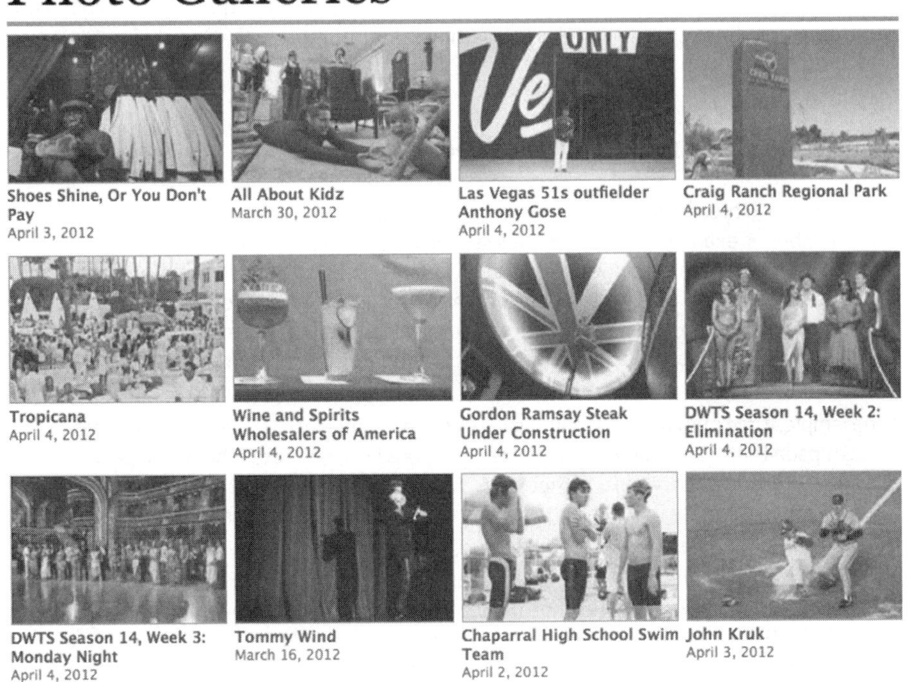

Figure 12.3 ■ Online photo galleries allow us to provide context through multiple images. This can benefit the reader, the subject of the story, and the news organization.

- *Sizing, resolution, levels.* Sizing, which sets the height and width, and resolution, the number of dots (pixels) per inch (dpi), are linked. An image 380 pixels wide is more than five inches across at 72 dpi but barely over two inches at 180 dpi. A photo only for the Web is normally saved at 72 dpi, but for any kind of print use it can require 180 or even 300 dpi. It's best to create two versions, starting with the higher resolution because once you remove information from a file, you can't restore it. For a photo going online, the program's color mode (in Photoshop, image/mode) is set to RGB. For print, it's CMYK. You might also have to tweak the photo's color hue and saturation or other levels. That's beyond our scope, but plenty of books and online sites explain how.

- *Saving and choosing file type and quality.* Once the image is ready, it must be saved using *Save As* or some option specifically for the Web if the photo is destined for online only. Create a separate copy by giving it a new name and, if necessary, file type. The most common image type for the Web is a compressed file with the JPG or JPEG extension. This produces smaller sizes without too much quality loss. Among others are PNG and GIF, a lower-quality type often used for smaller images and some animation.

If you've chosen JPG/JPEG, the program should ask you what quality to save it as. In most cases medium quality is OK. If you have only numbers, that's a 4, 5, or 6—a 40,

Box 12.1 Ethics: Notorious Doctored Photos

Image-altering software increases the danger of misinforming the public. There are a number of examples of news organizations that crossed the line with altered photos, but news organizations understandably rarely keep or provide the evidence for textbooks like this one. Still, various organizations (such as the Poynter Institute) provide some excellent case studies of such ethical lapses or dilemmas, and the Internet has numerous sites devoted to the falsification of photographs and their use by news organizations.

For example, *Time* magazine was famously criticized for the June 27, 1994 cover photo of O. J. Simpson that was clearly altered. When compared with the exact same image used on the cover of *Newsweek* magazine that week, Simpson's photo was clearly darkened and blurred in such a way as to make him look extremely menacing and dangerous.

A second famous media example occurred in April 2003, when the *Los Angeles Times* director of photography and a staff photographer were fired for distributing and publishing a composite image from Iraq. The photo was shared with other Tribune properties and published in the *Hartford Courant* and the *Chicago Tribune*. Details are available from Poynter online (http://www.poynter.org/how-tos/newsgathering-storytelling/9289/l-a-times-photographer-fired-over-altered-image/).

Another famously doctored photo was an image of Beirut, Lebanon, August 5, 2006, taken by photographer Adnan Hajj. The photo appeared shortly after a bombing by Israeli jets and was distributed by Reuters. The authenticity was questioned in a number of Internet blogs (see especially "Little Green Footballs" at http://www.littlegreenfootballs.com/weblog/?entry=21956&only&rss), and on August 7, 2006, Reuters removed this and all other associated photos from its Web site. In an April 2007 personal conversation, a representative of Reuters confirmed it no longer had any record of the photo in question, real or imagined.

More recently, some newspapers have justified photo alteration based on religious beliefs but later apologized. A *Time* magazine photo essay of "top ten doctored photos" noted that, in 2009, an Israeli newspaper was criticized for replacing images of women in the Israeli Cabinet with men. In May 2011, the noted "Situation Room" photograph of top U.S. officials standing by in the death of Osama bin Laden was similarly altered. The small conservative papers later apologized for erasing images of Secretary of State Hillary Clinton and director for counterterrorism Audrey Tomason.

50, or 60 in some programs. Once you have your photos, you can follow the instructions for uploading either to your site or that of your organization.

SOUND

As noted above, sound is as important as the visuals. There are three general categories: music, speech, and sounds (sound effects). Music has standard characteristics (tempo, rhythm) and can help set a mood or direct emotion, but its use in news items is controversial. Speech can be assessed according to traits such as accent, emphasis, inflection, and mood. Sounds are anything not speech or music; for our purposes, "sounds" refers generally to the "natural sound" of the world around us. Using sound effects (as they do in the movies) generally is considered an ethical lapse by a journalist.

Sound and Journalism

Sounds can be extremely powerful (as we know from music); gifted orators have been known throughout human history for their ideas and power of persuasion. Orson Welles sent Americans into a panic in 1938 with his "War of the Worlds" radio broadcast, and the words "Oh, the humanity" have long resonated from radio reporter Herbert Morrison's sorrowful recounting of the 1937 Hindenburg zeppelin disaster in Lakehurst, New Jersey.

Sound related to journalism is generally natural sound, sound bites, or narration. Natural sound is recorded at the scene, things like cheering, traffic, bits of background conversation, wind, and ambient noise. It helps bring the viewer or listener to the event. A report from a war zone sounds more authentic and dramatic with gunshots in the background; and a report of a sporting event comes alive when the roar of the crowd coincides with the winning goal.

Natural sound is often used as a transition. For instance, following a government official discussing the space program, we might softly hear the rumbling sound get louder and then we see the video of a rocket lifting off. In this way, natural sound makes the best transition element in shifting from one location to another.

Sound Bites

Sound bites, actual quotes from newsmakers and people affected by events, are key segments of news stories and are chosen according to length, quality, and content. The content—what is actually said—should emphasize opinion, emotion, or both. If the sound bite is simply information (e.g., the city council will vote next week), it's better said by the reporter.

Sound bites have shrunk to a standard of less than 15 seconds for broadcast. Longer ones tend to be used online, but as attention spans shorten, all but the most gripping content probably should not be longer than 30 to 45 seconds. Sound bites should also be of sufficient quality to be understood under normal conditions, with exceptions for especially gripping or significant segments. In these cases, the words should be transcribed and presented so that viewers can read as well as hear for themselves.

Emotion and opinion add drama and authenticity and cannot be made up or inserted into a story by reporters. All reporting textbooks emphasize asking "why" and "how" questions because these help to cut through the jargon and politically correct responses.

For more heavily produced reports, such as those in broadcasting and sometimes online, reporter narration puts the event into context and provides meaning for the listener by having a beginning, middle, and end. The reporter is also in part a performer and should use some professional vocalization techniques (see chapter 8).

Audio Tools

The capabilities now available in free or low-cost digital audio hardware and software mean there can be almost no difference between the professional and the amateur. The only limitation is time and imagination.

Sound is extremely versatile and can be combined with any visual presentation—still image, video, animation, or graphics. The sound may be added (narration, dialogue, music) or left natural (cheering at a football game). You will get better results if you understand the equipment used in audio production.

Microphones

Start with a professional-quality microphone and recording device. For microphones, the biggest issues will probably be power, impedance, pickup (or pattern), size and function, and the type of connector. Journalists need to be familiar with the terms because more and more they are being asked to gather sound on their own.

Power and Impedance

Microphones that need batteries or an outside power source are commonly called **condenser** mics. Those that don't need power are called **dynamic** microphones. You need to know the type of microphone you are working with because you may need to carry spare batteries with you (and the batteries might need to be a special type).

Impedance has to do with the flow of the electrical signal. Professional microphones tend to be low- rather than high-impedance. **Low-impedance** microphones can use longer cables without losing quality or volume (high impedance can't go longer than 25 feet versus 100 or more with low impedance).

Pickup (Pattern)

Pickup describes the radius of sound sensitivity. An **omnidirectional** microphone picks up sound in all directions. A directional microphone, commonly called a **cardioid** because the pattern plotted out looks like a heart, will block out at least some of the unwanted noise at a location (e.g., if you're interviewing someone near a busy highway).

You need to know what type of mic you are using so you know how to shield it and handle it. An omnidirectional microphone like the Electro-Voice 635 will pick up both the person being interviewed and you without the need to move the microphone (thus avoiding "mic noise"). But if you are in a noisy location, you'll need to pay more attention to pointing the microphone away from the racket, and even that might not help.

A cardioid microphone will shut out more of that noise, but it might also mean you have to move the mic to be heard with clarity on the recording.

Size and Function

The most common microphones are handheld **stick** mics like the directional Shure SM57 or the omnidirectional EV635 mentioned above. They are rugged and built for outdoor use. When recording, the mic should be held 6 to 12 inches from the person's mouth (see figure 12.4).

Lapel mics, commonly called **lavaliere** or **lavs**, are, as the name implies, clipped to a person's clothing around his or her chest. They are common to the studio and wireless versions have become common in the field. A "one-man band" reporter/videographer can clip it on the person, step back behind the camera, and shoot the interview.

Shotgun microphones have a tight directional (**hypercardioid**) pickup pattern. They are good for picking through crowd noise to isolate individual sound or comments. They need power, either from a battery or, in some cases, from the recording device.

Connector

The microphone must plug into a recorder, and how it plugs in is important. If you don't have the right cable, you're sunk.

There are three basic types of connectors: **XLR, quarter-inch,** and **mini-plug** (also known as an eighth-inch jack). The XLR connector is larger, and round, and has three pins in a triangle inside the larger ring (or three holes for those pins to fit in). XLR connectors are used on professional gear because they are more stable and remove external buzz that can be caused by radio frequencies.

The quarter-inch is common in high-impedance microphones. These consumer microphones are cheaper because the unbalanced line results in sound that is captured at noticeably lower quality. If the content is compelling, the quality is often still good enough to post online.

The mini-plug has become increasingly common because of MP3 players and other audio gear. Because of the small size, most recorders are fashioned with a mini-plug input. The mini-plug itself is a 3.5 mm metal shaft that will either be single channel or stereo. You have to look whether it has one or two dark rings around it (stereo is two). Depending on the microphone, to connect it to your recorder you might need an adaptor with either an XLR or a quarter-inch plug on one end and a mini-plug input on the other.

Digital Recorders

When buying a digital recorder, consider six things: recording length, battery life, weight, recording format, operating system, and external microphone input (not all recorders have them). Most standard digital recorders costing between $100 and $150 will do. They will record several hours of audio, especially voice, on their internal memory and usually use standard AA or AAA batteries (avoid proprietary rechargeable batteries, if possible). Some manufacturers also make plug-in microphone accessories that turn iPods into digital recorders for field use.

Try to get one that records in **WAV** ("wave") and **MP3** formats. Avoid those that use their makers' proprietary compressed formats and even those that record in **WMA** (Windows Media Audio). You will have to convert WMA into WAV before you edit it, and that requires file-conversion software that doesn't always work well, especially on Macintosh computers.

WAV is "uncompressed," meaning that no information has been removed from it as it is being recorded, and so it can be edited immediately in almost any editing program. The files are big. Use MP3 *only in an emergency when you know there will be no editing before posting.* You can post MP3 directly online, but when you go to edit it, MP3 will lose quality quickly because it is a "lossy" format (like JPG for pictures, information is actually removed in compressing the file).

Editing Audio

Editing audio is similar to word processing: highlight the portion of audio, cut, put the cursor where you want to move it, and paste.

Unless you are doing professional, high-end multitrack recording and mixing (a recording studio or documentary producer), a simple editing program is all you need. Audacity from Sourceforge is a common free program and does a pretty good job, though it has limitations. There are numerous low-cost programs too. What you need is a program that (1) allows you to split audio into multiple tracks, (2) allows some simple effects, like cross-fading, and (3) allows you to do some filtering and volume adjustment in case the recording is noisy.

Most of the editing you will be doing requires only one track from which you will be extracting sound bites. The multitrack function is good if you want to add in natural sound to some kind of more heavily produced piece, like a podcast.

Podcasting

As mentioned earlier in chapter 7, podcasting is both an ethos and a technical system. Technically, any audio recording that follows the ethos (detailed below) can be considered a podcast, even if the listener has to download it manually. But podcasting grew up around a system that combined the audio files with a system similar to an RSS feed to alert users when new audio files are available and allow them to be downloaded automatically. Another branch of this technology, v-casting, uses video instead of audio files.

VIDEO

As with audio, there are theoretically few constraints on what you can do with video online, especially as compression formats improve and higher-speed Internet service is adopted. The reality, however, is that newsrooms report their "ROI," or return on investment, is much lower on video than on slideshows. Users start the video, but they often click away before it finishes.

The other reality is that video takes more resources to produce, even if one person is doing all the shooting and editing. A standard guide is that it takes an hour of shooting and editing to produce one minute of finished video to basic professional standards. Documentaries and higher-quality efforts can be ten to one or more.

The more compelling the content, the more people will watch, no matter what the quality (think of all the grainy, jerky—but gripping—video from the 2011 tsunami that hit northern Japan). Still, the Internet is not TV. The traditional minute to 1:30 broadcast

(A)

(B)

Figure 12.4 ■ PROPER MIC TECHNIQUE. Whether you're using a handheld microphone or a studio mic, it should be about 6 to 12 inches from your mouth. Any closer and it will emphasize consonants such as "p" and "t"; any farther away and it will pick up too much background noise.

package does not play well online. Long shots lose detail, the sound bites are too short, the video shots too quickly cut. Here's the online reality:

- Your users have a limited attention span, aggravated by a medium that encourages interactivity and clicking from item to item. The TV viewer, on the other hand, is largely passive.

- The ever-growing TV screen (predicted to average 60 inches by 2015[1]) allows the viewer to quickly soak up large amounts of information. Digital theaters are also getting bigger and more realistic. Even small details become prominent in high definition and 3D, and filmmakers are now shooting at 48 frames per second (fps) (for a century 24 fps was the standard). But, online screen sizes are still generally 19 or 21 inches, and some video players only take a portion of that screen (Apple's iMovie program, e.g., exports video for the Web at only 240 × 180 pixels, or around three inches by two-and-a-half inches). Since streaming tends to be less than full-motion video (12 to 15 frames per second versus almost 30 fps under the U.S. TV standard, known as NTSC), Web video has some built-in constraints on resolution and picture quality.
- Online viewers need tighter shots without as much detail, and a little longer per shot to soak up what is there. The eight- or ten-second TV sound bite also does not work as well online. Although ideally video packages would be cut for the Web, they tend to be the same online as what is broadcast.
- What we are tending to see instead is that the sound bites are being offered as separate links in fuller versions that may run 20 or 30 seconds, sometimes longer, to capture the quote's full context and emotion.
- The online user can review the audio and video, but don't count on that too often. The medium is still spontaneous and unpredictable.
- In many cases, the most compelling video you can provide is raw and unedited, allowing someone who cares deeply about the story to see it develop from beginning to end. Raw video should be provided judiciously, but can be the most compelling way to share an event with the public.

Video Formats

There is no single online video standard, and online video is much more complex than most other online multimedia formats.

You have to briefly understand **containers** and **codecs.** Think of it as nested dolls. The container is the outer shell or format that you can recognize by the file type tag after the period, These include things like Quicktime (.mov), audio video interleave (.avi), Windows Media video (.wmv), Flash Video (.flv), Real Player (.rm, .rmvb, .rv, or .ra), and MPEG (.mp4 or .m4v, the most recent version of the MPEG container used by the iPod, among other devices).

Inside the container is the "codec," which tells the program how to decode the video and audio streams and play them together. A common one is H.264, but there are many. A codec can be used in several containers. As a user, you never really see the codec; it does its work behind the scenes.

The combination of containers and codecs you use will affect things like compression and file size which determine how the video is streamed and how the end user sees it on his or her computer monitor. It's important if you're editing and posting video regularly. There are numerous players, and all work across multiple formats. DivX has been noted

[1] D. Walker (January 2, 2008), "Average TV Size Up to 60-Inch by 2015 Says Sharp," http://www.techdigest.tv/2008/01/average_tv_size.html.

for playing online HD video. QuickTime is common on Apple computers. Flash is said to be the most friendly across operating systems. Shockwave is preferred by some high-end developers because it can do more than Flash, and VLC will play about anything.

For sizing, streaming, or other technical reasons (such as digital rights management), many organizations tend to use only one output format: Windows, QuickTime, or Flash.

Streaming

Streaming is how most news organizations and services such as YouTube provide video and audio. Because the full file is not delivered to the user's computer, the organization retains greater control over redistribution (although a quick Web search will turn up many programs designed to "capture" streams). Streaming generally requires special streaming servers and specific formats. It can be matched to different connection speeds and can start quickly on your computer before the entire stream is buffered. Many organizations also have their own "branded" players for streaming material so that they can frame the video with their logo or ads.

Capturing Mobile Video

Mobile video captured on a phone and uploaded to the Web may be the most exciting development these past few years and represents a huge shift in journalistic practice.

For decades, video was the domain of the professional broadcaster. Cameras and editing equipment were large, slow, heavy, and cumbersome. Now, as seen in figure 12.5, journalists and just about anyone else can record video on a mobile phone and upload it to YouTube or another file-sharing site. This rapid spread of information empowers people and enables conversation on virtually any topic, but there is less time to reflect or analyze, and short, grainy video clips hardly provide context. What you see is not always what happened.

To be able to transfer that video you've shot for breaking news or some other reason, your phone needs to be configured for easy uploading of video. Once that happens, though, you can begin immediately. Video is recorded using the MP4 format and file size can affect the time it takes to do a mobile upload. After you've captured the video, select the clip and upload it to your organization's website using whatever policies and procedures your company has set up.

Editing and Uploading Mobile Video

The basics of editing were previously covered in chapter 8 but will be touched on briefly here. For the highest quality video reports, journalists use professional DV cameras and nonlinear editing systems. When the report is aired over broadcast or cable systems, the viewer can appreciate the richness and quality. But on the smaller computer screen, short unedited clips tend to be more Web-friendly. Mobile video tends to be unedited and relies on the compelling nature of what's recorded to attract viewer interest.

How you upload your video online will depend on the specifications of your website or Internet service provider. Some sites allow you to browse for the file on your computer and then upload it, and the site's software takes care of any format conversion. Other sites require you to use software to convert the file on your computer before uploading or to use a separate computer to do the conversion and upload.

Figure 12.5 ■ Journalists can use their mobile devices to upload video reports from the field. The choice of shots is limited, and she or he must keep it short and to the point.

GRAPHICS

A graphic for this discussion is essentially any special visual element (as opposed to ordinary text) that is not video or a still picture and is designed to help tell the story (as distinguished from graphical elements that might be used to help navigate around a site). The key for graphics online is, "Keep it simple, make it interactive."

Maps, timelines, illustrations, and "pullout" boxes that list the key points of a story or key quotes are all examples. Graphics generally are drawn but do not have to be. A text box is simply text formatted in an easy-to-read way, such as a bulleted list and a larger size, designed to draw attention to itself and to be easy to digest.

The realities of online graphics are much the same as with video:

- Your fickle yet demanding audience wants to grasp things quickly.
- You have a smaller canvas than a newspaper or magazine page, and the user should not have to scroll up, down, or sideways to see the entire graphic.
- You have a restricted palette of "Web-safe" colors from which to choose, and newspaper graphics, generally done in the CMYK color scheme (cyan, magenta, yellow, black), must be redone for online in RGB (red, green, blue).

So the website is not the place for that full-page newspaper graphic of the inside of a battleship with minute detail and 87 individual labels. But the online user can get that kind of detail—make it interactive and instead of one detailed picture, layer many simpler elements. If the user clicks on one of the guns, up comes a page (or maybe a popup box) with a more detailed drawing and description of the typical guns, their size, and how they were used. Or click on the mess hall and get a typical week's menu. You can see how this can get to be a lot of work very quickly. This means more careful planning as a story develops.

Unlike photo programs like Photoshop, which use "bitmap" or "raster" graphics to build images pixel by pixel, the most popular graphics programs, such as Adobe Illustrator and CorelDraw, use vector graphics to build images from geometric shapes. Vector graphics can scale up or down infinitely, with no loss of quality. Raster graphics degrade quickly when enlarged.

If the complexity—and price—of those programs is out of reach, there are some simpler ways to create graphics. Open Office and Google Docs, for instance, have graphics programs, and Inkscape (http://inkscape.org) is an open source editor.

A spreadsheet program can create some simple graphs and charts using its graphing function, and then you can take a screenshot of just that graph or chart, save it as a JPEG, and post it as a still photo. If you own a Macintosh, the screenshot capability is built into the operating system. For Windows, freeware called Gadwin Print Screen (http://www.gadwin.com/printscreen/) will do the same thing.

You can create a text graphic the same way using a word processing program, a larger font, and perhaps a slightly different typeface. You can also create a rough but passable photo montage using a word processor and screen capture, too, as well as a timeline with photos.

OTHER INTERACTIVE ELEMENTS

The emphasis on interactive elements is because Web metrics repeatedly indicate the importance of time spent on a website, and the best way to keep people is to engage them. No video? No audio? No graphics? No problem—if you are thinking that a story is not just a river of text.

What about polls? There are a number of sites that will let you create a poll and post a widget (see chapter 12) on your site so people can click their choice then see the overall results.

How about quizzes? College students in particular show a fondness for creating and taking quizzes in connection with online stories. There are several free sites where you can create quizzes, but remember a few guidelines:

1. The user should be able to see the result of his or her quiz at the end. Some education-oriented sites are geared more toward reporting results back to the instructor. Don't pick a setting that shows the correct answer after each question because it slows things down.
2. Six to ten questions are good. The user should be able to complete the quiz in about two minutes, but there needs to be enough there to keep them engaged.

In the introductory material (first screen or top of first question), be sure to say how many questions there are.

3. Pick a site where you can upload images with the questions.
4. Multiple choice work best, and make sure they appear in the same order each time. This is especially important if the answers are in something like increasing amounts.

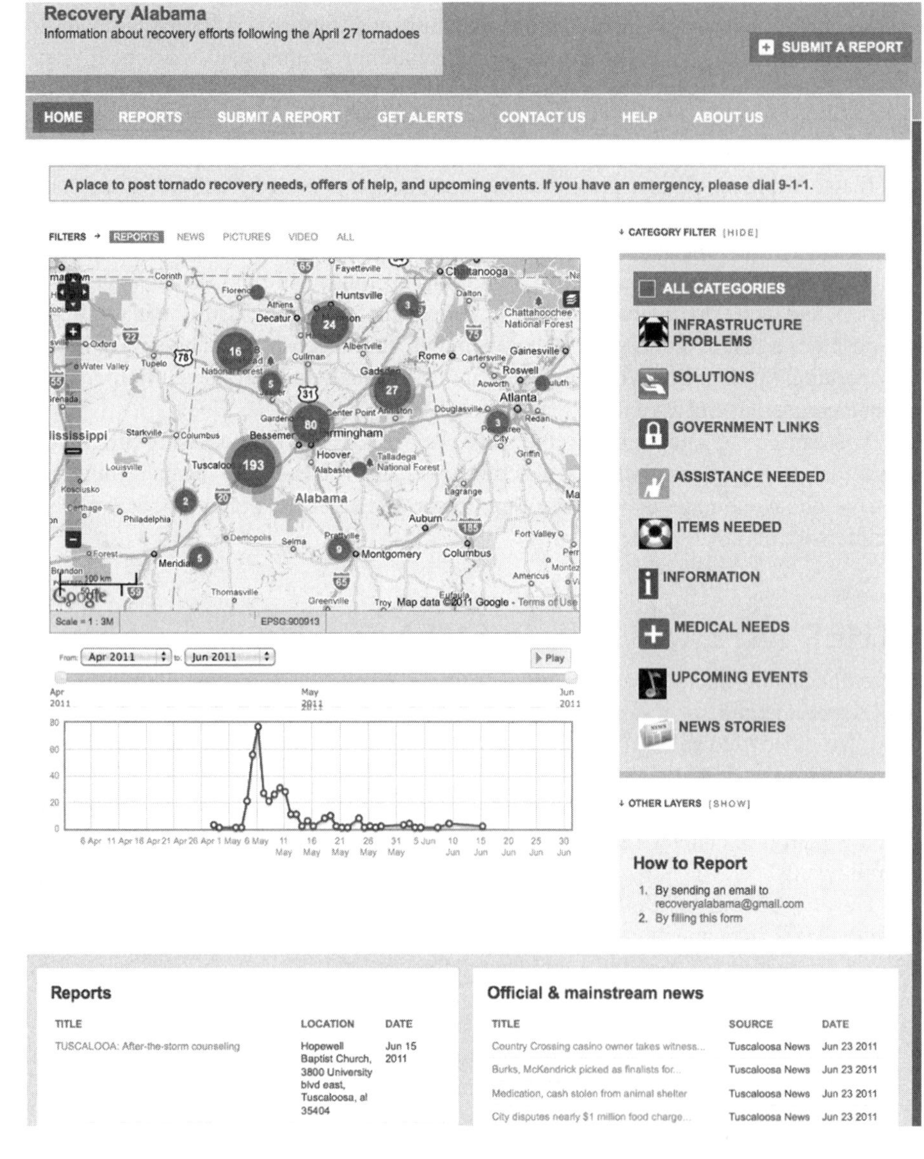

Figure 12.6 ■ New media tools enable us to create comprehensive interactive Web pages like this one for "Recovery Alabama." With such pages, recovery efforts can be coordinated and needs efficiently assessed to help the maximum number of people in the minimum amount of time.

This is part of something that has come to be known as **gamification**—the introduction of game-like elements in nongame situations. (A quiz, as long as the result doesn't count against you, can be seen as having game-like elements as you test your wits against the questions.)

One of the earliest examples was the *Virginian-Pilot*'s "Can You Spot the Shoplifters?" Users were asked to guess which people pictured in a store were shoplifters. As the cursor rolled over each person in the picture, the user learned whether his or her guess was right. Now, more sophisticated versions of these online interactives allow users, among other things, to help construct budgets, suggest ways to fix local transportation problems, or learn more about a foreign country in the news.

Maps lend themselves to a number of interactive possibilities. Many news organizations are taking Yahoo or Google maps and creating mashups by overlaying other data to illustrate things from crime reports to advertised yard sales. It is easy to create an interactive map on Google's My Maps, and it allows you to put some additional information into each of the popup boxes that corresponds to a point you have highlighted. Ushahidi, a Knight-Batten award-winner (see below), was used by the *Tuscaloosa News and Gadsden Times* after deadly tornadoes hit Alabama in early 2011 to create a crowd-sourced map of needs and resources at recoveryalabama.com (figure 12.6).

For a price, websites like iMapBuilder and MapsAlive allow you to quickly create mashups without having to do any coding. A well-crafted table or map can help explain a trend or action. The map in figure12.7 clearly and quickly indicates home addresses of convicted sex offenders in an area. Compare this to a lengthy listing of dates and addresses of the same incidents. The ethical issues involved with how and when to present such information are increasingly important in this information-rich age.

OTHER INNOVATIONS

Other ideas and possibilities for convergent journalism organizations to interact with the community can be found from the 2010 Knight-Batten award-winners, administered through J-Lab (http://www.j-lab.org/projects/knight-batten-awards-for-innovations-in-journalism/).

a. **Sunlight Live** project by the Sunlight Foundation, Washington, D.C. The nonprofit, nonpartisan watchdog group uses streaming, live blogging, and social networking to bring an openness to covering government events such as the U.S. House Government and Oversight Hearings. The blog posts verified facts and listed related links and was done in a fun and engaging way, demonstrating that government news can be a conversation. http://sunlightfoundation.com/live/archive/hcrsummit/.

b. **ProPublica Distributed Reporting** network systematically used crowdsourcing for ongoing investigative reporting projects. The nonprofit investigative news organization of more than thirty reporters operating out of Manhattan enlisted help from over 5,000 people. Projects included sifting through federal stimulus spending, looking into loan modification stories, and tracking oversight of a state nursing board.
http://www.propublica.org/special/reportingnetwork-signup.

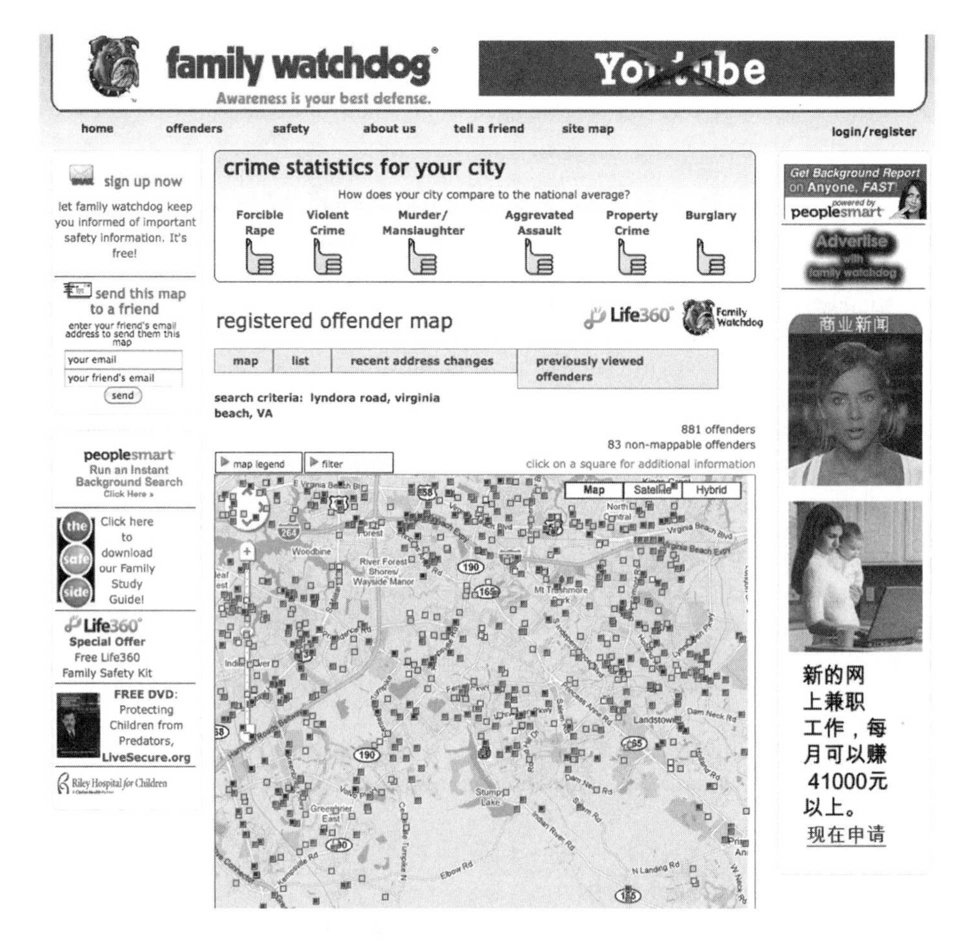

Figure 12.7 ■ Interactive Web sites allow users to get information specific to them or their families. Each user to an interactive site such as familywatchdog.us gets a personalized map, something that is not possible in other media.

c. **Ushahidi, Haiti**, operating out of Medford, Massachusetts, notably used map mashups to help with disaster relief efforts in Haiti after a January 2010 earthquake devastated Port-au-Prince and surrounding areas. Ushahidi used Skype, Twitter, Facebook, radio, and short codes to crowdsource local needs at that moment. http://haiti.ushahidi.com/.

d. **Sourcing Through Texting,** The Takeaway, WNYC, and Public Radio International in New York City worked with journalists from WDET Detroit to engage listeners and make a difference in their communities. Residents sent text tips about trucks speeding illegally down their side streets. Another project had residents send keywords describing their neighborhoods and the result was that nonlisteners became engaged and more informed. http://www.thetakeaway.org/.

As we see, it is now common for websites to solicit people to provide raw video, edited video, commentary, amateur reporting, photo essays, cell phone pictures, and just about any other form of content. Through these means we generate community involvement and excitement while strengthening our role in extending the conversation.

SUMMARY

Multimedia on the web can involve almost limitless permutations of content and delivery. Besides text, we can use still images packaged in galleries and slideshows, moving images, sound, graphics, animations, and other interactive elements to engage consumers and encourage them to become part of the greater community. A number of creative ventures and experiments in news organization, gathering, and delivery can serve as inspirations. The goal is to inspire us to become involved and make a difference in our own community and to break down barriers between the consumer of news and the journalist.

Although the tools constantly change, the basic function—telling the story in the best way—will always remain. Everyone wants to hear a good story that brings out the best (or perhaps the worst) of the human condition. Although you probably won't become expert in all of these tools, it is imperative to find the ones you seem to work best with and practice your craft. We learn best by doing, and there are no shortcuts. Each of the authors (and countless others) learned by reading the principles first and then going out and doing them. Now it's your turn.

EXERCISES

1. Create a photo gallery of interesting images (flowers, campus buildings, clouds) and experiment with processing and uploading them online.
2. Type a short script (30 lines, or about two minutes) of two or three news stories (it will be easier if you do this in 16- or 18-point type). Read the script into a recorder using a microphone. Listen to this (or if you don't like reviewing your own work, do this with a friend) and decide what works and what doesn't. Revise the script and do it again two or three times, seeking to smooth out the rough spots. Don't be afraid to simplify the language or split a sentence in two if you keep getting tripped up.
3. Read just the first story of your script two or three times. Start with the microphone about six inches from your mouth (you'll be holding it about mid-chest), then 12 inches, then about 18 inches (just above your waist). Which one sounds better? Now you'll know the best place to have the mic when you record.
4. Create your own podcast. Find an appropriate topic to analyze or critique, write up a script, and record three versions between one and three minutes each. Choose the best version and then find or create at least two appropriate sound effects to mix into your production. Upload the podcast to an appropriate site.
5. Use a cellphone or mobile video device to tell a story in a single-take of around :30. Do one version with the camera pointed at you; then do another one pointed toward the object and only provide voiceover. Which is more compelling, and why?
6. Put both of the items you created in exercise 5 on a video-sharing site and look at which one gets clicked on the most. Speculate as to why.

CHAPTER 13

CONVERGING WITH OTHER EMERGING MEDIA

When some people in journalism talk about "convergence," they think only in terms of adding a website to their newspaper or television station. But as discussed in the previous chapters, publishers, editors, and reporters increasingly discuss integrating print, broadcast, and online distribution of news in the same newsroom. "Convergence" is also not limited to these three forms of media. Social media have found a niche in almost every newsroom. And a plethora of other new technologies are emerging to offer a range of new opportunities to deliver news to the public.

These opportunities include text-only media, such as text messaging and RBDS (radio broadcast data systems); full-motion video; digital television multicasts; and digital signage. Delivery technologies can be as simple as a text message or as complicated as a fully formatted HTML email news service. Traditionally there are two ways to assess how content should be gathered, edited, and delivered through these emerging media. One is to start with the medium itself and its characteristics and then select and edit content to best reach the audience for that medium. The second starts with the story itself and considers what particular medium is best suited to tell each aspect of the story. Complicated financial stories demand graphics and text; celebrity features and dramatic scenes are more effective with video, or perhaps audio slideshows (if the video and audio are not synchronous).

The important thing is to look at the dimensions of each story and how the story can best be communicated through each medium. The key variable is the relative number of media choices available for distributing a story. Figure 13.1 illustrates the range of media

	Text	Graphics	Photos	Audio	Video	Interactivity
Newspapers	●●●	●●●	●●●			
Radio				●●●		
Television	●	●	●	●●	●●●	
Websites	●●●	●●●	●●●	●●●	●●●	●●●
Apps	●●●	●●●	●●●	●●	●●●	●●●
Digital Signage	●●	●●●	●●●		●●	●
RSS	●●●		●	●●●	●●●	
E-mail	●●●	●	●	●		
Text Messaging	●●●		●			
Enhanced Television	●	●	●	●●	●●●	●●●
RBDS	●					

Figure 13.1 ■ Comparison of new media.

available for each type of content. After reading this chapter, you'll see there are many options regarding additional distribution media.

The field of convergent journalism is too new to focus on any one medium in particular. Rather, you should think in terms of combinations of media, considering both the story and the medium's needs. This chapter presents a range of emerging media that may play an important part in the converged newsroom. Each medium is examined in terms of the audience, format, editorial considerations, timing factors, and basics of how it works. Ubiquitous technologies such as smartphone and tablet apps will be explored first, then the technologies that fill a more narrow newsroom niche.

APPS

The term "app" is shorthand for "application," which itself is a shorthand term created to refer to computer programs designed to deliver content to mobile devices. The term "app" now refers to programs that deliver content to tablet computers and other portable devices as well as smartphones. The key difference between apps and other types of computer programs is that apps generally are created to deliver content from a specific media organization, formatting that content for delivery on mobile devices.

Audience

Since 2010, apps have become the fastest-growing type of computer program as the two platforms they were created for, smartphones and tablet computers, gain market share. The audience reachable through apps consists of everyone who owns either device. As of 2011 less than half the U.S. population used either a tablet or a smartphone, but growth for both devices was strong, especially among the young and affluent, a valuable target for almost any media organization.

Timing

Apps are a "pull" technology, with users deciding when and where they will access information and entertainment. Usage patterns vary with the type of app: A sports app that delivers scores may be accessed more on weekends, for example, while a business app that delivers stock market quotes may be accessed more during weekday business hours.

Some apps are designed to emulate magazines, delivering a package of information every week or month to subscribers who have paid for or requested the content. Other apps, such as the ones provided by the *New York Times* and CBS News, deliver a continually updated menu of news organized by topic. As with websites and other pull technologies, there is a debate regarding whether routine content should be updated continually or on a schedule, but there is no debate regarding breaking news, which is always posted as soon as it is ready.

Editorial Considerations

An app's content can be as narrow or broad as you would like. The *New York Times* app, for example, provides almost all the news and information found in the newspaper (although the amount of advertising is greatly reduced as a proportion of space). However, the app's full features are available only to those who have a print or electronic subscription. Other organizations have simpler apps, with much less information, that are provided free as a tool for promoting content available in more depth on the Web, on TV, or in print.

If you are involved in designing or procuring apps for your organization, consider a few factors beyond traditional news value and other journalistic considerations. In this age of social media, the app should have a way to share content. Given that apps are primarily used in mobile devices whose users may have time initially to only sample content, they also should be able to save information for later use. Although users can't tear a page from an app as they could with a newspaper or magazine, you can provide the capability to bookmark and save content (as with the iPad's Readitlater app, for example). (For instance, rail or bus commuters might have a few minutes with good connectivity while waiting. Once on board, the connectivity could be spotty, but the app would have made it easy to save content during those few minutes for viewing during the ride.)

Finally, apps may present publishers with an opportunity to move to a content-based business model. But it's also good to keep in mind that a good app will not become a "walled garden" that seeks to keep the user only on the publisher's site. First, users are conditioned to being able to move around the digital world freely. Second, it is unlikely a publisher could ever match the vast amount of existing online content that can be used to augment and extend a publication. So a good app will let users follow links to discover other content, just as they could on a browser, as discussed in chapters 4 and 10.

Format Considerations

Theoretically, apps can deliver any type of media content that can be transmitted over the Internet. Most apps, however, are created to deliver specific types of content. The Weather Channel app, for example, delivers most of its information as plain text, but it also delivers images of weather maps and advertising banners. The most important consideration in formatting content for app delivery is the size of the screen that will be used to display the information. Much less detail is available on the screen of a smartphone than on a tablet, a television, or a regular computer screen, so images must be formatted appropriately (or enable users to zoom in on parts of the screen).

The size of text (font size) is another important consideration, and programmers should consider whether users want the same type of capability to increase font sizes for readability as they have had on traditional computers, or even whether the app should check for the display size and adjust fonts accordingly.

How They Work

For some smaller news organizations or journalists working on their own, apps could be a challenge for now. Creating apps requires specialized programming that takes skills beyond those needed to post content online for Web browsers. However, as has been the case with other technologies, it is likely that software improvements will make building apps easier and move much of the programming into the background.

Because apps are simply special-purpose computer programs, they can be programmed to emulate almost any kind of information delivery system, but most follow a few standards. First, the program must be designed for the operating system used by the device. For example, an app written for the iPhone won't work on an Android or Blackberry device—the app has to be rewritten specifically for each operating system. Second, the app must typically be selected and downloaded by the user. That means there is a major hurdle in promoting the app so that users can find and install it on their device(s). Then, information has to be available to be downloaded regularly upon user demand.

Some apps work primarily over the Internet. Others can use high-speed cellphone networks, and some can switch depending on the type of connection available. But in all cases, one or more computers (known as "servers") receive the content from a publisher (whether it is an organization or an individual) and forward it to the app upon request.

Other Issues

Apps represent an interesting multimedia challenge. It is easy to configure an app to deliver video, but getting a reliable video stream to the mobile device is sometimes more problematic. Although most devices that run apps are capable of playing audio, these devices are also frequently used in places where audio might be a distraction. In addition, Apple's early devices have not supported Flash, a common programming technology used to create and display video, animations, and other rich multimedia content. Newsrooms are still figuring out how to deal with these challenges, and the ultimate manner in which apps will be used in newsrooms will be important to watch over the next few years.

DIGITAL SIGNAGE

Signs are one of the most ubiquitous forms of print media, the original place-based communication medium. But almost all forms of signage, from small placards to billboards, can now be replaced by electronic displays known as "digital signage" that allow communication of almost any type of visual message. For journalists and media organizations, digital signage represents a new way of distributing news and information, illustrated in figure 13.2. Applications range from small computer-type displays that hang on the wall to large billboards and even stadium video displays. Digital signage is primarily used for advertising or commercial messages, but many news organizations have realized the potential for using digital signage to deliver the news.

Two examples illustrated in figure 13.2 show the range of digital signage: the *New York Times* has a partnership with RMG Networks to display continuously updated news headlines in 800 cafes in five major cities using standard television displays. At the other end of the spectrum, the *Las Vegas Sun* has experimented with using electronic billboards along highways to display headlines, hoping to attract visitors to its website.

The rules for delivering news via digital signage are not much different from those for billboard ads: The information must be brief, usually 10 words or fewer. Digital signage is thus most effectively used to transmit headlines.

Audience

Audiences for digital signage depend on location and the number of people who can see the display. A small display in a restaurant or coffee shop might be seen by no more than a few hundred people a day, while a similar sign in a shopping mall or subway station might be seen by thousands. Placement of digital signage will generally try to maximize the number of people who can see it, although the focus may be on specific audience segments and not a general audience. In most cases, people will pay more attention to news on digital signs when it is either breaking news or it relates to the specific environment (for example, sports information on a digital display in a stadium). In most, but not all cases, digital signage is used to drive traffic to your other outlets, so the critical question is what type of message will get attention and cause people to follow the story in another medium.

Timing

Most digital signs are like websites in that information tends to be updated continually. In cases where the sign's primary purpose is transmitting news, the updates reflect changing news headlines. But some organizations, such as hotels, have groupings of information (announcements, welcome messages, generic information about the hotel, ads, etc.) that rotate in a set cycle. Because many digital signs can be split into "zones," each of which can display different information, many signs in office buildings, hotels, and other public places display both types of content, often with headlines streaming across the bottom of the other messages.

Editorial Considerations

If you liken digital signage to traditional billboards and other signs, you'll see that the amount of information that can be conveyed is quite limited. It is possible to use smaller type to put more information on the screen, but the smaller the type, the closer someone has to be to read the sign.

At best, you can provide two headlines or perhaps a tease for another medium ("More police on the street... tonight on Channel 6"). As with all good teases, it has to be specific enough to attract reader interest. If it's too general, the audience may ignore it. At the same time, it should be careful to avoid ambiguity. For example, "President told of danger" is not a very good headline, even by newspaper standards, because of its

Figure 13.2 ■ An example of digital signage used to display headlines in a coffee shop.

ambiguity. Was the president told, or did he do the telling? "*President was told of danger*" is the better headline (as it is on the Web, where the headline is likely the link that leads readers to the story). Even better would be to specify what danger is in question.

Format Considerations

The word limit on most digital signage also restricts the decisions you can make regarding format. In some cases, you might be able to choose the color of the letters, but not to the point where the color becomes a distraction. Fonts should be kept simple and readable. Generally, blocky sans-serif fonts (think Arial instead of Times, for instance) work better for such "display" type.

Digital signs can deliver much more than text, including photos, graphics, and video. But you have to be selective—you might not have speakers for audio, for instance, so the visuals have to be self-explanatory and simple. You don't want to get too elaborate with color and effects that become a distraction. Video that is too elaborate also can require a passer-by to stop and watch. If the sign is in a high-traffic area such as the corridor of a train station or an airport, encouraging people to stop and watch can cause problems as they get in the way of others.

How It Works

Digital signs are connected to a computer that controls the display on the board. In turn, that small computer might use the Internet or telephone lines to download content from a larger host computer on which you have put the items. The host computer (sometimes also called a "server") lets the news staff manually upload stories, or it can be programmed to "scrape" headlines from the organization's website or other source. The system also has to be programmed to periodically change the message. This decision on how often to rotate headlines is critical; if the rotation is too fast, then some people won't be able to read what's on the screen, but if it is too slow, others will get bored and ignore it.

Other Issues

It can be expensive for a news organization to own or rent digital signs (such as those at airports or billboard-style signs along highways). But well-placed digital signs can attract extra traffic to a website, television broadcast, or other medium, increasing the advertising revenue from those outlets, and the signs themselves can be another outlet for the organization to sell ads.

However, a news organization might find opportunity without having to own or lease signs. With digital signs becoming more common in public places (as well as inside companies that use them for internal communication), news organizations such as CNN are syndicating content they already produce for display on those signs. There is no reason a local news organization couldn't look for similar opportunities in its market. The investment is relatively small, and it opens another stream of revenue at a time when media organizations' economic survival may depend on aggregating many smaller revenue streams.

Digital signage is a technology in its infancy. As with most new media, a great deal of experimentation will occur before industry standards emerge. In the meantime, the signs' increasing presence offers a tantalizing opportunity to reach consumers with news and information in those times and places they might need them most.

RSS

The term "RSS," short for "really simple syndication" or "rich site summary" (another version is called "Atom"), is an Internet tool to push content to users who have selected to receive that content. The content is delivered directly to an application on the user's computer, to a special website to which the person subscribes, or even to a person's Twitter feed or Facebook page. Some applications store the content until the user specifically requests that it be displayed; others display it immediately and automatically. You can tell that a website or blog has an RSS feed if you see an orange button that says "RSS" or "XML" or appears as a series of arcs depicting waves emitting from the lower left corner (see figure 13.3). Many browsers will now display that symbol in the site address bar when an RSS feed is present, and you can click to add the feed to your browser's bookmarks or favorites. Because of the ungainly and nonstandard names, some people have suggested calling all these "Web feeds." They think eventually most content will be delivered this way, with people rarely going to actual Web pages.

Audience

RSS users are a select number but are growing in number as RSS capabilities become standard in Web browsers. RSS subscribers have chosen to receive specific content and to trust your organization enough to allow you to deliver that content automatically. The most important thing to remember about RSS subscribers is that they have asked to receive the information but retain control of whether to read, listen to, view, or ignore what you send them.

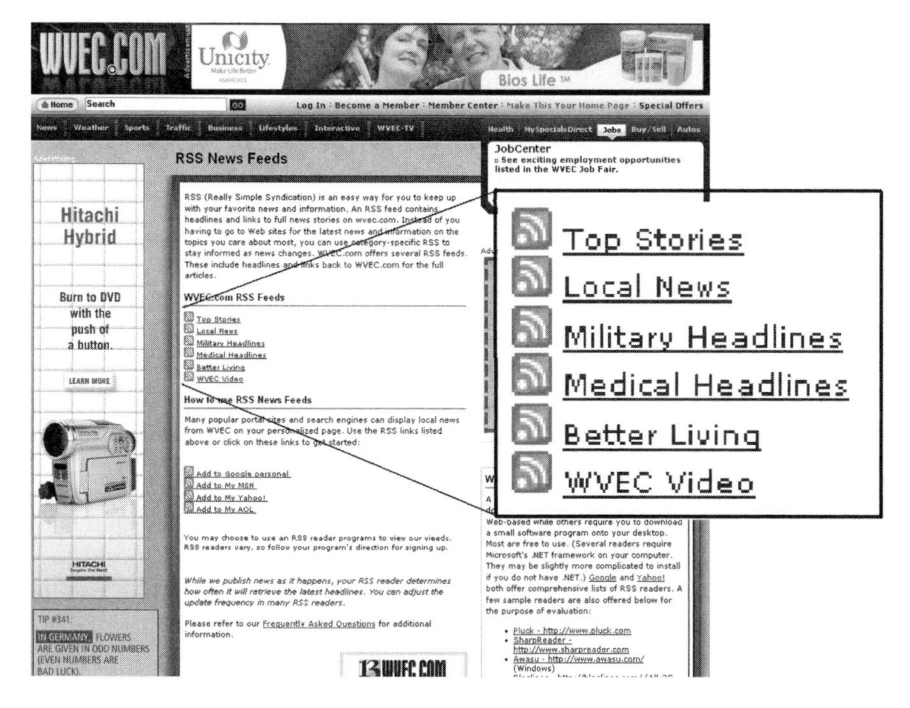

Figure 13.3 ■ The RSS button on a Web page indicates the presence of an RSS feed. By clicking on the button in some browsers or by copying and pasting the underlying link into a feed reader, you "subscribe" to the feed, and your computer automatically lets you know when new information is available.

Timing

An RSS item is generated, often automatically by the publishing system, primarily when another action takes place such as material being posted to a website or a blog. Therefore, the timing is tied to those actions and generally is not independent. Some efforts are being made to establish RSS feeds as their own independent, ad-supported channels; but so far those are rare. Some online sites that receive and aggregate the RSS feeds you want to monitor will also alert you via email or a message to your wireless device when a new item has been received. Everything in this world of new media is becoming interconnected.

One consideration in distributing information using RSS is whether it should be done on a regular schedule. People have distinct patterns of media consumption. They have specific times for watching television, reading the newspaper, and even surfing the Internet. Over time, they can and will condition themselves to expect new information at specific times if you take the effort to deliver that information on a regular schedule. On the other hand, some RSS content—blog postings, for example—takes place only when the sender has something new to say. The consideration is how you balance the habits of the audience with the availability of new information.

As with other media, the exception is always breaking news. However, distribution of breaking news using RSS presumes that your subscriber has an expectation of receiving breaking news or some other form of frequently updated information from your organization.

Editorial Considerations

The editorial content of your RSS feed will largely be determined by your Web publishing or blogging software. Settings in that software will determine, for instance, whether you send a "full" or "abbreviated" RSS feed. The full feed, as it implies, sends the entire item to your RSS reader, and you never have to go back to the original online site to read it. An abbreviated feed is usually just the first 250 characters or so—enough to entice you to click through to the online site to view the original item.

Some services send both kinds of feeds. The full feed is designed for private, noncommercial use, while the abbreviated feed can be used by sites that monitor various sources on a specialized topic and may display the RSS entries along with the monitoring sites' own ads.

Journalists should have a reader packed with feeds. For instance, many sites create an RSS when you perform a search. Download the feed into your reader, and you won't have to do that search again, but it will be updated. Want to follow someone on Twitter without having to check in all the time? There's a feed that will put those tweets into your reader for later.

We've mentioned following tags with an RSS feed and, of course, there are also just straight, old-fashioned news feeds. Especially if you are working a beat, there's probably a trade magazine or other specialty publication with an RSS feed. Many times those feeds can be narrowed down significantly to get you a minimum of nonrelevant items.

Besides, RSS still remains one of the ways to get your content out there to the wider world. Almost every digital publishing system these days has feed-creation built in.

Format Considerations

Since almost any kind of information, from plain text to full-motion video, can be distributed using RSS, the most important consideration regarding format is that it must be consistent. Since each member of the public has distinct patterns of media use, you want consumption of your message to be part of those patterns. This means you have to be consistent in providing and updating desired information.

How It Works

RSS requires two components: an RSS reader either online or as software on a user's computer (sometimes built into a browser) and a website that indexes content when it is updated. When you "subscribe" to an RSS feed, your browser or reader automatically checks the website for updated information. When new information is available, the updated full or abbreviated feed is downloaded to your computer and you can choose whether to read or ignore it.

Other Issues

RSS is not a new medium, but it represents enough of an enhancement to information delivery that it deserves special coverage in this chapter. The RSS technology allows any information to alert users when new information is available and, thus, has the potential to drive additional traffic to a website.

With the number of websites and the amount of information available from those sites increasing every day, news organizations will need every advantage they can get to attract attention from the public. RSS feeds are one of the best ways to ensure that someone who has found information on your site to be useful will come back to the site when new information is available. The primary barrier is the users themselves—although using RSS is comparatively simple for users, most people don't take the time to subscribe, limiting the effectiveness of the technology.

EMAIL NOTIFICATION

Email is so, well, 2005. So why do you still find a lot of news sites giving you the option of getting breaking news or a daily summary of stories sent to your inbox?

Email is still a powerful communications tool, especially in the business and professional communities. While smartphones are gaining ground, the Blackberry is still used by many executives and managers because of its built-in international email system. So when your economic survival depends on getting your content in front of people whenever, wherever, and however *they* want it, don't sell email short just yet.

Unlike text messages (or Twitter), you have more choices in the types and length of content you can deliver through email. The first step is to decide what type of service you're providing.

As shown in figure 13.4, email can be used to deliver almost any kind of content that can be delivered on the Web, including video, audio, pictures, and graphics—as long as that content can get past a growing phalanx of spam filters. As with apps, you also have to take into account the possibility that more of your email messages are being read on small screens, such as Blackberrys.

The big difference between delivering news on a website and delivering the same content in an email message is how involved the reader is in receiving the message. Email subscriptions are comparable to newspaper subscriptions. The reader gets the content regularly but can choose whether to read it now or later. Some systems also allow the reader to receive the entire report as an email, complete with images and other files, or as just a message with a link that can be followed to the complete report on a website (this gives an option to those whose antispam systems block some types of files). Email subscriptions may be more similar to picking up a newspaper off the rack—readers who have asked that it be delivered to them are more likely to have a specific motivation for reading the content because they have sought it out.

The danger is that if you overdo the messages, or if they don't continue to have things the user finds useful, they become spam, resulting in the user largely ignoring the messages or unsubscribing. On the other hand, email alerts and periodic summaries can position you as a valuable news source and increase the number of people visiting your website, watching your newscast, or picking up your newspaper. As with other converged media, a basic editorial and marketing decision is whether the news stories delivered through email are designed to stand on their own as self-contained reports or are a tease for content that is more completely delivered using other media.

Audience

Almost everyone who can receive your news stories through other media can receive them via email. The strength of email is that you can effectively segment your audience, delivering to each person only the types of news in which he or she is interested. With the proper programming, you can create a system that delivers sports scores and sports

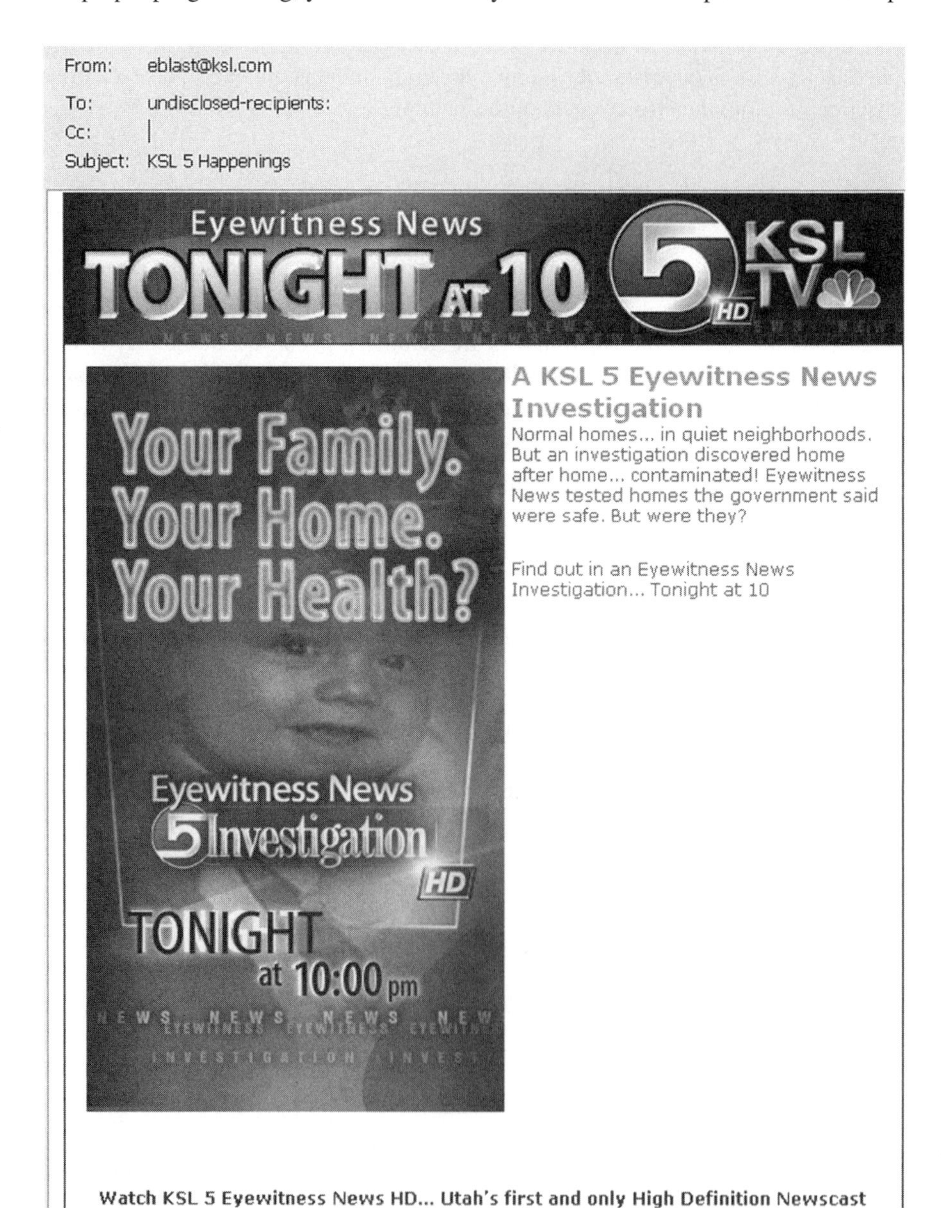

Figure 13.4 ■ Example of an emailed news report.

news to sports fans, political news to political junkies, entertainment news to those who are most interested in receiving it, and major breaking news stories to everyone.

You will have to decide the degree to which (1) you will enable people to select the specific types of stories to receive and (2) the amount of work your staff can put into customizing and delivering these stories. Although it is easy to create large menus of content that allow virtually every subscriber to receive his or her own personal combination of news, setting up such a system results in more day-to-day work for those responsible for the email product.

You will also have to decide on frequency of delivery and who decides what stories to include. As with other ancillary media, you can either allow the reporter or story-builder to decide whether a particular story should be included, let an editor make this decision across all stories you cover that day, or set up some combination, especially when there is breaking news.

Timing

Breaking news should be delivered as soon as the story is verified and is reasonably complete. Important changes must also be passed along quickly, but with email there is a caution—you can't bombard people's inboxes with every incremental development you might put online. The best solution is probably to deliver basic story information (the five W's and H) and then, judiciously, updates that include a link to where more details and developments can be found.

The delivery timing of other stories or summaries depends upon the type of news. Initial business news summaries, for example, are best delivered early in the morning before the stock market opens (especially any "look-ahead" stories) and then shortly after the stock market closes, with updates throughout the trading day as needed. Timing can also depend on your objectives. For example, if the goal is to get a person to watch the 6 P.M. news, the briefs should be delivered in the late afternoon. If the goal is to update a person on events that happened overnight, however, the best time is in the morning.

Editorial Considerations

Email allows stories of almost any length but works best for brief summaries and headlines. Stories should be selected that reflect interests the reader expressed when subscribing (if that was an option), but keep the stories short. Also, provide a link to a Web page or other source with additional information, instructions on where the reader can see or read a more complete story, or some combination of the two.

The easiest way to select stories for distribution via email is to let a computer choose according to relevant keywords or tags. But, as noted in chapter 5, tagging has not caught on in many newsrooms, and tags can fall prey to inconsistency. The danger is twofold: Some stories may be delivered that are not relevant to particular audience members, and some stories that should be delivered will not be. The solution is to ensure that at least one editor or producer examines and approves the content before distribution.

Format Considerations

Two big decisions must be made when formatting email news: the length of the stories and the appearance of the message. Some readers won't read more than a paragraph of a story delivered via email. Be brief and provide links to additional information.

Appearance is also important. The simplest email message consists of plain text. At the other extreme is HTML formatting, which allows you to embed pictures, graphics, and even full-motion video. Logos, pictures, and other information can help your organization's branding; but it can make the message file size so big that it takes too long to transmit or receive. It also can make it more vulnerable to antispam systems that may be programmed to reject messages with certain kinds of files or embedded pictures. Ask yourself whether that information can be better delivered through a Web page or another medium rather than an email.

How It Works

Many email summaries are generated automatically by services such as Google's Feedburner that turn the news organization's RSS feed into an email at least once a day (as long as there is new material). In that case, you are not going to get many formatting options except those that transmit in your RSS feed (which can include pictures and other multimedia, depending on how that feed is set up). Breaking news may be nothing more than a regular email message sent out through a mail-blast program that inserts the news organization's logo into the message.

More elaborate summaries are usually created using templates similar to those used to create Web pages. The template will identify your organization and include your logo, subscription information, and other material that brands your organization. Your job is to write the headlines, story summaries, and other text that goes into the message, and then select pictures or other information to accompany the text. These messages are then uploaded to a server that automatically generates messages to be delivered at predetermined times.

Other Issues

Because email spam is such a big problem, a special set of laws governs the use of emails by commercial organizations, including the media. In the United States, email news alerts usually must include information on how a reader can unsubscribe and include a street address for your organization.

How a user may subscribe to your organization's alerts can be as simple as having the person send you an email requesting to be added to your subscription list. Or you can place a form on your website where a user can type in his or her email address and be added. One problem with such a system is identity verification, so most organizations send a confirmation message when a person signs up, requesting they click on a link in the email to verify their interest in the subscription. This "double opt-in system" makes it a little more difficult for a person to subscribe as someone else but generally ensures that people who don't want their mailbox cluttered with your messages will not receive them.

TEXT MESSAGING

Cellphones are ubiquitous and versatile. Most cellphones now can send and receive text messages, making them an ideal way to deliver some news—generally, breaking stories and those requiring regular updates or that can be easily summarized—from a converged newsroom. Text messages are sometimes referred to as "SMS" (short-message system) and usually are limited to fewer than 150 characters, including spaces (one popular news website publishing system that allows the user to also send a text message at the time the story is moved online limits it to 133 characters).

Audience

Although cellphones are broadly distributed across the population, younger users are more likely to use them to send and receive text messages. Text messages interrupt conversations, work activities, and even driving, so remember that a story delivered via text message must be important enough to warrant the interruption.

Each text-messaging user must be able to easily opt-in to receive content as well as have a way to easily unsubscribe. You don't want users to become angry or frustrated with your newsroom because they are receiving (and perhaps paying for) content they no longer want.

You also need to consider the demographics of the people who choose to receive your text messages. It's easy to assume that they represent a cross section of your current readers or viewers, but that assumption is probably not correct. Rather, subscribers to text-message news delivery are probably younger on average than other media consumers. You should consider whether any research is needed regarding this audience to help you focus your text-messaged news on the needs and interests of these users.

Timing

There are two distinct options for the timing of content delivered using text messages. First is breaking news (discussed in the next section), and second is a summary of content at regular intervals (e.g., a stock market summary shortly after the market closes on weekdays or a scoreboard every hour during football season). Intuitively, text messaging appears best suited for breaking news. However, since most audience members consume news in a predictable pattern by time of day and day of week (reading newspapers, watching television newscasts, or visiting news-oriented websites), regular updates may also be desired. Again, the key is that the user must want and expect the information.

Editorial Considerations

The medium is too new to definitively say what type of news is best for text messaging. Newsrooms are experimenting with sending different types of stories at different times and in different formats. As mentioned earlier, the most effective use of text messaging appears to be distributing very short breaking news stories—information important enough to interrupt a person's activity.

Examples of breaking news that directly affect the reader include storm warnings, major accidents, and traffic problems. Done well, SMS news can strengthen the user's reliance upon your news operation for information that affects his or her daily life. A second type of content requires a user to subscribe to a feed from your newsroom. Such content could include, but is not limited to, sports scores, stock prices, or entertainment news. A third type of content is promotional or cross-branding, such as giving a reason for visiting your website or television station, perhaps by alerting the user to a longer enterprise story posted online, available in a printed edition, or to be broadcast in an upcoming newscast.

Format Considerations

Technology allows almost any type or length of message to be distributed using text messages. But at the common 150-character maximum, text messages are best used for delivering headlines or short summaries. The sender should think in terms of an "extreme inverted pyramid" style of writing. All the important information is crammed into the beginning of the story in as few words as possible. For example, a severe weather update could be simply: "Wx watch: T'storm this pm."

A news text message consists of three parts: a headline to get the attention of the user; a summary of the story, comparable to the lead in a print story; and information on where additional information is available. Most often today, the link takes the form of a short URL (explained previously in the Twitter discussion in chapter 11).

How It Works

Delivering news stories using text messaging is one of the easiest ways to deliver any type of news. Any computer can be loaded with the appropriate software, the story can be typed into the message body, and clicking a "send" button activates the software that delivers the message to your subscribers. As noted above, some news publishing systems also are integrating the ability to send a text message at the same time a story is uploaded to your website.

People generally subscribe to your service by signing up on your website, requesting the service from their cellular telephone provider, or receiving your stories as part of a larger package of information. From a reporter's perspective, this process is usually invisible; but if you can subscribe to the same service as your users, you will better understand their perspective.

One other important consideration in delivering news via text messaging is to be careful not to overuse such a service. Because it is an interruption and because some service providers may charge the consumer to receive each message, be selective about the news you send via SMS.

Other Issues

One of the most interesting capabilities of cellphones equipped with text messaging is that they let people alert a newsroom about breaking news. This capability becomes even more important because most cellphones also come equipped with cameras. People can snap a picture, create a caption, and instantly send it to your newsroom.

To take advantage of this capability requires three things:

1. The newsroom must be equipped to receive text messages (and pictures).
2. The public must be aware of the capability and the address or phone number they will use to send news tips, pictures, and other content.
3. The newsroom must have set procedures to verify content, the same way any content submitted by the public is verified before it is distributed.

Box 13.1 Ethics: Abuse of SMS Technology

In early 2003 a number of countries had to deal with outbreaks of severe acute respiratory syndrome (SARS). The sickness was especially severe in Asia, resulting in thousands of cases and several hundred deaths. The Special Administrative Region of Hong Kong, China, was especially hard hit, with dozens of new cases reported each day. In the midst of this frightening and uncertain time, a teenage boy set off a panic with a prank text message (SMS). On April Fool's Day, a text message allegedly from the Hong Kong government was widely distributed to cellphones, asserting it would immediately be quarantined as "an infected port." This designation is the most drastic of measures and means no one would be allowed to enter or leave the area. The notice sent the city into a panic, and there was an immediate run on stores for basic foodstuffs. But the panic was defused as quickly as it started when the Hong Kong government immediately began sending calming messages to millions of cellphones. The health director also held a live news conference in the afternoon, affirming the message was a hoax. This event demonstrated the power of the technology to disrupt as well as the ability of authorities to correct rumors.

Ownership of audience-submitted content could be an issue, but it is easily addressed with a disclaimer specifying that sending a picture or text to the newsroom's address gives the organization permission to publish this material. This notice should be delivered to every person who signs up to send and receive news from your newsroom.

The best place to ask people to submit content via text messages is through the news blurbs they already are getting via SMS. Audience members already receiving content from the newsroom both are more likely to submit content and will have the "address" for submitting content bookmarked on their cellphones.

OTHER TECHNOLOGIES

A few other technologies may soon provide new outlets for news and information. Some of these technologies are too new to know exactly how they will affect the newsroom; others are more established but haven't proved their value for news distribution. This section explores a few of these technologies.

Enhanced Television

In 2011 a new generation of "enhanced" televisions was introduced. In addition to receiving traditional video signals, these televisions include an Internet connection, enabling a new generation of interactive content. A few television manufacturers have embraced Internet-connected television in the hopes of selling more new sets, and a few companies such as Google are actively developing content to bring the interactivity of the computer to the television set. It is still too early to predict the impact of enhanced television in newsrooms, but journalists need to watch the development so they can provide content through this system when enough users have adopted it. Media historians might note that manufacturers have attempted to introduce television receivers with built-in computers since the early 1980s without much success, so adding Internet access to a television may result in a more interactive experience for the user, or just provide another set of channels to deliver reruns.

RBDS

Most listeners don't realize that every radio station in the United States can transmit a stream of digital information along with the music or talk. This information, designed to be displayed on the radio's faceplate, usually consists of the call letters of the station and the name of a song or a program.

This radio broadcast data service, or RBDS, can also be used to transmit short bursts of news. Traffic reports are the most frequent content, but transmitting virtually any kind of text information is possible. The problem is threefold: Most radios are not equipped to receive the information, most listeners don't look at their radios to see what information is being transmitted, and most radio stations don't bother to transmit information other than the call letters and information about the program. Nonetheless, with the advent of digital radio, RBDS has the potential to become an interesting tool for delivery of news by radio stations.

Although you might not make regular use of RBDS, it's a useful technology to know about. Especially as our information-gathering and monitoring devices become increasingly mobile, such technologies are likely to get additional consideration as channels for transmitting news, information, and advertising. For instance, why couldn't RBDS be used to reach users of mobile devices such as iPods if they have a special adapter? A station doing a live report at a store might seek to create hype by telling people with portable devices to check their displays for special deals. It demonstrates that even the most basic media have new dimensions in the converged environment.

Video Games

The latest generation of video game consoles, including the Nintendo Wii, Microsoft Xbox, and Sony Playstation 3, includes Internet connectivity so users can play against others around the world. The console manufacturers quickly realized this also transformed the game console into a powerful information retrieval device that could be used to deliver a variety of information, from high-quality digital movies to custom advertising messages within a game.

This opportunity is illustrated by the news reader built into Nintendo's Wii video game system. Any Wii that is connected to the Internet has the capability of delivering news organized for and targeted to Wii users. You don't normally think of a video game as a news medium, but a hard-core gamer who does not read a newspaper or watch television news might end up reading news on a TV screen, delivered through the video game system. The Associated Press, recognizing the opportunity, agreed to provide news to Wii users as early as 2007.

Widgets

Yet another way to distribute news and information is through "widgets" (also called "gadgets" in some software), those little snippets of computer code that can be embedded in a browser or sit on a computer's desktop screen and connect online to retrieve weather, headlines, scores, and stock listings, among other things. Early on, they were known as "desk accessories" on the Macintosh operating system and "active desktop" in Windows. The Poynter Institute has noted how some news organizations also have started using them as an interface to connect to online databases of information.

Their value is that they are always, but unobtrusively, in front of the user and able to be brought front and center with a click or a mouse movement. The potential variety of widgets seems almost endless, but they, along with SMS, RSS, and similar emerging means of distributing news and information, share the attributes of forcing the information stream into ever-tighter quarters that will put a premium on tight, bright writing; simple visual interfaces; and quick response in all quarters of the news operation.

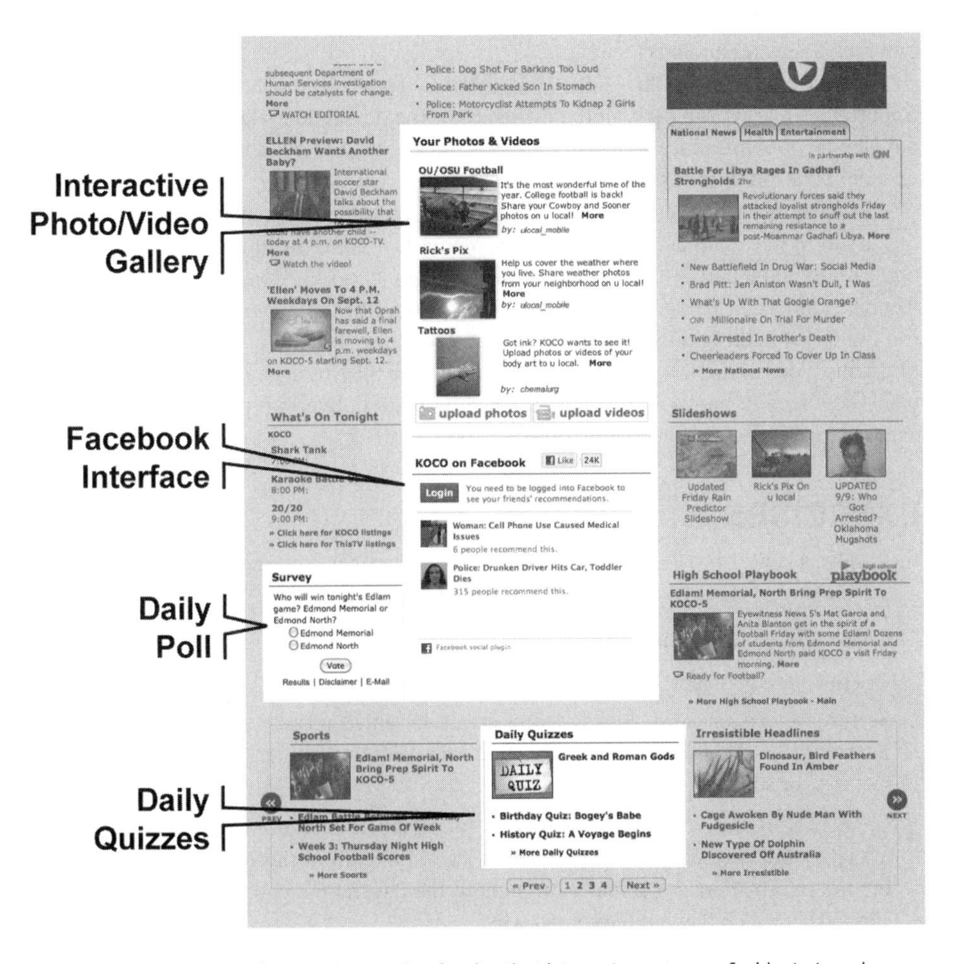

Figure 13.5 ■ KOCO.com is a good example of a site that integrates a range of widgets to enhance the reader experience. Included here is a daily poll, a quiz, interactive photo/video gallery, and a Facebook link.

It's instructive to know that creating the widgets themselves is also not as difficult as you might think. An interesting demonstration can be found at http://www.widgetbox.com/widgets/.

For example, most news organizations use the lower right section of the main Web page to place something devoted to soliciting feedback from people. It can be a daily poll asking about a major event or reflecting habit and personal lifestyle. A prime example is the Web page illustrated in figure 13.5. Not only are polls and interactive maps found at the bottom of the page, but there are additional ways of engaging visitors through links to advergaming and branded media; games, puzzles, and trivia; and even online coupons.

SUMMARY

Today's newsrooms have only begun to scratch the surface of possibilities for delivering news to the public. Among the challenges newsrooms face will be whether and when to embrace a new technology.

Consider the example of the Wii, above. The point is not that the Wii is so important—it is far too early in the diffusion of the device to make that claim—but that any device or communication system that is on any kind of network has the potential to be a delivery medium for news.

Over the next 10 years, news operations will experiment extensively with the media discussed in this chapter, as well as other media just being invented. You will have the opportunity to be part of this experimentation if you choose. Along the way, you'll have to make important decisions regarding format, timing, the audience, and other editorial issues. In making those decisions, always consider three interwoven considerations regarding your audience: where they are and what they're doing, what they want and what they need to know, and what you are capable of delivering to them using the tools available in your converged newsroom.

EXERCISES

1. Choose a story from the front page of today's newspaper. Rewrite the story as:
   a. A text-message alert.
   b. A headline for a billboard.
   c. An email message.
2. Select a television news package, and create an email message containing that story. In the process, consider what information you want to communicate using text, video, pictures, or audio.
3. Create a daily text-message news service for members of your class. Choose from five to eight stories to send, and experiment with sending all of the stories at once or sending the information sporadically throughout the day. At the end of the week, ask your classmates which they preferred and why.
4. Try the same experiment as in exercise 3 by sending the text-message alerts to your parents or other adults. At the end of the week, consider how their use of your news service differs from that of your classmates and why it is different.

5. For one day, make a list of all of the digital signage your encounter. For each one, make a note of:
   a. Where and when you saw the sign.
   b. How useful the information was on the sign.
   c. How the information was formatted.
   d. Whether you think it is possible to insert any type of news along with the content that is already being delivered.

CHAPTER 14

THE BUSINESS OF CONVERGENT JOURNALISM

Traditionally, American news media have maintained a separation between the news and advertising sales staffs. The rationale has been to preserve the credibility of the news, ensuring that advertisers—or others who might seek to influence news content—will not receive favored treatment. This separation has been so important it is often referred to as a "firewall" between the editorial and business aspects of a media organization.[1]

This firewall was easy to maintain when news organizations were extremely profitable. In the last part of the 20th century, for example, newspapers had typical profit margins of 20 to 30 percent, and television stations' profit margins were even higher. Such high profits allowed media organizations to report on wrongdoing by businesses that were also potential advertisers without substantially affecting the bottom line.

The firewall also meant most journalism textbooks did not cover the business aspects of news organizations, keeping the focus on the process of gathering, editing, and delivering the news. But as journalism has evolved, the need for journalists to know more about the business of journalism is increasing for at least three reasons:

- Profit margins are down, so the more you know about the business side, the better you can map your career.

---

[1] B. Kovach and T. Rosenstiel, *The Elements of Journalism: What Newspeople Should Know and the Public Should Expect,* completely updated and revised (New York: Three Rivers Press, 2007).

- The media system is in flux, with new opportunities for journalists emerging at an incredible rate. Taking advantage of these opportunities requires you to know as much about the business of journalism as about reporting, editing, or producing.
- More journalists are becoming entrepreneurs, spurred by the ease of creating a digital media outlet. To be successful, entrepreneurial journalists have to know as much about business as they do about journalism.

This chapter's purpose is to explore the business side so that you will be better prepared for a career in the rapidly evolving field of journalism. Three primary areas will be discussed, starting with the "basic equation" in business. Then, current and future business models for journalism will be explored. Finally, you will be introduced to the opportunities and challenges of entrepreneurial journalism.

THE "BASIC EQUATION"

Virtually all for-profit businesses are governed by a deceptively simple equation:

Revenues – Expenses = Profit
R – E = P

In order to make a profit, the total revenues—the money coming into a business—have to be greater than the total expenses. One implication of the firewall between journalism's editorial and business aspects is that most reporters and editors see only the expenses. Most news departments are given an expense budget, with only higher-level managers and executives seeing the connections between overall expenses and revenues. As long as the news department stays within its budget, further knowledge of the organization's finances is not needed.

But for this chapter, we will cross the firewall so we can understand revenues as well as expenses. In fact, for most businesses, the majority of management attention is on revenues, where there is more variance, rather than expenses. Put another way, before you can spend money, you have to know where it comes from.

Since the goal of most businesses is profit maximization, the two ways to increase profits are to increase revenues or decrease expenses. But both are short-term solutions, and a common managerial mistake is to apply the formula that way rather than for the long term.

The key to good business management is to learn how to apply this equation to maximize profits *over time*. The best way to increase long-term profits is to increase revenues rather than decreasing expenses, and the best way to increase revenues over the long term is actually to *increase* expenses—making an investment in personnel, equipment, marketing, and so on. Making such an investment will usually reduce short-term profits, but it is the best way to increase long-term profits.

(Businesses have special ways to account for expenses designed to yield a long-term payoff, and that discussion of financial accounting is beyond this book's scope. But if you plan a career as an owner, publisher, or general manager of any type of media outlet, you should study financial accounting so you know the different types of expenses and revenues.)

JOURNALISM BUSINESS MODELS

Traditional journalism organizations have been supported by three types of revenue: advertising, direct payment, and subsidy. As media organizations have evolved, they have experimented with a variety of business models, most depending upon multiple revenue sources. But the emergence of online media has expanded the options for news organizations to generate revenue. This section explores the variety of media revenue sources.

Advertising

Advertising support is the most common source of revenue for U.S. media organizations. There are numerous types of advertising and just as many business models. In this section, we'll discuss the most common ones used by media organizations.

Print Advertising

Most print publications have traditionally depended on display and classified advertising. Display advertising is typically sold to advertisers on a cost-per-space basis, either by the column inch (a column inch is one inch high and the width of one typical column on the page), or by the page, half-page, quarter-page, and so on. Each publication provides advertisers and advertising agencies with a "rate card" listing the different ad sizes available and their cost. There are discounts for buying a large quantity (usually measured in column inches or pages) and for long-term contracts.

Advertisers' difficulty is comparing the cost of ads from different publications. One local newspaper might sell a full-page ad for $800, with the paper in the next city selling a page for $1,200. You don't know which one is actually a better deal until you know how many people are reached by each ad, usually measured by each newspaper's circulation. To make it easier, those working in advertising break down the price to a "cost-per-thousand" of people reached, enabling advertisers to compare publications with different circulation numbers.

Because circulation numbers are so important in setting the price of advertising, they are a form of currency for the print media. Just as broadcasters have "ratings" that estimate the audience size for individual programs, print media have reports from the Audit Bureau of Circulation to verify the reach of publications.

One of the biggest changes in the newspaper business brought about by the Internet is the precipitous decline in classified advertising coincident with the growth of websites that specialize in consumer-to-consumer (C2C) advertising, especially eBay and Craigslist. Until the turn of the century, classified advertising generated between 25 and 40 percent of most newspapers' revenue, before falling to less than 5 percent just 10 years later.[2]

Newspapers have one additional source of advertising revenue. They charge retailers for advertising inserts that generally feature products or services from a single advertiser. Some are printed by the newspaper, but others are printed elsewhere and shipped to the newspaper to be inserted in a specific issue, usually the Sunday editions.

---

[2] R. G. Picard, "Shifts in Newspaper Advertising Expenditures and Their Implications for the Future of Newspapers," *Journalism Studies* 9, no. 5 (2008): 704–16.

Broadcast Advertising

Fewer options make advertising on television and radio stations simpler than print. An advertiser can buy a commercial "spot," a sponsorship, or an entire time slot. As opposed to print advertising, which is priced according to how much space is used, broadcast advertising is priced according to how much time is used. Typical spot lengths are 60 seconds, 30 seconds, and 15 seconds, although broadcasters have experimented with a wide variety of lengths to attract new business.

Broadcast advertising is also based more on the number of people reached than on the length of the spot. Commercials that run when the audiences are largest usually cost most. In television, this high-value time is known as "prime time" (8–11 P.M. in the Eastern and Pacific time zones; 7–10 P.M.in the Central and Mountain time zones). In radio, the most valuable time on most stations is "drive time" (6–10 A.M. and 4–7 P.M. when more people are listening to the radio in their cars on the way to or from work).

There are a few interesting exceptions. Some radio stations sell their most expensive commercials during midday when they have higher ratings because of a specific on-air personality. Some cable television networks get larger audiences at different times, and the cost of their ads varies accordingly.

You've probably heard the term "ratings" mentioned in relation to television programs. Ratings are estimates of the audience size for television and radio. The U.S. television ratings business is dominated by Nielsen Media Research, which provides separate services for broadcast television networks, cable television, local television stations, and even individual syndicated programs. The radio ratings business in the United States is dominated by Arbitron, which provides ratings for local radio stations and national networks. Arbitron also provides a variety of other research designed to help broadcasters understand their audiences and, in turn, sell advertisers access to those audiences.

It is easier to understand ratings if you understand the measures being used. As illustrated in figure 14.1, a **rating** is a percentage of the total potential audience watching or listening at a particular time. **Share**, on the other hand, is the percentage of just those tuned to any television or radio station who are watching or listening to a specific station at a particular time. Finally, **cume** is the number of different people who tune in at least once in a broad time period (for example, a day or a week). Most newsrooms care more about share than ratings because it tells you how you are doing against the competition. And most advertisers care more about rating than share because rating can always be translated into an estimate of the number of people reached by a commercial.

Rating is more useful to advertisers because it is the percentage of the entire population watching a specific program. A rating can thus be easily translated to audience size.

Share is more useful to programmers because it tells you how a program is doing against the competition, but it does not relate to the total audience size, so it can't be used to set the value of commercial spots.

There is one other basic principle to understand about broadcast advertising. Although print can add pages whenever advertising demand increases, broadcasters have a fixed number of commercial availabilities to sell each day. As a result, costs vary much more in the broadcast media than in print. The goal is to set the price low enough so all the availabilities are sold, but not so low that the demand exceeds

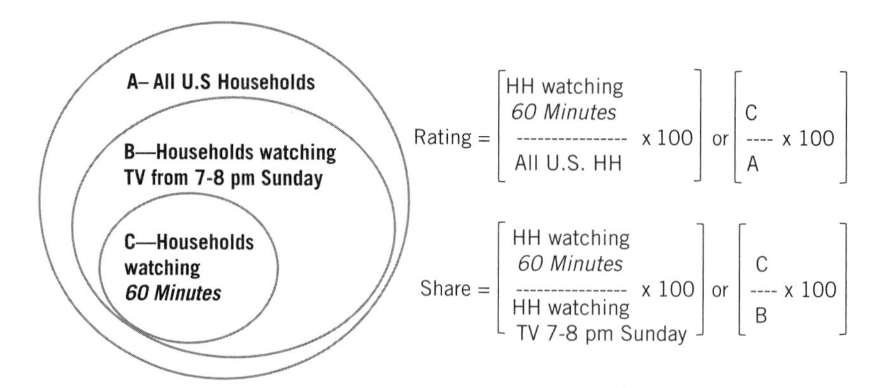

Figure 14.1 ■ Measures of Audience Size

the number. Broadcast commercial availabilities are perishable—if not sold, they are wasted.

Sponsorships

In addition to selling individual commercial spots, most broadcasters also sell sponsorships for specific programs or events. These sponsorships allow advertisers to become identified with specific programming, and since a sponsorship generally costs more, they offer additional revenue for broadcasters without reducing the amount of time available to sell in commercial spots.

Longer Time Slots

Occasionally, a broadcaster will sell an entire half-hour or hour to a single advertiser. There are two variations. The first is the "infomercial," a full-length program designed to sell a specific product or service. The broadcaster sells the block of time for a set price or gets a portion of the revenue from each sale (discussed below).

In the second variation, the advertiser buys an entire time slot, produces a program or other content for that time slot, and then keeps all of the advertising time during the program. This model was popular during the early days of television, but it has been used less as broadcasters seek to control their inventories.

Per-Inquiry Advertising

Not all advertising is sold at a preset price. Occasionally, broadcasters will air commercials offering to sell products or services directly and immediately. In this type of direct marketing, the advertiser pays the station a fixed amount for each order received as a direct result of the commercial. This type of advertising is known as "per-inquiry" or "PI" advertising because payment is made to the broadcaster for each "inquiry" made.

Online Advertising

Just as the Web can be used to deliver all the types of content discussed in the previous chapters, it can also be used to deliver almost all the types of advertising already discussed. The most prominent type is display advertising, which is comparable to display advertising in print media. But rather than buy entire pages, most online display advertising is sold by shape. The most popular shape is the "banner ad," a short and wide strip designed to take advantage of the size and shape of computer screens.

By far, the most lucrative form of online advertising is small text ads. These tiny ads are effective because the ad is not intrusive and always matches the content of the page, whether that page is news, entertainment, or search engine results. And logically, if a user is already interested in the content on a page, an ad related to that content is more effective than an unrelated one.

There is one big difference between online advertising and ads in traditional media. The cost of traditional ads rises as more people see the ad. Many online ads, on the other hand, are priced as "cost-per-click," where the advertiser pays a fixed amount (usually between 5 cents and a dollar) for each person who clicks on the ad. If no one clicks, the advertiser pays nothing.

Video ads similar to TV commercials have become more common online as online video has become more common. Typically, a user will have to watch one of these ads before watching a video and, in longer video streams, may also find ads in the middle, emulating TV commercials, which must be watched (or patiently waited through) in order to watch the program.

One other class of online advertising has become more annoying to users than most other forms. The technologies that allow us to integrate multimedia elements with almost any type of story also allow more intrusive ads, including popup windows, ads that float over content until someone clicks or closes them, "interstitial" ads that appear for 10 or 15 seconds before a requested page is delivered, ads that automatically start audio or video (a particular problem for some people browsing the Web at work), and others. The need for experimentation is clear from the business side, as online advertising does not yield as much revenue per user as traditional print or broadcast advertising. But when the ads dissuade users from returning to a website to consume more news, the consequence exceeds the revenue opportunity.

Demographics

Not all people have the same value to advertisers. Some, such as adults older than 65, consume much more media than average, while other groups, such as men 25 to , consume much less than average. In general, the more difficult it is to reach members of a demographic group, the more advertisers will pay for ads targeted at them.

Advertisers also care about people's spending habits—people with more money to spend are worth more to advertisers. So what a media organization charges for its advertising is a function of both how many people are being reached and how valuable those people are to advertisers. As a result, these demographic factors play a major role in how much content is produced and targeted at individual demographic groups.

Direct Payment

The simplest business model for any medium is direct payment, where consumers pay directly for specific content. Common examples are buying a newspaper or a book or paying to watch a movie. Although consumers spend billions of dollars on movies and other entertainment, they consume much more free than paid content. Some researchers attribute consumers' limited spending on media to the "Principle of Relative

Constancy," which says that, over time, the proportion of disposable income spent on media products by consumers is relatively constant.[3] Put more simply, there is only so much money consumers will spend on content, so any new purchases take money away from existing purchases.

Direct payment usually yields the greatest return per user to the media organization, whether from purchase of a magazine or download of a movie. But the media organization doesn't get all that money. Up to half is kept by the distributor is to cover its costs and profit.

Consumers have demonstrated that they are willing to pay directly only for the most valuable media content. For journalists, the most common content in this category is individual newspapers and magazines. A small number of people will pay to see documentary films (a form of journalism), but few will pay directly to see a television newscast or read a specific news article on a website.

Subscription

The next simplest form is subscription, where a consumer makes a periodic payment to receive a package of media content, such as daily delivery of a newspaper, a package of cable television channels, or access to a library of music. Subscriptions provide financial security for many media organizations, guaranteeing a continuing flow of revenue less susceptible to monthly fluctuations. Consumers enjoy subscriptions because they usually deliver a much greater variety of content than a person would get from buying access to individual stories, videos, images, and so on.

For media organizations, the subscription model is complicated by the cost of winning the initial subscription. Many media, especially magazines, offer steeply discounted rates to get consumers to sign up, counting on movement to "regular" subscription prices at renewal. A separate set of organizations has emerged that specialize in selling magazine subscriptions at these discounts; these organizations keep a substantial portion of the subscription revenue as their fee for selling the subscription.

As noted above, the most successful media organizations usually depend upon a combination of subscription and advertising revenues. This combination offers a more predictable and stable revenue stream, making it easier to plan and budget.

Subsidy

One of the oldest forms of revenue for media organizations is a subsidy, where a person or company finances the organization without direct remuneration. Examples range from public broadcasting in the United States and the BBC in the United Kingdom to information-oriented websites financed by political parties. In most cases, content is subsidized because it is deemed important enough by the sponsor to be produced and distributed, but it is not lucrative enough to be supported with advertising or subscription revenues. Sponsors include governments, political parties, philanthropists, businesses, and foundations.

---

[3] M. E. McCombs and J. Nolan, "The Relative Constancy Approach to Consumer Spending for Media," *Journal of Media Economics* 5, no. 2 (1992): 43–52.

Not-for-Profit Models

Not all media organizations are designed to generate profits. Your first stories are likely to be distributed on student media, which are typically subsidized by schools to help train journalists. Other nonprofit organizations that own media outlets include churches, city and state governments, and community foundations. Most of these organizations have budgetary constraints similar to for-profit media with one important difference: The budget is typically much less than in for-profit media. Most, but not all, news organizations supported by subsidies are nonprofit.

CUTTING-EDGE BUSINESS MODELS

New media outlets almost always create opportunities for new types of revenue, especially advertising revenue. For example, the emergence of social media will no doubt lead to new forms of "social advertising" that may more closely resemble a conversation or community than a sales pitch. Sites such as Facebook already are mining their vast trove of people's data to more precisely target ads.

Another new set of opportunities is related to the proliferation of tablet computers and ereaders. The failure of most media organizations to charge for content delivered on websites has haunted them as online advertising revenues have failed to keep up with revenues lost from advertising in traditional media. Many organizations have vowed to create subscription models for apps commonly used on mobile devices in the hope they will yield greater revenue.

The key to charging for content is the value of that content to the user. If content is either widely available elsewhere or has little value to the user, then a direct payment model (subscription or pay-per-user) is not likely to be successful. But consumers have consistently demonstrated that they will pay for content that has a high value and is not widely available, with movies, magazines, and financial information providing the best examples.[4]

Another perspective may become more important as the online news market matures—the "bottled water" analogy. When you look at how plentiful fresh water is in the United States, it is sometimes amazing to consider that the bottled water industry has U.S. revenues of more than $10 billion per year—almost as much as the entire American radio industry. There may be a lesson for news organizations in studying bottled water.

As with water, news and information is readily available from a variety of sources. Some is high in quality, but sometimes the quality is questionable. Bottled water offers convenience and assurance of quality. People are willing to pay for a product they could get for free because they want the convenience of the bottle, the quality of the product (e.g., filtered), or both. In order to sell bottled water, the marketers have to ensure the quality of the product as well as packaging it, distributing it, and, of course, investing heavily in marketing expenses such as advertising, branding, and sales promotion.

News organizations may consider whether consumers will place equal value on "filtered" news conveniently packaged and delivered. Even if *exactly* the same content

[4] For a detailed discussion of new business models, see J. Kaye and S. Quinn, *Funding Journalism in the Digital Age: Business Models, Strategies, Issues, and Trends* (New York: Peter Lang, 2010).

is available from other sources, some consumers may choose to go with the "name brand" of news rather than with an off brand. But applying the bottled water analogy presents an interesting ethical dilemma for a media organization. With a limited amount of money to invest in the news product, is it better to invest in a "better product," that is, more reporters, editors, photographers, designers, and so forth, or is it better to invest in strengthening and promoting your brand name so that consumers will be willing to pay to receive your content?

One somewhat related solution that has been proposed is the use of micropayment for media content. Rather than paying a larger amount for a monthly subscription, users might pay only a few cents every time they view a page or download content. The impact on the user's budget would, in most cases, be, well, micro, but the aggregate impact of this new source of revenue for the media organization could be significant.

As stated earlier, most news organizations depend upon more than one revenue source, mixing advertising, subscriptions, direct payment, and other elements. As illustrated in figure 14.2, media organizations are experimenting with even more sources of revenue, including text advertising, referral fees, and micropayments.

One major advantage of increasing the number of revenue sources is that the organization depends less on any single source of revenue, so changes in one source have less impact on the organization. An example occurred during the Great Recession of 2007–2009 when advertising revenues were disproportionately reduced as businesses cut their marketing budgets. Those organizations that relied exclusively on advertising were affected more than those relying on a combination of advertising, subscriptions, and other revenue sources. On the other hand, increasing the number of revenue sources complicates the organization's management.

THE SEARCH ENGINE CHALLENGE

The most lucrative form of online advertising is the tiny text ads that accompany the results from search engines including Google, Yahoo, and Bing. As noted earlier, these ads are especially effective because they are not intrusive and always relate to the content being sought.

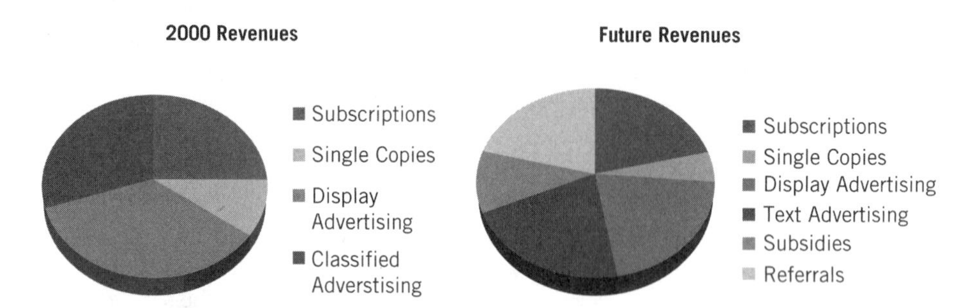

Figure 14.2 ■ Media Revenue Sources
As online business models evolve, the number of revenue sources available to support journalism should increase. Reliance upon multiple sources of revenue will complicate business models, but should provide more stable revenue flow.

The first online advertisements were display ads, similar to those in traditional print media. As the Web became more widely used to access news, information, and entertainment, new types of advertising emerged, including the simple text ad (comparable in format to traditional classified advertising) and interactive advertising, in which information input by the user alters the content delivered.

Journalists should be concerned about these text ads for two reasons. First, the ads sometimes appear on news organizations' websites alongside stories and photos (the news organizations agree to this for a cut of the revenue), but if an ad appears in the wrong context, it can be embarrassing (see box 14.1). Second, these ads, when they appear on search engine results pages, divert revenue from news organizations.

The text ads that appear along with search results on Google, Yahoo, and other search engines produced more than $12 billion in revenue in the United States alone in 2010, more than 7 percent of all advertising revenue.[5] But there is a negative side to these ads directly related to journalism.

Excerpts of news stories appear in many of these search results, but virtually all the revenue from associated text ads displayed on the results page is kept by the search engine. With advertisers moving billions of dollars of spending from traditional media to these search engines (and other new media such as social media), the amount of revenue to support content production is decreasing.

Search engines correctly argue that media organizations benefit from an increased number of visitors to their websites from these searches. The search engines also will not index any news organization's content if the pages are programmed to be invisible to searches. But the fact remains that a limited pool of money is spent on advertising every year, and when a large portion of advertising revenue does not pay for any of the content used, the money available to produce high-quality content decreases.

News organizations not only choose to have their pages indexed by the search engines but also engage in "search engine optimization" (SEO), the process discussed in chapter 4 of formatting a Web page to maximize the amount of traffic received from search engines.

EXPENSES

Media organizations have a cost structure different from most other industries. For example, instead of needing expensive, specialized equipment like manufacturers use to make cars or electronic devices, media rely primarily upon relatively inexpensive computer systems. Media, except for print, don't make extensive use of raw materials such as those used to build houses or supply energy. And media don't have to keep large inventories of products unlike retail businesses such as clothing or grocery stores.

To understand the expenses in a media organization, it helps to know the difference between fixed and variable costs. Fixed costs are those required no matter how many people consume your product. Variable costs, on the other hand, increase with every

[5] A. Enright, (April 13, 2011), "Online Ad Revenue Increases Nearly 15% in 2010, a Report Says," retrieved from http://www.internetretailer.com/2011/04/13/online-ad-revenue-increases-nearly-15-2010-report-says.

Box 14.1

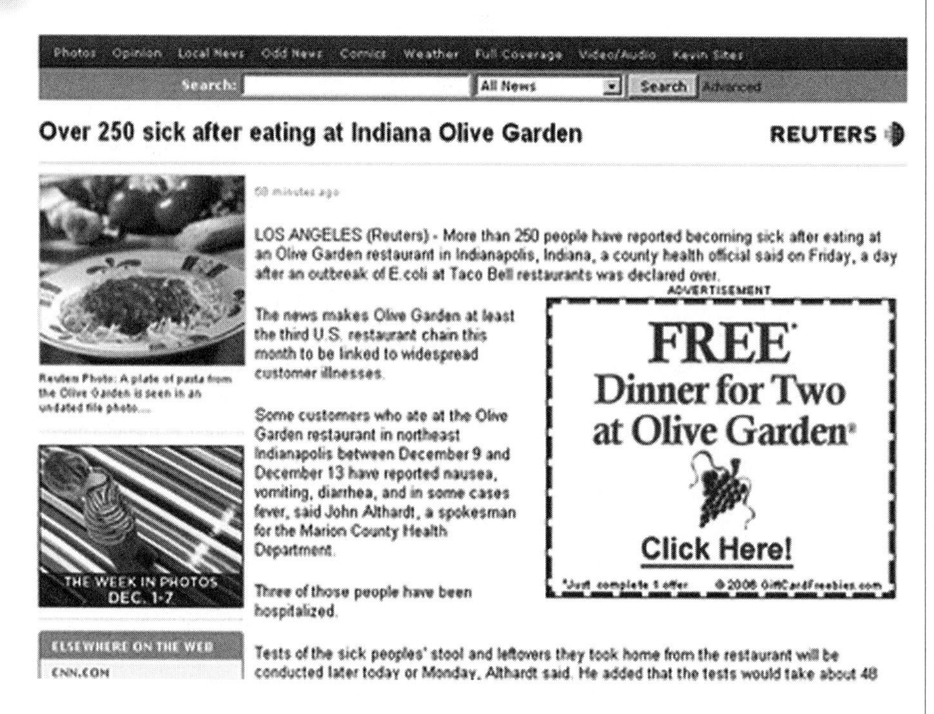

Photos Opinion Local News Odd News Comics Weather Full Coverage Video/Audio Kevin Sites

Over 250 sick after eating at Indiana Olive Garden REUTERS

LOS ANGELES (Reuters) - More than 250 people have reported becoming sick after eating at an Olive Garden restaurant in Indianapolis, Indiana, a county health official said on Friday, a day after an outbreak of E.coli at Taco Bell restaurants was declared over.

The news makes Olive Garden at least the third U.S. restaurant chain this month to be linked to widespread customer illnesses.

Some customers who ate at the Olive Garden restaurant in northeast Indianapolis between December 9 and December 13 have reported nausea, vomiting, diarrhea, and in some cases fever, said John Althardt, a spokesman for the Marion County Health Department.

Three of those people have been hospitalized.

Tests of the sick peoples' stool and leftovers they took home from the restaurant will be conducted later today or Monday, Althardt said. He added that the tests would take about 48

THE WEEK IN PHOTOS DEC. 1-7

ELSEWHERE ON THE WEB

CNN.COM

ADVERTISEMENT

FREE*
Dinner for Two
at Olive Garden®
Click Here!

Most banner advertising and text advertising is placed on a page by a computer algorithm that attempts to match the ad to either the content on the page or to the audience attracted by that content. But, as illustrated by the screen shot above, those computer algorithms don't always consider the full context of the ad.

additional user. For most media organizations, fixed costs are much larger than variable costs, meaning it usually costs a lot more to gather and edit the news than it does to distribute it to the public. The goal of most media organizations is therefore to attract as many users as possible to spread the fixed costs.

The number one expense for most news organizations is the fixed cost of personnel. Although journalists can correctly say their salaries are low compared to other degreed professionals with comparable years of experience, those salaries, and the related taxes and benefits, make up the largest expense for most media organizations.

The next most significant expense is marketing and promotion. The marketing budgets for news organizations are relatively small compared with other types of media content such as movies and music. One reason is that most media managers would rather put more money into content than into promoting that content. But in today's competitive news environment, expect to see news organizations making significant investments in attracting and keeping people's attention.

The next major category is distribution expenses. For newspapers, these can be comparatively large as a percentage of revenue because they include newsprint (the type of paper used for newspapers), ink, and vehicles and people to transport and deliver the paper. Magazines use less paper, but the paper and ink used are much more expensive. They also have the extra expense of mailing copies to subscribers, though at a special "periodicals" rate lower than most other postage rates. (It's not a coincidence our first postmaster general, Benjamin Franklin, was also a newspaper publisher.) For print media, the variable costs are high relative to other media, increasing with the number of copies printed and delivered.

The distribution expenses for broadcasters consist of transmission equipment and electricity, but those costs are the same whether a station reaches one person or a million people in its transmission area. Interestingly, all of a broadcaster's costs are fixed costs. Economists say over-the-air broadcasting may be considered the most "efficient" media because the marginal cost of adding additional users is zero!

Cable television, on the other hand, has a set of distribution expenses related to the cables, amplifiers, and network equipment needed in a modern cable system. They represent an interesting counterpoint to broadcasters because most cable systems have to pay those costs for every home passed, regardless of whether that home subscribes.

Online news also has a set of variable costs. The number of servers and the amount of bandwidth needed to deliver content to users increases with the number of users. It is common to hear that websites "crashed" because too many people were trying to get content from the site at the same time. How many simultaneous users the system should be prepared to serve is one of the most important decisions a media organization has to make regarding online distribution. If the organization guesses too high, it pays for servers and bandwidth it never uses, but if it guesses too low, users will occasionally fail to get the content they want when they want it.

In the Internet's earliest days, servers and bandwidth were vastly more expensive than they are today. As the bandwidth cost decreases and server power increases, capacity limits will become less of an issue for most media organizations. But there will always be the chance that sudden heavy demand for a small site will overwhelm the network infrastructure.

Other costs for media organizations include rent (or mortgages), utilities, computers, office supplies, and administrative services such as payroll. Compared to your household budget, the cost structures of media organizations are complex, but compared with the cost factors related to building automobiles or television sets, they are relatively simple.

One more note is needed regarding expenses. Any business has to separate "operating" expenses from "capital" expenses. Operating expenses are those incurred day to day, including personnel, utilities, rent, and office supplies. Capital expenses are for major items with life spans usually measured in years, including printing presses, cameras, computers, and network equipment. This distinction is important for two reasons. First, compared with most other industries, media organizations have relatively low capital expenses. Second, capital expenses are not counted as regular expenses on the budget but are divided over the equipment's expected lifetime, a concept called "depreciation." For example, if you buy a $20,000 car expected to last five years, you would not put all $20,000 in this year's budget. Instead, you would put $4,000 in each of the next five years' budgets. (If the concept is confusing, don't be concerned. Just know that you should take courses in accounting or business management if you plan to work in ownership or management at any point in your career.)

ENTREPRENEURIAL JOURNALISM

Your options for employment in journalism are not limited to being hired by a national or local news organization. You also can become an entrepreneurial journalist, working for yourself, choosing your own assignments, and then selling your work to existing publications. It's a tough way to make a living, but if you're good and can establish a network of buyers for your stories, you can make a living.

The most difficult part of freelancing is selling the first story. You have the most freedom when you decide what story you want to cover and then gather information, write the story, and, when it's done, look for a news organization to buy it. It is much easier from a financial perspective to find an organization looking for someone to cover a story and sell the editors on the idea that you are that reporter.

When working on an assignment, make sure you negotiate your fees and expenses beforehand, and don't forget that, as an independent contractor, you will be responsible for paying all the taxes on your income. You need to keep track of expenses so you can deduct them from your taxes and have a firm grasp of how much money you're making.

Pay attention to the contract terms being offered. Some organizations are demanding rights to use what you produce not only now, and for their publication, but also for other uses (such as compilations in books or online databases) and in forms "not yet invented" with no additional compensation. If you are unsure, it might be worth it to have a lawyer look over the terms.

You also have a new option afforded by the Internet—you can set up your own website to distribute your stories and support it with advertising. A number of services, including Google's AdWords, will place advertising on your site and then split the revenues with you. But it takes hundreds of visitors to your site to generate just a few dollars in revenue, and you may end up spending more time trying to attract visitors than you do actually reporting.

Entrepreneurial journalism is not for everyone, but if you are looking for maximum freedom and have the financial resources to help support yourself while you are waiting for your stories to sell, then you might consider it. Communication technology has provided us with a wealth of tools to gather news and distribute it directly to the public or sell it to other media organizations.

SUMMARY

This chapter has explored the business models for news organizations, and in the process, it has examined some of the possibilities that are emerging in converged media organizations. To understand the business side, you need to apply the "basic equation" that *revenues minus expenses equals profit*. But the best way to increase profit is not by decreasing expenses but by increasing them today—making an investment—so that revenues go up tomorrow.

News organizations may rely upon many different types of advertising, as well as direct payments, subscriptions, and subsidies. The most stable media organizations don't rely on just one source of revenue but rather have a number of sources that support the operation.

The comparatively low revenue from online news distribution is forcing news organizations to look for new types of advertising and other new revenue sources. Along the way, these organizations may invest significantly more money in marketing and promotion as they seek to maximize the number of people who are reached by the news products produced by the organization.

EXERCISES

1. Keep a log of your media use for a day, writing down all of the media you use, including news, other information, entertainment, and social media. For each one, make a note regarding whether you paid for that content or received it for free. Then, at the end of the day, analyze how much you "spent" for the content that you consumed that day. Was it worth it?
2. Choose three comparable news sources: a daily newspaper, a television news program, and a website. Count the amount of advertising you find on each, then estimate which one provided greater revenue that particular day.
3. Imagine what your first job will be, then make a list of every expense your employer will have to make in order to employ you. (Don't forget taxes and benefits.) How much of your employer's expenses for you will you actually receive in salary—after taxes?
4. Compare the list of courses you must take as a journalism major with those required for a business major. Then think about the skills needed to manage the revenues and expenses discussed in this chapter. How many of those business courses would it be helpful for you to take if you plan to move from being a journalist to being an editor, manager, or publisher?

CHAPTER 15

YOUR FUTURE IN CONVERGENT JOURNALISM

OVERVIEW: WE DON'T MAKE THE RULES . . . BUT WE CAN MAKE THEM WORK FOR US

The future of journalism becomes clearer and muddier at the same time as "journalist" becomes more of a function than a title. With journalism freed from its traditional economic moorings based on scarcity of output channels, some see the profession becoming a kind of survival of the fittest. Increasingly, anyone who writes nonfiction may argue that he or she is practicing journalism. As ebooks outnumber paper books, we see it is easier for writers to get published. Blogs are considered by many to be as credible as newspaper columns. So who's to say someone is or is not a journalist? We may not like it and we may disagree with good reason, but, more importantly, we can use this trend to our advantage. Think of modern journalism as more of a contest where the winners are those who produce the best content and provide the best utility for interacting with that content. Online newspapers are confirming that good journalism is not only in demand but that the best stories attract the most readers. Having completed this book and its exercises, you have the tools to compete for—and win—the most readers.

The purpose of this book is to prepare you to work as a journalist and develop a career in a world increasingly dominated by digital media. In a converged media environment, employers still want the basics: people who can report the facts accurately and quickly and who can tell a clear story. They also look for people who can effortlessly repurpose stories for the Web, who can work across media, and who understand the importance of branding—both corporate and personal—in this evolving media world. You will invariably develop expertise in at least one of the modes of reporting, but you should have functional skills in all of them.

To prepare yourself for a career in new media, you also have to understand the big picture. It is one thing to enter the field but another to move up quickly to achieve your life goals and aspirations. There are numerous paths to becoming a leader in this field; the traditional means of entering low and working your way up remains, but it's not the path everyone has to follow.

Familiarity with some big-picture issues will help you grow professionally from an entry-level employee to perhaps a manager, employer, or entrepreneur. These include media management and employment trends; changes in law, policy, and regulation; brand management; and employee-employer contracts and negotiations.

EVOLVING MEDIA, EVOLVING JOBS

Deciding where you want to work and in what capacity is influenced by the changing media landscape. Companies differ in where they are on the "convergence continuum."[1] Some are more Web-oriented than others, but all involve developing rich, interactive media content. But even as old barriers and lines are erased inside the organization, follow common sense when you're interviewing for a job. Don't apply for a radio position and say, "I just want to do this until something opens up on the Web side." Similarly, be careful applying for a broadcast editor or producer position if you wish to be a reporter, anchor, or other on-air talent. This kind of a jump is not as easy as you might think.

There are a number of new positions with roles and titles yet to be developed. We've noted a few new roles in this book. Some newsrooms are still looking for editors to help them transition from print to digital; others need help handling content submitted by community members.

For example, in chapter 11 we noted "social media manager" positions have proliferated in newsrooms and other companies, especially those with a consumer orientation. Even professional associations have set up their own private networks. LinkedIn has its own group devoted to sharing tips and best practices for online community management.

One of the popular terms is "curation." Unlike aggregation of stories from other sources that can largely be done by machine algorithm, curation seeks out the most influential, authoritative, or trusted voices on a topic. It may display or link to their work, but it also pulls those disparate threads together into a cohesive narrative with wider context and perspective. Slate magazine's The Slatest (slatest.slate.com) is a good example.

Some familiarity with social media is being baked into almost every position, it seems. A wire editor now must know how to scan all media (including blogs, social networks, and talk radio), what stories are being talked about and pictures are being posted, and how to use the Web to identify the highest-interest stories that grab and keep readers' attention.

---

[1] L. Dailey, L. Demo, and M. Spillman, "The Convergence Continuum: A Model for Studying Collaboration Between Media Newsrooms," *Atlantic Journal of Communication* 13, no. 3 (2005): 150–68.

As this chapter was being written, a search for the term on JournalismJobs.com, a widely used industry jobs board, listed 96 positions that in some way required skill in "social media," from Web developers to sports reporters and copy editors.

Industry recruiters say they are not looking so much for those who know all the latest tools but for those who understand the underlying philosophies and practices—and pitfalls—and who are willing to continue learning because the tools are almost sure to change. For instance, Steve Buttry, a former newspaper editor who moved to TBD.com, a Washington, D.C.–area online news site, when it started, told Poynter's Joe Grimm: "I'm not interested in somebody who claims to be a social media expert, but I am interested in someone who claims to be a social media student. Somebody who thinks they understand it all indicates that they don't."[2]

According to the annual survey of radio and television stations by Hofstra University and the Radio Television Digital News Association (RTDNA), TV employment figures remained stable in 2009, and even increased in 2010, as local news remained profitable. Most of the new hires in broadcast news fell into one of four categories: reporters, producers, photographers, and editors. Several local TV stations continue to add news programming, which could mean more positions with an improved economy. But expect lots of competition for those jobs. U.S. government labor projections expect a continuing downward trend through 2018 for the positions of news analyst, reporter, or correspondent.

Thousands of newspaper jobs have been lost in recent years, but others have been added on digital staffs both in those publishing companies and in new ventures. The 2011 national launch of Patch.com hyperlocal news websites in 797 markets came with the news there would be an equal number of jobs available (one per market).[3] And Patch, a division of AOL, continues to expand along with other ventures like Main Street Connect that are trying to sink roots into neighborhood news. Still being debated is whether these jobs are entry-level positions or genuine long-term career options.

As a good journalist, you should take the gloom and doom projections with some skepticism and look behind the scenes. The industry is evolving, not dying. That evolution was already under way before the Great Recession of 2007–2009, but the economic problems collapsed what might have been a more orderly shift over a decade or more into just a few years. It will take time to find a new equilibrium and economic models, but journalism is hardly like buggy whips. Study after study shows that people have become heavier news consumers, but they want their news and information on demand and in the forms they desire. As one study put it, they aren't seeking to become citizen reporters, but they are asserting their power as editors.[4]

---

[2] J. Grimm (February 2010), "The Social Media Skills You Need to Qualify for Journalism Jobs," retrieved from http://www.poynter.org/how-tos/career-development/ask-the-recruiter/100762/the-social-media-skills-you-need-to-qualify-for-journalism-jobs/.

[3] Brett Pulley (April 13, 2011), "AOL's Huffington to Add News Staff in Local Site Revamp," retrieved from http://www.bloomberg.com/news/2011-04-12/aol-to-add-800-news-employees-to-revive-sales-growth-after-huffington-deal.html.

[4] Pew Research Center Project for Excellence in Journalism (August 20, 2008), *The how vs. where of news consumption*, retrieved from http://www.journalism.org/node/12448.

Figure 15.1 ■ Being an eyewitness to history while helping to change your community are just some of the rewards of being a multiskilled journalist.

The upshot is that if you are dedicated to journalism, you should be encouraged because people are being hired. Partly it's because of turnover—the business encourages people not to stay too long in a market—plus there are new positions as revenue from digital operations grows. Whether filling a replacement position or a new one, however, employees increasingly are expected to have multimedia and social media knowledge as well as the rock-solid basics of journalism. They also are being asked to understand the business better and how their roles relate to the overall health of the organization, as well as to be more willing to take entrepreneurial risks.

CROSS-OWNERSHIP AND A GLOBAL PERSPECTIVE

In 2007 the Federal Communications Commission changed a longstanding rule and announced it would consider some proposals for a single company to own both a newspaper and a television station in the same market.[5] The FCC ruled that in the top 20 markets (measured by Nielsen as "Designated Market Area" or DMA) it would be in the public interest to allow such cross-ownership. In other words, this type of ownership is seen as promoting competition, localism, and diversity. But two conditions would also have to be met: (1) the television station was not ranked among the top four in that market and (2) there remained at least eight other companies owning the market's other

[5] Federal Communications Commission (n.d.), "Review of the Broadcast Ownership Rules." retrieved from http://www.fcc.gov/guides/review-broadcast-ownership-rules.

major newspapers or full-power TV stations. In smaller markets, the separation between newspapers and TV stations would remain. So at least in the larger cities, there may be additional new positions in converged newsrooms.

As the world becomes globally interconnected, you may also want to look to other countries for opportunities. Some European companies not encumbered by U.S. regulations are moving ahead in creating consolidated newsrooms and exploring new ways to deliver news, such as through text messaging and other mobile devices. Similarly, some Asian publishers are taking advantage of the public's quicker and more widespread adoption of several new technologies in that part of the world to develop new media initiatives. One of the most widely watched citizen journalism sites in the world, for instance, has been South Korea's Oh My News.

If you wish to work in another country as a multiskilled journalist, however, there are as many cautions as opportunities, and you will need to do some homework. Language, culture, and local laws are important no matter where you are but especially in a field such as journalism. Whether you're freelancing or employed by a multinational corporation, you may no longer enjoy certain freedoms and benefits you understand about your home country. China, for example, formally acknowledges freedom of speech. But there are some not-too-subtle differences, and your blog advocating a free Tibet might not evoke the reaction you intended. And once your words are published, it's too late to take them back. Even in some European countries, the rules can be markedly different; Britain's libel laws, for instance, put much more of the onus on the journalist to show that what is published is truthful.

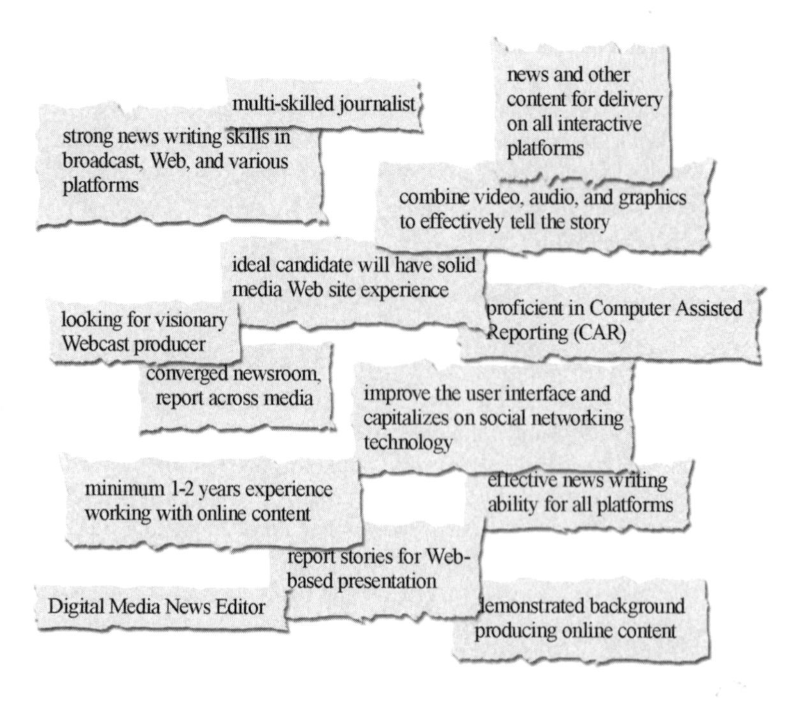

Figure 15.2 ■ Excerpts from recent journalism help-wanted ads.

The Public

In this era of "slivercasting," there remains great uncertainty regarding business models that would aggregate these slivers into an audience sizable enough to support and sustain news organizations as government and societal watchdogs. In fact, debate continues about whether such "general-purpose" news organizations are even needed any longer. This debate is a critical factor as you plot your career path, and considering the wants and needs of the public can help you avoid steering your career toward a dead end.

As noted above, audiences now expect choice and content on demand—when and where they want it. Even if they are loyal to your organization, they will immediately look someplace else if you don't have the information they want. If this happens often enough, you may be bumped to the person's second, third, or fourth choice—or abandoned.

Audiences remain the same in some key aspects, too. In the early days of the Internet, people visited a variety of websites, sampling and choosing from an unmatched array of information selections. But as the Web matures, people tend to revert to the same pattern of surfing as found in cable television viewing. Some research suggests that people are creatures of habit and end up mostly going to a relatively few favorite channels. In the same way, Web-surfing habits for news and information inevitably bring people to rely on a few websites they like and trust.

The matter becomes a bit complicated because the algorithms being developed to personalize our searches are making choices for us that may preclude us from finding information that doesn't "fit" our profile. The efforts to create an intelligent Web may end up shielding us from information we may not want—but, in fact, may need. This underscores the importance of journalism in the next decade. Keep this old formula in mind as we work to retain and build audience: Give them what they want, when they want it. Give it to them better than the competition, and give them pleasant surprises from time to time. The way to do all these things is the same as before. Find the best people, hire them, and let them do their jobs. The old saying, "A reporter is only as good as his or her sources," remains true today.

SOURCES: ANOTHER SOCIAL NETWORK

Developing and maintaining professional news sources is one of the most important things a journalist can do. Our increasingly online world offers greater opportunity to find and develop sources but also greater potential for abuse. One of the greatest dangers is that you will spend more time at your desk with your head buried in a computer screen than talking with people. Developing news sources requires networking—making friends and influencing people—and effective networking is hard work, requiring time and personal contact.

Another danger of easily finding sources online is that it can be too easy to overlook sources that are powerless and unknown. These sources may be struggling to make ends meet and survive in the 21st century. They may even not have a computer or a Web page or an email address. They might not have a phone, and they probably don't show up in an online search. You can only find them by getting out of the office. But their stories and information are just as compelling and valuable—often more so—than those of your community's established institutions. As with all sources, go by the golden rule and treat them with respect and care. Listen to what they say without overly committing to their view. Developing these sources is an art, and it improves with experience.

COMPETITION AMONG MEDIA

You also have to appreciate the dynamics of professional competition. The ranks of journalists are actually comparatively small (government forecasts are for fewer than 60,000 reporters and correspondents by 2018, compared with 105,000 predicted to be travel agents), and, as with news sources, you have to be careful to pick your battles and how you fight. A common practice for certain events is for journalists from competing organizations to pool resources. In some courtrooms, for example, a judge may allow only one video camera, which will then be used to provide the video of the proceedings to all the other news organizations. You don't want to be "accidentally on purpose" left out. One of this book's authors saw firsthand what can happen when you're paired with an unpopular camera operator: things malfunction, tapes get lost, cables don't fit, delays happen.

A better approach to working and competing with others might be to think of the competition as siblings. It's OK to squabble among yourselves, but at the end of the day, you're all in this together. Be sure to actively seek out like-minded co-workers, and you'll be able to withstand the ones you consider obnoxious divas.

Although convergence implies more cooperation among journalists to produce a multifaceted news report, as in the rest of life there are unintended consequences. The intense drive to survive leads news organizations to get journalists to produce higher-quality reports more often. "Print" journalists used to meeting one or two deadlines a day now may have a half-dozen or more. Broadcast reporters used to dealing in stories rarely more than 100 to 150 words may now be required to produce additional online or print stories twice that long and with details far beyond what broadcast standards require. The ease with which news outlets are created online means that even as convergence and cooperation increase, so does competition.

THE MULTISKILLED JOURNALIST

This book has provided a checklist of sorts for developing the skills and aptitudes you need to become a multiskilled journalist. You have to be able to write across platforms, including print, radio, television, online, and mobile. You need to be able to report and gather information from the field. You have to know whom to interview and how to do it. You need to know how to synthesize and organize (sometimes contradictory) information from diverse sources into a logical, coherent whole. You need to know how to incorporate text, still images, moving images, audio, animation, and graphics for the "three screens"—60-inch plasma TVs, 17-inch computer monitors, and 2-inch cellphones—and you must be able to accurately decide what will work best for each. If you work within a traditional newsroom, you likely will have to work with many others to make that happen; the day of the lone wolf is waning in those settings. On the other hand, if you are willing to learn all these skills and to keep learning throughout your life, the opportunities to strike out on your own have never been greater.

Complicating matters, you also must be able to reach your target audience or audiences. You need to know how to present the story so that it appeals to a grandmother watching television or to a teenager or young professional with an iPod, smartphone, or tablet computer. You will need to be aware of the newest apps on next-generation smartphones in order to reach all the slivers needed to generate the economic support for your, or your employer's, journalistic endeavors. And after all of this, you need to think about yourself as a marketable brand. Will you appear on camera (webcam, phonecam, HDTV), and if so, do you play it straight, hip, flip, combative, or conciliatory? Outdoor, indoor, studio, or on-site? What will you wear, and how will you sound? What will your social media presence be? A thousand tiny decisions like these will ultimately reflect on you as a name-brand, multiskilled journalist.

LEVERAGING CONVERGENT SKILLS TO GET A JOB TODAY

One important development is that more people who wish to be converged journalists will find they must begin to strategically and systematically build a marketable personality. "Brand management" is one of the hot areas being discussed among journalists.[6] Just as celebrities need agents to negotiate million-dollar contracts, you may need an agent who can honestly assess the worth of your journalism. You may be worth more than you think!

At the very least, you need to do periodic assessments of how your work and image are being projected online. It is becoming clear that getting a job may depend just as much on networking skills and your social media presence as formerly it was based on landing internships at "good" newspapers or broadcast operations.[7]

Begin by planning. You need a standard resume and a portfolio that includes samples of your work. Depending on the job you desire, those samples could include video packages, photos, writing samples, podcasts, Web pages, or some combination of these. Building your own professional website and creating a blog for your work is a perfect place to start. Choose the name carefully, and think in terms of a potential employer. PartyDog101 may sound cool now, but you may regret that identification later. Keep in mind that your public "persona" includes your Facebook, Twitter, Myspace, or other social networking pages as well as stories or columns you've written for internships at professional publications or on student media websites. The Internet has brought us the "long tail"—the ability to find items that may have been posted many years ago (and for some organizations, to continue making money from them). If you have a blog, you may know this phenomenon as new comments occasionally pop up on popular or controversial posts from years earlier, posts newly discovered in most cases by someone's search engine inquiry.

---

[6] A. Hermida (August 19, 2009), "Journalism Students Need to Develop Their Personal Brand," *MediaShift*, retrieved from http://www.pbs.org/mediashift/2009/08/journalism-students-need-to-develop-their-personal-brand231.html.

[7] J. Halliday (May 9, 2011), "Personal Branding Is Key for Would-be Journalists," *BBC College of Journalism blog*, retrieved from http://www.bbc.co.uk/journalism/blog/2011/05/personal-branding-for-would-be.shtml.

It is now common for prospective employers to do an online background search on you. Any work you've done that appears on the Web can be accessed, for better or worse. One of the authors has had appeals from former students hunting for their second or third job to take down stories they did for the journalism school's practicum newspaper and website. Similar appeals have come from some people interviewed and photographed for past stories—their views or their appearance may have significantly changed. Such "unpublishing" requests discussed earlier in chapter 4 pose an ethical challenge: Do we, in essence, rewrite history by deleting some of it?

Next, you need to consider what to put on your site. For example, if you blog, you should remember the ethos we mentioned earlier (see chapters 4 and 7). Also, include at least one photo (tasteful, professional), displayed prominently. If you have video clips or podcasts you can post, even better. But again, do not post things online just to have things online. The content must be informational or entertaining enough to withstand the test of time. And, of course, there is that old admonition that if you wouldn't want your mother—or certainly a potential employer—to see it, get it out of the social media sites (figure 15.3).

Remember, the goal of all this content is to market yourself and show others that you're credible, interesting, exciting, entertaining, and professional. As mentioned in chapter 8, begin developing your on-camera persona. Work at ways to bring out your personality. If you have any hobbies or interests, add a link with photos.

To demonstrate your commitment to your community, join and be active in a local nonprofit organization. Allocate time every week or two to help out in a nonmedia capacity. But use your experiences as the foundation for content. Write about your thoughts and insights on issues that are meaningful for those involved. Especially when you're younger, it may not be so attractive to spend your time with people with whom you have little in common. Take senior citizens, for example. It can be a real sacrifice

(A)

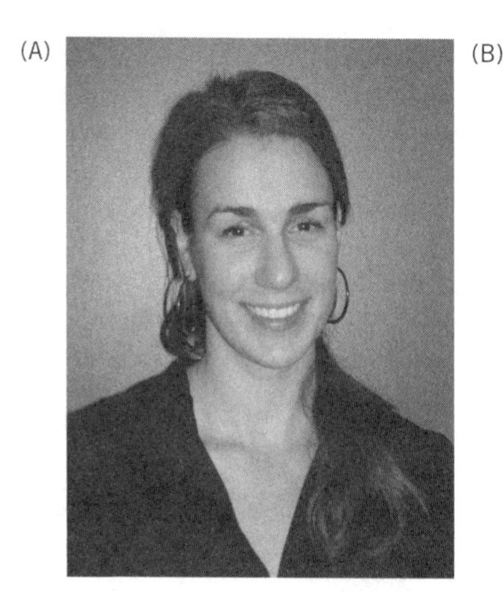

(B)

Figure 15.3 ■ We want prospective employers to see us at our best, as in A. But you have to make sure that a Web search won't also reveal another side of your personality, as in B (taken from the Facebook page of the same student and used with permission). (*Source*: Stephanie Margalis.)

to give up a night to help out in a home or senior center. But if you can spend time and sincere effort with them, you'll soon grow to hold a genuine love and compassion that can't be manufactured as well as gain a deeper understanding of issues you might have to cover as a journalist.

Spending time with others who are different from you can in many ways help you grow as a journalist. As a jack or jill of all trades, you will spend your life communicating with and reporting on people different from you in age, outlook, culture, beliefs, values, and perspectives. By meeting and talking to them, you will become more rounded and knowledgeable about the world around you. Using that knowledge to add perspective and insight to your reporting will make your stories more powerful and more popular. Eventually, you'll discover that all these diverse experiences provide you with an expanded worldview and a greater understanding of society in general, as well as a better understanding of the actions and motivations of the individuals you report on. Traditionally, reporters who have this insight have been the best journalists.

LIFE PLANNING AND POSITIONING YOURSELF

Get used to the idea that no one cares about your career more than you. Unless you have an agent (whom you pay or who gets part of what's paid to you), no one else will always be on your side, pushing you and promoting you and your accomplishments, your skills, and your talents.

Take some time and invest in yourself by working on a strategic life plan. Develop three- to five-year goals as a professional that are specific enough for direction, realistic enough to be attainable, and flexible enough for you to change course when something unexpected appears. Get input from at least one person you respect as a teacher or mentor (professor, boss, friend of the family, etc.). Pull out your long-range plan at least once a year and re-evaluate it because circumstances change, and as you grow, your goals in life will change too.

When you interview for a job, it is important to keep these points in mind because negotiating your career can be a central point in your happiness with life. Take the time to establish your work conditions and expectations at the job interview, but do it through polite negotiation. Until you have established your credentials, you are unlikely to be in a position to dictate terms, but there also is less opportunity to change your working conditions or requirements once you begin working someplace.

There are a number of strategies for positioning yourself at a job interview. A lot of it is attitude; the rest is providing the evidence that supports your argument that you are worth hiring and should be treated well.

FINDING A JOB AS A MULTISKILLED JOURNALIST

The first part of the hiring process—before you ever get an interview—can be impersonal and is becoming more so as media companies adopt modern human-resources practices common to other corporations. This does not, however, eliminate the need for networking; many a job notice is posted because of legal requirements when an editor already knows whom he or she wants for the job.

There are many places to find journalism jobs, some better than others. General sites like Monster or CareerBuilder are not the best places, but you should become familiar with more specialized sites such as JournalismJobs.com.

Many professional associations also have job boards for their members. Join some of those associations and go to meetings—local, regional, and national—to get to know editors, news directors, and executive producers. When the time comes to look for a job, such contacts can be invaluable, and you may hear about jobs that have not yet been posted publicly. The Society of Professional Journalists, Investigative Reporters and Editors, the American Copy Editors Society, the Online News Association, and the culturally specific journalists' organizations under UNITY/Journalists of Color Inc. all provide excellent opportunities.

The Radio Television Digital News Association annual meeting has opportunities for young journalists to circulate their resumes, and if you are interested in a specific subject, numerous journalists' organizations cover things such as the environmental, health care, business, and science beats; state capital reporting; and agriculture reporting. Many journalists can tell you they got that first job—or later were able to move up to a better one—because of contacts made this way.

The skills needed to be a journalist will help you to get into related fields too. For example, just as reporters need to study areas like government and history, if your interest is to be a weather reporter or meteorologist you need the right knowledge base. The work of a meteorologist has changed dramatically over the years. From the days of raincoat-clad weather clowns, broadcast meteorology is now a respected and competitive field that combines science training with on-air skills. You should become a member of the National Weather Association (NWA), which has hundreds of members and awards the NWA Radio and Television Weathercaster Seals of Approval. The organization sponsors award programs, college scholarships, grants, and other programs and can help you begin to network.

Similarly, those wanting to cover sports have always known you have to live, eat, and breathe sports. Attending games and matches and knowing the rules and strategies is just as important as knowing the people. It's best to focus on your favorite sport, but remember that almost everyone wants to cover the big ones (football, baseball, basketball). You can find more opportunity with the lesser-known sports. Either way, it's vital you begin in college (or sooner) and build up skills in play-by-play, interviewing, scores and statistics, and color and analysis.

Becoming a member of a sports-related journalism organization is an important place to start. Among those you might consider are the American Sportscasters Association, the Association for Women in Sports Media, or the Sports Journalists' Association of Great Britain. A good site for free sports journalism resources is the Associated Press Sports Editors (http://apsportseditors.org).

Many organizations and related meetings have dues, registration fees, and other costs, of course. And you should be budgeting for your job search throughout your career. While you are in college, expect to spend as much as $2,000 to get that first job. If your dream job is in Texas and you are in Wisconsin, you will have to drive or fly to Texas for the interview and possible tryout. Prospective employers rarely pay these expenses for entry-level jobs, but it never hurts to ask. After that, some experts say you should save at least $500 a year toward your next job search because you never know when or where the next opportunity will appear. Job hopping no longer has the stigma it once had on a resume, although too many changes still can raise questions.

The process of applying for jobs can be arduous. You have to make sure your skill set and experience match the employer's needs, and you are competing with dozens (perhaps hundreds) of other journalists who believe they are as qualified as you. Getting the offer is the result of both your skill and luck—sometimes it can take several months and dozens of inquiries, while in other cases an offer emerges quickly. As you go through your career, you may find yourself in both situations.

Remember that the hiring decision often is not about you or your skills; it can be as much about timing (and friendships) and other factors beyond your control. One of the authors landed a job in radio news because he walked through the station's door less than one hour after the station's newsperson had unexpectedly walked off the job!

Perhaps an editor or news director may be losing an experienced person and wants to replace that person with the same level of experience and pay so that the money is not lost from the newsroom budget. If you have only a couple of years' experience, you won't be considered, no matter how good you are. Conversely, it may be that the position calls only for a low-paid, entry-level person because of budget cuts. Or the person who will be the supervising editor has a specific need to fill but does not want to be too specific in the ad because it would limit the number of applicants (one of this book's authors once got a job because he was the first to say yes, he'd cover the farm beat, although his knowledge about it was limited). The ads seldom make such hidden agendas clear, but getting wide experience in how institutions and society work and broadening your skill set to include multiple media increase the chances you will fit into someone's plan.

In the Interview: Negotiation and Presentation

The interview is when both of you are testing each other and looking to see if it's a good match. You don't have to be arrogant, but we've all worked for companies that were lucky to have us. The real world of business is full of stories of frauds, liars, malcontents, whiners, malingerers, and thieves. If you work hard and are talented, enthusiastic, and full of potential, you are special. Remember this when you're asked, "Why do you think our company would be interested in you? What do YOU have to offer us?" Don't undersell yourself. Make sure your answer to this question addresses how your skills and experience meet the specific needs of the company.

In the Interview: Supporting Evidence

Being able to interview well is a skill everyone can develop. But that's only half the job. Besides showing yourself to be a wonderful person, you need the supporting evidence to bolster your claims and give you more firepower in negotiating the work conditions you seek.

Make sure you always have an up-to-date resume. The general form for media jobs is a resume of no more than one page that stresses your professional experience over your education. Numerous books and software programs can help you. A well-written cover letter can also make a huge difference in how you are perceived. Job candidates

Box 15.1 Materials to Help You Land the Job

There are some things common to ALL job interviews, and there are some things unique to working in media.

1. In advance/preparation:

   Plan what to bring, what to wear, how to get there and back (transportation), topics to discuss, topics to avoid; make sure you get a good rest the night before; and be sure to leave in plenty of time in case of the unexpected (traffic jam, car trouble).

   Men:

   Well-groomed (hair cut and/or tied back appropriately, facial hair trimmed)

   Wear a dark-colored suit with light-colored shirt (light blue, white) and matching tie (solid or basic pattern; avoid strange and eye-catching designs or motifs)

   Dark socks, polished shoes (black or brown)

   Avoid cologne, jewelry (earrings, noserings), visible tattoos (if possible)

   Women:

   Well-groomed (hair cut and/or clipped appropriately)

   Dark-colored pant or skirt suit with light-colored blouse

   Use dark socks with pants; pantyhose with skirt, polished shoes (heels no higher than 3 inches)

   Avoid perfume, excessive makeup

   Jewelry: earrings (one on each ear, conservative is best), a necklace or pin, one ring per hand, and no pierced nose, tongue, cheek, or eyebrow or visible tattoos

   Accessories:

   Briefcase/portfolio with pad and pen

   Copy of cover letter

   Copy of resume

   Copy of posted job announcement (if any)

   Extra DVD or VHS (depending on the position)

   Valid driver's license

   List of questions you have regarding your salary requirements, job responsibilities, and opportunities for advancement and retirement

2. The interview itself:

   Be punctual, arrive on time

   Be upbeat and ready to talk about yourself and the organization to which you are applying

   Don't chew gum, make sure teeth are clean

   Trim nails, clean hands

3. Specific types of media positions:

   a. Reporter

      You need clips (PDFs) of your stories including where and when you wrote them.

Box 15.1 (continued)

b. On-air positions (anchor, reporter)

You must have recorded video of your work. What you put on your resume tape or DVD is extremely important.

News directors often say they make their decision in the first 10 seconds, so don't waste time. Begin with a rapid-fire montage (:10 or so) of you—stand-ups, sign-outs, bridges, taking an anchor toss, going live, etc.

Then go immediately into a full stand-up or bridge from a field report. Use a good live shot if you have it, and the stronger the story, the better.

Next, include a short segment of you in the studio. You should show your relaxed side and your ability to interact seamlessly with the anchors.

Finish your tape with what you believe to be your best package, the one that shows you to be the potential award-winning reporter you were meant to be.

c. Producer, editor positions

If you seek a producer or assignment editor position, you'll need a resume and list of references.

Producers may also be asked to provide a tape or DVD of a recent show they produced. Be ready to talk about why you selected that show to highlight your ability as a producer.

d. Visual journalist positions

If you're seeking a videographer/photographer position, you need a resume, but probably most important are references and your demo reel. This should highlight your abilities to (1) compose basic shots, (2) creatively construct images (without manipulation or ethics issues), (3) show initiative (hard-to-get shots), and (4) work as part of a team. In addition, you may have to discuss your abilities as an editor and a satellite truck operator.

e. Web positions

If you're seeking a Web position, you may need bits and pieces of all of the above, depending on how the position is written/envisioned by the hiring company. Web designers in particular need to know a variety of software languages (including HTML, JavaScript, Flash, and Photoshop). You will definitely need something online to show off your Web skills.

whose cover letters and resumes have spelling errors and grammatical mistakes—even just one—seldom get called back. A cover letter that is well-written and to the point will help create an atmosphere of credibility and the idea you're a serious candidate.

Besides the resume and cover letter, it's also standard to include samples of your work, including copies of newspaper or online articles and a copy of your best video work. Editors and news directors generally say their first look at portfolio material is quick so that they can focus on the best candidates and ignore the others.

In television, for example, news directors watch most applicant video with one eye as they're engaged in some other activity, and you often have 10 seconds or less to make your impression. So don't waste the first 10 seconds on anything except YOU. Start with a couple of simple sign-offs/sig-outs and then demonstrate your single best writing and performance in a news story.

Editors in more traditional print-oriented newsrooms will read the first few paragraphs of a story as they imagine a regular reader would, and if they aren't persuaded to continue reading after those first few paragraphs, the candidate may drop to the bottom of the pile.

Box 15.2 Career Path for Journalists

Typical/possible career path for modern journalism students:

If you're especially driven, you can enter the workforce pretty much any time you meet the legal age requirements. Increasingly, there are teen news programs and organizations that enable you to work and gain practice on air and writing. Most of the stories are feature- and fun-oriented, and the key is to give you your first demo tape and on-camera experience.

This is also the time you can begin to blog and contribute your thoughts and ideas on any number of topics. But be careful—there are few substitutes for age and experience, and any teenager trying to tackle a 40-year-old about politics is asking for trouble (not that you can't "win," but statistically the odds are way against you).

During the ages of 18 to 22, this is a great time to be in school, majoring in journalism and mass media and taking specific courses to give you experience and training in writing, reporting, Web design, audio and video production, and on-camera/performance work. At some point it's good to have a management course to give you "the big picture" and keep you abreast of trends and changes in the industry. Finally, be a part of your school (department, college, university) media outlet's newsroom, working on either the Website, newspaper, radio station, cable or TV station, or whatever else they might have. Again, the goal is to give you more experience in (1) writing, (2) reporting, (3) performing, (4) producing, (5) managing, (6) selling, and (7) creating any and every form of media content.

The first job. Getting the first full-time job in media is a watershed event. It marks a change in your status and is society's right-of-passage and recognition that you're able to be lauded/congratulated as well as sued/fired/put in jail. This text provides details on getting the job and holding it.

During this time, you establish your first "three- to five-year plan."

By your mid-20s you have enough experience (one to three years) to make any of the following moves (for better pay, better working conditions, or both):

a. Having started in a small market, it's time to move to a larger one.
b. Having started in an entry-level position, it's time to move up the organization into a more senior position.
c. Having started in one medium, you have made enough media friends and contacts to move to another (say, from TV to newspaper or newspaper to radio).
d. Having had your fill of 50- to 60-hour workweeks and working holidays, you decide to get into another line of work and leave the media for good.
e. Having had your fill of everything, you decide it's time to get an advanced degree.

Pay careful attention, however, to the *exact requirements* for submitting material as set out in the job notice. Many employers now want material submitted electronically; some use email, and others require you to use the forms on their website. Many say they want the information in the body of the email and do not want resumes attached as word processing documents; others want the attachment. Some also say they do not immediately want samples of your work.

As mentioned earlier, the day of the paper resume may be waning and the online portfolio is clearly ascending, so be sure you have your own website or space to display your work and resume. In a pinch, you can refer someone there or, through serendipity, they can find you. Once an employer gets truly interested, he or she may want to see a full electronic portfolio of what you can do.

Increasingly, employers are doing automated screening of resumes, looking for keywords and basic eligibility for the job. They will contact you later for support material and references if you make the first cut. (However, as noted above, personal contacts you have made through professional organizations can come in handy at this stage if you feel you are unfairly being cut. Telling an editor or news director whom you know of your interest in a position can have amazing palliative effects on an otherwise overlooked application. Even better, of course, is if that editor or news director alerts you to the upcoming position before it is even posted and suggests you might apply.)

The Contract and Your Job

Your skills as a reporter will serve you well once you have a job offer. You will need to research salaries, responsibilities, living expenses, and so on for comparable jobs in your area so that you can negotiate appropriate pay and other terms of employment. Your negotiating power will be limited by the number of qualified people who want the same position; the higher your qualifications and greater your experience, the better position you'll be to negotiate.

Once you have settled on a salary and other terms, your prospective employer, especially in broadcasting, may offer you a contract or another type of employment agreement. As with any legal document, be sure to consult an attorney before signing. Some agreements are simple, limited to listing your job responsibilities and pay. Others may include the length, conditions under which you or the employer can negate the agreement, and specific conditions that will govern your work for the company.

Especially when starting your career, be mindful of company policies involving comp time versus overtime, hourly rates versus a salary, and benefits. For example, federal regulations amended in 2004 set a level of $455 a week for a salaried worker to be ineligible for overtime pay, which comes out to roughly $24,000 per year.

In addition, some contracts might include a "noncompete clause," which prohibits you from taking another job in the same area or with any company that competes with your employer. Generally, the restriction is for a set time after your employment ends, regardless of whose decision it was for you to leave. An attorney who specializes in employment law *in the state in which you will be working* can examine your employment agreement and provide advice. The contract review may cost you a few hundred dollars, but it is an investment in your future.

LAUNCHING AND FINE-TUNING YOUR CAREER

Your work doesn't end once you get the job offer—as the field evolves, you must keep up with the latest techniques, trends, and technologies in journalism. Just as the most experienced reporters today have had to adapt to the Internet, you will have to adapt to new technologies and opportunities that may create fundamental changes in the way you practice journalism.

The best way to keep up is to be a regular consumer of news from all media, from print and broadcast to online and other electronic media. As noted earlier, you should join and participate in professional organizations, such as the Society for Professional Journalists and the Online News Association. These organizations have regular meetings and conventions where you can keep up with new techniques, trends, and technologies; and most distribute publications that serve the same purpose.

Gil Thelen, the former *Tampa Tribune* publisher who oversaw one of the largest experiments in convergence when he combined the *Tribune,* WFLA-TV, and the online site TBO.com under one roof, has two pieces of advice for journalists working in a converged media environment. First, he says, tomorrow's journalists must be committed to lifelong learning and skills acquisition. Second, the most important skill to be developed is learning how to work and produce news content as part of a team.[8]

The other important task is keeping your portfolio up to date. Always have fresh copies of articles, Web pages, and video packages that demonstrate your skills. News organizations have been known to cut staff without warning, and you always need to be prepared to begin a new employment search. In addition to portfolio materials, you need to have a good network of contacts and references who can be as important as your portfolio in your next job search.

SUMMARY

This chapter examines the employment challenges and pitfalls facing those who want to work as multiskilled journalists. The news industry continues to evolve and change, and breaking in can be difficult. But most organizations are looking for someone with a variety of skills and a good blend of reporting instincts, writing ability, and comfort with technology. Technology skills include shooting and editing photos and video, as well as Web design, computer programming, and even some knowledge of using wireless technology, although rarely would you be expected to know all of those in depth.

The job interview is an opportunity for both sides to test each other. It gives the organization a chance to look at someone who is young, bright, and enthusiastic; and it gives you a chance to see if the company values what you have to offer. Some simple things are important. Wear nice clothes, be well-groomed, and have all the appropriate materials such as a tape or writing or editing examples and an error-free resume and cover letter. You are looking for a match between your skills and the needs of the organization; make sure you discuss both in the interview.

---

[8] G. Thelen (2006), "Rogues, Rascals, Nostrums, & Hard Truths," retrieved from http://www.jour.sc.edu/news/newsann/Fall06/Buchheit.

You should have some sort of guiding plan or direction to cover short- and long-term goals (as discussed in box 15.2). Because of the nature of modern journalism, you have to take advantage of all the tools at your disposal to stay competitive. For example, you should already have a professional website or blog that demonstrates your talent, but remember such things can be discovered by future employers for many years, so be deliberate and careful in what you put on them. Combine these showcases with public service work and skillful negotiating to land the type of job that becomes a career.

Box 15.3 Ethics: Little Lies and an Honest Application

Realistically, it is impossible to go through life and *never* lie. Lying is universally condemned for many reasons that are beyond the scope of the discussion here. But basically people do it for the ends it accomplishes. For example, we learn to lie or spin the truth to avoid conflict or embarrassment ("I was studying in the library" versus flirting at a bar), or we may lie to gain status or win some benefit ("I was having lunch with the general manager and he said …"). Through experience and situations we learn to bend truth for what we believe to be the "greater good"—our greater good.

Lying is bad. Professionally it can be called libel or fraud. But when it comes to getting the job we want or need, the situation becomes tricky and full of temptation. The world is not fair and we hear stories of people who embellished the truth and were rewarded with either a great job or a promotion we feel was undeserved. We struggle to get our dream job at the salary we deserve. But the job interviewing process lends itself to games and trick questions. HR directors ask you to divulge your greatest weakness or describe a time when you failed at something. Instinctively we know that downgrading ourselves is not the path to beating out other applicants. We learn to defend ourselves by offering ambiguous character flaws like 'being stubborn about finishing projects on time" or having "a near obsession with taking care of details and saving the company money." We can engage in such wordplay in an interview, but the resume is a different matter.

What you put on your resume is actionable, in the sense that you can (and often will) be fired for not telling the truth. All the authors have known people—good people—who were caught putting something in their resume that was not true. The long tail of the Internet allows others to track your past accomplishments. Also, the adage "it's a small world" applies to working in the media. People know other people. The ones you put down as references may not be the ones they call. If your resume says you were a reporter at a certain newspaper for 10 months, it can come back to haunt you if you actually were in the mailroom for six of those months. It is better to just state that you were a reporter for only four of the 10 months and take it from there. The point in all this is to remember the rule you were taught as a child: Tell the truth. Just as the journalist must be accurate and honest when writing about others, so also you have to do the same when writing about yourself.

EXERCISES

1. Choose a city or region where you want to work and list all the major media properties (newspapers, broadcast stations, magazines) there. Pay special attention to corporate ownership and event coverage (Fourth of July, Labor Day). Look for cross-promotional work that demonstrates partnership and sharing of resources or content.
2. Put together your own tape/portfolio/resume/employment package and prepare yourself for three different types of positions (e.g., one reporter position, a Web designer/page editor position, and an assistant broadcast producer position). Be sure your materials are distinctly different and appropriate to go with matching cover letters.
3. Find at least two written works dealing specifically with negotiating contracts. Adapt what's written to your specific case and apply the principles of contract negotiation with your next job interview. Decide on three nonmonetary benefits that could be used to offset being hired at less than your ideal wage.
4. Evaluate various journalism-specific online job boards for the past month. How many jobs are available in your geographic area? In your skills area (reporter, copy editor, designer, etc.)? Overall? Is there a pattern among the ads in the types and amount of experience desired? Do some jobs, regions, and media types predominate? How many specify some kind of new media skill or multiple skills across media? Do you see any patterns in how they want resumes and supporting material submitted? How will this affect your job search?
5. Choose a city that you would like to be working in after graduation. Use your information-gathering skills to research:
    a. Entry-level salaries for journalists.
    b. Cost-of-living factors (rent, transportation, living expenses, etc.).
    c. Professional expenses (dues, wardrobe, etc.).

    Then create a personal budget that balances your income against your expected expenses. Use your reporting skills to identify and interview an entry-level reporter in that city to find out how accurate your estimates were.

GLOSSARY

The media are Towers of Babel. There are few standardized terms between print and broadcast, within print or broadcast newsrooms (such as radio vs. TV), or sometimes even among newsrooms within the same organization. Online has added more to the lingo. These linguistic and cultural differences have been cited as the main impediments to working across media.

What follows are various terms referenced in this book or used in the field in general that may be helpful in understanding the language of print, broadcast, and online as we increasingly work across media.

-30- or ###: Marks signaling the end of a story. Often used when a story is edited by hand but generally not used when it is edited by computer.

actuality: A radio term for a **sound bite.**

add: Subsequent pages of copy (see also **take**), so page 2 is also the "first add," etc.

advergaming: A special type of **gamification** that incorporates advertising messages and interaction.

algorithm: A set of rules or a process that is followed to solve a problem, usually used in the context of computers.

ambush interview: Confronting an interview subject without prior warning.

analog: Using continuously variable physical properties, such as the shape and frequency of waves, to carry information such as that required to reproduce sound or video. Analog recorders, for instance, generally use magnetic tape. See also **digital.**

anchor: Member of a broadcast news team who regularly appears on camera to present a newscast, as opposed to a reporter who gathers information and usually works in the field.

anchor lead: Copy the anchor reads before introducing a **package.** Also called an **intro.**

app: A dedicated computer program or application that is designed to run on a mobile device such as a smartphone or tablet computer.

assigning editors: The editors in a print newsroom who work directly with reporters to develop stories. They also usually give those stories the first read for content, structure, completeness, and clarity before sending them to the copy desk. Sometimes called "line editors."

assignment desk (news desk): In broadcast newsrooms, where the **assignment editor** and assistants work to coordinate the coverage of stories.

assignment editor: The primary person in a broadcast newsroom responsible for coordinating story coverage and for keeping track of potential future stories. Most news releases and public relations calls, for instance, will go to the assignment editor or an assistant for evaluation of news potential.

backgrounder: A fact sheet or file with basic facts and history on a person or company that can be quickly used in a news story. It also can refer to a story that delves more deeply into an event or issue and tries to explain what led up to it.

backhaul: The transmission of a broadcast signal from a remote location back to a studio or network control room.

backlight: Light coming from behind a subject or the fixture used to provide such light. Too much backlight will wash out video or a photo.

backtiming: A way of timing a newscast that keeps track from the show's end. So if a newscast is to end at 11:28:30 and the closing theme is 20 seconds long, the music should start at 11:28:10 (11:28:30 minus :20). This is done for each element of the show to the beginning. See also **forward timing.**

banner: A print newsroom term for a large headline, usually at the top of the page and stretching the entire page width. Also a term for a display advertisement on the Internet stretching most of the width of a Web page, usually at the top.

beat: A reporter's area of specialization.

bird: Another term for satellite.

Bluetooth: A short-range (under 100 meters) wireless connectivity standard commonly used to transfer data among mobile devices.

block: A broadcast term for segments of a newscast. The segment between the opening and the first commercial break is the A-block, the next segment the B-block, etc.

blog/blogging: Both a system for publishing online and an ethos for how it is done. Each entry is a "post," each post has its own unique **URL** or Web address, and the posts are presented with the most recent appearing first. The ethos for news and information blogs is that you have something to say, that you link to other sources to bolster your story or argument, and that you do it regularly.

blue screen: See **chroma key.**

boilerplate: Wording that tends to get used repeatedly in stories about the same subject. Take, for example, the phrase "Smith, who was charged in 1994 with embezzlement. . . ." But 10 years later, if nothing ever came of the case and Smith has had no other problems, she might decide to take legal action for continuing to bring it up. Errors that creep into boilerplate also can be repeated unknowingly when someone pulls the phrasing out of the archive. The same wording over and over is dull writing, so be careful with boilerplate.

bot: see **spider.**

bridge: Reporter or **anchor** narration between two **sound bites.**

brief: A short print or Web story, usually fewer than 200 words and generally without a byline. Several briefs run together on a page are sometimes called a "briefs package."

broadsheet: A newspaper printed on wider sheets of paper in the traditional format most people know. The sheets are usually 50 inches wide or a little narrower, although as newspapers' fortunes decline, they continue to narrow the width. See also **tabloid.**

B-roll: Video footage other than **sound bites** or the reporter's **stand-up** that is shot to be used under the reporter's or **anchor**'s narration or sometimes under a **sound bite**. Sometimes called **cover video.**

budget: In a print or wire service newsroom, a listing of the stories being worked on or likely to happen that need coverage. (Broadcasters often call this a **rundown**)

budget line: An entry on the budget, usually no more than two **grafs** long, that fully and accurately summarizes the individual story. The line itself usually should tell a small story because it needs to sell the story for better placement.

bug: News organization logo unobtrusively embedded in the corner of video reports. Used for identification and copyright.

bumper: Video transition common in TV news programs used to advertise or tease upcoming stories.

CG: Computer graphic, character generator. Now a generic term for onscreen text.

chroma key: A system to insert images electronically into an area of solid color. Also known as **blue screen** or **green screen.** That weather map behind the forecaster is usually inserted this way. The forecaster is actually standing in front of a green or blue wall.

close: In television, the final portion of the script or the final shot(s).

close-up (CU): A visual image where a single item fills the entire shot.

cloud, cloud services: Used in relation to computing to designate those programs or databases that are not kept on a local computer or server but are accessed and used or manipulated online, usually through a Web browser. One of the advantages is that they are potentially available anywhere the user has online access.

column: A news item usually written with a point of view—that of the columnist. A column often can be identified by the use of the first person. Most columns also run with a "signer"—a picture or special graphic, along with the columnist's name.

column inch: One inch of a print story in one column. A five-column story with each column three inches long (also known as deep) is 15 column inches.

consortium: A group of stations that share video and information, often by satellite.

content management system (CMS): A computer program(s) that merges authoring tools with a database in which content elements are stored. New elements can be created and entered in the database, or existing elements can be called up and manipulated according to the publication needs of a medium—online, print, and broadcast—or even potentially to create DVDs, CDs, etc. Every story, graphic, photograph, video clip, or audio clip is its own "element" with a separate ID in the database. A CMS also can record when and where content is used, keeping track of copyright, authorship, etc.

copy: A story or stories. In broadcast, about 15 full lines (completely across the page) of copy take about a minute to read. In newspapers, slightly more than 30 words usually fit in a **column inch.**

copy editor: In print newsrooms, often the last person to see the copy before it goes to be printed. Copy editors specialize in grammar, style, brevity, and clarity and are the surrogate for the reader. See also **rim** and **slot.**

count: The maximum width of a headline. It is based on the width of each letter, space, and punctuation mark. Each letter, space, or punctuation mark can be a half-count, a full count, one and a half counts, or two counts, depending on whether it is in lower case or upper case, the typeface, etc. See also **schedule** or **sked.** Because of "tight counts," headline writers tend to use a stripped-down form that omits articles and helping verbs and uses the comma to stand for "and." These restrictions generally are looser online, where headlines also serve as links and should be written in a more natural sentence form.

cover video: See **B-roll.**

CQ: "Correct as shown." The origin of this term is cloudy, but it's a common way in print newsrooms of signaling that a questionable item, such as an odd name spelling, has been checked and is correct.

cross-ownership: Where the same company, organization, or person owns more than one type of media outlet (say a TV station and a newspaper) in the same market.

crowdsourcing: Using a swarm of people—often experts but not normally journalists—to help report a multifaceted story. The technique, although a management challenge, can produce comprehensive results more quickly than relying on a small team of reporters. One example is the use of crowdsourcing to help ferret out hundreds of "earmarks," or special funding requests, buried in congressional budget bills. In another, a Florida newspaper used retired engineers and other experts in its community to dig into government records that uncovered overcharges on utility assessments.

CSS: Cascading Style Sheets, a method of coding the styles used in a Web page into one master document that can be accessed as needed instead of styles being coded into each line of **HTML**. See also **XML**

curator (*noun*): In converged newsrooms, journalists (formerly editors), who not only do traditional work editing stories but also engage in curation (*verb*) which is finding or confirming related links and monitoring online posts for relevant content from other sources such as **blogs** and Twitter feeds.

cut: (*noun*) Another term for a recorded **sound bite,** most often used in radio. (*verb*) Another word for "to edit."

cutaway: Video that shows other than the main action, such as people applauding at a concert. Cutaways are most often used to bridge separate parts of interviews or transitions in the main action. See **jump cut.**

cutline: Another word for "caption" in print newsrooms from the days when photographs had to be physically cut or etched onto a printing plate.

cutting: In broadcast, editing tape or film. In print, trimming a story to fit available space.

dateline: The city (and usually the state) at the beginning of a story that gives its place of origin. It is common on wire-service stories but not so much on local print stories, and broadcast almost never uses it except in graphics showing where video was shot.

deck: This has two common meanings: the subordinate **hed** under the main hed or the individual lines of a headline.

desk: In print newsrooms, the copy desk. In broadcast newsrooms, the assigning desk. In converged newsrooms, sometimes called the "superdesk," where editors and producers from print, broadcast, and online sources interact.

diamond style: A broadcast term for using a specific person or small group to tell the story of something that affects a large group of people.

digital: A type of signal or encoding that uses discrete representations of numerical values to convey information, as opposed to **analog,** which uses continuously variable physical properties. Computer chips process digital values into **analog** signals that we can physically sense. Digitally encoded information can be replicated without degradation.

digital rights management: A system designed to limit access to media content to those users who have paid for access.

director: In a television control room, the person who selects and coordinates the assembly of live cameras, video recording, audio, and graphics into a complete television program.

donut: A TV term for when the reporter is live in the field or in the studio or newsroom before or after a packaged report. A donut usually does not have a **stand-up** or **sig-out.**

double truck: A print term for a story (or ad) displayed on two inside facing pages on the same sheet of paper. The term derives from when printing plates were so heavy they had to be taken to the pressroom on hand trucks, and a double truck took two of them.

DPI: Dots per inch, an indicator of print resolution.

dub: *(noun)* A copy of a tape or film. *(verb)* To make a copy or to replace one soundtrack with another.

dupe: Another word for "duplicate," a dubbed tape or film.

DV: Digital video. The information to produce the video is in bits and bytes processed by a computer chip as opposed to older **analog** forms, such as VHS and Beta. Digital video is edited with a computer program, such as Apple's iMovie or Final Cut Pro or Avid's Newscutter, instead of mechanically with electronic assist (linear editing) as were the older forms.

editor: In print newsrooms, the person who fixes or changes copy or who directs the work of reporters. In broadcast newsrooms, the person who processes video segments into stories or packages.

enterprise: A story developed by original reporting, digging, and research as opposed to primarily augmenting a news release or covering **spot news.**

fade: To gradually increase or decrease the video or audio signal, as in "fade to black."

feed: Broadcast term for sending a program or a signal from one point to another. Also a noun meaning that program or signal.

file: *(noun)* An old-fashioned term for a story, especially a wire-service story, or a newer term for a named grouping of computer data that can represent anything from a word processing document to a photo to a program. *(verb)* To submit a story for publication. Primarily a print term.

flame, flamer: See **troll.**

forward timing: Another way of timing a newscast (see also **backtiming**). Usually used when a particular story must air at an exact time in a newscast (such as a live satellite feed). Timing is done from the beginning of the newscast, not the end.

frame: The smallest measure of videotape. In the U.S. system (National Television Standards Committee), 30 frames = one second. Also, to correctly set up an image for taking a photo or recording video.

full-screen graphic (FSG): A graphic that takes up the full TV screen. See also **over-the-shoulder graphic.**

future file: The filing system by which editors and reporters keep track of upcoming events that may be worthy of coverage. Also known as a **tickler file.**

gamification: The trend toward making technology and websites more "fun" by using interactive elements such as quizzes, polls, and games to keep people engaged in the content.

geolocative: Programs or services that track or use a device's or user's location, often to customize the information delivered.

graf: Shortened spelling of "paragraph" (the "f" helps prevent accidental printing so that it is not confused with the real word, "graph").

graphic: In print, any kind of artwork that accompanies a story or that stands on its own to impart information; however, the term more commonly is applied to drawn artwork rather than photographs. In TV, it usually means a visual element used in place of video.

green screen: See **chroma key.**

hammer: A headline style where the top line is shorter, essentially a **kicker,** but is much bigger than the main lines.

headroom: In photography, the space between a subject's head and the top of the screen.

hed: Abbreviated term for "headline." Not spelled "head" to avoid confusing it with the actual word and lessen the possibility it could be printed accidentally.

hit: Each time someone visits a particular Web site.

hook or peg: The reason we should care about a story now.

hourglass: A journalistic writing form that starts with an **inverted pyramid** of the most important facts but then takes a "turn" and shifts into a more narrative, timeline form. It is being used more widely in print and is especially useful for telling a broadcast story.

HTK: "Hed to kum" (used in places where there is to be a headline but it's not yet written). Spelled this way so it is not accidentally printed.

HTML (hypertext markup language): The markup computer language that ushered in the modern Web by providing a way for browsers to display graphical pages over the Internet. HTML is not a true programming language but one that directs another program (usually a browser) how to display various elements. See also **CSS** and **XML.**

IFB: How broadcast reporters and **anchors** hear some or all of the station's programming through an earpiece. Derived from the term "interruptible feedback," it also allows a producer or director to speak to them during a broadcast.

in-cue: The first words of a recorded **sound bite.**

interactive: Especially online, an element that invites reader, viewer, or user input and responds to that, sometimes by leading the person to additional information.

intro: See **anchor lead.**

inverted pyramid: A journalism writing style that puts most of the important information at the beginning. It is handy for quick scanning and is easier to cut from the bottom. This form has made somewhat of a comeback online.

jump: When a story continues on another page. Also, that part of the story on the other page.

jump cut: An unnatural visual transition, usually within a scene where two related actions separated in time are edited together without a **cutaway.** For instance, say you start with a shot of a boy holding a cup at a picnic and the next shot is of the cup sitting on a picnic table. How did the glass get there? That's a jump cut. Inserting a cutaway showing a friend calling the boy to come play between the two scenes of the cup smoothes the transition.

key light: Principal source of light.

kicker: In print, a headline with a shorter and smaller top line over the main **hed.** It's often underlined or in italics. The best have some "kick" to them, a bit of sprightliness. In broadcast, a lighter story at the end of a newscast or the end of a newscast **block.** In radio, these are sometimes called "*zingers.*"

lav, lavaliere: A small microphone clipped to clothing.

lead: The top story in a television news program. See also **lede.**

lead-in: The first sentence or two a news **anchor** reads to introduce a video **package.**

lede: The first paragraph or two of the story—the "lead"—but deliberately misspelled to lessen the chances an editor's note could get in the paper.

level: Strength of an audio signal. As in "give me a mike level."

lineup: See **rundown.**

live shot: A news or other event broadcast in real time from other than the studio. A reporter or **anchor** need not be featured in a live shot, especially when the pictures, such as a massive fire, are gripping; but one usually is. When the "other event" is more entertainment- or advertising-oriented, this is usually called a "remote."

lockout: See **sig-out.**

logging: Listing scenes, **sound bites, natural sound,** etc. on a videotape; how long each runs; and at what time each is located so it is easy to go back and find them.

lower third: The place on a screen where text computer graphics typically go.

managing editor: The person who usually leads a print newsroom.

mashup: In online journalism, taking two or more elements, often from third parties, and bringing them together through a

digital interface to produce new information or a new representation of information that aids understanding. Many mashups involve taking databases and overlaying the information onto maps. A classic is chicagocrime.org, which maps where crimes were happening by combining police department data with Google Maps.

masthead: Listing of a publication's key editors, publisher, and other executives, as well as mailing and other contact information often required by postal authorities.

microsite: See **Web shell.**

mike or mic: Shorthand for "microphone." Some people prefer the first spelling because the second can also be an ethnic slur.

mobile journalist (mojo): Reporter working in the field who uses technical tools (camera, notebook PC, and wireless connection) to send stories in to the home office.

moblog: Short for "mobile Web log," an online space that allows remote uploading of pictures, captions, and other information and presents them in a **blog** structure. Can be used to present a multidimensional perspective on a story or event.

mom rule: Writing a story the same way you'd tell it to your mom; an especially popular term in broadcasting.

MOS, MOTS: Man-on-the-street interviews.

multiskilled journalist: A journalist trained in reporting, photography, videography, and editing, capable of producing stories for a range of media.

nameplate: The stylized rendition of a newspaper's name on the front page.

narration: Voice-over track for a news report given by **anchor** or reporter.

natural sound (NAT): Any sound other than a formal interview. See also **wild sound.** NAT can include people talking if they are not being formally interviewed.

news director: The person who usually leads a radio or TV newsroom.

news hole: The total space (print) or time (broadcast) available for news, as opposed to ads and other elements.

newsflow editor: The editor responsible for deciding which stories will be delivered through each output medium, as well as when these stories are delivered.

NTSC video: The **analog** video standard formerly used in most of North America including the United States, Canada, and Mexico, commonly identified by the frame rate, 29.97 frames per second, compared with 25 fps for PAL video used in Europe and Asia.

nut or nut graf: A term for the key **graf** or **grafs** in a story that tell you why you are reading it and its broader significance.

on demand: Stories, images, and other elements stored in a way that the viewer or reader can call them up as desired, sometimes for free and sometimes for a fee.

one-man band: One person doing the work of several (reporter, videographer, editor, producer, engineer).

op-ed: The page opposite the editorial page on which many newspapers run syndicated and local columnists.

open: The beginning of a broadcast news program.

orphan: One or two words of a paragraph at the top of a newspaper column.

out-cue: The final few words of a **sound bite** or **package.**

over-the-shoulder (OTS) graphic: A graphic over one of the **anchor**'s shoulders as he or she reads copy.

Oxford or serial comma: The comma before the conjunction that precedes the last element in a series. More common in the United States than in the United Kingdom. However, in journalism it often is still not used (because—a carryover from the "hot type" days when saving lead was important—it "saves space and money").

package: A TV term for a complete recorded story. The typical package is by a reporter and usually includes **sound bites,** narration over **B-roll,** and a **stand-up.** However, there also can be an *anchor package* in which the **anchor** does the narration (typically without a stand-up) and a *natural sound package* that uses only that.

pad: Extra copy either in print or broadcast designed to fill in if a story runs short.

PAL video: See **NTSC video.**

passive: Passive writing makes the normal object the subject. It can be ponderous but is not always wrong. "Mayor Bill Smith was indicted Friday on 27 fraud charges" is passive but is preferred to "A grand jury indicted Mayor Bill Smith on 27 fraud charges Friday." The story is about Mayor Smith being indicted, and that should lead the **lede,** not about a jury indicting. Passive voice can be especially useful with crime stories where we want to be careful about making the target of the investigation the subject, lest we inadvertently convict or impart guilt.

ping: (1) A simple electronic query that indicates whether a path is available to a specific server or computer. (2) A short message that indicates whether a person is available for further communication.

pingback: A message notifying a website or **blog** that it has been referenced by another website or **blog**, usually with a link to the reference.

pixel: Short for "picture element," reflects degree of image resolution. Each individual dot on the computer monitor is a pixel, and **digital** cameras are listed in terms of megapixels (millions of dots).

podcasting: Melding audio files with a system similar to **RSS** that notifies users when new files are available to download and that can download them automatically. Like **blogging,** podcasting has an ethos, a set of generally followed practices: have something to say, make the audio segments interesting using various production elements, and produce the podcasts regularly.

producer: The person in charge of getting a TV or radio program on the air with all the elements in correct order and properly timed.

prompter: A system for displaying words in front of the TV camera lens so an **anchor** can appear to be looking at the viewer while reading the script.

pronouncer: Phonetically spelling out a word to help an announcer read it aloud.

PSA: "Public service announcement."

pull quote: A quote taken from a story that is enlarged and given special graphical treatment to make it stand out.

Q&A: "Question and answer." In print, a story form where the reporter's questions are shown, each one followed by the interviewee's answer. Both the questions and answers are lightly edited, if at all. In broadcast, a format in which the **anchor** or a reporter conducts the interview, which is live or recorded for use later. As some broadcasters and newspapers cooperate more closely, it has become a popular way to bring the expertise of print reporters into the newscast without making them do a produced package

rapid relevance: The concept of delivering content that satisfies the user's needs and desires when, where, and how the user wants it.

raster graphics: A method of creating an image by assembling it line-by-line in a display device. Programs like Photoshop that convert images into pixels for display on a computer monitor are said to have "rasterized" an image. However, when severely magnified, rasterized images degrade to an unfocused mass of pixels or are said to have "pixelated." (Contrast with **vector graphics.**)

raw sound: See **natural sound** and **wild sound.**

reader: In TV, copy read by an **anchor** without any video or graphic. In radio, copy read by an **anchor** without any **sound bite.** In print, sometimes used to praise a well-written story ("That's a good reader" or "That's a good read").

rim: Generic term for rank-and-file copy editors. Copy editors used to sit on the "rim" of large, U-shaped desks, with the **slot** in the middle. The terms still hold.

roll cue: The final few words from a reporter doing a live introduction to a **package** that let the director know when to start the video.

RSS: "Rich site summary" or "really simple syndication." A system using online files coded in **XML** to tell a Web site or a special computer program that new information is available to download. Currently, RSS feeds are generally a by-product of other online publishing operations; however, some entrepreneurs are examining whether RSS could be a **digital** media form of its own.

rundown: The document listing the stories for a newscast, their order, and other information about how each is to be presented. Sometimes called a **lineup.** See also **budget.**

schedule or sked: The listing of the headline count for each letter, number, space, or punctuation mark. (Each typeface has a different count and thus a different **sked**) Also, the total number of units a designer has allowed for a **hed.** Some broadcast newsrooms use this term for the **rundown.**

script: In general, all the material to be read during a newscast. The *anchor script* contains all elements to be read and cues as to who will read them, as well as **in-cues** and **out-cues.** An *editing script* usually has just enough information so that the videographer can put together the video for a **package.** The *producer script* contains timing and other cues needed to make sure the show runs exactly as designed.

segue (SEG'-way): A smooth transition from one show element to the next.

setup: Same as **shirttail.**

shell: An online page or pages structured to make it easy for a user to find all relevant information and multimedia elements on a topic.

shirttail: Part of a story written ahead to be topped with fresher information, often when time is critical. For instance, a company schedules a "major" announcement. The reporter has a tip it will announce a new plant with 1,000 jobs but does not have enough confirmation to publish. The reporter will write a shirttail with background on the company, maybe what he or she can find out about what led up to the announcement, etc. Then, when the announcement is made, the reporter will phone in details, fashion a few **grafs** for the top, and send the story. Especially important for wire service reporters and, now, for feeding the Web.

shooter: Another name for videographer.

shotgun mike (or mic): A microphone designed to pick up sound from directly in front of it and block out most background noise.

shovelware: Largely a term of derision referring to online content originally created for another medium and just "shoveled" online without any changes that acknowledge the benefits or limitations of the online space.

sidebar: A shorter story related to a longer one. The sidebar will usually focus on a narrower or additional aspect of the overall story.

sig-out: The standard line a broadcast reporter typically uses to end a packaged story, such as "Jane Smith, Channel 2 News, at City Hall." Also called a *signature out-cue* or **standard out-cue** and sometimes called a *lockout* (more common in radio).

slot: This person supervises a shift of copy editors. He or she runs the copy desk, parcels out stories and graphics to be edited, and reviews the final work. See also **rim** and **copy editor.**

slug: The brief name assigned to a story. In print, a slug may also include the number of words, the date, and information identifying the reporters and editors who have handled it. In broadcast, it may include the estimated running time. Improperly slugged copy can get lost in the computer system or, worse, cause the wrong version of the story to make it into the publication or on the air.

SMS: "Short message service." The text messaging found on cellphones and many other mobile devices. Because SMS uses the cellphone system's control channel, not its voice channels, text messages sometimes continue to operate even when cellphone systems are overloaded with voice calls (such as in disasters). SMS messages generally are limited to 160 characters; but that is not absolute, and some carriers allow longer messages or automatically break up the text into several messages of conforming length. SMS is growing as a way to deliver news alerts, stock quotes, weather information, and other premium information services.

sockpuppet: See **troll.**

SOT: "Sound on tape." Recorded sound from an interview for use in a broadcast story.

sound bite: A short segment of audio from a person expressing an opinion, emotion, or information (or some combination). See **actuality, cut, SOT.**

spider: In the context of online, a small program that roams the Internet, visiting websites, determining what information is there and how it is linked (mapping), and then returning that information to a search engine for its index. Also known as a **bot**. Websites can prevent being indexed by search engines or control what pages are indexed by including a file called "norobots.txt."

split: In headlines, when one line ends in a preposition, conjunction, or adjective or when a compound term is partly on one line and partly on the other (e.g., "Students will receive report / cards this week").

spot news: Coverage of unplanned events, such as fires, accidents, crime, sudden resignations, etc.

stack, stacking: When a broadcast producer puts all the stories and elements together for a show.

standard out-cue (SOC, SOQ): See **sig-out.**

stand-up: When a reporter appears on camera, usually at the scene, and says a sentence or two. Stand-ups most commonly are seen at the close of a **package** but can appear anywhere, including in the middle to bridge elements.

stet: A copy-editing term that says "Oops, I made a mistake. Put it back the way it was." In other words, "return to original."

stills: Term for still photographs. Now that many newsrooms are expanding into multimedia, it often is used to distinguish from video.

sting, stinger: A transition sound effect common in TV news programs.

story editor: In a converged newsroom, the individuals responsible for all aspects of a single story, coordinating reporters, photographers, researchers, and others to produce appropriate output stories for each medium.

super: Graphics information superimposed over video, usually a person's name and title or the location from where the report is coming.

tablet: A portable computer with the size and thickness of a pad of paper that is predominated by a large touch-screen surface used for both input and display. Tablets may be connected to keyboards, printers, or other peripheral devices so that they can perform the same functions as laptops, but they are more often used to access and display information.

tabloid: A style of newspaper printed on sheets smaller than a **broadsheet.** There are variations, such as *compact* and *Berliner* (compact also often is used to refer to a paper that was a traditional broadsheet but switched to tabloid). The term has a yellow-journalism reputation, but some of the world's well-respected papers are tabloids, such as *The Times* of London.

tag: In broadcast, **anchor** copy that follows a reporter's package or a **VO/SOT** to bridge to the next story or segment break. Online, a way of assigning labels to Web pages, **blog** posts, etc., so that a user can click on the tag and see all related material similarly tagged. Online services such as Technorati also gather tag information from around the Web to provide a broad picture of what many people are saying on the same topic.

tag cloud: A visual representation of the relative popularity of **tags** used to classify posts on a **blog** or other content on a Web site. Color and size are most often used, with larger type indicating more popular tags.

take: A page of copy (also see **add**). This term is often used when copy is being produced in short chunks as a bulletin or urgent material on the wires or on deadline.

talking head: Video (head-and-shoulders shot) of a person just talking. Not very interesting to watch and, after a brief amount of time, should be avoided.

tease, teaser: Short items in a newscast previewing items to come, usually just before a commercial break. Writing a good tease is a balance of intriguing the viewer or listener but not giving away the story.

template: A preset format for a Web page (or any other document) specifying layout, font, text size, etc. so that content can be formatted and posted quickly and uniformly.

text messaging: See **SMS.**

tickler file: See **future file.**

toss or throw: When an **anchor** in a news broadcast introduces another person on the set (such as the weather or sports **anchor**) or sends the story to a reporter doing a live shot.

troll (and related terms): A person who (usually without using his or her real name) posts on a discussion board or in a comments section in a way designed to promote angry or derisive responses. Related terms: A "flamer" is someone who posts angry, sometimes incoherent, messages designed to inflame the conversation. The messages, called "flames," often are written in all-caps to mimic shouting. A "sockpuppet" is someone who registers several fake names and then uses them to support and bolster each other's comments in an attempt to make it appear there is more support or opposition for a person or issue than there is.

tweet: (*noun*) Shorthand for a message sent on Twitter, the social media short message service. It is limited to 140 characters, spaces, and punctuation. (*verb*) To send a message on Twitter.

upload: Sending a **digital** file to a computer or server for use online or in a content management system.

UGC: "User-generated content." Content created by consumers and distributed directly or through traditional media channels. A term despised by some because it treats the content as just another element to be plugged in rather than representing "news as a conversation" with the audience.

URL: "Uniform resource locator," or Web address. The identifier for each Web page and other online element that allows a browser or other specialized computer program to reach it.

vector graphics: In the context of computers, a way of drawing graphics using straight lines and mathematical formulas so that the resulting image can be enlarged to almost any size without breaking up. (Contrast with **raster graphics.**)

videographer: A photographer who shoots videotape, usually for a TV news operation.

v-log: Short for "video blog" because it's too hard to say the other way. A type of **blog** that conveys information with video and other multimedia information rather than just text.

VNR: "Video news release," a news release sent out as a video report instead of printed. Using VNRs without properly telling viewers the material came from a corporate or government entity has been controversial and has brought threats of federal action.

VO: "Voice-over." A short TV story read by an **anchor** over video or a full-screen graphic.

voicer: In radio, a **reader;** but instead of being read by the **anchor**, it is recorded by a reporter with no **sound bites.**

VO/SOT: "Voice-over/sound on tape." A story in which a TV **anchor** reads some of the copy over video or a graphic, then waits while a **sound bite** is played, and then finishes the story by reading more copy on camera. Sometimes also referred to as *VO/B* ("voice-over with **sound bite**"). A variation is *VO/SOT/VO*, where the **anchor** finishes the story by reading more copy over video or a graphic.

wallpaper: Generic video that does not really relate to the copy the reporter or **anchor** is reading. It often happens when archival video is paired with a script covering more current developments in a story.

webcast: A live or on-demand broadcast that can be watched online. The *Spokesman-Review* in Spokane, Wash., has become known for webcasting daily news meetings at which editors and reporters decide what will be in the paper the next day.

webchat: A live online session in which several people exchange and respond to messages among themselves. The *Washington Post* has used the format successfully to introduce its reporters and editors—and their thinking—to an online audience.

Web services: A set of protocols designed to translate data from one format to another, allowing networked computers running different programs or operating systems to share data.

Web shell: Also known as "microsite." A set of online pages that gathers all the related elements of a story into one place for easy access, updating, and continuity.

white balance: A technical setting on a video camera to make sure it renders colors correctly. It involves pointing the lens at a pure white area and then making the adjustment.

widget: A snippet of computer code that can be embedded in one website to bring in information from another website or online service. For instance, a **blog** could also display the blogger's **tweets** by embedding a Twitter widget on the **blog**.

widow: A line of only a few words at the end of a caption or paragraph, which then leaves a large trailing white space. Such captions are often sent back for rewrite.

wild sound: Often interchangeable for **natural sound** or **NAT** but sometimes used to differentiate sound that truly is ambient and "wild," from the sounds of nature to the traffic noise of a city.

window: Time leased from a satellite broker to transmit video or audio.

World Wide Web: The protocols that allow and control access to information over the Internet using a graphical user interface so that users can interact with their computers using intuitive elements such as icons and a mouse rather than complex text commands.

wrap(around): Radio's term for a **package**—a reporter records the item, which includes one or more **actualities.** Derived from the idea that the report "wraps around" the **sound bites.** In film and video production, the term is used to signify the end of shooting a scene or segment ("That's a wrap").

WX: A shorthand journalistic form for "whether" (and sometimes "weather"). Often used in notes for speed and to prevent accidental printing of the real term. (Formerly, also the AP designation for the Washington, D.C., bureau. That's now "WDC.")

XGR: A shorthand journalistic form for "legislature." Often used in notes to distinguish from the real word and prevent accidental printing.

XML: "Extensible markup language." Similar to **HTML** but more exacting and powerful because users can define individual **tags** to allow easier customization and sharing of information. See also **CSS.**

zoom: A lens movement from a wider starting shot to a closer shot.

INDEX